Intermediate Robot Building

DAVID COOK

Intermediate Robot Building
Copyright ©2004 by David Cook

ISBN-13 (pbk): 978-1-59059-373-8
ISBN-10 (pbk): 1-59059-373-1

Printed and bound in the United States of America 9 8 7 6 5 4 3 2

Trademarked names may appear in this book. Rather than use a trademark symbol with every occurrence of a trademarked name, we use the names only in an editorial fashion and to the benefit of the trademark owner, with no intention of infringement of the trademark.

Technical Reviewers: Don Kerste

Editorial Board: Steve Anglin, Dan Appleman, Gary Cornell, James Cox, Tony Davis, John Franklin, Chris Mills, Steve Rycroft, Dominic Shakeshaft, Julian Skinner, Jim Sumser, Karen Watterson, Gavin Wray, John Zukowski

Assistant Publisher: Grace Wong

Project Manager: Sofia Marchant

Copy Editor: Kim Wimpsett

Production Manager: Kari Brooks

Production Editor: Kelly Winquist

Proofreader: Patrick Vincent

Compositor: Dina Quan

Indexer: Kevin Broccoli

Artist: Kinetic Publishing Services, LLC

Cover Designer: Kurt Krames

Manufacturing Manager: Tom Debolski

Distributed to the book trade in the United States by Springer-Verlag New York, Inc., 233 Spring Street, 6th Floor, New York, NY, 10013, and outside the United States by Springer-Verlag GmbH & Co. KG, Tiergartenstr. 17, 69112 Heidelberg, Germany.

In the United States: phone 1-800-SPRINGER, email orders@springer-ny.com, or visit http://www.springer-ny.com. Outside the United States: fax +49 6221 345229, email orders@springer.de, or visit http://www.springer.de.

For information on translations, please contact Apress directly at 2560 Ninth Street, Suite 219, Berkeley, CA 94710. Phone 510-549-5930, fax 510-549-5939, email info@apress.com, or visit http://www.apress.com.

For my future robot builders, James and Samuel

Contents at a Glance

About the Author ....*xi*
About the Technical Reviewer ....*xiii*
Acknowledgments ....*xv*
Preface ....*xvii*

Chapter 1   Assembling a Modular Robot 1

Chapter 2   Comparing Two Types of Homemade Motor
Couplers and Common Errors to Avoid 11

Chapter 3   Making a Fixture and Drilling
Solid Rods for a Coupler 21

Chapter 4   Finishing the Solid-Rod Motor Coupler 43

Chapter 5   Building a Motor Inside a Wheel 51

Chapter 6   Understanding the Standards and Setup
for Electronic Experiments 73

Chapter 7   Creating a Linear Voltage-Regulated
Power Supply 95

Chapter 8   Making Robot Power Supply Improvements 121

Chapter 9   Driving Miss Motor 143

Chapter 10   Driving Mister Motor 173

Chapter 11   Creating an Infrared Modulated Obstacle,
Opponent, and Wall Detector 213

Chapter 12   Fine-Tuning the Reflector Detector 233

Chapter 13   Roundabout Robot! 247

Chapter 14   Test Driving Roundabout 285

Chapter 15   If I Only Had a Brain 309

Chapter 16   Building Roundabout's Daughterboard 341

Chapter 17   Adding the Floor Sensor Module 369

Chapter 18   Cooking Up Some Robot Stew 393

Appendix   Internet References 421

Index 423

Contents

About the Author..xi

About the Technical Reviewer..xiii

Acknowledgments..xv

Preface...xvii

Intended Audience xviii
Volatile Parts xxi
Safety Rules xxi
Preferring the Metric System..xxii
Getting Updates and Seeing What's New...xxii

Chapter 1 Assembling a Modular Robot.......................................1

Building Modules 1
Getting Comfortable with Machining 3
Putting It All Together 8
Applying Parts and Techniques to Other Robots................................9

Chapter 2 Comparing Two Types of Homemade Motor
              Couplers and Common Errors to Avoid.............11

Comparing Two Homemade Coupler Technologies...........................12
Identifying Desired Results in Coupler Drill Holes,
Along with Common Errors and Their Effects....................................14
Getting Ready to Make a Solid-Rod Coupler.....................................20

Chapter 3 Making a Fixture and Drilling
              Solid Rods for a Coupler....................................21

Gathering Tools and Parts 21
Preparing Lengths of Solid Rod for the Couplers 22
Making a Coupler Fixture 27
Getting the Money Shot..37
Drilling the Motor-Shaft and LEGO Axle Coupler Holes.............38
Examining the Coupler So Far...42

Chapter 4 Finishing the Solid-Rod Motor Coupler 43

Installing the Coupler Setscrew 43
Adding the LEGO Axle 48
Summary 50

Chapter 5 Building a Motor Inside a Wheel 51

Encountering Danger: Bent Shafts Ahead 52
Making a Hub-Adapter Coupler 54
Summary 72

Chapter 6 Understanding the Standards and Setup for Electronic Experiments 73

Reading Schematics 73
Using Solderless Breadboards 84
Understanding Oscilloscope Traces 89
Riding the Bandwagon of Modern Electronics 89
Summary 93

Chapter 7 Creating a Linear Voltage-Regulated Power Supply 95

Understanding Voltage Regulators 95
Understanding Linear Voltage-Regulated Power Supplies 96
Heading into Optimizations 119

Chapter 8 Making Robot Power Supply Improvements 121

Bulking Up the Input and Output Capacitors 122
Adding Voodoo Capacitors 127
Sprinkling with Bypass/Decoupling Capacitors 128
Preventing Damage from Short Circuits or Overcurrent 131
Preventing Damage from Overvoltage in a Regulated Circuit 136
Putting It All Together for a Robust Robot Power Supply 140

Chapter 9 Driving Miss Motor 143

Why a Motor Driver? 143
Demonstrating the Four Modes of a Motor 146

Driving Simply with a Single Transistor.................................149
Putting the NPN and PNP Motor Drivers Together 156
The Classic Bipolar H-Bridge...158
Interfacing with the High Side...163
Mastering Motor Control 171

Chapter 10 Driving Mister Motor 173

Driving Motors with MOSFETs...173
Driving Motors with Chips 194
Evaluating Motor Drivers 206
Summary..211

Chapter 11 Creating an Infrared Modulated Obstacle, Opponent, and Wall Detector 213

Detecting Modulated Infrared with a Popular Module, or,
Another Reason to Hog the Remote Control.........................214
Expanding the Detection Circuit to Include an
LED Indicator 218
Completing the Reflector Detector Circuit...........................222
Making It Work 231

Chapter 12 Fine-Tuning the Reflector Detector.............233

Tuning In 38 kHz...233
Limitations of the Reflector Detector 242
Getting Ready for a Practical Robot Application 246

Chapter 13 Roundabout Robot! 247

Examining Roundabout..248
Roundabout's Circuitry..250
Building Roundabout's Body 254
Summarizing Roundabout...282

Chapter 14 Test Driving Roundabout.........................285

Preparing for the Test Drive...285
Preparing the Robot and Correcting Minor Glitches 291
Evaluating Roundabout's Performance 293
Getting Stuck 300

Chapter 15 If I Only Had a Brain.................................*309*

Considering the Motorola KX8 Microcontroller
As an Example..*310*
Comparing a Microcontroller to a Logic Chip.....................*310*
Programming a Microcontroller..*313*
Exploring Common Microcontroller Features.......................*320*
Choosing a Microcontroller..*335*
Graduating Your Robot..*340*

Chapter 16 Building Roundabout's Daughterboard..........*341*

Converting to a Two-Story Configuration............................*342*
Intercepting Signals: Meeting the New Boss.......................*358*
Expanding Functionality..*360*
Upgrading a Robot..*368*

Chapter 17 Adding the Floor Sensor Module......................*369*

Sensing Brightness with Photoresistors...............................*370*
Sensing Brightness with a Photodiode IC............................*378*
Following a Line...*386*
Competing in Robot Sumo..*389*
Expanding Possibilities...*392*

Chapter 18 Cooking Up Some Robot Stew.............................*393*

Making Music...*393*
Scaling Up...*399*
Mounting Motors..*403*
Roaming the Solar Terrain..*412*
Standing in a Robot's Shoes for a While.............................*418*
Thank You...*419*

Appendix   Internet References.................................*421*

Index...*423*

About the Author

David Cook hosts the popular robotics Web site, RobotRoom.com. Having taught himself electronics and mechanics, David can explain his years of robot experiences to the average backyard scientist in a comfortable and helpful way without scholarly intimidation.

David is currently a software engineering manager for Motorola. He manages up to 20 developers who write and support software for mobile public safety (police, fire, emergency medical services) around the world. David's software is installed in more than 10,000 police vehicles in the United States. So, if you're pulled over and your driver's license is being run, chances are the data is passing through a piece of David's team's code.

Longtime Macintosh devotees may remember David's award-winning computer games, TaskMaker and MacSki, along with Tomb of the TaskMaker, Asterbamm, and Technical Snapshot. Yes, there are still fan sites out there!

When not writing books and building robots, David enjoys spending time with his family, growing really enormous sunflowers, playing with his cats, and eating home-grown vegetables.

About the Technical Reviewer

Don Kerste began experimenting with things electrical at age two, when he stuck a hairpin into an electrical outlet. Somewhat daunted, but nevertheless undeterred by this and other near-disasters, he eventually graduated from Northwestern University in 1959 with a bachelor's degree in electrical engineering. Over the next four years he took many courses in biological sciences at the University of Illinois while serving as a consultant to the Physical Medicine Department of VA Research Hospital in Chicago.

Over the years Don has been mostly self-employed and for a while ran his own small electronics design and prototyping company. His first computer programming course was on an IBM 650 in 1958, and he still owns a working model of the famous Altair 8800. Don's interest in robotics was kindled by a project in the late 80s that involved the design and prototyping of a computer-coordinated, remote-control video camera system with automated zoom-tilt-focus compensation. His early forays into robotics were hampered by the absence of microcontrollers and a lack of suitable power semiconductors. Thus, early robotics used bulky motor driver boards, used crude sensors, and were controlled via a double-handful of logic chips or a desktop computer port. Eventually a CMOS version of the 6502 became available, which allowed the computer to travel with the robot.

Now that Don has retired from full-time work he looks forward to having ample time to pursue his primary interest of amateur robotics. Although serving as chief information officer of Catalyst Integrations and still helping a few old clients two days a week, he now finds time to be the program chairman of the ChiBots Computer Club and is writing several robotics-related articles that will appear later this year on the ChiBots Web site.

Acknowledgments

IT'S AMAZING THE AMOUNT OF SUPPORT an author needs to write a book. Imagine the level of assistance required to write a Web page or magazine article and then multiply that by a 100.

Appreciating My Technical Editor

Few authors are lucky enough to have a technical editor that they can truly trust to thoroughly read draft material, catch errors, and offer improvements. For this book, Don Kerste took on the challenge with great pride and intensity.

I met Don at the Chicago Area Robotics Club (ChiBots), http://www.chibots.org/. Because we lived in the same town at the time, we struck up a friendship carpooling to meetings together. Don's editing approach is a deep dive, where he visits the manufacturers' Web sites, reproduces critical experiments, and then notes any contradictory data in detail. Don's years of experience in electronics were particularly beneficial.

With a pool of knowledge to test, Don swam laps to get a feel for the user's experience and then inspected the bottom of the pool for cracks. The combination was perfect. Thank you for your time, attention, and friendship.

Exchanging Ideas with Robot Club Members

Another person I met at ChiBots, Terry Surma, proofed the machining sections for me. Terry always brings the most interesting parts and thought-provoking experiments to robot club meetings to share with others.

Terry's generosity epitomizes the dedication to the exchange of scientific goodwill and camaraderie that's found in robot club members. Those sentiments apply to Scott Williamson, Tom Gralewicz, Joe and Dustin Martin, John Orlando, John Patrick, Jim Fiocca, Eddy Wright, Paul Jurczak, Nabeel Rasheed, and Mike Davey. Thanks, guys!

Learning a Lesson in Photography

Disaster struck about halfway through writing this book—the storage mechanism broke on my digital camera. "No big deal," I thought, "I'll just buy a newer, better camera." It turns out that the latest batch of consumer digital cameras have relatively poor macro lenses. The close-up pictures lacked depth of field, were out of focus, and suffered from barrel distortion. I guess not enough people use cameras for that type of photography to make it a must-have feature.

After buying and returning several high-end cameras, I decided to send my old camera out for servicing. (In this rare instance, I regret declining the extended warranty.) In the meantime, Stacey Kacek was kind enough to loan me her camera, which is identical to my original camera. A large number of photographs in the middle chapters of this book are directly attributable to her charity.

Getting Support at Work

I work for Stacey at Motorola. She encourages her staff to reach beyond their workday roles, with this book being an example. As such, she attracts and retains a talented group of well-rounded achievers.

Speaking of which, thank you to my friends and colleagues: Dan Schwimmer, Tom Zehner, Trung Le, Rim Yoo, Tom O'Toole, Kanda Arunachalam, Aaron Thomason, Jon Kishkunas, Gupta Narayanam, Mark Prukalski, Darren Roberts, Craig Detter, Aspi Havewala, Mike Klein, Tom Moore, Tim Marlow, Chuck Olson, Richard Smith, Roy Qian, Nasser Amer, Dave Layer, and Chuck Bland.

Tom Gavin, another friend at work, was the technical editor on my first book. Despite globe-trotting travel to the other side of the world throughout the year, Tom took the time to help me with a number of chapters of this book. Thanks, Tom!

Getting Support from the Field

There are a few people in the field of amateur robotics that deserve special mention. The first two are Cheryl and Dave Hrynkiw. I think they have done more for robot hobbyists than all academics and authors combined.

Together, they have brought inexpensive, interesting projects to the masses. Through their company, Solarbotics, they have introduced unique parts (gearmotors, solarcells, and so on) and made them available from a dependable source, rather than the spotty salvage to which robot builders are usually subjected. Dave regularly tours North America visiting robot events and teaching classes. I wonder how many budding builders his work has touched?

Some other noteworthy contributors to the field are Jake Mendelssohn, Pete Miles, Dale Heatherington, Jim Frye, Roger Arrick, Dave Lavery, Gordon McComb, Mark Tilden, and Bill Harrison. I have had the opportunity to talk with a few of these individuals, but for many, I've simply admired and benefited from their work from afar.

Support at Home

Robotics is an expensive hobby. As any robot builder knows, you need a sympathetic significant other to overlook the thousands of dollars (or tens of thousands of dollars) worth of robot parts and tools.

I'd like to thank my family for their sacrifices, especially my wife, Rachel. She took the boys on adventures to the park, library, and the houses of out-of-town friends to provide me with a quiet workplace on the weekends in order to write this book. She smiles and nods faux-attentively as I explain the in-depth particulars of each "amazing" new discovery. She accepts the milling machine in the basement and the truckloads of plastics and metals that arrive for obliteration. I love you, darling.

Preface

Prerequisites, Target Audience, Safety, and Getting Updates

GREETINGS, ROBOT BUILDER!

Over the years, I've created many homemade robots (some of which, only the builder could love). However, with each successive robotic generation, I try to gradually expand my knowledge of electronics, mechanics, machining, software, and art by experimenting with new techniques, features, or parts (keeping in mind, all the time, it's a hobby to be enjoyed; see Figure P-1).

Figure P-1. Author, growing a robot

Rarely will my latest robot be composed entirely of new technologies. Instead, each robot takes a small evolutionary step with a few changes from a collection of tried-and-true modules. In a self-contained way, this book follows that trend by tracing the stages of growth of a single robot, Roundabout, from mindless prototype to virtuoso.

My approach is to delve deeply into a particular part or subject, rather than skimming the surface of an entire design. This focus on modules and segments allows you to create your own *personalized* robot from desired pieces, rather than necessarily replicating exactly what I've made.

I invite you, now, into my laboratory (straight through the living room, turn left at the kitchen) for friendly conversations about robot secrets and designs.

Intended Audience

This book is aimed at college students, adults, and advanced teenagers. Family participation in robot building is highly encouraged. Adult supervision of minors is always required because some tasks can be performed safely only by a competent adult.

Prerequisites

You should have basic experience in electronics and intermediate experience in software development. There are many different modules and versions of the robot throughout this book. All readers should be able to build the first generation of Roundabout (presented in Chapter 13). With greater working knowledge and further development, construction of the advanced version of the robot is possible.

Required Electronics and Machine Shop Experience

You must already be familiar with the following:

- Where to obtain electronic and material supplies, such as from retail stores, mail-order catalogs, and the Internet

- Safety rules (summarized later in this preface)

- Metric prefixes, particularly mega, kilo, milli, micro, nano, and pico, along with their associated abbreviations and symbols

- Using a multimeter for testing DC voltage, DC amperage, resistance, diodes, and transistors

- The difference between voltage and current

- Hand tools such as wire strippers, wire cutters, needle-nose pliers, screwdrivers, crimp tools, and tap wrenches

- Power tools such as variable-speed rotary tools (Dremel; http://www.dremel.com/), drills, and drill presses

- Sandpaper, glues, and vises

- Jumpers, test leads, wire, and breadboards

- Consumer batteries (particularly 9 V batteries)

- Switches, resistors, potentiometers, and photoresistors

- LEDs and diodes

- Basic bipolar (NPN/PNP) transistors

- Ordinary two-wire DC gearmotors (permanent-magnet brush)

- Reading simple schematics and wiring diagrams

- Soldering and soldering equipment such as solder wire, soldering iron, flux, sponges, helping-hand holders, and desoldering bulbs

- Crimp connectors and heat-shrink tubing

- Screws, nuts, washers, and spacers

The preceding subjects are covered in detail in my book *Robot Building for Beginners* (Apress, 2002). I highly encourage you to purchase my first book, or at least read through a library copy. This book assumes that you have the knowledge presented in the beginner's book.

I make a lot of comparisons throughout this book to Sandwich, the line-following robot from *Robot Building for Beginners*. Descriptions, images, and a movie of Sandwich are available online at http://www.robotroom.com/Sandwich.html *(this address is case sensitive)*. Therefore, you don't have to run out and buy the first book to understand the references made to Sandwich.

Required Software Development Experience

The reader should be proficient with personal computers and software programming. The more advanced robot in this book makes heavy use of a microcontroller without providing step-by-step programming instructions. Therefore, you must understand how to program and use a microcontroller of your choosing, you must purchase a preprogrammed version of the one featured in this book, or you must be prepared to acquire the necessary microcontroller programming instructions independent of this book.

Although the software prerequisites are significant, it allows the book to focus on robots. There is a universe of material available on computers and software development. As for microcontrollers, there are books, as well as lots of material and tools available directly from the microcontroller manufacturers. Put another way, if I had put in enough information about microcontrollers into this book, it'd be a book about microcontrollers, not robots.

This book tries to show no favoritism regarding operating systems, programming languages, and microcontrollers. I personally develop in Motorola (http://www.motorola.com/) HC08 assembly language on a Microsoft Windows–based computer. However, the wide array of microcontrollers and the staunchness of the loyalty of embedded developers (my technical editor has asked me to change that to "cadre of enthusiastic supporters") necessitated that all of the examples were generalized to device-independent algorithms. In other words, you can use any computer, programming language, or brain parts that you prefer.

> **NOTE** *As this book goes to print, Motorola is divesting itself of its semiconductor division. The Motorola parts referred to in this book will likely be manufactured by Freescale Semiconductor by the time you read this.*

Preferred Robot Building Experience

Because this book delves into interesting parts, features, or algorithms, it's helpful to have already experienced the rush and confidence of having built at least one simple robot. Building Sandwich, the line-following robot from the book *Robot Building for Beginners*, is an excellent start. A lot of interesting robot kits are also available, such as the Parallax Boe-Bot (http://www.parallax.com/) or the Mark III (http://www.junun.org/MarkIII/Store.jsp).

If you're saying to yourself, "Okay, I successfully built an easy robot. Now I want to make a better one or make one from scratch," then this book is for you.

Would LEGO MINDSTORMS Be Better for You?

If you're younger, have a limited financial budget, negligible free time, or haven't ever drilled or soldered, then I highly recommend you begin with LEGO MINDSTORMS (http://mindstorms.lego.com/). The LEGO robot kit is very friendly and should have you building robots quickly. My handbuilt, custom-tailored robots have lost in enough contests to Steve Hassenplug's (http://www.geocities.com/stevehassenplug/) LEGO creations for me to offer due respect to the capabilities of the LEGO kits in the hands of a master builder.

If you decide to go the LEGO route, pick up a LEGO MINDSTORMS Robotics Invention System, some batteries, and the book *Definitive Guide To LEGO MINDSTORMS*, Second Edition, by Dave Baum (Apress, 2002).

Would BEAM Robots Be Better for You?

Another popular branch of robotics is based on not programming the robot at all. BEAM robots generally have simple circuits that result in complex behavior. Most, but not all, BEAM robots are solar powered. Most, but not all, BEAM robots are small and resemble insects. You can build an interesting BEAM robot in a weekend with minimal expense and without a microcontroller.

Take a few minutes (or hours or days) to visit http://www.solarbotics.com/ and http://www.solarbotics.net/ to explore the world of BEAM robots. Solarbotics stocks many parts that are equally at home on non-BEAM robots.

If you want to build a BEAM robot, I highly recommend the book *Junkbots, Bugbots, and Bots on Wheels* by Dave Hrynkiw and Mark W. Tilden (McGraw-Hill/Osborne, 2002). Actually, even if you decide you don't want to build a BEAM robot, pick up the book anyway. It's that good.

No Remote-Controlled Armageddon

This book isn't about destructive or remote-controlled robots. Instead, this book focuses on lunch-box-sized autonomous (self-controlled) robots, with emphasis on semi-intelligent behavior. However, you can apply the modules and tips presented to mechanical beasts that shake the bolts out of their brethren, if you so choose.

Volatile Parts

Whenever possible, descriptions of tools and parts mentioned in this book are accompanied by listings of resellers, part numbers, and approximate prices. No favoritism to a particular supplier or part is intended.

Prices are listed in U.S. dollars. Keep in mind that prices change and that part numbers may no longer be available after this book is published.

Safety Rules

Don't mess around.

Robot building involves the use of electrical power sources, power tools, ignition sources, and chemicals. Any one of these can maim or kill you. Always, always, always read and follow the manufacturer's instructions and lab/machine shop's rules. Because my directions are generalized, follow the manufacturer's specific directions if they conflict with mine:

- Adults must supervise minors at all times.

- Tools and parts should be put away and locked up when not in use.

- Read and retain product labels and material safety datasheets (MSDS).

- Wear safety goggles.

- Wear boots, long pants, and long-sleeved clothing. Although ballroom gowns technically meet the requirements for "long-sleeved," they're loose enough that they might catch in a power machine or touch a soldering iron.

- Wear a dust mask and ensure adequate ventilation.

- Avoid lead-based solder. Use tin-silver solder or other lead-free alternatives.

- Avoid mercury and cadmium.

- Use low voltages and consumer batteries instead of household electrical lines.

- Use circuit breakers, fuses, and GFCI outlets.

- Don't cut off or fail to utilize the ground prong on three-prong plugs. Also, don't trim the polarized two-prong plugs.

- Never touch a live circuit with both hands.

- Beware of creating dangerous robots or robots with weapons.

- Powerful motors with parts attached can act like weapons.

- Maintain a well-lit, clean, and uncluttered work area.

- Stay rested and alert—fatigue can cause serious accidents.

You've only got one set of eyes and one complete set of digits. Take extreme care to preserve them. You're obviously smart enough to read articles and books in order to make better robots. So, let me assure you of this: Work performed in safe conditions always turns out better than pieces built in a hurry or without regard to health.

Preferring the Metric System

The metric system is used throughout this book whenever possible. However, the imperial system is used whenever a part is actually manufactured in imperial units. For example, a ½-inch rod won't be described as "12.7 mm" if it really is a ½-inch rod. Admittedly, the mixing of measurement systems in this book leads to such bizarre sentences as "Drill a ⅛-inch hole 2.6 cm from the side of the workpiece."

Getting Updates and Seeing What's New

My Web site is at http://www.robotroom.com/IRBGoodies.html *(this is case sensitive).* Please drop by and visit to find book updates, source code, PCB files, and a parts list. On the root level of Robot Room, you'll also find other robots, plus links to numerous robot-related clubs and sites.

CHAPTER 1

Assembling a Modular Robot

THIS BOOK WAS MUCH MORE DIFFICULT to write than the first book, *Robot Building for Beginners* (Apress, 2002). In the first book, I assumed the reader knew nothing about electronics or machining. That neatly limited the subjects to the trunk of the "robot tree of knowledge."

But a funny thing happens after that. Robots are so diverse in their capabilities and purposes that the robot tree of knowledge explodes with braches in all sorts of directions after you understand the basics.

Therefore, it's impossible to select a single type of robot that would encompass a direction that all immediate builders would want to take. Once armed with (almost) enough knowledge, each builder is already heading down in his or her own unique path. Therefore, this book is about how to grow a robot, not what type of robot to grow.

Building Modules

Rather than building a robot, build modules. Build power supply modules, motor driver modules, sensor modules, sound modules, and brain modules. After that, don't build a robot—assemble a robot!

You achieve many benefits by assembling a robot from modules:

- You can handcraft the modules you're interested in, but purchase off-the-shelf modules for the ones you aren't interested in (or for those modules that require professional quality for a certain critical aspect of the robot).

- You can upgrade the robot by simply swapping out a module rather than replacing the entire robot.

- You can replicate and reuse successful modules on other robots.

- You can reduce the time from idea to outcome.

- You can get a functional base going (gaining that feeling of accomplishment) and build it up from there. Many times the most ambitious projects lie in partially completed piles because they're just too complicated to finish in one or two (or 20) sittings.

Assembling Roundabout, or Not

This book shows you how to assemble a robot named Roundabout. Chapter 13 shows you how to assemble the simplest model of Roundabout (see the left side of Figure 1-1) from the modules and techniques presented in Chapters 2 through 12. This version of the robot contains a voltage regulator, infrared object/wall sensors, and motor drivers. By using a logic chip for brains, the robot requires no programming and uses only off-the-shelf electronics.

Beginning in Chapter 16, you'll upgrade Roundabout by attaching a second board on top and a third board below (see the right side of Figure 1-1). Because the upgraded robot uses a microcontroller for brains, it can perform a wider variety of functions. Roundabout can be a room explorer, line follower, or sumo robot. Perhaps you'll add a maze-solving algorithm?

Figure 1-1. The simpler version of Roundabout (left). The upgraded version of Roundabout (right).

Because Roundabout consists of modules, you don't have to build the same robot as presented in this book. With a few alterations, you can create a robot with a substantially different set of objectives and behaviors. Roundabout is merely a framework to bring together the discrete units and demonstrate their functionality as part of a whole.

Arranging Chapters

As you might expect from the preceding paragraphs, the chapters in this book are grouped by module. And just as you don't need to create every module that goes into a robot, you also don't need to fully read and understand each chapter to create the final robot in this book.

Some chapters, such as those describing motor drivers, can be a little intimidating. You can skip some chapters and sections within chapters, such as those describing machining, by building the robot using the Sandwich robot base (see Figure 1-2) presented in the book *Robot Building for Beginners*. This can save you time and money.

For those readers interested in the more complex subjects, many chapters include enough depth to fully explore certain topics. However, you may choose to skim those chapters or read only to the point that your brain becomes full. Later, when you want to learn more, pick up the book again and give those heavier chapters a second read.

Figure 1-2. Roundabout's circuit board installed inside of Sandwich's base (left). The same switches, couplers, battery, and Ziploc container but arranged in a centered-shaft configuration with Roundabout's circuit board mounted on top (right).

The point is that not every facet of robot building is interesting to all robot builders. Have fun by concentrating on the parts you like the most.

Getting Comfortable with Machining

As previously stated, by reusing the Sandwich body and machining techniques described in the first book, you can get away without any additional machine tools or skills to create the robot (Roundabout) in this book. In fact, less than one-third of the book (Chapters 2 through 5 and some of Chapters 13, 16, 17, and 18) contains machining content. But I encourage you to consider gaining machining competency if you don't already have it because it's very freeing to be able to make almost whatever part your heart desires.

At the Chicago Area Robotics Club (ChiBots) meetings, almost all newcomers profess comfort with software programming and tolerate their electronics skills but confess a fear of machining. So, you're not alone if you feel uncomfortable with machining. But just like anything else, you can overcome those anxieties with a little bit of practice.

Probably the best way to learn about machining is to take a machine shop class at a local community college. Alternatively, spend a few afternoons with a local robot builder who is fortunate enough to own a power tool that you don't. It's amazing what you can learn from witnessing a machining operation firsthand. (It's really not possible to learn that in a book.) Most machinists are happy to share their experience and wisdom, especially because the number of people interested in the craft has declined over the years.

Stocking Your Machine Shop

You can assemble a reasonably useful home machine shop for about the same price as a midrange home computer. Most people already own common tools such as screwdrivers, wrenches, hammers, sandpaper/files, saws, rulers/squares, snips, pliers, vises/clamps, and drills. Taps and dies are a little more unusual but are neither expensive nor intimidating. Of course, you also need a well-lit workbench or other flat, solid surface.

I use a few power tools all the time for robotics:

- High-speed rotary tool, such as a Dremel

- Drill press

- Milling machine

- Cutoff disc/chop saw (see Figure 1-3)

Figure 1-3. A large, abrasive cutoff disc machine for cutting lengths of raw material faster and straighter than using a hacksaw

Many robot builders would also argue for the following:

- Lathe

- Router or scroll saw

- Grinder

- Press/brake/bender/punch

- Welder

Lots of kinds of machines are available, along with machines that combine various functions, so this list isn't intended to be exhaustive. This book uses the first list of power tools extensively.

Looking at a Miniature Milling Machine

A favorite power tool for robotics is a miniature combination milling/drilling machine. My whole life opened up when I got this tool.

In a fundamental sense, a vertical milling machine is a power tool that can take a raw material (such as plastic or metal) and cut it flat and square. Also, the milling machine can add grooves, slots, holes, and even bevel (round) edges. With additional accessories, there's almost no limit to the kinds of pieces you can create on a milling machine. If you find your robot needing "a small, unique piece with a notch and a couple of holes," then you want a milling machine to make it.

Industrial milling machines weigh several thousand pounds or more, are as tall as or taller than a refrigerator, and are as wide as a one-car garage door. Used models start at several thousand dollars. Most modern milling machines are controlled by computer for high precision, speed, and repeatability. Obviously, industrial milling machines are outside the budget and storage facilities of most hobbyists.

Many miniature milling machines are more appropriately sized (33 pounds to 110 pounds and about the size of a large computer) for home use and are relatively affordable ($650 to $900 with the necessary accessories and shipping). Sherline Products, Harbor Freight Tools, Grizzly Industrial, Enco, and Micro-Mark all sell a variety of smaller milling machines. Most milling machines double as functional drill presses.

I have the MicroLux milling/drilling machine ($509.95, #82573) from Micro-Mark (http://www.micromark.com/). A few required accessories are end mills ($39.95, #82576) for cutting and a vise ($59.95, #82577) for holding the workpiece. But that's just the beginning of all the wonderful accessories you can buy. Over the years, don't be surprised if you find yourself surrounded with accessories that, in total, cost many times the original price of the mill itself.

I selected the MicroLux machine because it was the largest and heaviest for the price. Hobbyists with limited space may prefer the Sherline model.

Using a Milling Machine

A milling machine is easy to use but difficult to master. The following are the most important things to learn:

- A milling machine is for precision work only. First make large rough cuts using a saw or similar tool, and then fine-tune the workpiece on the milling machine.

- Always tightly secure the workpiece. Any vibration or sudden movement will cause damage to the cutting tool, the workpiece, the machine, or you.

- Be patient! Take slow, thin cuts.

The following is a common milling procedure (refer to Figure 1-4):

1. Cut the material (plastic, brass, or aluminum for miniature milling machines) to roughly the desired size with a hacksaw or cutoff disc machine.

2. Secure the workpiece directly on the milling machine table or in a vise ①.

3. Insert a drill or end mill (which looks like a drill but with a flattened tip and side cutting edges) into the drill chuck ② or mill collet.

4. Position the workpiece by turning the handwheels to adjust the side-to-side position ③, the forward or back position ④, or the up and down position ⑤.

5. Turn on the power, and fine-tune the speed ⑥.

6. Adjust the position of the workpiece using the handwheels, allowing the drill to plunge into the workpiece or the end mill to shave/chip away at the workpiece.

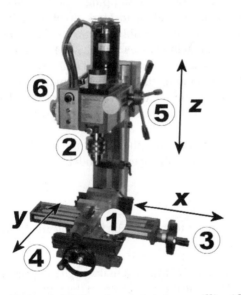

Figure 1-4. MicroLux miniature milling/drilling machine

Precisely Positioning the Workpiece with Handwheels

I tend to be a bit clumsy, and I'm usually unable to position things accurately by hand. What I like the most about a milling machine is that the handwheels make fine adjustments in the position of the workpiece, even with relatively large rotations of the handwheels. If the workpiece needs to move to the left just a little bit, a quick turn of the handwheel is all that's required. Now up a bit? No problem. Spin the other handwheel a little. Too far? No big deal. Spin the handwheel back. I can take my time using the handwheels to nudge the workpiece exactly where I want it.

Because each handwheel adjusts a separate axis, you can position the workpiece one axis at a time without messing up the position of the other axes. To cut a straight groove, just turn one of the handwheels while the other handwheels are locked in place. It's just that easy.

One of the most elegant uses of a combination milling/drilling machine is making homemade circuit boards. Simply mount the etched board in the vise and nudge it (tap the side of the vise with a rubber mallet) parallel to the table. Using the handwheels, line up one of the circuit board holes with the drill and drill the first hole. Then turn only one of the handwheels (the x-axis, for example) to line up and drill each hole on that board that's along the same line (imagine one-half of a DIP socket—say, eight holes in a row). If your handwheels are in the same units as your circuit board holes are spaced (such as tenths of an inch), then each turn (or two turns or a half turn) of the handwheel advances the board exactly to the next hole.

After all the holes are drilled, swap out the drill for an end mill. Position the end mill of the outside edge of the circuit board to begin cutting. Rotate one handwheel (the x-axis for example) to cleanly cut and square up one edge of the board. Next, rotate the other handwheel (the y-axis, for example), then rotate back to the first handwheel (x-axis), and finally rotate the other handwheel again (y-axis). In this example, the table moves the board left, back, right, and forward to perfectly square off all edges of the circuit board.

Correcting Circuit Board Errors

Another good use for the milling/drilling machine is to correct errors in a circuit board. In Figure 1-5, an end mill has carefully shaved off an errant copper trace ①, and then a drill has made a hole ② for the replacement wire to be inserted. Was it difficult to position the end mill and drill in this example? No, each rotation of the handwheel gradually positioned the board exactly where I wanted it before cutting.

Figure 1-5. A combination milling/drilling machine can help correct errors on circuit boards by cutting traces ① and drilling new holes ②.

Admitting a Bias Toward Milling

I admit that I really enjoy milling. It's very relaxing. I truly find a milling/drilling machine an indispensable tool in robot building. You won't believe it until you see it or try it yourself.

This book starts out with Chapter 2 through Chapter 5 concentrating on machining. If you remain unconvinced as to how this applies to you, feel free to skip ahead to the electronics stuff, which begins at Chapter 6.

Putting It All Together

The birth of a robot exercises many different disciplines of the builder. One of my favorite things about building robots is that when I get bored with one aspect, I can turn to a different task that feels completely fresh but is still "building robots."

For example, sometimes I'll feel like machining, sometimes I'll want to prototype with LEGO bricks, sometimes I'll experiment with circuits on solderless breadboards, other times I'll design printed circuit boards on the computer, sometimes I'll stuff boards full of components and soldering, sometimes I'll assemble boards and parts together, other times I'll write software, sometimes I'll test a robot, and other times I'll dig out my collection of robots to enjoy them in action.

This book reflects on all of those different aspects. About one-third of the way through the book, you may lose sight of the book's goal (or may think I've lost sight of that goal). So, what follows is an overall summary of the different parts, modules, and processes throughout the book and how they all fit together.

Grouping Machining Parts

You can group the significant parts machined in this book as follows:

- **Motor couplers (for connecting motors to wheels)**: Chapter 2 through Chapter 5 and the middle of Chapter 18.

- **Circular robot platforms**: Some of Chapter 5, Chapter 13, and Chapter 18. A testing insight appears in Chapter 14.

- **Motor brackets (for securing motors to the robot's body)**: Some of Chapter 13 and Chapter 18.

Grouping Stand-Alone Electronic Modules

You can group the stand-alone electronic modules in this book as follows:

- **Power supply**: Chapter 7 and Chapter 8

- **Motor drivers (for supplying power to the motors)**: Chapter 9 and Chapter 10

- **Wall and object sensor**: Chapter 11 and Chapter 12

- **Light and floor sensing**: Chapter 17

- **Sound (tones and music)**: First half of Chapter 18

Assembling and Testing a Robot

Although you can use the machined parts and electronic modules however you want on your own robot, you build Roundabout as follows:

- Combine the power supply, motor driver, and object sensor onto a single printed circuit board in Chapter 13

- Connect the motor, coupler, and bracket in Chapter 13

- Bring together the power train and circuit board on a platform in Chapter 13

- Power up and test Roundabout in Chapter 14

So, by the end of Chapter 13, you've assembled Roundabout from everything described in the book up to that point. By the end of Chapter 14, you'll see many reasons for improvement. But rather than discarding the existing robot, you can upgrade Roundabout as follows:

- Chapter 15 describes microcontrollers, and you'll add one to the robot in Chapter 16, along with a push button and DIP switch for configurability

- You'll add floor sensing in Chapter 17

- You'll add tones and music in Chapter 18

Applying Parts and Techniques to Other Robots

When a Web site, magazine article, or fellow builder shows off a particularly well-designed robot, it can be easy to be a little intimidated or even discouraged. This is an illusion caused by seeing the robot as a whole rather than for its parts, many of which are likely no more sophisticated than sample circuits recommended by part manufacturers.

After building numerous robots, you begin to gain an eye for breaking down these complex machines into common pieces. You'll then see your compatriot's robot for its modular patterns and the few, but special, differences that make it outstanding.

In this book, a handful of robots besides Roundabout provide cameo appearances. Some portions of Sandwich, Soup, Bugdozer, Have a Nice Day, Hard2C, Lightspeed, and Carefree will illustrate a particular technique, part, or alternative. Although each robot is unique in its own way, they all can be broken down into the classic elements demonstrated by Roundabout.

For example, Soup appears to be a very different robot on the surface (see Figure 1-6). Yet, it has a power switch ①, power supply ②, motor driver ③, motor brackets and couplers ④, microcontroller ⑤, push buttons ⑥, and DIP switches ⑦ that serve the same purposes as on Roundabout.

A few of the parts on Soup are fancier than on Roundabout. For example, the power switch is a key switch ① salvaged from an old computer, the power supply is an inductor-based switching power supply ② that conserves battery power, and the display is an LCD ⑧ instead of LEDs. Yet, the robot isn't that far from Roundabout on the "robot tree of knowledge."

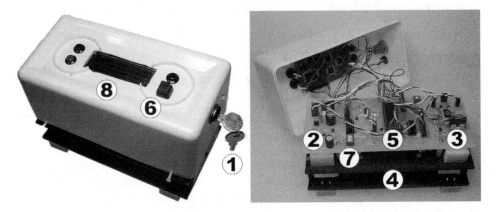

Figure 1-6. Soup has many of the same elements as Roundabout—and any other robot for that matter. (Incidentally, the plastic body cover comes from a consumer container of baby wipes.)

When you're done with this book, I hope you'll look at other robots differently than when you first started. Visually break them down into modules, reproduce the modules you find most interesting or valuable, and then put your own twist on the rest of the robot.

Okay? Ready? Let's go!

CHAPTER 2

Comparing Two Types of Homemade Motor Couplers and Common Errors to Avoid

UNTIL PEOPLE ACTUALLY TRY to build a robot themselves, they don't realize that one of the more difficult tasks is finding a precise and reliable way to connect a motor to a wheel. The selection of motors and wheels is endless, and, unfortunately, few were designed to mate easily (fit snugly together).

At first, it seems like the solution should be obvious: "I'll just drill a hole in the wheel, add some glue, and jam the motor shaft into the hole." But then reality sets in. Failure to drill a straight, centered hole results in a wobbly wheel. Also, the hole can end up either slightly larger or slightly smaller than the motor shaft. And with glue, you run the risk that either the glue affixes the motor in perpetuity (forever eliminating the ability to swap parts) or the glue doesn't stick well enough to the parts and the wheel falls off. In the end, you'll know it didn't turn out well when you resort to using a big piece of tape to hold the whole thing together.

A better choice is to use a *coupler*, which is a removable piece that connects a motor shaft to a gear or wheel. Think of a coupler as an adapter with one end compatible with a motor shaft and the other end compatible with a wheel hub.

Unfortunately, miniature couplers aren't readily available for purchase, again because of the lack of standardization of motor shafts and wheel hubs. Therefore, most of the time, robot builders must custom make couplers suited for their particular parts.

The next few chapters focus on making a coupler that connects any small (⅜-inch diameter or smaller) motor shaft to a standard LEGO cross axle (see Figure 2-1). The LEGO axle provides most off-the-shelf miniature motors access to a large variety of high-quality, standardized LEGO parts. However, if you don't desire LEGO compatibility, you can omit the LEGO axle and substitute another kind of axle instead.

This chapter begins by comparing the coupler technology presented in my earlier book, *Robot Building for Beginners* (Apress, 2002), to the coupler technology presented in this book. Then the chapter discusses common errors that occur when making homemade couplers, such as angular offset and parallel offset.

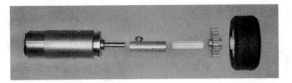

Figure 2-1. Motor with motor shaft, coupler with setscrew, white LEGO cross axle (normally epoxied into the coupler), and example LEGO gear and wheel (left to right)

Chapter 3 and Chapter 4 describe a technique for making solid-rod couplers on a drill press, emphasizing the tools and methods that reduce errors and increase your ability to produce high-quality parts. Working with hand tools and power tools can be intimidating for some people. However, with a little courage and patience, you'll soon know the joy of machining a robotic element with your own hands.

Comparing Two Homemade Coupler Technologies

Chapter 20 of *Robot Building for Beginners* provides steps for making a coupler out of several telescoping tubes. This book shows how to make a similar coupler out of a solid, round rod instead of tubes. There are trade-offs to both methods.

Examining Telescoping-Tube Couplers

Figure 2-2 shows a telescoping-tube coupler. You place the tubes inside one another, thus ensuring the shaft and axle holes are centered on both ends and parallel to each other. You can place a half-length, smaller-diameter tube in either end if the motor shaft is a different size than the LEGO axle. Epoxy permanently holds the LEGO axle in place, and a setscrew holds the coupler to the motor shaft to permit easy disassembly.

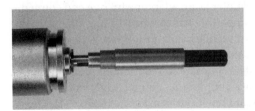

Figure 2-2. Telescoping tubes (center) slide together to connect a motor shaft (left) to a black LEGO cross axle (right). This is an unfinished coupler for illustrative purposes. Usually the tubes would be fully inserted into the largest tube and then glued together. You would add a setscrew to hold the tubes to the motor shaft.

The telescoping-tube method works well, especially for hobbyists without either access to a drill press or the skill to drill parallel-aligned, centered holes in a solid rod.

Telescoping tubes are readily available at hobby shops and hardware stores. However, several limitations to the telescoping-tubing coupler exist:

- The inner diameter of standardized telescoping tubing may not match the outer diameter of a motor shaft (robot builders are often stuck with whatever motors happen to be available). In those cases, the resulting lack of a tight fit can cause wobble or other problems.

- Telescoping tubing is usually available in only brass and aluminum. This construction method isn't applicable if you prefer a different type of material, such as plastic.

- Thicker tube walls increase durability and rigidity, but you could cut and glue together layer after layer of telescoping tubing to increase thickness, which is time-consuming; a similar problem exists if the motor shaft diameter is vastly smaller or larger than the diameter of a LEGO cross axle, which is $\frac{3}{16}$ inch. In either case, you must cut and assemble lots of tubing.

- The setscrew threads aren't as strong or reliable as those formed in a solid rod.

Comparing with Solid-Rod Couplers

On the outside, a finished solid-rod coupler looks identical to a finished telescoping-tube coupler. But, instead of gluing tubes together, you make a solid-rod coupler from a single piece of material, with appropriately sized holes drilled in both ends. You employ epoxy and a setscrew in both types of couplers to hold the LEGO axle and motor shaft, respectively.

The following are the biggest advantages of the solid-rod coupler:

- Hole sizes are limited only by drill availability—and lots of drill sizes are available.

NOTE *I grew up calling the part you insert into the drilling machine a drill bit. The power tool you plug into a wall I called a drill. Despite temptation, I'm trying to keep on friendly terms with the local machinist union by using the formal term, drills, to refer to the sharp, metal, spiral thingies instead of drill bits. The thing you plug into the wall is called a drill machine or drill press. In the process I've worn out the Find and Replace feature in my word processor.*

- Many more types of materials are available in only solid-rod form, as opposed to telescoping tubing. For example, fluorescent acrylic is available in solid rods but not in telescoping tubing; the acrylic is too brittle for manufacturers to produce the thin walls required for narrow-diameter (smaller than ¼ inch) telescoping tubing.

- Many more diameters of solid rod are available; so it can be as thick and sturdy as desired, without a lot of extra work. Additionally, because only one piece of rod must be cut and then sanded smooth, as opposed to multiple layers of telescoping tube, the solid-rod process can be a little faster.

One disadvantage of solid-rod couplers (as opposed to telescoping tubing) is that two holes must be meticulously drilled in the solid rod. A drill press or metalworking lathe is absolutely required. Drilling consumes some time and, even worse, can be frustrating or difficult to perform accurately if the correct steps aren't followed. Fortunately, the next couple of chapters provide all the steps necessary to reliably produce high-quality, solid-rod couplers.

Identifying Desired Results in Coupler Drill Holes, Along with Common Errors and Their Effects

Throughout these next few examples, I selected a ½-inch diameter, round, clear-plastic rod for the coupler material to illustrate how the drilled holes should (or shouldn't) align with one another. Neither the large diameter nor the clear plastic is actually necessary for a coupler in practice, but it looks pretty cool on a robot.

....

Picking a Plastic

The clear plastic material in these examples happens to be acrylic (often referred to by the trade name Plexiglas). Natural acrylic is inexpensive, lightweight, immune to ultraviolet light (present in sunshine), easy to machine, and available in many colors. Unfortunately, acrylic is brittle and easily scratched.

Alternatively, natural polycarbonate (often referred to by the trade name LEXAN) is almost as clear as acrylic, but natural polycarbonate is a little more expensive and can be damaged by ultraviolet light (additives can protect against this). On the plus side, polycarbonate tends to bend and stretch rather than shatter.

If you want to make see-through motor couplers that will actually be installed on a working robot, choose polycarbonate (or even clear PVC) for its resiliency. Avoid acrylic, as it is too brittle and will eventually crack and fail. Transparency is not usually necessary for a motor coupler, so ABS and standard PVC are good choices for opaque plastic.

....

Figure 2-3 shows a good example of the finished solid-rod coupler.

Figure 2-3. Motor (left) shaft inserted into clear plastic coupler (center) with setscrew (center top) holding the motor shaft in place. LEGO cross axle (right) glued into the other side of coupler. Three holes of different sizes were drilled into the plastic coupler: ① for the motor shaft, ② for the setscrew, and ③ for the LEGO axle.

Connecting the Setscrew Hole to the Motor Shaft Hole

The most obvious requirement for the setscrew hole ② is that it must meet up with the motor shaft hole ① to press against the motor shaft. When the setscrew is tightened, it prevents the motor shaft from turning within the coupler, and it also prevents the motor shaft from sliding out of the coupler.

The purpose of the coupler is to attach the motor shaft to the LEGO axle as though they were one solid piece so that they turn together.

Interestingly, all the physical energy from the motor shaft is transmitted via the setscrew to the coupler body. Therefore, the coupler body material shouldn't be too thin or flexible at the location of the setscrew hole. Generally this isn't a problem, but you should keep it in mind if you try to make a really slender coupler out of wiggly plastic.

Aligning the Hole Angles and Hole Centers

To keep things simple, the next few couplers pictured don't have setscrew holes drilled in them. Concentrate your attention on the motor shaft hole and the LEGO axle hole. At the top of Figure 2-4, notice that the hole is nicely centered within the coupler body. Within the coupler itself, notice that the holes are centered with respect to each other, and the axes of the holes are parallel and meet. A line formed by the two end-to-end axes should be absolutely straight. For appearances, it's attractive to have the combined axis concentric (centered and parallel) with the rod's surface, but this isn't essential for acceptable function.

Figure 2-4. Desirable: Coupler with nicely centered, straight-angled holes

This is what you're striving to achieve. Perfection isn't required. But the closer your finished coupler approaches this ideal, the smoother the rotation of the axle, gear, and wheel will be.

Accepting Parallel Offset Between the Holes and the Coupler Body

Figure 2-5 demonstrates an exaggeration of the most likely error in drilling the coupler: The holes won't be exactly centered within the coupler body. Believe it or not, this doesn't matter much.

Figure 2-5. Permissible: Although each hole is nicely centered with respect to the other and they have nice, straight, parallel alignment, the holes aren't centered within the coupler body itself.

Vibrating motors work by offsetting a large mass from the center of a motor shaft (see Figure 2-6). However, homemade couplers are relatively lightweight, and the offset error, and thus the center of mass, is rarely wrong by more than a millimeter or two. The resulting amount of vibration is negligible. If this is the biggest error in your homemade coupler, don't worry about it.

Figure 2-6. A motor with a heavy, offset mass causes vibrations when spun. (This motor was removed from a "force feedback" joystick.)

Avoiding Parallel Offset Between the Holes Themselves

Figure 2-7 demonstrates an exaggeration of an undesirable error in drilling the coupler: the holes not centered with respect to each other (even though the holes' axes are parallel to one another).

Figure 2-7. Avoid this: Although each hole is straight and parallel with respect to the other and the coupler body, the holes aren't centered with one another.

Misaligned shaft and axle holes (called *parallel offset*) cause the axle to rotate around a circle rather than a central fixed point. On the right side of Figure 2-8, the attached wheel tends to move up, left, down, and right as it rotates. Figure 2-8 was constructed using the actual couplers pictured in Figures 2-4 and 2-7. The offset in the coupler really causes that much disturbance in the wheel rotation!

A wheel spinning in a wide orbit causes the robot to bob up and down. This alters sensor readings and vibrates the robot, potentially into pieces. I suppose this could be a cute effect if purposeful—perhaps in a robot duck.

Figure 2-8. The lack of parallel offset allows the wheel to properly spin in place, which is good (left). Excessive parallel offset causes the wheel to move up, left, down, and right as it spins, which is bad (right).

Now imagine that the bad coupler is attached to a gear. A gear spinning in a wide orbit doesn't mesh evenly with a mating gear throughout each rotation. If the offset is excessive, the gear will stray too far from the mating gear and skip a tooth (or completely disengage) or stray too near and jam. This results in noise, wear (grinding and chipped teeth), and a loss of power because of friction or skip.

A wee bit of parallel offset isn't a disaster. But the process used to create the coupler should attempt to minimize this error. Two specific steps (which are described in more detail later in this chapter) help minimize parallel offset:

- Drill the narrower hole all the way through the coupler rod, not just halfway, so that the narrower hole acts as a pilot hole for centering the wider hole.

- Don't move the coupler rod or vise between drilling; instead, swap drills and immediately drill the wider hole over the narrower hole to the desired depth. This causes both the narrower and wider holes to be drilled in the same spot and thus to be centered with respect to one another.

Avoiding Angular Offset Between the Holes Themselves

Figure 2-9 demonstrates an exaggeration of an even more undesirable error in drilling the coupler: the holes drilled at different angles with respect to each other (even though the holes may be closely centered with respect to each other). This is called *angular offset*.

Figure 2-9. Avoid like the plague: Although the holes are somewhat centered over each other, the angles are horribly different.

Angular offset causes the axle to precess (see the right side of Figure 2-10) like a toy top that's slowing down. Figure 2-10 was constructed using the actual couplers pictured in Figures 2-4 and 2-9.

Figure 2-10. Lack of angular offset allows the wheel to properly spin in a single vertical plane, which is good (left). Excessive angular offset causes the wheel to wiggle back and forth and not make flat contact with the surface, which is really bad (right).

Precession is highly undesirable. Not only does precession cause wobbling, but also the attached gears and wheels don't make flat contact with adjoining surfaces. That results in uneven wear and loss of traction.

Soft tires counteract the detrimental effects of minor precession. The tires' flexibility causes them to elastically deform against the surface to retain even contact.

A drill press can help eliminate almost all angular offset because it plunges the drill straight down into the work surface. However, a long, dull, or narrow drill can bend a little and can cause some angular offset. You can avoid this by using short, sharp drills. Also, a spotting drill can provide an accurate hole to get narrow drills started in the correct place and at the correct angle.

Reiterating the Advantages of Telescoping Tubing

Building a coupler out of telescoping tubing avoids both parallel offset and angular offset errors because the manufacturer is providing you with straight tubing and centered holes. If you don't care about the advantages of solid-rod construction, or if you're having difficulty avoiding offset errors, you may want to consider making telescoping-tubing couplers instead of solid-rod couplers.

Getting Ready to Make a Solid-Rod Coupler

The straightness of the connection between the motor and the wheel or gear can significantly affect the motion of the robot. In the worst cases, wheels can slip, gears can fail, and the robot can be diverted off course. Avoiding parallel offset and angular offset are the key principles that guide construction of a good coupler.

The next chapter introduces some simple machining techniques that allow you to create solid-rod couplers that steer clear of the most severe problems described in this chapter.

CHAPTER 3

Making a Fixture and Drilling Solid Rods for a Coupler

Provides Machining Tips for Drilling Centered Holes

THE PREVIOUS CHAPTER INTRODUCED solid-rod couplers and compared them to telescoping-tube couplers. The prior chapter also described some problem areas to watch out for when drilling your own couplers.

This chapter provides step-by-step instructions for making a fixture to use with a drill press. With the fixture, you can reliably create decent solid-rod couplers. This chapter provides the initial steps for making the couplers.

This chapter contains many valuable machinist tips, such as selecting drills and accurately drilling holes. Therefore, this material is worth reading even if you aren't interested in making the coupler.

Gathering Tools and Parts

To make a solid-rod coupler, you'll need a lot of tools and supplies:

- The motor's datasheet listing motor-shaft dimensions (preferred) or calipers to measure the motor-shaft dimensions yourself.

- Round, solid rod in a material and diameter desired. The upcoming example uses a ¼-inch aluminum round rod.

- Measuring ruler and marker to indicate lengths of rod to cut and to mark the setscrew hole in the fixture.

- Safety glasses and protective clothing to wear during machining.

- Hacksaw and vise for roughly cutting the rod to length and for cutting out the fixture. Alternatively, a power cutoff saw is even better for cutting the rod to length.

- V-groove vise or block, rubber-grip material, and/or short parallel block if you're having difficulty keeping the round rod tightly held at the desired height in the vise.

- Metal file, sandpaper, or vertical milling machine for smoothing the ends of the cut rod.

- A block in which to hold the rod during drilling. In the upcoming example, 16-mm thick by 26-mm wide aluminum rectangular bar stock is cut down to 14-mm long. Larger sizes are fine. Plastic or wood may be an acceptable substitute for light duty use.

- Light machining oil or other suitable lubricant for drilling and tapping.

- Drill press or vertical milling machine with vise for drilling holes.

- Four split-point, short-length, high-speed steel (HSS) drills. In the upcoming example, you'll use a $\frac{1}{4}$-inch drill for the rod, either #12 or $\frac{3}{16}$-inch drill for the LEGO axle, a 3-mm drill for the motor shaft, and a #43 drill for the setscrew.

- #4-40 hand tap and tap wrench.

- One $\frac{3}{8}$-inch long #4-40 setscrew for the fixture.

- One #4-40 setscrew for each coupler. The upcoming example uses $\frac{1}{8}$-inch long for $\frac{1}{4}$-inch couplers.

- One approximately 3 LEGO unit (LU) in length LEGO axle for each coupler. Or a 5 LU in length cross axle cut to half length. An LU is $\frac{5}{16}$ inch. So, 3 LUs equal $\frac{15}{16}$ inch.

- Vinyl gloves to wear when using epoxy.

- Five-minute clear epoxy.

This list may seem overwhelming at first, but most of the tools and parts are used throughout robot building and thus aren't unique to this project.

Preparing Lengths of Solid Rod for the Couplers

The first steps in making the coupler are determining the length of rod required, cutting a few pieces, and smoothing the ends of the cut pieces.

Measuring the Motor and Axle

The length and diameter of the desired coupler vary depending on the motor and axle sizes. The best source of motor information is from the motor manufacturer's datasheets, if available. In any case, you can easily determine the motor-shaft length, motor-shaft diameter, and axle diameter by using dial or digital calipers.

If you don't have calipers (get some!), you can compare the shaft and axle diameters by eye against known diameters, such as the plain ends (the *shanks*) of known sizes of drills. You can measure the length of the motor shaft with a ruler.

Selecting a Solid Rod for the Coupler Body

To select an appropriately sized solid rod for the coupler body, you'll need to calculate a length and diameter. Your choice of rod material affects the minimum diameter required for adequate support.

Calculating the Coupler Length

You'll calculate the desired coupler length first. Consider both the motor-shaft length and the amount that the LEGO axle will be inserted into the coupler.

For my example motor, the motor-shaft length is 12 mm. For the LEGO axle, a depth of $\frac{5}{16}$ inch (about 8 mm) generally provides a straight and sturdy connection. This is consistent with the width of a LEGO brick. Greater depth might be preferable for longer axle lengths.

Thus, the *minimum* length of this coupler should be 12 mm (the motor-shaft length) plus 8 mm (the LEGO axle depth), which equals 20 mm.

Calculating the Coupler Diameter

Now you'll calculate the desired coupler diameter. Consider both the motor-shaft diameter and the LEGO axle diameter. Then pick a size bigger than the larger of the two diameters.

For my example motor, the motor-shaft diameter is 3 mm. The LEGO cross axle diameter is $\frac{3}{16}$ inch (about 4.76 mm). Because the LEGO axle is wider, the *minimum* diameter must be greater than $\frac{3}{16}$ inch.

Aluminum and brass are strong enough that you can use a $\frac{4}{16}$-inch (¼-inch) diameter rod (see Figure 3-1). However, if you have difficulty centering your drill or if you prefer plastic couplers, it'd be safer to step up to a $\frac{3}{8}$-inch rod or larger.

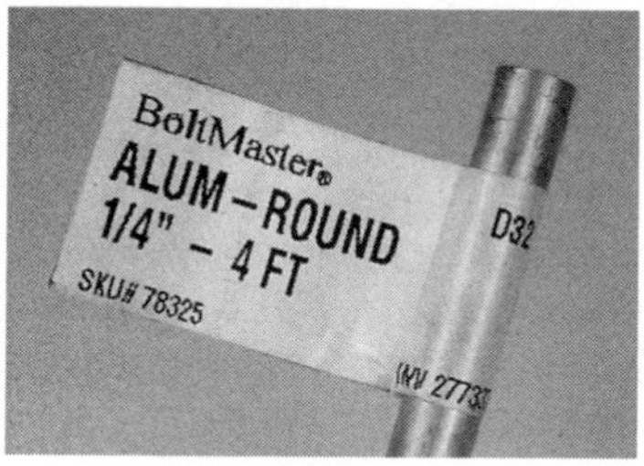

Figure 3-1. A ¼-inch diameter round aluminum rod

Selecting the Coupler Material

You can find round aluminum rod in local hardware stores, hobby shops, or online. Local stores are the most convenient because ordering long lengths of rod online will likely result in irregular shipping charges. Hexagonal (six-sided) rod, square rod, or other shapes are rarer and would be perfectly adequate as couplers except that they won't work with the instructions in this chapter.

For this application, you can substitute brass for aluminum. Brass is easier to machine at the expense of more mass.

ABS, acrylic, polycarbonate (LEXAN), and PVC are acceptable plastics that you can substitute for metals in this application. Plastics are cheap, easy to machine, and light-weight but are generally weaker than aluminum. Therefore, select a larger diameter rod if you choose plastic.

Stay away from iron or steel because they're too difficult for a hobbyist to machine. Avoid polypropylene, polyethylene, nylon, acetal (Delrin), and PTFE (Teflon) plastics because they tend to be too flexible or the epoxy for the LEGO axle won't stick.

For this example, I obtained the ¼-inch diameter, round, aluminum rod from a local hardware store. Alternately, you can purchase a 2-foot length from MSC Industrial Supply ($1.56, #32000515) at http://www.mscdirect.com/.

Cutting the Solid Rod into Coupler-Size Pieces

With a ruler and marker, indicate on the rod the lengths to cut for the couplers. Be sure to add a bit more length to each mark because you'll remove some of the material during cutting and filing. For example, if you want 20-mm couplers, mark every 22 mm or more.

Put the marked rod into a vise and tighten. Sometimes a V-block (see Figure 5-22 in Chapter 5) or V-grooved vise is necessary to hold round stock. The *V* refers to a trian-gular cut in which the round rod is placed so that it's surrounded and held on multiple sides, which prevents it from popping out under pressure.

Put on your safety glasses. Now use a hacksaw with a fine blade (24 teeth per inch) to cut on the waste side of your mark (see Figure 3-2). Alternatively, a power cutoff saw (see Figure 3-3) is better than a hacksaw because the cut will be straighter and smoother.

Figure 3-2. Hacksaw cutting lengths of solid aluminum rod gripped in vise. By the way, I'm left-handed. Those of you who are right-handed may want to extend the workpiece over the right side of the vise for cutting.

Figure 3-3. A small cutoff machine with built-in V-groove vise ($134.95, #15218 at Micro-Mark) cuts rod smoothly and at the proper angle so that sanding or filing may not be necessary. Larger machines are available at local hardware stores.

TIP *This is a golden rule of home machining (along with "Wear your safety glasses"): Use a hacksaw or other cutoff tool to cut down stock material to slightly oversized pieces. Then use more precise tools, such as a file or vertical milling machine, to clean up or make the final cuts.*

I'll usually make a dozen or more couplers at a time, depending on how many motors of a similar size I purchased together. Making a bunch of couplers at the same time spreads out the overhead involved with making only a pair of couplers because it reduces the overall time spent per coupler. Think of it as an assembly line where efficiency is gained in volume.

Additionally, later, having a bunch of couplers already made allows me to concentrate on the robot I'm designing rather than dragging myself to the basement to make yet another pair of couplers. I store my couplers in the same box as the motors they were made to fit.

Smoothing the Ends of the Coupler Body Pieces

The hacksaw leaves the pieces of rod with fairly rough ends. Depending on your hacksaw skills, the angle may be slightly off as well. But the rough ends won't affect the rotation of the wheels.

However, rough edges are unsightly and pose a cutting risk to humans and adjoining robot parts. Also, rough ends may cause the drill to cut off-center. Therefore, it's recommended you sand or file the ends smooth and square (at 90 degrees to the rod's surface), as shown in Figures 3-4 and 3-5.

Figure 3-4. Filing smooth the edges of the cut rod by holding the rod piece in one hand and drawing it across the file, which is held in the other hand. What? No! That's not how you're supposed to file!

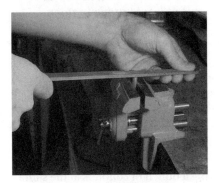

Figure 3-5. This is the proper way to file. The workpiece (cut rod) is held firmly in a vise. Hold the file with both hands and push it across the end of the rod. A V-block may be necessary to hold the cut rod in the vise.

Okay, I admit that for quick, small jobs I actually file like the method shown in Figure 3-4. However, I rarely file. Instead, I use a vertical milling machine (see Figure 3-6) followed by a light sanding if necessary.

Figure 3-6. A vertical milling machine smoothly cutting the tops of the rods. Note that in this picture, the shaft holes have already been drilled in the coupler bodies. This is because I'll often cut the rods smooth both before drilling and after drilling.

If you choose to file or mill multiple rods in a vise at the same time, it may be necessary to insert a piece of rubber to prevent individual rod pieces from being loose in the vise (see Figure 3-7). There's a grippy rubber mesh sold in grocery stores and hardware stores as a shelf liner or to aid in opening household items that seems to work well.

Figure 3-7. Rubber-grip material allows the vise to firmly hold multiple rods at the same time. A small, rectangular piece (parallel stock) evenly raises the tops of the rods above the top of the vise.

Depending on the depth of your vise, you may also find it necessary to insert a small, rectangular piece (called a *parallel* in such uses) to lift the rods high enough out of the vise for milling or filing. The parallel must be narrower than the rod diameter, or the vise will grip the parallel and not the rods.

Another advantage of a parallel is that it aligns the lower ends of all of the rods. If you file or mill the tops of the rods evenly, all the rods will become the same length.

At this point, some professional machinists are cringing. Throwing a bunch of rods into a vise at the same time won't result in ends that are nicely squared (90-degree angles) to their sides. That's not important to the function of this piece. However, if it's important to you, at the end of this whole process you can use a V-block or the fixture (described in the "Making a Coupler Fixture" section) to squarely cut each end. This minimizes drill-tip wandering when making holes for the motor shaft and wheel axle.

Setting Aside the Lengths of Rod

Now you should have two or more pieces of cut rod, with approximately the same length and reasonably smooth ends. Set them aside for a while.

Making a Coupler Fixture

Believe it or not, it's often necessary to make another part just to be able to make the final part you actually want. In this case, you need something to hold each round rod during drilling so that the drill press is accurately centered for each piece. When you make a holder or positioning device to aid in the manufacturing of another piece, the holder is called a *fixture*.

NOTE *A jig positions and holds the workpiece and guides the cutting tool. A fixture just positions or holds the workpiece; it doesn't guide the cutting tool.*

The coupler fixture (see Figure 3-8) is a block of aluminum with a hole drilled in it to the diameter and partial depth of the desired coupler. The rod piece is placed into the fixture's hole. A setscrew on the side holds the rod in place and prevents it from spinning while being drilled. The coupler fixture has flat sides so it fits firmly in a vise.

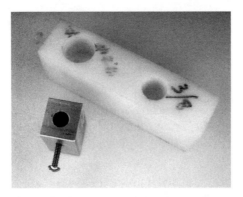

Figure 3-8. Rectangular aluminum coupler fixture with a hole for a ¼-inch rod and a screw to hold the rod in place (lower left). Another fixture, this time a "dual" model, made of nylon block with ½-inch and ⅜-inch holes for rods of those diameters (top right).

The coupler fixture is made from metal to dissipate heat during drilling and to resist wear so you can use it repeatedly. You could substitute a block of plastic for metal, but it won't provide the aforementioned benefits. Another problem with some plastics is that they compress during drilling and expand slightly afterward. So, the hole ends up being slightly too narrow to insert the rod. I highly recommend aluminum or brass instead of plastic.

For this example, I obtained a scrap rectangular bar of aluminum from Machinist Materials (http://www.machinistmaterials.com/). MSC Industrial Supply carries 6-foot lengths of 1-inch square bars of aluminum ($40.95, #32012064) or brass ($62.66, #32001737). Six feet should last you a while. Perhaps you could split the cost with a friend or a club?

Alternately, Online Metals (http://www.onlinemetals.com/) has 1-foot lengths of 1-inch square bars of aluminum for $5.62 or brass for $12.16. (Sorry, Online Metals doesn't seem to have part numbers, so you'll have to navigate the site.)

Cutting the Coupler Fixture Block

Place a chunk of aluminum (bar, square rod, or flat plate) in a vise. It must be large enough to hold the specified diameter of rod to at least 50 percent of the rod's length, with room to spare to avoid drilling into the vise beneath the fixture. In this case, I had a scrap piece 16-mm thick by 26-mm wide. That's more than enough to hold a ¼-inch rod (6.35 mm) to a depth of 20 mm (the total length). I cut off an arbitrarily sized 14-mm piece with a hacksaw (see Figure 3-9).

Figure 3-9. Using a hacksaw to cut off a piece of aluminum bar stock held in a vise

Only three sides of the fixture block (the shape is technically a rectangular prism) must be flat and square (90-degree angles to each other). To sit firmly in the vise, the important sides are the ones that touch the jaws and the bottom of the vise (see Figure 3-10).

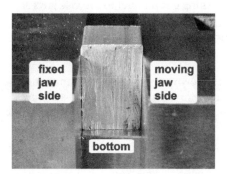

Figure 3-10. The three important sides of the fixture

If you cut your fixture block from appropriately sized stock, you don't actually need to clean it up because it retains at least four decent manufactured sides after cutting. However, if you have a vertical milling machine, you could take just a minute to finish off the rough-cut sides (see Figure 3-11) or square it up to your own personal standards.

Figure 3-11. Milling off the rough-cut sides of the fixture. Each rough side is placed face up and milled flat with a four-flute ¼-inch end mill. A parallel (barely in view between the vise jaws) raises the fixture block high enough in the vise to be milled flat.

Drilling the Coupler Fixture Setscrew Hole

When installed in the vise, a short side of the fixture is going to be on top. Peek ahead to Figures 3-21 and 3-22 to see how the coupler fixture will be situated in the vise during use. Notice that a long side has the setscrew coming out parallel to the vise jaws so the setscrew can be loosened and tightened with the fixture in place in the vise. To make the following instructions more understandable, pay attention to the location of the setscrew in those figures:

1. From the top of the fixture block, measure down approximately 8.5 mm and mark in the center widthwise. That's where you'll drill a hole for the setscrew. If you've left a side rough, that's the side you'll want to choose for marking the setscrew hole.

2. Install a #43 drill in the drill press or vertical milling machine. If you're not familiar with drills, then the label *#43* may confuse you. Some drill sizes are labeled with imperial fractions (for example, $\frac{5}{64}$ inch), some with metric (for example, 2 mm), some with letters (for example, F), and some with numbers (for example, #43). The standard machinist tables list a #43 as being 0.0890 inch, which equals 2.26 mm.

    You should be able to purchase a drill actually labeled "#43" at a good hardware store, usually near the taps and dies. For instance, MSC Industrial Supply has a #43 drill ($2.16, #80120439). I'm a big fan of the parabolic cobalt TiAlN #43 drill ($5.47, #01348259).

3. Place the fixture in the vise with the marked face pointing up (see Figure 3-12).

Figure 3-12. Drilling the fixture setscrew hole

4. Position the vise or milling table so the drill is generally centered over the setscrew mark.

5. Lock the vise or table. *The y-axis should remain locked from this point on in the process.* That is, the relationship between the table/vise/fixture and drill can change from left to right or from up to down, but not toward you or away from you. This will ensure that all subsequent holes are drilled in the same spot in that axis. If you have a milling machine, simply lock the y-axis on the table. If you have a drill press, simply secure the vise in place on the table.

6. Drill the setscrew hole to a depth of about halfway. In this example, 14 mm divided by 2 equals 7 mm deep. It's not critical to drill exactly halfway, but if you drill too deep, then you'll drill into the vise or parallel stock below.

During drilling, consider using a little light oil if you're drilling into a metal fixture.

Tapping the Coupler Fixture Setscrew Hole

Remove the fixture from the vise and use a #4-40 tap and tap wrench (see Figure 3-13) to create threads in the setscrew hole. If you've never tapped before, you can find some tapping tips in the next chapter.

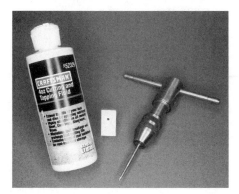

Figure 3-13. Tapping fluid, coupler fixture with setscrew hole drilled in it, and tap wrench with #4-40 tap (left to right)

A drop of tapping fluid or light oil is recommended when tapping aluminum. Terry Surma, a friend of mine from the Chicago Area Robotics Group (ChiBots), swears by kerosene when working with aluminum. No oily mess, either. Of course, you should always be aware of potential ignition sources and provide adequate ventilation when working with flammable liquids or chemicals.

Drilling the Coupler Rod Hole in the Coupler Fixture

At this point, you've cut the fixture block to size and drilled and tapped a setscrew hole. Now you'll make the hole in which the round rod will be held during drilling.

The next holes to be drilled are crucial. Any amount of misalignment, bending, or walking will result in parallel offset or angular offset in the coupler. The previous chapter documents the evils of these errors.

Selecting Drills

A good hole starts with a good drill. For accurate centering, this is what you should look for in a drill:

Machining drill is required: Don't use drills labeled for woodworking or masonry only because they're shaped differently for those purposes. Drills labeled specifically for aluminum are preferred in this example, but drills labeled generally for metal, wood, or plastic are also fine.

Right-hand rotation is required: Left-hand rotation drills require the drilling machine to rotate in a reversed direction. Left-hand rotation drills are unusual, so if the drill isn't labeled "left-hand," then it's right-hand.

Split-point (also called *crankshaft*) is required (see Figure 3-14): A split-point self-centers the drill and resists walking (rolling away from the center). This is opposed to a conventional point, which is more general purpose and can walk. Many other drill point types are available; the acceptable ones for this purpose are the ones that describe themselves as "self-centering."

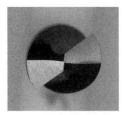

Figure 3-14. A split-point drill. The tip of the point is split into two parts, whose forces tend to draw the drill into the center of rotation.

Screw-machine length (also called *stubby* or *short length*) is recommended (see Figure 3-15): Jobber-length drills are longer and are the standard, but a shorter drill has less flex and is less likely to result in angular offset. Also, shorter lengths leave more vertical clearance for the workpiece at the expense of not being able to drill as deeply as jobber drills. Avoid extra-long or extended-length drills for this task.

Figure 3-15. Standard-length (jobber-length) drill (top). Machine-screw length drill (bottom)

Either 118-degree or 135-degree drill point angle is fine: 118 degrees is generally more common, but self-centering split-point drills seem to appear most often with 135-degree drill point angles.

Sharp and undamaged is required: Worn or broken drills slide around.

HSS or cobalt drills are recommended: Carbide drills are sharper and longer lasting but are much more expensive and brittle. Smaller (hobbyist-sized) machining equipment tends to vibrate a lot, which often chips and shatters narrow-diameter carbide drills.

Ordinary bright-finish drills are fine: Titanium nitride (TiN), titanium carbonitride (TiCN), and titanium aluminum nitride (TiAlN) coatings are good, but hobbyists rarely require their added performance attributes. Avoid drilling aluminum with drills coated with black oxide coatings because the aluminum tends to "stick." If you want a high-performance coating for aluminum, choose TiAlN or TiCN.

Parabolic wide-land is recommended: Parabolic drills are designed to improve chip flow (material removed in making the hole). This permits much deeper holes to be drilled, and it prevents clogging in "stringy" materials such as plastics and aluminum. Although recommended, parabolic drills aren't absolutely necessary unless you're drilling deep holes (greater than four times the diameter of the drill).

Fixing the Depth

To obtain the desired depth for the coupler rod hole, you could drill a little, pull the drill out, measure, drill a little more, and so on. But this is an easier and more accurate way:

1. Place the coupler fixture block into the vise. Make sure the bottom of the fixture sits flat against the bottom of the vise—otherwise the hole will be drilled at an angle.

2. Insert a drill with a diameter equal to the diameter of the coupler rod. In this example, use a ¼-inch drill. You must use the proper drill diameter for this step because different drills have different lengths. If you swap in a different drill to perform the actual drilling, you may end up with a depth you didn't intend.

    MSC Industrial Supply has an HSS, ¼-inch diameter, screw-machine length, 135-degree, split-point drill ($3.72, #80110166). Even better, it sells a cobalt, TiAlN-coated, parabolic, screw-machine length, 130-degree, split-point drill ($13.40, #01349307).

3. Don't move the y-axis because it's currently set in the identical position as the location of the setscrew. But, for the moment, you want the fixture block beside the drill, not under it. If you have a vertical milling machine, simply adjust the x-axis. Otherwise, slide the fixture block over in the vise (don't move the vise in a drill press because the y-axis might change).

4. Lower the drill beside the fixture block until the drill body reaches the desired depth (see Figure 3-16). In this example, it's about 12.5 mm. Make sure to measure to where the widest circumference of the drill first appears. This is because the drill point makes a conical hole, which is fine for chips, but it won't fit the rod to that depth.

Figure 3-16. Side view of the vise. The drill is lowered beside the fixture block to determine the desired depth.

In this example, the fixture's setscrew hole is 12.5 mm minus 8.5 mm, which equals 4 mm above the bottom of where the coupler will rest. Because the fixture setscrew often leaves a little scratch on the coupler rod, it can be used to mark the location where you want to drill the setscrew hole on the coupler itself. Although you can always measure and drill the coupler setscrew wherever you please, a little thinking ahead can take advantage of a consistent scratch.

5. Most drill presses and vertical milling machines have a limit block. Slide the limit block up the headstock and lock it in place (see Figure 3-17). This allows the drill to move up but not to move down any farther than the depth just measured.

Figure 3-17. Limit block being slid up the headstock. In this figure, the limit block needs to be moved up a little more before it's locked in position.

Great! The y-axis was positioned and locked before drilling the setscrew. Now the z-axis maximum (depth) is positioned and locked by the limit block.

Drilling

To continue with the project and start drilling, follow these steps:

1. Raise the drill so you can move the coupler fixture block underneath.

2. Horizontally center the fixture block underneath the drill by adjusting its x-axis only. It doesn't need to be exactly centered horizontally—generally centered is good enough.

3. Lock the x-axis or vise jaws. The x-axis and fixture should remain locked in place from this point.

When a drill first touches the workpiece, the vibrations, flexing of the drill, sharpness of the drill, straightness of the drill, drill point, and roughness of the material surface all contribute to determining if the tip starts cutting exactly in the center of the drill's rotation. Obviously, a bent drill or damaged tip will cut a little to one side or another. This will self-correct as the drill continues to spin and cut, or the starting hole will continue to lead the drill astray, bending the drill and creating a hole that's slightly off-angle.

A special kind of drill, called a *spotting drill* (see Figure 3-18), is especially precise and especially rigid. The more exact the starting hole, the more likely the drill will continue straight. In fact, if the drill is headed straight when the full drill diameter enters the workpiece, the sidewalls of the hole will help aim the drill so that it continues straight.

Figure 3-18. A spotting drill for making precise starting holes

MSC Industrial Supply has an HSS, TiN-coated, short-length, 120-degree, ¼-inch diameter spotting drill ($26.66, #63735328). Even though you'll drill a ¼-inch hole in this example, you could use a ¼-inch diameter spotting drill to get the hole started. Plunge the drill tip only partway into the material so that the tip starts the hole.

If you have a long enough spotting drill (remember, you set the limit block earlier for the ¼-inch drill), you should insert it and drill a nice, clean starting hole until the hole diameter matches the diameter of the coupler rod. Plunge slowly to allow the drill time to remove chips and to work out any surface roughness. Also, don't attempt to drill the full depth with a spotting drill. They're designed for rigidity. They *aren't* designed for drilling efficiency or for chip removal. When you're done, replace the spotting drill with the normal drill you intend to use for the hole.

TIP *Take care when removing or inserting a drill. Each time you must hold the drill tightly against the chuck's internal stop while tightening the jaws. Any variation in drill insertion is equivalent to having moved the limit block.*

To finish, drill the coupler rod hole (see Figure 3-19) down to the depth allowed by the limit block. Pull out frequently to clear chips and prevent the material from clogging the flutes of the drill.

Figure 3-19. Drilling the coupler rod hole

The coupler fixture is now finished.

Getting the Money Shot

Okay, here's the big tip. This is key to the whole chapter. This is why you've been carefully following each step: You know the drill is absolutely centered over the hole it just drilled. When you drop a matching-diameter rod into the hole, the drill is absolutely centered over the rod. Good trick, huh? Just don't move the fixture block or vise (or x-axis and y-axis locks on a vertical milling machine).

You can switch to a smaller drill, drop in a rod, drill perfectly centered holes in the rod, pull the rod out, drop in another rod, drill perfectly centered holes in that rod, and so on. Each hole will be perfectly, absolutely, and completely centered.

Okay, perhaps I got overly dramatic with *perfectly* and *absolutely*.

In reality, the rotational imperfections of the machine (the *runout*), the vibrations of the machine, the bending of the drills, any dullness, and so forth contribute to a little bit of offset from rod to rod. Even though it should be theoretically centered, the limits of the tools and materials foil perfection somewhat. But the quality ends up being good and consistent for a homemade part. Make more than you need, and keep the best ones.

Enlarging Tight Fits

Depending on the materials you select, you may find that the rods you made earlier aren't easily inserted or removed from the fixture. This can especially be true with certain kinds of plastic fixtures, where the material contracted during drilling and expanded after drilling.

As your drill is directly centered over the fixture at this time, you can do one of the following:

- Redrill the hole a couple of times to get a looser fit.

- Bore out the hole with a boring bar, or ream it with a reamer.

- Insert a slightly bigger drill. Depending on the coupler rod diameter, you can usually find a weirdly numbered or decimal-sized drill that's a bit larger.

 CAUTION *If you choose too large of a diameter, the hole will be enlarged too much, and the coupler rod will wiggle. This results in a poorly centered hole in the coupler rods themselves.*

I haven't had a problem with too tight of a hole when the fixture is made from aluminum or brass. However, I've seen this occur with nylon fixtures.

Remember, too, that the diameter of the rod itself has been manufactured to within a certain tolerance. It may be that the specific rod you chose is a little wider diameter than labeled. Again, simply enlarge the fixture hole a tiny amount.

Adding a Setscrew to the Coupler Fixture

Insert a #4-40 screw (in this example, ⅜-inch long) into the fixture's setscrew hole you drilled earlier. Don't move the fixture!

Check that the screw can be turned all the way in so that it extends into the hole drilled for the rod. Turn the screw out to insert a rod, and then turn the screw in to check that the screw tip locks the rod in place for drilling.

Repositioning the Coupler Fixture

You can't move or use the drill press or vertical milling machine for other work until you've drilled all the couplers. That's fine for a dozen couplers or so, but eventually you'll want to free your locked machine for other services. This is an amateur method for recentering the fixture beneath the drill:

1. Put the coupler fixture into the vise.

2. Insert a decent length of suitable-diameter round rod into the drill press or vertical milling machine as though it were a drill. In this example, insert a ¼-inch round rod approximately 4 inches long.

3. Position the table or vise so you can plunge the round rod (see Figure 3-20) into the coupler fixture hole. It may take a couple of tries and some adjusting.

Figure 3-20. Recentering the fixture in the vise by inserting a round rod instead of a drill into the chuck

The drill is now reasonably centered once again over the coupler fixture hole. (A professional method for recentering the fixture is to use a dial indicator or an edge finder.)

Drilling the Motor-Shaft and LEGO Axle Coupler Holes

Believe it or not, you've completed most of the difficult steps. You should have a pile of smooth, cut round rods from earlier in this process. To drill the motor-shaft and LEGO axle coupler holes, follow these steps:

1. The finished fixture should still be tight in the vise and centered.

2. Insert the drill of the narrower of either the motor-shaft diameter or the LEGO axle diameter. In this example, the motor shaft is only 3 mm, so you insert that diameter drill into the drill press.

3. The fixture shouldn't have a rod inserted at this point—only a bare hole.

4. Lower the drill into the hole until it touches the bottom.

5. Set the limit block. This prevents the drill from drilling into the fixture.

6. Raise the drill.

7. Loosen the fixture setscrew.

8. Insert a precut rod into the fixture.

9. Tighten the fixture setscrew so the rod won't rotate during drilling and it can't accidentally lift out when the drill is being withdrawn.

10. If desired, remove the drill and replace it with a spotting drill to make the start of the hole. Drill the start hole, and restore the original drill (see Figure 3-21).

Figure 3-21. You can use a spotting drill (left) to drill a fairly accurate (but shallow) pilot hole or starting mark. You then use a regular drill of the narrower diameter (right) to drill straight through the coupler rod.

11. Drill about a centimeter into the rod, and then pull up to clear the chips. Repeat this process until you reach the limit block.

12. Without moving the coupler fixture or newly drilled rod, switch out to a larger diameter drill. In this example, this is the diameter of the LEGO axle, which is $\frac{3}{16}$ inch. If the coupler is plastic, you might want to use the slightly wider diameter (#12) drill to compensate for compression.

13. Plunge slowly at first so that the narrower diameter hole in the rod acts as a center for the wider drill.

14. Drill a little (see Figure 3-22), pull up and measure the hole, and drill again. For the LEGO axle, a $\frac{5}{16}$-inch deep hole is fine. Deeper holes are appropriate for longer axles.

One method of checking the hole's depth is to insert a LEGO Technic pin friction connector to see if it fits in all the way.

Figure 3-22. Drilling a wider hole in the top of the coupler rod (left). Inserting a LEGO Technic pin friction connector to check depth (right).

Unfortunately, the limit block is in place to indicate the maximum depth that prevents the narrower drill from drilling into the fixture bottom. There's no danger of that occurring with this second drill because it's only plunging partway into the coupler. However, it'd be nice to find a way to be consistent with the depth other than cautiously drilling a little and pulling back up. Many drill presses and milling machines have numbered indicators you can use to measure the depth of a perfected hole and repeat. However, even with the indicators, swapping drills results in some variance.

15. Loosen the fixture setscrew, and remove the drilled coupler rod.

Inspect the coupler rod. Even if the two holes aren't centered exactly within the rod itself (see Figure 3-23), the two holes are likely centered within each other. That's all that affects parallel offset—so, that's all that really matters.

Why would the holes not be centered in relation to the coupler rod? And why isn't the miscentering consistent from rod to rod?

The texture on the top of the rod can cause the drill to "walk" from the true center. A smooth surface is an advantage, but also remember you can use a spotting drill to drill a fairly accurate (shallow) pilot hole or starting mark.

Even if the surface of the rod is smooth, narrow drills tend to vibrate and bend, which contributes to parallel offset and angular offset. Again, a spotting drill starting mark helps a lot here.

Ultimately, the runout (rotational error) in my cheap, imported milling/drilling machine is to blame for most of my inconsistencies.

Repeat steps 8 through 15 until you've drilled all the precut rods.

Figure 3-23. Axle and motor-shaft holes well centered within each other and the coupler rod body itself (left). Holes well centerted within each other, but not as well in relation to the coupler rod (right). No big deal. Both couplers perform beautifully.

Swapping Drills, Not Coupler Rods

Why not keep the same narrow drill in place and drill holes through all of the rods in the pile before switching to the wider drill? Admittedly, it's a royal pain to switch drills for each coupler one at a time.

However, if the drill press isn't exactly centered over the coupler fixture, there will be a slight offset in relation to the coupler rod. That's not harmful as long as the second drilling takes place at the same offset so both motor-shaft and LEGO axle holes are centered within each other.

If instead you were to pull out the rod after the first drilling, when you insert it later you'll likely have rotated the rod so that the drill press's offset now aims at a different spot on the rod. Although the narrow first hole may still help guide the wider drill, some parallel offset will be introduced along with perhaps some angular offset because the wider drill is bent toward the center of the narrow hole.

Add the Finishing Touch: Squaring the Ends

Now that you've drilled all the motor-shaft and axle holes, you can clean the ends of the couplers. If you chose aluminum for your coupler, the drilling has likely left some burrs on the drill's exit hole at the bottom of each coupler. A metal file, a high-speed rotary tool (such as a Dremel), or some sandpaper can clear that up.

Even better, if you have a milling machine, reinsert the couplers into the fixture one at a time to hold them straight up and down. This makes it easy to mill each end flat and square in relation to the sides. Although not functionally necessary, it makes the part look more professional.

Examining the Coupler So Far

Some simple machining techniques allow you to create professional couplers of almost any diameter or material desired, even with hobbyist tools. These techniques are also applicable to making other parts:

- Select a material that's easy to work with, such as aluminum, brass, or most plastics. Avoid plastics that are difficult to glue or metals that are too tough to machine.

- Use a hacksaw for cutting material to a little larger than needed. Avoid using a precision machine for rough cuts.

- Smooth the cut ends.

- When selecting material for the fixture, save yourself time and take advantage of the smooth, squared sides and sizes of stock ready-made by manufacturers.

- Make a fixture to position and hold your workpiece. In fact, don't be surprised if you find yourself creating different fixtures for various steps in a process. I've got a box full of homemade fixtures. They've made an enormous difference in the quality of my work.

- Position the drill to the side of a piece to center it visually. At the same time, determine the desired depth and fix it with the limit block on a drill press or milling machine.

- To drill in the center of a rod, drill a hole the diameter of the rod in a stock piece (now your fixture). Then, without moving the milling/drilling machine table, vise, or workpiece, insert the rod into the hole. The rod is now centered beneath the drill.

- Later, you can reasonably recenter the fixture by inserting a rod into the drill chuck.

- A flat surface on the material, slow drilling when first entering the workpiece, a spotting drill, a short-length drill, and a self-centering drill point all aid in drilling straight and centered holes.

- To drill one hole centered in another, first drill the narrower-diameter hole. Then, without moving the milling/drilling machine table, vise, or workpiece, switch drills and drill the wider-diameter hole. The narrower hole acts as a pilot hole for the wider drill.

Now that you have a pile of coupler rods with beautiful holes drilled in them, you need to finish them with setscrews and LEGO axles. The next chapter describes how to cut threads into the coupler rod for a setscrew and how to attach a LEGO axle with epoxy. Soon you'll have turned a $1.50 aluminum rod into useful bits of robot anatomy!

CHAPTER 4

Finishing the Solid-Rod Motor Coupler

Covers Tapping Holes and Selecting Setscrews

IN THE PREVIOUS CHAPTER, you cut a solid rod down into coupler lengths by using a hacksaw. With a fixture on a drill press, you drilled holes in the cut rod pieces for the motor shaft and the LEGO cross axle.

In this chapter, at long last, you'll finish your coupler with a setscrew and LEGO axle. This chapter contains some interesting information on tap styles, as well as a grooving technique for making sure the LEGO axle stays in place in the coupler.

Installing the Coupler Setscrew

Recall that the setscrew connects the coupler to the motor shaft. With the setscrew loosened, you can easily remove the coupler. With the setscrew tightened, the motor shaft is held firmly inside the coupler.

Determining the Location for the Coupler Setscrew

If you took the time to measure and drill accurately when you created the fixture, the setscrew on the fixture may conveniently mar the coupler exactly where you want to drill the coupler's setscrew hole (see Figure 4-1). By the way, this trick works only if the motor shaft is narrower or equal in size to the LEGO axle because the end with the narrower hole is at the bottom of the fixture being held in place by the fixture's setscrew that leaves the mark.

The setscrew for the coupler must be located on the end of the coupler in which the motor will be inserted. After all, the setscrew's purpose is to tighten against the motor shaft to keep the shaft from spinning and from falling out. Don't accidentally drill the setscrew on the end of the rod where the LEGO axle will be mounted.

I prefer to locate the setscrew generally closer to the motor. That way, if the motor shaft slips out a bit, the setscrew will still be able to hold onto some length of shaft. Most motor shafts have a *flat* (a flat spot on the otherwise cylindrical shaft) only toward the very tip, which limits how close to the motor body you can go.

Figure 4-1. The setscrew on the fixture can conveniently leave a little mark on the coupler.

If the flat continues all the way up to the motor body, resist the temptation to drill too closely to the coupler's end. First, the coupler hole may weaken the end of the coupler because of the little amount of material surrounding the hole on the end. Considering that the motor force transmits to the coupler body through the threads in the coupler hole, it's important that the hole be surrounded by enough material to provide strength. Second, many motors mount to a bracket in the front of the motor. If the coupler setscrew is too close to the end, then the motor bracket may block setscrew access when the coupler is slipped into place.

For the example of the coupler in this chapter, the coupler setscrew is located about 4 mm from the end of the coupler. Mark that location if it hasn't already been done for you by the fixture's setscrew.

Drilling the Coupler Setscrew Hole

Follow these steps for drilling the coupler setscrew hole:

1. Insert a #43 drill.

2. Place a coupler rod into the vise. A parallel may be necessary to lift it to a height for easy viewing. Some people prefer to use a V-block for this step. It may get in the way of the hole you want to drill, depending on the size of the block and on the length of the coupler. I find that a vise has sufficient gripping force for drilling this fairly narrow-diameter, shallow hole in the coupler rod.

3. With the drill off to one side of the coupler, lower the drill to a depth of half the diameter of the coupler (see left side of Figure 4-2) and set the drill machine's limit block.

4. Also use this opportunity to center the drill in the Y direction (front to back) in reference to the motor shaft hole in the coupler (again, see the left side of Figure 4-2). Lock the vise or y-axis.

5. Position the coupler or drill so that the mark lines up underneath the drill.

6. Drill the setscrew hole (see the right side of Figure 4-2). The limit block should prevent the drill from plunging into (or through) the lower side of the coupler. A careful eye and a gentle hand on the drill press lever also suffice.

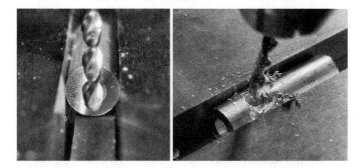

Figure 4-2. Centering the drill in relation to the coupler's motor shaft hole and also locating the maximum depth that can be drilled without breaching the lower wall of the coupler (left). Drilling the setscrew hole (right).

7. Remove the coupler, and repeat steps 5 and 6 for the remaining couplers.

Tapping the Coupler Setscrew Hole

The setscrew holes now need threads tapped into them so they'll accept screws. You can choose from a couple of tap styles, as well as from some tapping techniques that are helpful.

Selecting a Bottom-Style Tap

Depending on the diameter of the coupler and the diameter of the motor shaft hole, a bottom-style tap may be required to make the full threads in the coupler hole. A bottom-style tap differs from a plug-style or taper-style tap in that only the first one to two threads are *chamfered* (ground down) to guide the insertion of the tap (see Figure 4-3). This has the advantage of making full threads to almost the complete depth of the hole.

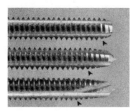

Figure 4-3. Bottom-style taps have one or two threads chamfered (top). Standard or plug-style taps have three to six chamfered (middle). Taper-style or starter taps have seven to ten threads chamfered (bottom).

Bottom-style taps are normally used in tapping *blind* holes—holes that don't go all the way through the material. In this case, the motor shaft diameter can be so narrow that the tap doesn't have enough room to extend beyond the setscrew hole such that the full cutters (farther up the tap) are engaged throughout the entire setscrew hole.

If you can't find them at your local hardware store, MSC Industrial Supply at http://www.mscdirect.com/ has bottom-style ($5.32, #74924416), plug-style (($5.32, #74924408), and taper-style ($5.32, #74924424) three-fluted taps.

Comparing to a Taper-Style Tap

A taper-style tap does a good job of guiding itself straight in the hole because the hole threads are formed more gradually. Also, less force is required. However, if the taper-style tap isn't permitted to penetrate deeply enough, the deepest seven to ten threads won't be fully cut.

Forcing a setscrew into less-than-full-cut threads stresses the material. Aluminum and brass may be strong and malleable enough to accept this mistake. However, brittle materials, such as acrylic, form cracks over time or may even shatter (see Figure 4-4).

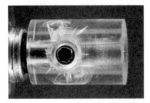

Figure 4-4. Stress cracks in an acrylic coupler because of failure to fully cut the bottom threads in the setscrew hole. Believe me, this started out as a beautiful, clean, clear piece. It developed the cracks over a period of several days.

Tapping Tips

A smart compromise is to use a plug-style or taper-style tap to start the hole. Tap as deeply as you can and then remove the tap and switch to the bottom style to make the deepest threads. This combination gives you the straightness and ease of cutting of the more tapered varieties, with the full-cut depth of the bottom-style tap.

A couple of other practices can further improve tapping:

- Use some tapping fluid or light cutting oil when working with metals or oil-compatible plastics. The oil helps remove the chips and makes turning easier, which reduces the likelihood of breaking the tap in the hole. The lubrication reduces friction (and thus heat), which extends the tap's life by keeping it sharper for a longer period of time. Ooooh, one more thing: The oil keeps the tap from rusting.

- Turn the tap back a quarter- or half-turn for every full turn. This helps break up the material and prevents the tap from binding.

- For hand tapping in relatively soft materials (such as plastic, aluminum, and brass), try a spiral or three-fluted tap instead of a straight or two-fluted tap. The balance of cutting edges tends to keep the tap a little more centered.

- Use only gentle downward pressure, if any. The turning motion pulls the tap into the threads as it cuts.

Selecting a Setscrew

Technically, a real setscrew sets itself apart from a standard screw by the lack of an obvious head and by the variety of points (tips) available. Only the middle sections appear similar (see Figure 4-5).

Figure 4-5. A #4-40 panhead ⅛-inch long screw (left) in comparison to a #4-40 socket head ⅛-inch long setscrew with a flat point (right). Notice both the tops and tips are different.

MSC Industrial Supply sells #4-40, ⅛-inch long, socket head, flat point, stainless steel setscrews ($0.14, #64100985).

One nice thing about a real setscrew is that the lack of a protruding head allows it to fit snugly within the coupler (see Figure 4-6). Nothing sticks out to become entangled! Also, the engineered tip presses firmly against the motor shaft without digging into it. (A cone point is available if you want it to dig in.) Furthermore, real setscrews are usually made out of hardened steel for increased toughness.

Figure 4-6. Setscrew nicely flush in a finished coupler. The 0.050-inch key located at the bottom right of the figure tightens or loosens the setscrew.

On the other hand, ordinary machine screws are more commonly available. Also, they're more often designed with Phillips or slotted heads. That isn't to say there aren't any setscrews with slotted heads, just that socket heads are the standard, especially in setscrews with smaller diameters. There isn't anything significantly wrong with socket heads apart from requiring another tool—usually a 0.050-inch key ($0.51, #05051032).

Regardless of the type of screw you choose, I recommend you always purchase stainless steel screws over alloy or zinc-plated steel screws. The few extra cents in cost may save you hours of painstaking work from having a screw corroded or stripped in place.

Adding the LEGO Axle

The coupler is almost complete.

For this example, a LEGO axle is going to be epoxied in the coupler. A LEGO axle provides a friction fit to many LEGO parts, including wheels, gears, cranks, and differentials. The quick-change friction fit encourages experimentation with your robot, not to mention easy-to-replace parts.

Epoxy is required instead of thin adhesives because the X shape of the LEGO cross axle leaves lots of gaps that must be filled. Also, the LEGO axle is made of polypropylene, which is extremely difficult to glue. So, you're going to take advantage of the shape-forming properties of epoxy to create a physical bond where a chemical bond would likely fail under load.

Follow these steps to add the LEGO axle:

1. Obtain a LEGO cross axle in a length desired. In this example, I cut a 6 LEGO unit (LU) length axle in half.

TIP *LEGO axles have become available in a variety of colors. Although black is still the most common, you can find colors such as red, white, and gray. Visit the auction site at* http://www.bricklink.com/.

2. With the sharp corner edge of a file, make notches (see Figure 4-7) in the end of the LEGO axle that will be inserted into the coupler. If you cut down a longer axle, put the notches in the cut end because the tapered end accepts LEGO parts more easily.

   The notches don't have to be straight, similar, all the way across, or parallel. The depth and position can vary. For longer axles, you can make multiple sets of notches. The purpose of the notches is to have the epoxy harden into a shape that physically prevents the axle from being able to be pulled out.

3. Besides the notches, roughen the sides of the inserted end a little. Each groove and scratch is an opportunity for the epoxy to grab hold.

Figure 4-7. A small triangular file (upper left) can make notches and grooves in the end of a LEGO axle (center).

4. Clean the axle with a mild detergent and water or with isopropyl alcohol to try to remove oil, dirt, and other contaminants from the axle surface. The idea is to provide the best possible surface with which the epoxy can bond. In the case of polypropylene, the epoxy needs all the help it can get. Allow the axle to dry completely.

5. Obtain some quick-setting epoxy. I prefer Devcon High-Strength All Purpose 5-Minute Epoxy—clear. It comes in a two-part dispenser. An opaque tan color is also available but can be unattractive if the couplers are visible on the robot.

6. Wearing vinyl gloves (not latex) and with adequate ventilation, follow the instructions on the epoxy to mix a small amount on a scrap of cardboard.

7. Apply enough epoxy to the notched end of the axle so it can fill the voids and gaps between the X shape of the axle and the O shape of the coupler hole (see Figure 4-8). Often, I'll use a toothpick to gently poke and brush the epoxy to make sure it reaches the inside corners of the X shape.

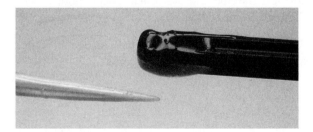

Figure 4-8. A notched LEGO cross axle coated with epoxy, ready to be inserted into the coupler. You can use a toothpick to nudge the epoxy into the grooves in the cross axle.

8. Swirl the axle around as you insert it. You want maximum coverage and contact. If the LEGO axle hole is a larger diameter than the motor shaft hole, then you can insert the axle as far as it'll go. The LEGO axle hole eventually bottoms out against the narrower motor shaft hole.

9. Repeat these steps for the remaining couplers.

10. Give the epoxy plenty of time to harden. Five minutes is the maximum amount of working time, not the time for a complete cure. Refer to the product package to determine the time until maximum strength. It can commonly be between an hour and 24 hours.

11. If you applied too much epoxy, sand or chip off the external residue. If some epoxy leaked into the motor shaft portion of the coupler, you can easily remove it with a drill size slightly narrower than the diameter of the motor shaft.

Summary

You've finished the solid-rod couplers. Even if it seems like a lot of work at first reading, the serviceability, reliability, and versatility of the couplers more than compensate for the time spent making them. I use couplers in every robot I build.

This chapter in the coupler saga presented some information applicable to machining in general:

- There are advantages and disadvantages to various tap styles. Picking the right tap and using it correctly makes subtle but important differences in the creation of threads. Better still, use a combination of tap styles and tap the hole twice.

- Scratching and grooving a material improves the physical bond, as well as exposes a greater surface area for chemical bonds.

- Where even a gel-type superglue would fail, a thick epoxy can fill voids and gaps between materials, providing a strong and lasting joint.

CHAPTER 5

Building a Motor Inside a Wheel

Covers Skills Perfect for Building Compact Sumo Robots, Machining Round Parts (Including Making Homemade Wheels), Using Step Blocks, Mating with Unthreaded Holes, and Using Really Large Drills

MOST HOMEMADE ROBOTS ARE BUILT around their method of locomotion. First you choose the motors and the wheels, then you decide how to position the motors in relation to the wheels so that you can deliver mechanical power, and finally you build the rest of the robot from this base.

Because of the difficulty of accurately positioning wheels, motors, and everything in-between (gears, belts, brackets), it's usually best to build the simplest drive train possible. Oftentimes, it's worthwhile to sacrifice drive-train space in exchange for drive-train simplicity. But what do you do when a robot's dimensions demand a compact solution?

This chapter describes a technique that avoids external gears and offset motors, without compromising either the robot's width or the wheels' width, by installing the motors inside the wheels themselves (see Figure 5-1). This is great for creating a robot similar to the Mars Rover or for meeting contest requirements such as mini-sumo (10-cm wide or smaller).

Figure 5-1. A small motor built into a slightly altered LEGO 49.6 by 28 VR wheel

However, this chapter is just an excuse to discuss a few more machining techniques, such as how to make a circle from a square sheet, why two adjacent pieces shouldn't both be threaded, the purpose of a Silver & Deming drill, and the use of Teflon to create a gluing fixture. Don't be put off that this chapter includes specific instructions on using a rotary table with a milling machine to make discs or wheels. Even if you don't have access to such equipment, it's still interesting to see how a hobbyist could do it.

Encountering Danger: Bent Shafts Ahead

I'm generally not a big fan of driving a wheel directly from a motor unless the wheel's axle is supported on both sides. By *driving a wheel directly*, I mean when the motor's shaft is connected directly to the wheel axle rather than through a series of external gears or belts. Although a direct connection provides a simple and efficient method for delivering motor power to a wheel, it provides an equally efficient path for harmful road forces to travel from the wheel back to the motor.

Driving Properly with Bearings

Figure 5-2 shows a motor directly driving a wheel. The motor shaft is attached to the wheel's axle by a rigid coupler.

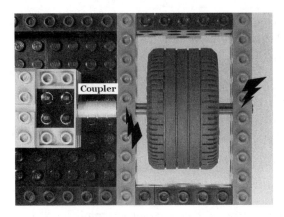

Figure 5-2. The LEGO motor is connected directly to the wheel's axle. However, the axle (and therefore the wheel) is supported on both sides to absorb bumps.

Protecting Against Bumps and Falls

A good thing about the design illustrated in Figure 5-2 is that both sides of the wheel are supported on the axle by LEGO Technic bricks. Therefore, the LEGO bricks, as opposed to the motor shaft, carry the weight of the robot. When this robot hits a bump or takes a fall, the amount of force transmitted to the motor is minimized.

Shifting Against the Coupler, Laterally

It also happens that in this design, the coupler reduces lateral (side-to-side) forces. When the axle is pushed one way (pushed left in Figure 5-2), the coupler presses against the motor case. When the axle is pushed the other way (pushed right in Figure 5-2), the coupler presses against the LEGO brick.

LEGO bricks, motors, and wheels are carefully manufactured to tight tolerances so they line up exactly. In a structure built from handmade parts, a flexible coupler would be a better choice than a rigid coupler. A flexible coupler would not only stretch and compress to reduce and absorb lateral forces, but it'd also bend to compensate for any misalignment between the motor shaft and the wheel axle.

Flexible material wasn't recommended in Chapter 4 for making a solid-rod coupler because flexible material is difficult to drill and glue. More important, flexible material is almost impossible to thread for a setscrew.

Bending Without Support

Many smaller robots are designed without support for wheels or axles other than the bearings built into the motors. A potential risk of an unsupported wheel is that when the wheel hits a bump, it could bend the motor's shaft. It's one thing to replace a cheap axle that has slowly worn away against a support, but it's entirely another thing to replace an expensive miniature gearhead motor whose shaft bent at the first sign of real action.

Driving a wheel directly from a motor without any additional support is acceptable under certain conditions:

- The motor should have a thick output shaft that's supported by internal bearings

- The wheel should have a small diameter to limit leverage on the axle and motor shaft

- The wheel should be as near to the motor as possible, again to limit leverage on the axle and motor shaft

- The robot's mass should be relatively low

- The robot's tasks should be performed at moderate speeds to reduce stress

The motor described in this chapter has to be small enough to fit within the wheel. Conversely, the wheel has to be large enough to have the motor fit within it. That translates into a tiny motor with a tiny shaft holding a large wheel whose large diameter results in the production of a lot of torque and bending force on the tiny motor shaft. All of this and no support!

Making a Hub-Adapter Coupler

LEGO wheels are plentiful, lightweight, and terrific quality. They remain my robot wheels of choice. To attach a non-LEGO motor to a LEGO wheel, I'll usually make a coupler rod with a motor-shaft hole at one end and a LEGO cross axle at the other end. Unfortunately, that type of coupler is fairly long.

What's needed in this example is a compact coupler that consumes little room itself and permits reuse of interior hub space by allowing the motor to be embedded as deeply as possible inside the wheel hub. As always, the coupler should provide a simple method of detaching the motor from the wheel for maintenance.

Adapting the Motor Shaft's Outer Diameter to the LEGO Wheel's Inner Diameter

The hub-adapter coupler design consists of several pieces, as pictured in Figure 5-3.

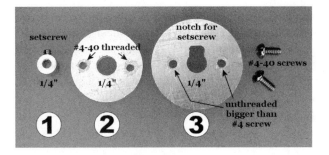

Figure 5-3. The various parts of the hub-adapter coupler

This hub-adapter coupler consists of the following:

- A ¼-inch diameter rod ① drilled to fit the motor shaft, with a setscrew to hold the rod in place on the motor shaft.

- An inner disc ② with a ¼-inch diameter center hole for the rod ① and two #4-40 threaded screw holes.

- An outer disc ③ with a ¼-inch diameter center hole for the rod ① and a notch for the setscrew. Also, it consists of two screw holes that are unthreaded and slightly larger (about ⅛ inch) than those on the inner disc ② so that the pair of #4-40 screws can slip through and pull the inner disc ② flush against the outer disc ③ when the screws are tightened.

When attached to the motor, the hub-adapter coupler appears as shown in Figure 5-4.

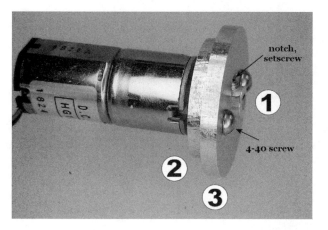

Figure 5-4. The hub-adapter coupler as attached to the motor. Normally, the wheel hub (not pictured) would be covering the coupler and most of the motor.

The rod ① is held onto the motor shaft with a removable setscrew. The notch in the outer disc ③ allows the outer disc to fit on the rod ① with the setscrew in place. If the setscrew were short enough to fit flush inside the rod, then the notch wouldn't be necessary.

The inner disc ② is attached to the rod ① with a permanent adhesive. The outer disc ③ is held to the inner disc ② with a pair of #4-40 screws. The outer disc is attached to the wheel hub (not pictured) with a permanent adhesive.

I've made a couple of references to adhesive. "Glue?" you exclaim in shock. Relax. There's nothing wrong with glue in a robot, as long as it's being used appropriately.

Despite the glued pieces, you can easily remove the wheel/hub/outer disc assembly from the coupler by unscrewing the two #4-40 screws. You can then remove the coupler from the motor shaft by loosening the setscrew. The glue exists only to bond parts that would've been made out of a single piece of material had it been possible or practical to do so.

Starting Simply with the Coupler Rod

Chapters 3 and 4 presented instructions for making a solid-rod coupler. The rod portion of this hub-adapter coupler is identical to the solid-rod coupler, except the LEGO axle portion is chopped off (see Figure 5-5).

 NOTE *Nothing precludes using telescoping tubing instead of a solid rod if you prefer. Also, although this example uses ¼-inch diameter aluminum rods, larger diameters or different materials are also suitable.*

Figure 5-5. A stubby solid-rod coupler whose length and inner diameter mirror the motor's shaft. Only one coupler is necessary per motor. However, the two couplers shown in this picture illustrate the coupler's length and the coupler's interior hole.

You make the hub-adapter rod in a manner similar to how you made the solid-rod coupler (as per the previous chapters):

1. Cut a piece of ¼-inch diameter rod to the length of the motor shaft. Additional length to incorporate a LEGO axle is unnecessary and undesirable because this is intended to be as compact as possible.

2. File or mill the ends of the rod flat.

3. Position the drill over the center of the rod (use a fixture), and drill a hole that matches the diameter of the motor shaft. A single hole is all that is necessary because a LEGO axle isn't being used.

4. If desired, file or mill the ends of the rod flat again to clean off burrs that occurred in drilling.

5. Mark the position for the setscrew so that at least half the length of the outside of the rod remains unobstructed. That is, don't drill the setscrew in the center of the length of the rod. Pick one end or the other. Later, you're going to glue the inner disc to the rod in the space you've saved.

6. Drill the setscrew hole, and tap it.

Making the Inner and Outer Hub-Adapter Discs

Two pieces adapt the rod's outer diameter to the wheel hub's inner diameter. One piece glues to the rod, and the other piece glues to the wheel. The two pieces attach to each other with screws.

Choosing a Shape

Technically, the piece that attaches to the hub can be any shape. However, a disc (a circle with depth) is the easiest shape to center within the hub, and a disc makes the most contact for gluing.

The piece that attaches to the rod can also be any shape, as long as it fits within the hub. However, a disc provides good balance as the rod and the wheel rotate. Because you're going to the trouble of making at least one disc, both pieces might as well be discs.

Determining the Size

My motor's shaft is 8 mm long. Therefore, each disc can be up to 4 mm thick and still fit on the rod.

The internal diameter of the outside end of the LEGO 49.6 by 28 VR wheel's hub is $1\frac{3}{16}$ inch (1.1875 inches or about 30 mm). As shown in Figure 5-6, this was measured using calipers. Because the final diameter of the outer disc needs to be $1\frac{3}{16}$ inch, the raw material cut from a stock sheet must be at least $1\frac{3}{16}$-inch square to start.

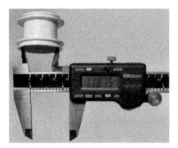

Figure 5-6. Measuring the internal diameter of the outside of a LEGO 49.6 by 28 VR wheel hub using digital calipers

Choosing the Raw Material

Any raw material that can be attached with glue and tapped for screws will do for the discs. The weight of the material could be a consideration for this application depending upon what the robot will be doing. Generally speaking, wheels and couplers with less mass react faster because they require less energy to change motion (start and stop).

Many plastics, such as PTFE (Teflon), polypropylene, polyethylene, nylon, and acetal (Delrin), are too slippery for adhesive. But other plastics are fine, such as ABS, PVC, and acrylic. All of the aforementioned plastics are easy to machine, but softer materials, such as Teflon, won't provide enough thread strength for setscrews.

Some metals do well. Brass is attractive and easy to machine. Stainless steel is gorgeous but difficult to machine.

Ultimately, I chose aluminum. It's lightweight, strong, easy to machine, can be tapped, and can be glued. Also, I had a $\frac{1}{8}$-inch thick (3.175 mm) sheet lying around. The sheet is a little bit thinner than desired (4 mm), but $\frac{3}{16}$ inch was the next standard thickness available in the United States, and I didn't feel like milling it down to 4 mm.

NOTE *A flat, wide, long raw material with a uniform thickness of a ¼ inch (some sources say ³⁄₁₆ inch, and some say as little as 3 mm) or more is commonly called plate. Material thinner than that is commonly called sheet (for example, think of a sheet of paper). A relatively narrow plate is called a bar. A relatively narrow sheet is called a strip.*

You can purchase aluminum sheets from MSC Industrial Supply (http://www.mscdirect.com/) that are ⅛-inch thick, 12 inches wide, and 12 inches long ($17.78, #09425455). The same size sheet is available from OnlineMetals.com (http://www.onlinemetals.com/) for $11.10.

Cutting the Raw Sheet Down to Size

You need to cut the raw material down to four pieces (two for each hub), 1³⁄₁₆-inch square. Because the inner disc is going to be a smaller diameter, two of the pieces could be cut smaller. However, it's easier just to cut four roughly similar pieces.

The pieces don't have to be exactly square, and they can be larger than 1³⁄₁₆ inch. Therefore, making a rough cut with a hacksaw is the quickest and easiest method. Measure and mark the pieces to be slightly larger than ultimately desired because a hacksaw is imprecise and because some material is going to be wasted in the cut.

Being between 3 mm and 4 mm thick, the raw material bends easily, making it more difficult to cut. To increase rigidity, you can cut multiple back-to-back sheets down at the same time. Or, you can sandwich the sheet between thicker pieces of scrap material, such as wood. Or, a pair of vises can hold the sheet down (see Figure 5-7) rather than hanging out the end of a single vise.

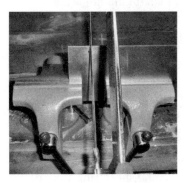

Figure 5-7. Aluminum sheet held between two bench vises while being cut by a hacksaw

Regardless of how you secure the material, you should select a fine-pitch (24-tooth or 32-tooth per inch) blade for the hacksaw because the sheet is thin. Each tooth of a coarse-pitch blade would catch on and rip up the raw material.

Drilling the ¼-Inch in Diameter Center Hole

After cutting, stack the four squares of raw material together. Sometimes a little masking tape around the edges helps keep the squares together in a neat stack. Mark the center of the top square.

At the point just marked, drill a ¼-inch diameter hole through the stack (see Figure 5-8). Use a drill press or milling machine to drill the hole because a handheld drill will likely result in a slightly angled hole. An angled hole would cause the attached hub to be held at an angle in relation to the motor shaft. This angular offset would cause the wheel to precess and roll imperfectly.

Figure 5-8. Rough-cut aluminum squares held down firmly by step blocks ① and raised up to protect the table by use of parallel stock ②

Although light drilling doesn't present nearly the same forces as milling, holding rough-cut stock safely can be a challenge.

 CAUTION *Never use your body weight, fingers, or hands to hold or steady a workpiece. You must always use mechanical clamps of some form. If you find any part of your body entering the machining area during operation, you really have to stop and question what you're doing.*

Step blocks provide parallel downward force to prevent the workpiece from lifting up or turning during machining. Parallel flat stock underneath the workpiece raises up the workpiece so that the drill can punch through without damaging the table underneath. Adding a flat scrap piece (not shown in Figure 5-8) underneath the workpiece minimizes burrs.

Again, Why Measure Oversize?

Recall that the pieces were measured, marked, and cut slightly larger than the final diameter desired. This compensates for all the things that could have gone wrong in the subsequent steps. Poor measuring, cutting, and centering, along with the drill walking during drilling, all contribute some error.

If the rough-cut pieces are sufficiently oversized, then none of the errors (unless absolutely grotesque) will cause the center of the resulting hole to be so close to the edge that it prevents a full $1\frac{3}{16}$-inch disc from being cut out of the rough-cut pieces.

Milling Circles with a Rotary Table

Two popular machines can convert square-shaped stock into cylindrical or rod-shaped stock. A lathe is one choice. But I don't have a lathe. Another choice is a milling machine with a rotary table.

The Sherline rotary table ($270, #3700 at Solarbotics) is high quality and is just the right size for hobbyist projects. To fit the rotary table to my MicroLux milling machine, I drilled the correctly sized sets of holes in a piece of PVC-plastic plate stock, attached the rotary table to the PVC with screws, and attached the PVC to the milling machine table with standard T-slot screws (see Figure 5-9).

Figure 5-9. A Sherline rotary table mounted on a home-cut PVC plate with holes the proper diameter to secure it to a milling machine table

Adapting the Rotary Table for Small Pieces

The top of the Sherline rotary table features four T-shaped slots for securing the workpiece. Unfortunately, the T-nuts and T-slots don't come close enough to the center of the rotary table to allow very small pieces to be mounted.

You can make a simple adapter that takes advantage of the factory precision alignment of the T-slots. This enables a bolt to be accurately centered on the rotary table for securing smaller workpieces (see Figure 5-10).

Placing the Square Rough-Cut Stock in a Stack on the Rotary Table with the Candlestick in the Billiard Room

To make a circle from a square, you have to remove a lot of corner material. Because a milling machine is designed for slow, precision work, you could speed the process by first cutting down the corners of the square by hand with a hacksaw (see Figure 5-11).

Figure 5-10. A stock plate with five holes carefully drilled in it and a ¼-inch bolt inserted in the center allows smaller stock to be secured about in the center of the rotary table. Actually, the center hole of the stock plate was originally drilled under-size and then milled out to a ¼ inch while on the rotary table to make sure the hole was centered.

Figure 5-11. For larger pieces, you can reduce milling time considerably by using a hacksaw to cut off the corners of the square.

When arranging the workpieces on the rotary table, stagger the square stock so that the mill doesn't have to cut into all four corners at the same time (see Figure 5-12). It makes the transitions less abrupt and reduces the stress on the securing bolt.

Figure 5-12. A stack of staggered aluminum squares (left) slowly being milled down to discs (center). The final stack almost looks like a single piece (right).

Place flat scrap material beneath the stack of squares to prevent the rotary table adapter from being cut by the end of the mill. If possible, place one or two washers atop the stack to distribute the compressing forces and prevent the stock material from being marred by the nuts. Tighten one nut just enough to flatten the stack and hold it all in place.

Add a nut to prevent the first nut from twisting off during milling. The second nut can be standard thickness or can be a thinner, jam nut. Tighten (jam) the second nut against the firmly installed first nut while holding it stationary with a wrench. This "stretches" the bolt between the nuts. Internal forces are sufficient to lock the two nuts and bolt together.

Rotating, Cutting, and Approaching the Center

Lower the mill to just above the top of the rotary table and lock it in place. Using the mill table's horizontal (x-axis) handwheel, bring the stack almost against the mill. Power up the mill, and bring the stack a little closer until the mill begins cutting. With the rotary table handwheel, rotate the stack so that it's cut evenly all the way around (see Figure 5-13).

Figure 5-13. The mill slowly approaches the center of the rotary table as you turn the handwheel to cut the stock evenly on all sides.

 CAUTION *Rotating the table clockwise into the mill has the advantage of being the smoothest method; called conventional milling, this removes a chip from its thinnest point to its thickest point. However, there's a danger. The clockwise table rotation causes the mill to present a counterclockwise force against the workpiece, which can unscrew the center bolt and nuts. This wouldn't be a problem if the workpiece were attached to multiple points, such as the four bolts and nuts in the four T-slots. So, if you choose to make your own center bolt adapter or use a chuck on a rotary table, then only make light cuts and make sure the workpiece stays securely fashioned. Alternatively, you can use a left-hand threaded bolt and nut.*

From time to time, stop and measure the diameter of the discs using calipers (see Figure 5-14). While you're at it, check that the bolt and nuts are still firmly in place. Continue to bring the mill closer to the center of the stack while rotating until the desired diameter is achieved.

Figure 5-14. Periodically measuring the diameter of the discs with a caliper

Drilling Screw Holes in the Discs

After reaching the proper diameter, the discs need holes for the #4-40 screws. You can perform this operation either in a vise with a V-block for holding round stock or on the rotary table. The discs are already secured on the rotary table, so you might as well drill them in place.

A #43 drill makes the correctly sized hole for tapping threads for #4-40 screws. A #43 drill is fairly short. Depending on your setup, you may need to add flat stock to raise up the stack of discs to drill through without the drill chuck contacting the top of the securing bolt. It's better to drill through the entire stack, rather than one disc at a time, so that the holes line up from disc to disc. If that isn't possible, at least drill two discs (a mating pair) at a time.

To place drill holes near the center of the discs, remove the top washer and rotate the table so that a side of the securing hex nut is adjacent to the drill (see Figure 5-15).

Figure 5-15. Drilling the stack of discs while they're still on the rotary table. They've been raised up on flat stock so that the drill chuck won't rub against the top of the securing bolt when the drill is plunged into the discs. Also, the table has been rotated to the flat side of the securing hex nut to drill closer to the center of the discs. There's only room for one nut now, but the jam nut is no longer necessary because rotational milling has been completed.

Accurately Positioning More Than One Screw Hole

Accurate placement of a screw hole isn't a big issue if you want only a single hole in the discs. Actually, even the position of multiple holes isn't important for the purpose of the hub-adapter coupler, as long as the holes match from disc to disc. And, unless the drill really bends, a stack of discs on a drill press is going to have holes that match fairly decently from disc to disc.

If, for whatever reason, you want to position the holes evenly around the disc, equidistant from the center, it's really easy to do on a rotary table. On the side of the rotary table are engraved markings that divide the circumference into 360 degrees (see Figure 5-16).

Figure 5-16. The 0-degree mark on the side of a rotary table

For two holes, simply rotate the rotary table to 0 degrees, position the drill the desired distance from the center of the disc, and make the first hole. I chose to drill the first hole about 8 mm from the center. Then, rotate the rotary table to 180 degrees and drill the second hole. Voilà! Two holes spaced evenly on the disc, equidistant from the center.

Making Cool Wheels Instead of Hub Adapters

With the steps already described previously, you could use the discs and rod couplers as wheels by themselves. By stepping up to a larger drill size and drilling more holes, say at 0 degrees, 60 degrees, 120 degrees, 180 degrees, 240 degrees, and 300 degrees, you can make the wheels shown in Figure 5-17.

Figure 5-17. Two custom-made aluminum wheels with speed holes every 60 degrees and clear acrylic couplers (left). Wheels attached to a miniature solar-powered line-following robot (right).

You can make an additional improvement if the discs are going to be used as wheels. A ball-end mill can groove the outside of each disc while the stack is still attached to the rotary table but with the rotary table set up vertically on the table. That way, you can slip rubber O-rings onto the custom wheels to make them grip better.

With thicker materials, you can mill away a portion of the inside while on the rotary table (see Figure 5-18). This results in giving the wheel a little depth, which is a nice touch.

Figure 5-18. Creating depth by milling away some disc material while mounted on the rotary table (left). Partially drilling three holes from the opposite side resulted in the plastic melting and deforming to match the contour of the drill point (right).

Finishing the Inner and Outer Hub-Adapter Discs

To use the discs as hub adapters, you need to complete a few more machining tasks on them.

Enlarging the Holes on the Outer Discs

Without moving the table from the position used to drill the screw holes, remove two of the discs. The two discs remaining on the rotary table will be the outer discs. The holes in these outer discs need to be enlarged. The holes that already exist there will act as pilot holes to aid positioning.

Why not tap all the existing holes? If both the inner disc and outer disc have threaded holes, the threads in each consecutive hole must line up perfectly or else the parts will push away slightly from each other as the screw is inserted (see Figure 5-19). This results in some angular displacement that causes wheel precession.

To ensure the threads run consecutively, I suppose you could tap an inner and outer disc while the discs are pressed together. But then you're going to have to label each pair of discs and holes to make sure they mate to each other every time.

A more reliable method is to allow the screw to slip through the outer disc's hole and thread the inner disc's hole. The head of the screw will pull the outer disc flush against the inner disc, resulting in a nice, flat mating (see Figure 5-20).

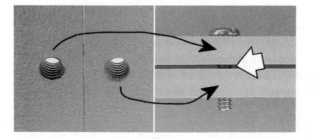

Figure 5-19. Two independently tapped parts (left). Those same parts, one on top of the other (right). The parts are forcibly separated by the screw's threads as much as necessary to rotate around to the next hole's thread. Even if the threads line up exactly, a gap also results if the parts aren't pressed together when the screw is driven.

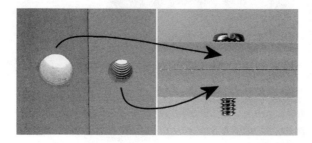

Figure 5-20. One untapped part with a slightly larger hole and one tapped part (left). Those same parts, with the untapped part on top of the tapped part (right). The parts can consistently be brought together without a gap. In fact, as the screw tightens, the screw head brings the parts together, even if a gap existed when the screw was first being driven.

Enlarge the holes of the two outer discs by drilling through them with a $\frac{1}{8}$-inch diameter drill. Because the rotary table hasn't been moved and because pilot holes have already been drilled, it shouldn't be difficult for the $\frac{1}{8}$-inch diameter drill to fairly accurately enlarge the old holes. The remaining discs may have rotated a little when the other two discs were removed. That's not a big deal. Simply line them up as best you can.

The $\frac{1}{8}$-inch diameter hole in the outer disc provides a bit of wiggle room to line up the inner and outer discs as the screw is being inserted. So, lining up the finished inner/outer pair of discs should be easy, despite any inaccuracies during the drilling process. After the screws are tightened, the heads of the screws compress the discs together to prevent any looseness between the discs that you might think would occur because of the larger $\frac{1}{8}$-inch diameter holes.

If desired, the outer screw holes can be countersunk (drilled wider at the top). This would permit the top of the screw heads to sit flush with the outer disc's face rather than sticking out.

Making a Setscrew Notch in the Outer Discs

The shortest-length #4-40 setscrew I could locate is ⅛-inch long. That's going to stick out from a ¼-inch diameter coupler rod with a motor shaft centered inside the rod. You might be able to find a shorter setscrew, or you might choose to use a larger-diameter coupler rod. If your setscrew sticks out beyond the coupler like mine does, drill or file a notch in the outer discs to leave room for the setscrew. Refer to Figures 5-3 and 5-4 for notch placement.

Reducing the Diameter of the Inner Discs

The two discs remaining on the rotary table will become the inner discs. They need to be reduced in diameter, using the same rotary milling process described earlier, until the discs fit inside the narrower portion of the LEGO 49.6 by 28 VR hub. The exact minimum diameter of the inner discs is unimportant, as long as the screw holes remain uncompromised. I chose a diameter of about 0.95 inches, which was about as large as the inner discs could get and yet still fit within the narrowest portion of the LEGO hub.

After milling down to the desired diameter, tap the #43 holes in the inner discs to accept #4-40 screws.

Sanding the Discs

Depending on the raw material selected, the screw holes (whether tapped or plain), center holes, and setscrew notches probably have some burrs or raised edges. With either a high-speed rotary tool (such as a Dremel) or a bit of sandpaper, remove any burrs or raised edges so that the inner and outer discs can truly fit together flatly.

All Done?

You've finished the pieces for the hub-adapter coupler. They should look like and fit together the same as those pictured in Figures 5-3 and 5-4, presented earlier in this chapter. But don't glue anything yet! You need to drill out the centers of the LEGO wheel hubs to allow a final fitting before gluing.

Coring the LEGO Hubs

Usually a coupler is made to adapt a motor shaft to fit the standard LEGO cross axle socket present on almost all LEGO wheels. But because this project requires a more compact design, the finely molded cross axle socket in the LEGO hub is unnecessary. Actually, because the motor mounts within the LEGO hub, the LEGO cross axle socket isn't only unnecessary, but it's also unwanted (see Figure 5-21).

Figure 5-21. LEGO 49.6 by 28 VR wheel (left), tire pulled off with only the hub remaining (second to left), center of hub drilled out to make room for the motor (second to right), and inner portion of the hub sanded smooth (right)

The LEGO hub is made from ABS thermoplastic. It's lightweight and easy to machine.

Securing the Hub During Machining

Because of the circular shape of the hub, it helps to use a V-block (see Figure 5-22) to hold the hub in place in a vise during machining. In fact, a pair of V-blocks, one on each vise jaw, is preferable. Matching pairs of V-blocks are available from most industrial or hobbyist supply companies.

Figure 5-22. A V-block partially surrounds a cylindrical object and holds it at two points to prevent it from popping out of a vise during machining.

Selecting a Silver & Deming Drill

The inner portion of the LEGO hub is wider than ordinary drills and wider than the maximum shank most drill presses can accept. As such, you'll employ a special kind of drill. A Silver & Deming drill has a ½-inch diameter shank with a wider diameter body (see Figure 5-23) so that larger holes can be drilled using drill chucks that only accept a maximum of ½ inch.

NOTE *Silver & Deming was the name of a company in the 1800s. It now generically refers to a reduced shank type drill rather than a brand name or company name.*

Figure 5-23. A Silver & Deming drill consists of a ½-inch diameter shank and a wider diameter body.

For the LEGO 49.6 by 28 VR wheel hub, a ⅞-inch diameter Silver & Deming drill removes most of the inner portion.

Drilling Out the Center of the Hub

To drill out the center of the hub, follow these steps:

1. Place the hub into a vise with a V-block or pair of V-blocks.

2. Insert the ⅞ drill into the drill chuck, and lower it to one side of the hub to determine the proper depth to drill without damaging the vise (see left side of Figure 5-24). Write down or note the depth on the milling/drilling machine's z-axis gauge because the limit block can't be set until after the next step.

3. Insert a LEGO cross axle into the drill chuck, and roughly center the hub until the axle can slide into the hub's axle socket (see the center of Figure 5-24). Lock the vise and milling/drilling machine's x-axis and y-axis locks.

4. Move the milling/drilling machine's limit block to the depth noted earlier.

5. Reinsert the ⅞ drill into the drill chuck and drill out the center of the hub (see the right of Figure 5-24), all the way through.

Figure 5-24. Checking depth (left), centering with a LEGO cross axle (center), drilling (right)

Sanding Away the Remains of the Center of the Hub

After drilling out the hub with a ⅞ drill, some minor remnants of the spokes remain (see the left side of Figure 5-25). Depending on the diameter of your motor or depending on your desire for finishing touches, you can cleanly remove the last bits with a high-speed rotary tool and some sandpaper (see the right side of Figure 5-25).

Figure 5-25. The inside of the hub is rough after drilling (left). A handheld rotary tool and sandpaper provide smooth clean up (right).

I used a Dremel #932 aluminum oxide grinding stone followed by 100-grit sand-paper. The grinding stone can become clogged with plastic, so you may prefer disposable sanding bands.

Fitting and Gluing the Parts Together

Other than being glued and screwed together, the pieces are finished. Before gluing, it's worth assembling them to test the fit. It's going to be easier to make minor alterations and touch-ups while they are still in their component forms, rather than after they've been glued together.

Fitting and Gluing the Outer Disc into the Hub

The outer disc snaps into the wider-diameter end of the cored LEGO hub (see Figure 5-26). If the fit is without gaps, apply a thin layer of gel-type cyanoacrylate-based glue (superglue) around the inner diameter of the hub and insert the outer disc. If the fit is loose or contains gaps, a thick epoxy is more appropriate than cyanoacrylate adhesive.

Figure 5-26. The outer disc is inserted and glued into the wide end of the LEGO hub.

Fitting and Gluing the Inner Disc onto the Rod

The inner disc attaches to the half of the rod that doesn't contain the setscrew. It's important that the inner disc is as square (perpendicular) to the rod as possible. Any angle here greatly affects the rotation of the wheel.

Making a Fixture for Gluing

Because the angle of the rod to the inner disc is so critical, I found it helpful to make a fixture for gluing any kind of flat part perpendicular to any kind of ¼-inch diameter rod. First I squared up a block of Teflon (glue won't stick to this material) on a milling machine. Then I spot-drilled a starting hole, followed by drilling a ¼-inch in diameter hole straight through the block. Without removing the Teflon block, I resurfaced the top face with a mill. This removed any raised portions caused by the drilling, and it made sure the face, as it rested in the vise for drilling, was truly square with the hole, even if it wasn't absolutely square with the rest of the block.

You don't have to make a gluing fixture, especially if you've got a good tight fit. The fixture is just an aid to hold the parts at the correct angle while the glue dries.

From time to time, you can purchase scrap blocks of Teflon from Machinist Materials for a considerable discount from retail. United States Plastic Corporation (http://www.usplastic.com/) has a 1-foot long, 1-inch-square bar ($29, #47546). MSC Industrial Supply also has that same size available ($58.27, #32014169). However, if it's suitable for your fixture, you can reduce the price in half at MSC Industrial Supply by selecting a 1-foot long, ½-inch thick (height), 1-inch wide rectangular bar ($25.54, #32018871).

Gluing the Inner Disc to the Rod

Before gluing, make sure to rotate the setscrew hole to a position that allows it to fit into the outer disc's notch at the same time that the #4-40 screws line up. If you're going to use a gluing fixture, you may have to mark this location on the backside of the rod and inner disc to know that they're in the correct orientation as they're inserted into the fixture.

The rod coupler without the setscrew is inserted halfway into the ¼-inch diameter hole in the gluing fixture. Then, the inner disc is placed on top (see the left side of Figure 5-27). Whether or not you use a fixture, the finished inner disc/rod with setscrew combination should look like that pictured on the right side of Figure 5-27.

Waiting for Glue to Dry

After you finish gluing all the parts together, please be patient and give them lots of time to dry before assembling them as a whole. You've gone to a lot of trouble to machine an easily removable hub and motor adapter—an errant dab of moist glue could make the assembly permanent.

Figure 5-27. Glued disc and rod drying on a Teflon fixture (left).
Finished part with setscrew inserted (right)

Summary

When pressed for space, you can build drive motors into the robot's wheels. Although it involves a little more machining on the hub, that effort is offset by the less complicated direct drive train (no gears or belts to align). Remember either to choose a motor with a thick axle and built-in bearings or to support the wheel axle externally.

A rotary table is a terrific tool for making circular cuts on a milling machine. After cutting down the raw material with a hacksaw, you can attach the workpiece to the rotary table using multiple bolts (preferable) or a single center bolt (for smaller pieces). The rotary table is also nice for drilling evenly spaced holes about a center point. You can even use the resulting workpiece as a wheel by itself.

A few points in this chapter apply to general construction techniques. For example, avoid threading two adjoining pieces of material. Instead, tap one piece and drill a slightly larger hole in the piece that will be held down by the screw head. Another general construction technique you learned in this chapter is that fixtures made out of Teflon can hold a workpiece in the desired position as glue dries.

CHAPTER 6

Understanding the Standards and Setup for Electronic Experiments

Covers Reading Schematics, Using a Wall Wart Power Supply, Frosting an LED, Understanding Hardware Push Button Debouncing, and Understanding Surface-Mount Technology

THIS CHAPTER EXPRESSES THE STANDARDS for schematics and the arrangements used for solderless breadboards throughout the book. For some types of components, this chapter describes default attributes, such as maximum wattage and working voltages, which can be assumed unless otherwise noted in a particular circuit.

Reading Schematics

Truth be told, my schematics are actually wiring diagrams. For example, proper schematics would show stand-alone logic-gate symbols (see the left side of Figure 6-1) where my "schematics" show a full chip (see the right side of Figure 6-1).

A *schematic* is a logical representation, and a *wiring diagram* is a physical implementation. Most builders prefer wiring diagrams over formal schematics. I just wanted to point out that I know the difference, but I still insist on calling mine *schematics*.

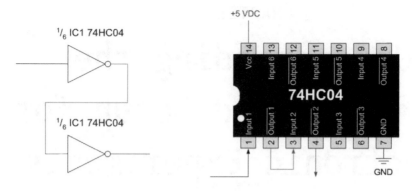

Figure 6-1. Formal schematics use logical symbols (left). This book uses implementation-based wiring diagrams (right).

Connecting Wires

In this book's schematics, a little jog in crossing wires indicates wires that *aren't* connected to one another (see the left side of Figure 6-2). A little dot where wires cross indicates wires that *are* connected to one another (see the right side of Figure 6-2).

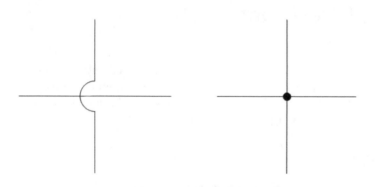

Figure 6-2. Crossing wires with a jog don't connect (left). Crossing or touching wires with a dot do connect (right).

A jog in unconnected crossing wires is admittedly redundant and old-fashioned. After all, if the wires don't have a little jog, they must be connected; there's no need for a little dot. Still, the redundancy of a dot without a jog *emphasizes* that the wires are connected.

One of my technical editors strongly recommended (I think his comment was, "Ah, the 1950s were great times, weren't they?") that I drop the jog, not only because it's outdated but also because it makes the schematic look busy. But the purpose of a schematic or wiring diagram is to precisely communicate a strict connective arrangement. Because so many magazines and books have errors in their schematics, it seems appropriate to use additional techniques to decrease or catch errors in both schematic creation (the author) and schematic interpretation (the reader).

Because extra work is required for me to add a jog or a dot, I must stop and think about whether the lines need to be crossing or connecting, thus reducing errors in the schematic creation process. I mean, it's easy to draw lines on top of each other, but it requires conscious consideration to mark the intersection one way or another.

Furthermore, nontechnical proofreaders can quickly check all crossing lines on a schematic. If no mark is present, that's an error. In addition, a reader may not see a dot, depending on how large a schematic appears when finally printed in the book. Or, a printer's glitch may cause an errant dot to appear.

In closing, if the jogs offend your sensibilities, please print little stickers with plus (+) signs to cover all the jogs.

Designating Parts

In a circuit, each individual part has a unique identifier so that the part can be referenced and discussed without confusing it with another part. For example, if a schematic contains four resistors, they might be designated R1, R2, R3, and R4. Now, instead of saying, "Connect the second 100-ohm resistor to the fourth 100-ohm resistor," the instructions can say, "Connect R2 to R4."

Lettering Designations

Table 6-1 describes the letters that begin a part designation in this book.

Table 6-1. Letter Designations

Letter	Part Type
B	Battery
C	Capacitor
CB	Circuit breaker, resettable current-protection devices
D	Diode
IC	Integrated circuit
IED	Infrared-emitting diode
L	Inductor
LED	Light-emitting diode
M	Motor
OSC	Canned oscillator
Q	Transistor
R	Resistor, photoresistor, potentiometer
SW	Switch
TP	Test point
VR	Voltage regulator
ZD	Zener diode

My designations are different from some older standards. Classically, B is supposed to be for blower, and M is supposed to be for meter or oscilloscope. Also, classically, switch is S, integrated circuit is U, zener diode is VR when used to regulate voltage, and canned oscillator is Y.

You'll notice that each book, magazine, or Web author uses a slightly different set of designation standards. The designations C, D, L, Q, and R seem to be the only ones used consistently from author to author.

Numbering Designations

In this book, whenever possible, part designations are numbered in associated groups even if a bunch of numbers in-between must then be skipped. For example, an LED and current-limiting resistor would normally be labeled "LED1 and R1" to show that they function together. However, if 64 other resistors are already in the schematic, I'll bump up the number on the LED designation so that the LED's number matches the number of the paired resistor, as in "LED65 and R65."

Because a complete robot tends to be a collection of modules or subcircuits, the designation numbers in an entire module may be increased to show the association. For example, a power circuit might normally be SW1, D1, C1, VR1, and C2. However, as part of a complete robot circuit, the module's parts might be designated SW101, D101, C101, VR101, and C102. This numbering convention helps distinguish modules.

The downside to the approach of skipping numbers is that you may mistakenly try to locate a part that doesn't exist: "I see R1, R2, R3, R4, R6, R7, and R8. What happened to R5?"

Labeling Parts

Besides a unique designation, the schematics in this book usually include informational labels that specify part values or important characteristics for each part in the schematic. The types of information contained in the label depend upon the part.

Labeling Resistors

All resistors are labeled in the schematic with their resistance in ohms (Ω). A through-hole resistor shape (see the left side of Figure 6-3) is used rather than the schematic-standard triangular squiggle (see the right side of Figure 6-3).

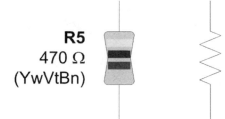

Figure 6-3. Resistor labeled with a designation (R5), resistance value in standard notation (470 Ω), and resistance value represented with color-coded bands (YwVtBn) (left). The classic schematic symbol for a resistor isn't used in this book…uh…except in this figure, of course (right).

Because resistances span such a large range in most circuits, a modifier can reduce the number of digits. Common multipliers and dividers are applied to represent fractional units or larger units (see Table 6-2).

Table 6-2. Common Resistor Multipliers

Amount	Multiplier	Prefix	Abbreviation
Million	1,000,000	Mega	Uppercase M
Thousand	1,000	Kilo	Lowercase k
Thousandth	0.001	Milli	Lowercase m

Megohm resistances are commonly seen in IC inputs and feedback circuits. A resistor labeled 15 MΩ equals 15,000,000 Ω. Kilohm resistances are commonly seen throughout circuits but usually in timing or default-value pull-up applications. A resistor labeled 4.7 kΩ equals 4,700 Ω. Milliohm resistances are commonly seen in wiring, MOSFETs, and H-bridge chips. A MOSFET labeled as 125 mΩ equals 0.125 Ω.

Coloring Resistors

Because most hobbyists still use through-hole resistors that come in cylindrical packages, an abbreviated description of the associated color bands (see Table 6-3) is included in the part label in the schematic (refer to Figure 6-3). For example, a 470 Ω resistor would be labeled YwVtBn to indicate a resistance value of ('4' '7') times 10 equals 470.

Table 6-3. Resistor Color Value Bands

Color	Abbreviation	First Band	Second Band	Third Band
Black	Bk	('0'	'0')	✕ 1
Brown	Bn	('1'	'1')	✕ 10
Red	Rd	('2'	'2')	✕ 100
Orange	Oe	('3'	'3')	✕ 1 000 *(kilo-)*
Yellow	Yw	('4'	'4')	✕ 10 000
Green	Gn	('5'	'5')	✕ 100 000
Blue	Be	('6'	'6')	✕ 1 000 000 *(mega-)*
Violet	Vt	('7'	'7')	..
Gray	Gy	('8'	'8')	..
White	We	('9'	'9')	..

Selecting Resistor Construction, Tolerance, and Wattage

Unless stated otherwise, all circuits can be built with carbon-film resistors rated for ¼ watt and 5 percent value tolerance. Of course, you can substitute resistors rated for higher wattage (such as ½ watt), improved construction (such as metal film, metal oxide, or thick film), or increased precision (such as 1 percent tolerance). I use ½-watt resistors throughout this book because they show up better in photographs.

For the circuits in this book, you should avoid resistors with poorer precision (such as 20 percent tolerance) or alternate construction (such as wire-wound or carbon composition). This isn't because those kinds of resistors are necessarily bad; it's just that I haven't tested the circuits with those kinds of resistors.

Substituting Lower-Wattage Resistors

Resistors function by converting electricity to heat. The more power they're subjected to, the more heat they must dissipate. As such, resistors are rated in watts to express how much power they can consume without resulting in damage.

You shouldn't substitute lower-wattage-rated resistors for any circuit in this book unless you've done the math and then derated by 50 percent. So, for a 100 Ω resistor with 30 mA passing through it, you'd use this calculation:

```
power in watts = (current in amps)² ✕ resistance in ohms
power in watts = (0.03 amps) ² ✕ 100 ohms
power in watts = 0.09 watts
```

Based on the previous calculations, a ⅛-watt (0.125 watts) resistor would technically be correct. However, a ¼-watt resistor provides for a safer margin of error. Of course, the manufacturer has likely already added a margin of error, so the ⅛-watt resistor is probably just fine. But, why risk it on a robot that's going to take you tens or hundreds of hours to build?

Most of the digital circuits have extremely small amounts of current flowing through them and can easily accept $\frac{1}{8}$-watt resistors. Therefore, the only times you'll likely need to be concerned with calculating resistor wattage is for resistors connected to output devices such as LEDs, motors, displays, speakers, and so on.

Including Other Parts As Resistors

Photoresistors, potentiometers (or trimpots), and any other parts whose purpose is to change resistance are labeled as resistors in this book's schematics. Basically, if you can get a legitimate reading by hooking up the part to an ohmmeter (or a multimeter in ohm or resistance-measurement mode), then that part is lumped into the resistor category in this book.

Labeling Capacitors

To represent capacitors in a schematic, this book uses a double-straight line to indicate a nonpolarized capacitor (see the left side of Figure 6-4). This means you can insert the capacitor with either lead connected to either wire.

In this book, a straight-and-curvy line along with a plus (+) sign indicates a polarized capacitor (see the right side of Figure 6-4). This means the capacitor must have its positive lead connected to the wire with the plus (+) sign in the schematic. Inserting the capacitor in the wrong direction can prevent it from functioning and may destroy the capacitor.

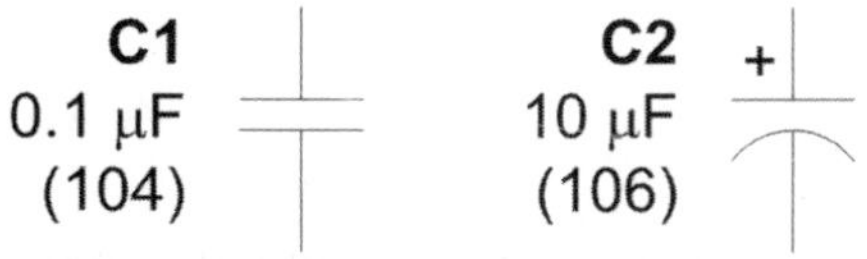

C1
0.1 μF
(104)

C2 +
10 μF
(106)

Figure 6-4. Nonpolarized capacitor labeled with a designation (C1), value in standard notation (0.1 μF), and value in three-digit notation (104) (left). A polarized capacitor with the same kind of label but different attributes. The plus (+) sign indicates that the positive lead of the capacitor must be connected exactly as shown in the schematic (right). You'll find variation between authors, with some using a curvy line for all capacitors and others using only straight lines. However, polarized capacitors should always have the positive (+) lead labeled.

Indicating Capacitor Values

Capacitance is measured in farads. However, because a farad is such a large amount of capacitance, most circuits use smaller-value parts. Table 6-4 describes the most common multipliers for capacitors.

Table 6-4. Common Capacitor Multipliers

Amount	Multiplier	Prefix	Abbreviation
Millionth	0.000 001	Micro	Greek μ or lowercase u
Billionth	0.000 000 001	Nano	Lowercase n
Trillionth	0.000 000 000 001	Pico	Lowercase p

Micro capacitances are the most common. In fact, the micromultiplier is so popular that it often bleeds a little above and below its range. The micromultiplier frequently appears on labels for capacitors with values as large as 22,000 µF (a really large value used in power supplies) to as little as 0.1 µF (a smaller value used as a local power source for an individual chip).

Nano capacitances are used mostly in timing circuits. A 1 nF capacitor equals 0.001 µF. Pico capacitances are used mostly in radio frequency (RF) and timing circuits, particularly in relation to crystal oscillators. A 1 pF capacitor equals 0.001 nF, which equals 0.000 001 µF.

Another method of indicating a capacitor value is with a three-digit number printed on the case. Take the first two numbers and add an additional number of zeros indicated by the third number, and that's the value in pF. So, the following are true:

- 102 = 1000 pF.

- 333 = 33,000 pF.

- 104 = 100,000 pF = 0.1 µF (very common).

- 105 = 1,000,000 pF = 1 µF (very common).

- 106 = 10,000,000 pF = 10 µF (very common).

The schematics in this book label the capacitor value in both conventional notation, such as 1 µF, and with three-digit notation, such as 105. This should reduce errors in selecting the wrong part from your parts box because you can match the label on the schematic to the label on the actual part.

Selecting Capacitor Construction

Unless noted otherwise, it's assumed that acceptable capacitor construction can be aluminum electrolytic for 10 µF or larger, tantalum for 47 µF to 1 µF, and ceramic or plastic for 1 µF or smaller values. (Therefore, there's some crossover from 10 µF to 47 µF where either aluminum electrolytic or tantalum is suitable.) Usually retail part numbers are suggested in the text that accompanies the schematic, so preferred construction isn't left for you guess.

Selecting Capacitor Working Voltage and Temperature

Unless noted otherwise, I've chosen a capacitor's working voltage to be double the highest voltage to which it's subjected. For example, a capacitor connected to a 12 V battery should be rated for at least 24 working voltage (WV) continuous duty. A capacitor connected to a 5 V regulated power supply should be rated for at least 10 WV continuous duty.

The three most significant factors leading to capacitor failure are, in order of significance, temperature, voltage, and age. For example, if you select a 6.3 WV, 2000 hour, 85° Celsius (C) maximum, aluminum electrolytic capacitor to run on a 5 V board at 70° C, the capacitor's life span may be as short as 6,000 hours (less than a year of continuous operation). A 10 WV capacitor run under the same conditions would have double the expected life span. A 10 WV capacitor run at 30° C would have an expected life span of 30 times longer (180,000 continuous hours; about 20 years) than a 6.3 WV capacitor running at 70° C.

Consider potential heat sources when placing capacitors on a circuit board or in your robot. Motors, batteries, and power supplies can all run fairly hot.

Another heat source is less avoidable: The capacitor generates heat internally during use because of its small amount of resistance—usually stated as equivalent series resistance (ESR). A lot of current flowing in and out of the capacitor will increase its temperature. Adequate spacing and air flow helps a lot. Alternatively, multiple capacitors taking the place of a single capacitor can reduce the amount of internal heat generated by each capacitor.

You can find information about the working voltage and maximum temperature of a particular capacitor from the vendor or manufacturer. For example, Digi-Key Corporation (http://www.digikey.com/) prints that kind of information prominently at the beginning of each capacitor product from each vendor.

Don't be overly concerned with capacitor limits. Just make sure your robot isn't getting too hot, and buy capacitors rated at double the maximum voltage for which you expect to use them. Most of my capacitors are rated at 25 WV, 35 WV, or more, so I don't spend any time thinking about working voltages on a 12 V robot. If I select a 16 WV or 10 WV capacitor for the benefit of its smaller physical size, I simply double-check that the capacitor is going to be placed in a 5 V regulated circuit.

Labeling LEDs and IEDs

Figure 6-5 shows the schematic symbol for either an LED or an IED. All diodes are polarized. In the schematic symbol, the cathode is indicated by a line, and the anode is indicated by an arrow pointing toward the cathode (which is also the direction of conventional current flow).

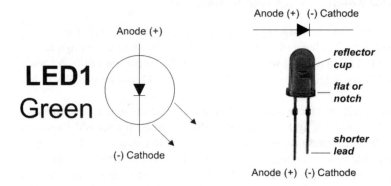

Figure 6-5. Schematic symbol and label for an LED (left). The symbol for a standard diode is the same but doesn't have the arrow(s) pointing away from it. LEDs are polarized (right). Look for the flat or notch on the side of the actual LED to determine the cathode lead. Usually (but not always), the cathode side also has the reflector cup and shorter lead.

On an LED, the cathode is usually physically indicated by a flat or notch on the side. If not, check the manufacturer's datasheet or use the diode test mode on a multimeter.

A color is suggested for each LED in this book's schematics. You can substitute a different color, but you may become confused when I refer to the "green" LED that's blue on your robot.

For IEDs, the schematic label also suggests a wavelength, which is the equivalent of a color if you were able to see it with your bare eyes. Substituting a wavelength that's slightly different, such as 940 nm instead of 950 nm, is usually just fine. However, substituting 880 nm for 950 nm may result in the circuit not functioning well, if at all. Avoid purchasing infrared devices that don't clearly indicate their wavelengths.

Labeling Other Parts

All other parts not mentioned so far are accompanied by enough detailed information in the text to make it easy to purchase and use them.

Specifying Power Supply

This book uses the conventional notion of current flowing from a higher voltage point—often indicated with a plus (+) symbol for polarity sensitive devices and significant circuit locations—to a lower voltage point. The highest point in the power supply is considered the positive voltage supply. The lowest point in the power supply is considered ground (GND), or 0 V. No circuits in this book require a negative (below ground) voltage supply.

Simplifying the Positive Voltage Supply Label

Most professional electrical engineers label the positive voltage supply on their schematics with a V+, V_{CC}, or V_{DD}. At some point they define that to be a value between 4.75 V and 5.25 V, between 2 V and 6 V, or whatever the circuit requires.

This method of assigning the positive voltage supply with a representative label provides great simplification in defining other voltage values based on the supply. For example, a test point on the board below a diode might be V_{DD}–1.2 V. That's a lot easier than saying "6 V–1.2 V or 2 V–1.2 V or some value in-between based on your power supply voltage."

Unfortunately, hobbyists (including myself) are often confused by the professional voltage supply labels and tend to prefer a fixed number. For that reason, I use +9 VDC (assuming a 9 V battery is attached) to label the unregulated positive battery voltage going to the robot's motors and +5 VDC (assuming a 5 V regulator chip is being used) to label the regulated positive voltage going to the robot's chips.

Of course, a real alkaline 9 V battery begins at 9.6 V and drops to 6 V (or less) as it's consumed. A real regulated power supply fluctuates up or down by a couple tenths of a volt without upsetting most chips or circuits. My choice of positive voltage labels, such as +5 VDC and +9 VDC, aren't meant to be taken too literally. For example, your circuit is within the normal range if your multimeter indicates 4.92 V instead of 5 V or indicates 9.16 V instead of 9 V.

Symbolizing Ground and Simplifying Wiring

The left side of Figure 6-6 shows the symbol for ground (or GND), and the right side of Figure 6-6 shows a circuit with a couple of connections to ground.

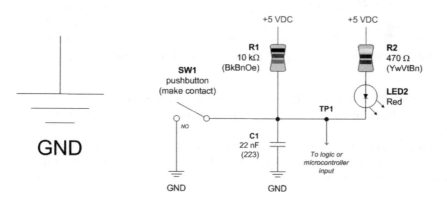

Figure 6-6. Schematic symbol for ground. Ground is connected to the negative terminal on the battery (left). A circuit with multiple connections to the positive power supply and ground (right). This particular circuit, a switch debouncer, cleans up the noisy signal produced when a switch, SW1, is pressed and released.

To prevent more complicated schematics from looking like a sea of wires, the power and ground sources aren't visually shown as being tied together. However, in this book, all of the +5 VDC sources are tied to one another, and all of the GND sources are tied to one another.

For example, in Figure 6-6, you don't need two 5 V power supplies and two GND supplies. Both of the +5 VDC wires connect at a single 5 V source, and both of the GND wires connect at a single ground return.

There are no dual or split power supplies in any of the robots or circuits in this book.

Using Solderless Breadboards

Almost all of the schematics presented in this book are followed by photographs of the working circuit constructed on a solderless breadboard (see Figure 6-7). The parts are labeled in the photograph to match the parts in the schematic.

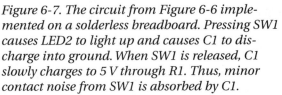

Figure 6-7. The circuit from Figure 6-6 implemented on a solderless breadboard. Pressing SW1 causes LED2 to light up and causes C1 to discharge into ground. When SW1 is released, C1 slowly charges to 5 V through R1. Thus, minor contact noise from SW1 is absorbed by C1.

The photograph can be helpful in suggesting a layout. However, you should feel free to arrange the components differently as long as the connections match the schematic.

I highly encourage you to build the circuits on a solderless breadboard before assembling them more permanently with solder. A solderless breadboard provides an opportunity for experimentation and rapid error correction.

Selecting a Solderless Breadboard

I prefer 3M 840 tie-point solderless breadboards ($19 to $22; #922309 at Digi-Key and #N03SB02 at Electronix Express). Conversely, most of the inexpensive boards I've tried have connectors that don't line up properly with the holes or that don't grip the leads and wires firmly. The whole experience can be frustrating or worthless if your solderless breadboard gives you trouble.

Setting Up a Solderless Breadboard to Match the Photographs

The photographs should be labeled with enough information to allow you to re-create the circuits on any kind of board with any kind of setup. However, it may be helpful for you to understand how I set up my breadboards.

To provide power to the breadboard, a battery or other power source is connected to the binding posts (see Figure 6-8). The positive binding post—connected to the positive (+) terminal of the battery—is connected to a power switch on the board. The power switch then either connects to the very top row of the breadboard or connects through a voltage regulator to the top row of the breadboard. The top row of the breadboard is connected to the second-to-the-bottom row to provide convenient access to positive voltage for the circuits in the middle of the breadboard.

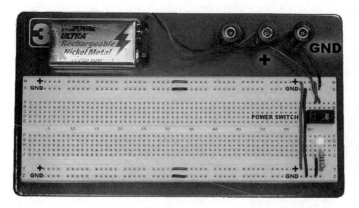

Figure 6-8. Standard setup for an 840 tie-point solderless breadboard. This particular board has a power switch and indicator LED, but it doesn't have a voltage regulator. When the power switch is turned on, it allows power from the positive (+) terminal of the battery to reach the breadboard distribution buses. Circuits on this board would receive approximately 9 V.

The ground binding post—connected to the negative (-) terminal of the battery—is connected directly to the second-to-the-top row of the solderless breadboard, without going through the power switch. The second-to-the-top row of the breadboard is connected to the bottom row to provide convenient access to ground for the circuits in the middle of the breadboard.

The left side of each of the top two rows and bottom two rows is connected in the center to the right side so that power is distributed in the top and bottom rows across the board. These rows are often referred to as the *power distribution buses*.

TIP *If you're still confused about how to set up or use a solderless breadboard, consult Chapters 12 and 13 of* Robot Building for Beginners *(Apress, 2002) for detailed instructions.*

Powering a Solderless Breadboard

For most of my experiments, power is provided by a Rayovac rechargeable nickel-metal hydride (NiMH) 9 V battery. Not only does a consumer battery make the board portable, but also this type of power source is relatively inexpensive enough to have a bunch of independently powered boards lying around the desk at the same time. Another benefit to battery power is that it replicates the conditions under which the circuits operate when installed in a robot.

Lastly, consumer battery power is fairly safe. A 9 V consumer battery just doesn't contain enough energy to do much damage.

Selecting an AC Power Adapter

You can use an AC power adapter (a *wall wart*) for longer-running experiments or for those experiments that require a voltage that mustn't vary with use. RadioShack (http://www.radioshack.com/) carries voltage-adjustable models that can provide up to 800 mA of current (see Figure 6-9). Although the RadioShack model works fine for most hobbyist purposes, it doesn't have any fancy features because it's really intended to replace lost adapters from consumer appliances.

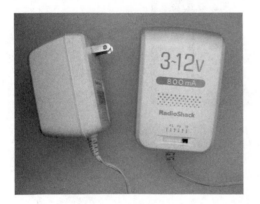

Figure 6-9. The RadioShack AC Adapter 273-1667, $15.99, provides regulated 3 V, 4.5 V, 6 V, 7.5 V, 9 V, or 12 V with up to 800 mA of current.

Choosing a Professional Power Supply

If you want to step up from the RadioShack model, a professional variable DC power supply is readily available from electronic catalogs such as Electronix Express. For between $60 and $600, you can get a power supply in which you can select the voltage and limit the maximum current by turning a couple of knobs. The power supplies usually have built-in displays for the voltage and current actually being supplied.

Professional power supplies have safety features such as protection against short circuits, thermal overload, and other overload conditions. They feature standard connectors for wires, cables, or test jumpers. Also, they tend to regulate the voltage well, even in the face of varying loads and electrical noise. Many have filters to reduce AC ripple to a negligible level.

There are two other important features in professional power supplies. First, they have the ability to be set to any particular voltage in a range—say, to 4.67 V rather than a limited specific preset value such as 4.5 V or 6 V. Second, they can output more current (between 1.5 amps and 10 amps) than can consumer power adapters (commonly able to deliver between 0.1 amp and 1 amp).

The better power supplies also feature a constant-current mode. With this, the power supply provides the same amount of current to the attached load/circuit by automatically varying the voltage. This is useful for charging certain kinds of batteries or determining voltage drop across a semiconductor under various conditions.

The downsides to professional power supplies are the cost and the size.

Reusing a Consumer Appliance AC Power Adapter

With some care, it's possible to reuse power adapters from discarded consumer appliances. Be sure to avoid adapters that appear damaged, emit smoke, make noises, overheat, or smell funny. The label should include either an Underwriters Laboratory (UL) listing mark or a Conformité Européenne (CE) marking.

A reused AC power adapter should be labeled well with the voltage output and maximum current (which you shouldn't exceed). The voltage output must be labeled as DC. As with any power source, you must determine the polarity of the output with certainty before attempting to use it.

Unlike the RadioShack model or a professional power supply, most consumer AC power adapters are unregulated. This means that the actual AC voltage level present at your AC power outlet will alter the DC voltage output by the adapter. If the label reads "OUTPUT: 9 VDC," it could actually output 8 V to 10 V, depending upon whether your AC outlet is 110 V or 120 V (or somewhere in-between). And when your significant other starts vacuuming (not you, obviously) and the lights momentarily dim, the AC voltage may sag to 90 V, causing the DC voltage to briefly droop to somewhere in the 6 V range.

Lack of regulation also causes voltage to fluctuate depending on DC circuit load. For example, an AC adapter labeled 6 V at 500 mA may actually supply 10 V at 5 mA.

Risking Electrocution

I avoid AC experiments, and I usually stay away from altering anything that plugs into an electrical outlet. I'll leave playing with 120 V to a professional. The whole thought becomes even more gruesome when one considers that, unlike a battery, the household electrical supply is relatively infinite. The last thing in this world I want are people standing around the office telling the funny story about the know-it-all hobbyist author who electrocuted himself. I can imagine the sound effects.

If I've dissuaded you, great! Stick with household consumer batteries. If not, as the lawyers are fond of saying, proceed at your own risk.

Adding a Few Amenities

Back to the solderless breadboard! An on/off switch and a power-indicating LED are located on the right side of the board. Most of my boards also include a 5 V regulator and capacitors to convert the 6 V to 9.6 V coming from the battery into a steady, clean 5 V supply for the circuits (see Figure 6-10). The next chapter describes voltage regulators in detail.

Figure 6-10. A power switch, voltage regulator, and capacitors for providing a clean 5 V power supply from a 9 V battery

The majority of LEDs on the market feature either a colored lens or a water-clear lens. The problem with the colored lens is that sometimes it can be difficult to discern whether the LED is lit. The problem with a water-clear lens is that it tends to be focused forward, making it hard to tell from the side whether the LED is lit. And then, when you do look straight down into a water-clear lens, the ultra-bright LEDs can be painful to the eye.

Here's a neat trick I use for my solderless breadboard power indicator LEDs: Take an ultra-bright water-clear lens LED, and scuff it up with 400-grit sandpaper (available at most hardware stores). Don't use lower-numbered sandpaper because it tends to groove and scratch the LED body instead of providing a frosted appearance. Sometimes it helps to wet the sandpaper to prevent it from clogging up.

Figure 6-11 shows a pair of LEDs that started out identically. The hand-diffused LED is easier to differentiate between on and off.

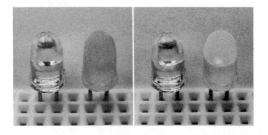

Figure 6-11. An unaltered water-clear lens versus a finely sanded water-clear lens. Unlit (left pair) and lit (right pair)

Understanding Oscilloscope Traces

Sometimes a circuit performs a function whose electrical detail is best viewed on an oscilloscope. In this book, interesting oscilloscope traces (see Figure 6-12) occasionally follow the associated schematic and solderless-breadboard photograph.

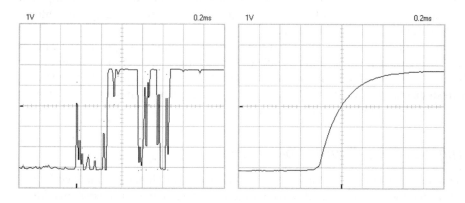

Figure 6-12. Oscilliscope traces of the circuit presented in Figures 6-6 and 6-7 (earlier in this chapter). As measured at TP1, a noisy push button doesn't rise in an electrically clean manner with C1 removed from the circuit (left). With C1 installed, the rise is smoothed, eliminating what would otherwise appear to be multiple button presses (right).

The oscilloscope traces are intended to provide fascinating insights that wouldn't otherwise be available to most hobbyists, who usually don't own an oscilloscope. These traces aren't intended to suggest that an oscilloscope is required to build the circuits in this book.

Riding the Bandwagon of Modern Electronics

We robot builders are fortunate to live in a period of rapid growth in the speed, reliability, feature set, ruggedness, and miniaturization of electronics all coupled with a decrease in power usage and price. Robot designers should take advantage of the solutions produced by the genius engineers in the trillion-dollar electronics market.

Getting Past the Learning Curve Barrier

One of the most significant obstacles to adopting new technology is the learning curve. If you're familiar with a particular part, you're less likely to be willing to learn about a moderately better part unless it functions and can be wired in an almost identical way (backward compatible). Additionally, a component isn't likely to be adopted until instructions and circuit examples are available, either informally through a knowledgeable colleague or through documentation available from the manufacturer or a Web site.

Avoiding Obsolete Technology

It's interesting to see books and Web sites continue the hobbyist demand for obsolete parts. This is especially apparent in motor driver chips, voltage regulators, and logic chips. Hobbyist builders don't consider or care about some of the attributes that a professional electrical engineer does. The hobbyist just wants the exact chip that appears in some author's circuit. Unfortunately, the high-volume production engineers rule the market, so the hobbyist must keep up.

All of the logic chips presented in the circuits in this book are high-speed CMOS or better (HC, VHC, AC). Please don't try substituting a bipolar logic chip, an older CMOS chip, or a TTL-compatible CMOS chip (HCT or ACT). Ironically, some robot parts remain stuck in the 5 V world, so don't try substituting any of the newer low voltage (3.3 V, 2.5 V, or, God help us all, 1.8 V) chips.

Using Surface-Mount Components

I generally design a module on a solderless breadboard and then combine it with previously tested modules onto a printed circuit board that I etch in my basement. I've pretty much gotten away from point-to-point soldering, except for very small boards, such as a board for a sensor located at a robot's extremity. As such, the industry changeover to surface-mount components isn't as prohibitive for me as it is for beginners or die-hard through-hole designers.

 TIP *For instructions on creating homemade printed circuit boards, see* http://www.robotroom.com/PCB.html *(case sensitive).*

Sizing Down Surface-Mount

Surface-mount components (SMT, or SMD) are designed to be soldered to copper pads on a single side of a board. Through-hole components have leads (wires) that are inserted into holes going through the board to be soldered onto the opposite side. Through-hole components are larger and easier to keep in place during soldering.

Except for high-value capacitors, the difference in through-hole versus surface-mount component size is usually quite significant (see Figure 6-13). But some of the apparent space savings in surface-mount technology is offset by the exchange of vertical area for horizontal area. For a hobbyist, the resulting board is thinner but wider.

Another space loser is that surface-mount components provide little or no room to route traces underneath. In fact, through-hole resistors were the perfect way to jump over a bunch of traces (thus creating an additional plane) rather than having to pass traces to the opposite side of the board and back again. Mass-production surface-mount component printed circuit boards (PCBs) often have four or more layers with plated through holes, so trace jumping isn't much of an issue for them.

Yet another space loser is that surface-mount chips have such a high density of tiny pins that traces have to be drawn away from the chip to have room to maneuver and make connections. That is, there isn't enough room between tiny pins to squeeze in a small capacitor or a resistor. Instead, the traces from the pins must be directed away from the chip to a different location where there's room enough to spread out. The total amount of space taken up by this extra trace routing often exceeds the space a DIP chip would've required.

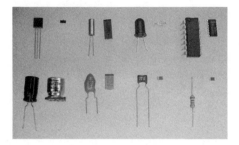

Figure 6-13. Through-hole components (the left side of each pair) beside their sur-face-mount equivalents (the right side of each pair). Bipolar NPN 2222A transis-tors, 32.768 kHz crystals, red LEDs, 74AC14 inverter chips (top row). One hundred µF 25 V aluminum electrolytic capacitors, 22 µF 20 V tantalum capacitors, 0.1 µF ceramic capacitors, 10 kΩ resistors (bottom row).

Saying "Good-Bye" to Through-Hole

Surface-mount components are easier for a machine to install. How paradoxical that parts designed for placement by industrial robots (automated manufacturing) can make robot building so difficult!

An additional manufacturing advantage of surface-mount parts is that they can be mass soldered. This occurs by screening solder paste onto a board, dropping the parts in place with a pick-and-place machine, and then heating the entire board so that the solder paste melts simultaneously throughout the board.

Except for high-wattage and high-voltage components or components that undergo physical exertions (switches and connectors), through-hole packages are going away. Even now, most of the latest chip designs aren't being offered in through-hole packages at all. Sadly, even the through-hole varieties of some older components are being phased out. So, through-hole varieties are becoming more expensive than the surface-mount packages, or they're simply not available in the first place.

Working with Surface-Mount Components

As long as you have a PCB (as opposed to a solderless breadboard or solderable perforated board), you can solder most surface-mount components by hand. I use a toothpick to put a tiny dot of silicone adhesive at each desired location, place the surface-mount components with tweezers, and then, after they've dried in place, solder them to their copper traces.

Soldering surface-mount components isn't so hard with a good work light, good eyes, and a steady hand. It just takes some practice. Really!

For surface-mount chips with a lot of pins, you can apply a line of solder straight across the pins. Then, add a little liquid flux and reheat the pins. Unless you've used a truly disgusting amount of solder, it tends to wick up properly onto individual pins and traces, leaving a clean, perfectly soldered chip without solder bridges. If that doesn't work completely, use a solder sucker to remove excess solder or draw the solder out onto the copper traces using just the point of the soldering iron.

Converting Surface-Mount Components to Through-Hole

Generic PCBs with surface-mount leads are available (see Figure 6-14) to aid in experimenting with surface-mount components on solderless breadboards.

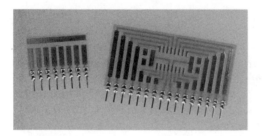

Figure 6-14. Surfboards are available from Digi-Key ($2.51, #6008CA, and $6.53, #9164CA) and Electronix Express for converting surface-mount components to through-hole.

Larger composite PCBs (see Figure 6-15) with surface-mount pads connected to holes (instead of pins) are also available for experimentation. Usually the boards are designed with lots of different part styles in mind so you can cut out or snap out the sections desired. Of course, you can always etch your own surface-mount adapter boards.

Figure 6-15. A larger board with many different pads for lots of different styles of surface-mount components. Each trace goes to one or more holes to which wires can be attached. Pads for surface-mount capacitors and resistors surround many of the chip pads. The designer of this board anticipated the armada of general support components needed by most ICs.

Mixing and Matching Package Technologies

One theoretical advantage of using surface-mount components is that you don't need to drill so many holes in your home-etched PCBs. Unfortunately, sometimes that's offset by a lot of pass-through holes to get around trace logjams. However, there's nothing that says you can't use a 0 Ω resistor (or a piece of wire) to jump over PCB traces.

Better still, mix and match surface-mount components with through-hole components as needed to best arrange circuits on your homemade robots. Such mixing can make production boards difficult to manufacture, but that's not a concern for one-off robot designs.

In fact, in the last couple of years, nearly all of my robots have been built with a mix of component packages. That being said, out of respect for readers, the circuits in this book are built strictly from through-hole components, where available.

Shrinking Below Hand-Labor Level

Unfortunately, surface-mount components continue to get smaller and smaller. Their leads are getting skinnier and skinnier and closer and closer together. In fact, some surface-mount technologies, such as ball-grid arrays (BGA), are almost literally impossible to hand solder (with the possible exception of the toaster oven approach).

There will come a day, sooner than you think, when you'll have to purchase a prototyping machine to work with commercially available electronic components. I can see it now: There will be your all-in-one handheld digital multimeter oscilloscope, your miniature computer numerically controlled (CNC) milling machine body-part maker and PCB router, your macro-lens video pick-and-place soldering machine, and your laptop schematic-routing-CAD-and-simulation software.

Then again, maybe a robot will just do all of the work for you.

Summary

This chapter has described the labels and conventions for the schematics in this book. Schematics are usually followed by photographs of the circuit laid out on an 840 tie-point solderless breadboard, set up in a consistent manner.

As for components, this chapter has established the minimum wattage and working voltage values, unless specifically called out otherwise in a later chapter. The chapter has also covered default component chemistry, as well as chip technology. Finally, through-hole packaged components have been selected to ease prototyping, wherever possible.

Now it's time to move on to some actual circuits commonly used in the robots.

Creating a Linear Voltage-Regulated Power Supply

Includes Classic 5V 7805, Reverse-Battery Protection, Low Dropout Regulators, Simple but Improved Reverse-Battery Protection, Variable Power Supply, and a Head-to-Head Match-Up

IN THIS CHAPTER, YOU'LL LEARN how to build and evaluate a +5 VDC linear voltage-regulated power supply, which is used to provide a consistent voltage to chips, sensors, and circuits. Although some robots, such as low-voltage solar robots, can accept a varying voltage, most require a power supply such as the one presented in this chapter.

Understanding Voltage Regulators

A battery's voltage steadily decreases as the battery is discharged and transiently decreases when the battery is subject to heavy demands (for example, when a motor starts). Additionally, the base chemistry of the battery determines the minimum and maximum voltages it can supply. Therefore, a battery by itself can't be relied upon either for selection of a particular voltage or for supplying that voltage consistently.

The raw output from the battery is called the *unregulated* power supply. To deliver maximum power, unregulated power is usually applied to motors and other heavy loads.

Voltage regulation is a technique to modify the battery's varying unregulated voltage to create a clean supply at a predetermined, steady voltage. Voltage regulation makes current, wattage, and other circuit calculations easier because you can rely on a consistent voltage in your equations.

The output from the voltage regulator is called the *regulated* power supply. To prevent logic errors or unreliable sensor readings, regulated power is usually applied to chips, sensors, and other complex or delicate circuits.

There are two basic types of voltage regulators: linear and switching. Within the class of switching regulators, there's either buck or boost. There's also a type of combination regulator that contains a boost-switching regulator followed by a linear regulator.

For now, you'll concentrate on the simplest type, the linear voltage regulator. Also, because all of the robots in this book have 5 V circuits, this book focuses on regulators that provide a fixed 5 V output. However, you'll find one circuit for an adjustable voltage regulator located in the "Introducing the LM1117 Adjustable Voltage Regulator" section.

Understanding Linear Voltage-Regulated Power Supplies

A linear voltage-regulated power supply requires an unregulated voltage that's higher than the desired regulated voltage. For example, a 9 V battery can supply power to a linear voltage regulator that outputs 5 V. But two AA batteries putting out a total of 3 V can't supply enough voltage to a linear regulator that intends to output 5 V.

A linear voltage regulator discards the extra power as heat. So, a 5 V regulator receiving 9 V dissipates 4 V (times the current) as heat. Obviously that's not very efficient. In this example, the regulator is only 5 V divided by 9 V, which equals 55 percent efficient. Almost half of the battery's power is wasted.

However, linear voltage regulators are relatively inexpensive, require few additional components, and generate little electrical noise. The complete circuits are easy to build and take up very little space.

Linear voltage regulators are popular for the following uses:

- Quick, small, simple circuits

- Low-cost, high-volume products, such as inexpensive consumer electronics

- Circuits that consume small amounts (100 mA or less) of current

- Regulated voltage that's just slightly less than the unregulated voltage

The 7805 Linear Voltage Regulator

The venerable 7805 linear voltage regulator is an inexpensive, well-documented, widely available component. Many varieties of the 7805 exist, but the 7805C, 7805CT, 7805T, and 78L05 are the most easily obtained (see Figure 7-1).

Figure 7-1. The 7805C regulator in a TO-220 through-hole package that can handle up to 1 amp of current (left). The 78L05 regulator in a TO-92 through-hole package that can handle up to 100 mA of current (right)

Probably any 7805 variety (7805B, 7805K, 78M05, and so on) will succeed in the 7805 circuits presented in this chapter—I just haven't tested them myself. If you're working on a solderless breadboard, be sure the component package is compatible. For example, neither the thick pins of a TO-3 package nor the flat tiny pins of a surface-mount package fit in a solderless breadboard.

The 7805CT/7805T ($0.35 to $0.48; #MC7805CT at Digi-Key, #N107805-T at Electronix Express, and #51262 at Jameco) in the TO-220 package provides up to 1 amp of current. The 78L05 ($0.22 to $0.40; #296-1365 at Digi-Key, #N107805-L at Electronix Express, and #51182 at Jameco) in the TO-92 package provides up to 100 mA of current.

Other than the difference in maximum current output, the 7805CT and 78L05 function identically. If your circuit requires only 100 mA, you can save space and a little money by choosing the 78L05.

Introducing a 7805-Based 5 V Power Supply

Figure 7-2 shows the generic circuit for a 7805-based power supply.

The capacitor values have been bumped up from the suggested values so that this circuit is drop-in compatible with the other linear voltage regulators presented later in the chapter. It's worth noting that the manufacturers' specifications (datasheets) say the 7805 will perform acceptably without any capacitors at all.

As you can see in Figure 7-2, there's not much to the circuit. Put in 7 V to 20 V, and get out approximately 5 V. R1 and LED1 are the first to utilize the regulated power source to provide a power indication light.

VR1 is the 7805. Positive unregulated voltage flows into pin 1 (the leftmost pin). Positive 5 V regulated voltage flows out of pin 3 (the rightmost pin). Pin 2 (the middle pin) is simply connected to ground.

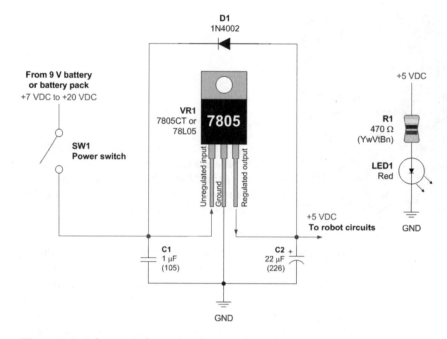

Figure 7-2. Schematic for a simple 7805-based power supply

Assisting the Batteries and Voltage Regulator

C1 and C2 are capacitors. Their role is to store and release electricity to smooth out noise, surges, and sags. Without the capacitors, the 7805 would still output 5 V but wouldn't react as quickly to changes in supply and demand, and thus it wouldn't provide as clean of a regulated output.

The operation of these capacitors is fairly simple. C1 is connected to the battery. When the power switch (SW1) is turned on, C1 charges up to the same voltage level as the battery. If a short-term demand occurs, the battery voltage may drop a little. C1 would then have a slightly higher voltage than the burdened battery, so some of the power stored in C1 would flow back out to assist the battery and to support VR1. In this circuit, C1 has such a small value that its *speed* in flattening out electrical noise is more useful than its total capacity for storing power reserves.

Capacitors react much more quickly than batteries. They're perfect for storing and releasing small bursts of energy very quickly. Under normal conditions, capacitors can be charged and discharged over and over again for decades. Capacitors are relatively small, so they can be located directly beside the chips or components that they're intended to support. It's like having a fast, short-term, private rechargeable battery.

C2 performs in the same manner as C1 except that C2 is connected to the output of the voltage regulator. When the power switch (SW1) is turned on, C2 charges up from the 5 V provided by the voltage regulator. When the robot's circuits temporarily demand more power than the regulator can supply, the regulator's voltage dips below 5 V, which is slightly lower than C2's voltage level, so C2 drains to supplement the short-term demand of the circuit.

Both C1 and C2 have fairly small values of capacitance. As such, they can't provide power for long. They're great at absorbing a spike (charging) and good at covering up a sag (discharging to supplement the power supply). However, their total storage is too small to supply full power to the circuit for any useful length of time when the power switch is turned off or when the battery is disconnected.

You can increase the values of the capacitors if desired. Also, you don't have to use exactly 1 µF and exactly 22 µF if you don't have them handy. "Close enough" is acceptable for these capacitors in this application.

Protecting the Voltage Regulator Against Reverse Flows

In Figure 7-2, D1 is an optional safety feature. If someone disconnects the battery with the power switch still turned on and then connects the unregulated voltage wire to the ground wire, the unregulated input to the voltage regulator (pin 1) will drop to 0 V. Without D1, the power stored in capacitor C2 (and all of the other capacitors in the robot's circuits) would try to force itself backward through pin 3 of the voltage regulator to pin 1.

According to the manufacturer, you can destroy the 7805 by a reverse current if the total capacitance on the regulated side is 10 µF or more. Placing D1 over VR1 permits any reverse power flow to go through the diode rather than the voltage regulator.

Unfortunately, D1 also provides the perfect path for a battery connected in reverse to run rampant through the circuit. This is sort of a self-centered preservation technique on the part of the manufacturer. The rest of your circuit is fried, but the regulator is fine!

Instead, I prefer the layout shown in Figure 7-3. Now diode D1 protects against reverse batteries (no current can flow from a reverse battery because it'd be against the direction permitted by diode D1) and protects against shorted power wires (no current can flow from regulated capacitors because the flow would also be against the direction permitted by diode D1). The downside, however, is a loss of between 0.3 V and 0.45 V dropped across the diode when operated in the correct direction.

The part specified for D1 in Figure 7-2 is a 1N4002 diode ($0.03 to $0.04; #1N4002 at All Electronics, #1N4002GICT at Digi-Key, #N11 1N4002 at Electronix Express, and #76961 at Jameco). The part specified for D1 in Figure 7-3 is a #1N5817 diode ($0.29 to $0.39; #1N5817 at All Electronics, #1N5817DICT at Digi-Key, and #177949 at Jameco).

The difference between the diodes is that a 1N4002 is less expensive and leaks little current in the reverse direction (0.5 mA versus 10 mA is the worst case for the 1N5817). However, the 1N5817 diode has a much lower voltage drop (0.45 V versus 1.1 V is the worst case for the 1N4002). In Figure 7-2, the voltage drop didn't matter because current wasn't flowing through the diode in normal operation. But in Figure 7-3, the voltage drop occurs constantly during normal use.

Later in the "Substituting a Power MOSFET for the 1N5817" section, I'll describe a method to protect against a reverse battery without a significant voltage drop. However, using a diode is a straightforward, inexpensive, and popular protection method.

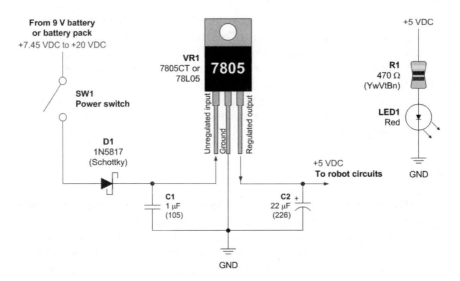

Figure 7-3. Revised schematic for a 7805-based power supply that includes reverse-battery protection

Building the 7805-Based Power Supply

The 7805 linear voltage-regulator power supply is easy to build on a breadboard. In Figure 7-4, the power supply has been built on the right side of an 840 tie-point solderless breadboard because the binding posts appear on that side of the board. The only disadvantage to placing the power supply on the right side is that you have to insert the 7805 with the label facing away, as shown in Figure 7-4 (metal tab facing front), or you have to use a bunch of jumper wires to get the pins in the correct order.

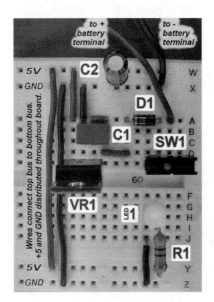

Figure 7-4. A 7805-based power supply with reverse-battery protection. The circuit has been built onto the right side of a solderless breadboard.

Readers of *Robot Building for Beginners* (Apress, 2002) will recognize this setup of the solderless breadboard. The battery, switch, LED, and distribution wires are the same as before. The addition of a voltage regulator circuit provides +5 VDC to the board, as opposed to the unregulated 6 V to 9.6 V from the 9 V battery as presented in my prior book.

Tracing the Power Flow of the 7805-Based Power Supply Circuit

Unregulated voltage flows from the positive (+) terminal of the battery (not shown) through the power switch (SW1) through the reverse-protecting diode (D1) to the battery-filter capacitor (C1) and to the voltage regulator (VR1). The voltage regulator (VR1) outputs 5 V to the regulator-reserve capacitor (C2) and to the rest of the circuits on the board.

Wires on the solderless breadboard route power from the top distribution bus to the bottom distribution bus. From the bottom distribution bus, 5 V goes through the current-limiting resistor (R1) to light the power-indication LED (LED1) and back to ground (GND). Power returns through the distribution buses and wires to reach the negative (–) terminal of the battery (not shown).

Note that ground isn't "regulated," per se. Only the positive voltage is regulated. Ground is 0 V and is connected to both the regulated circuits and unregulated circuits. In this arrangement, ground is often referred to as *common ground*.

Obtaining Capacitors for the 7805-Based Power Supply Circuit

Because C1 is acting as an electrical noise filter, the frequency response of the capacitor is important. Also, because C1 is exposed to the unregulated voltage, a working voltage higher than the maximum unregulated voltage is required. That makes metallized film technology the top choice for a capacitor that has the value required by C1. A 1 µF, 63 working voltage (WV) metallized polyester capacitor with radial leads spaced at 5.08 mm (which fits well in a solderless breadboard) is a good choice ($0.41; #BC1622 at Digi-Key). As an alternate to metallized films, a 50 WV monolithic ceramic would be a legitimate second choice ($0.58 to $0.60; #81509 at Jameco; CP1.0µF at Solarbotics).

Because C2 is acting as storage for reserve power, a large capacitance value is important. However, because it's connected to only 5 V, the working voltage can be as low as 10 WV. Aluminum electrolytic capacitors are inexpensive ($0.05 to $0.22; #22/25VR at All Electronics, #P960 or #P967 at Digi-Key, #198846 at Jameco, and #CP22µF at Solarbotics). As an alternative to aluminum electrolytic capacitors, tantalum-dipped capacitors are more expensive but smaller in size and are more responsive ($0.50 to $1.45; #DT-2215 at All Electronics, #399-1393 at Digi-Key, and #N14TA02522U Electronix Express).

Obtaining the Power Switch

I really like the EG1903 slide switch available from Digi-Key for $0.71. It fits nicely in a solderless breadboard and doesn't take up much room. Unfortunately, it's rated only at 200 mA.

For more current, the N17SLDH251 is available from Electronix Express for $1. It also fits nicely in a solderless breadboard but is twice as wide (as well as generally larger). However, it can handle 1 amp of current.

Improving the Power Supply by Reducing the Minimum Required Unregulated Voltage

One of the first things you may have noticed about the 7805-based power supply is that the manufacturer's guaranteed minimum input voltage is 7 V. My preferred location for D1 (for reverse-battery protection) makes things worse, with the minimum input voltage rising to 7.45 V. A four pack of alkaline batteries (1.6 V times 4 equals 6.4 V) isn't adequate to power the circuits of a robot with a 7805-based power supply.

Admittedly, the manufacturer determines the minimum input voltage value conservatively to guarantee that the 7805 meets all the specifications at maximum rated current. For example, at room temperature, if you draw only 50 mA from the 1000 mA (1 amp) rated 7805CT, the minimum input voltage may only be 6.3 V instead of 7 V. Additionally, the 1N5817 diode consumes only about 0.3 V at 50 mA, bringing the total to 6.6 V.

That's still not very good. Two component substitutions can greatly decrease the minimum input voltage requirement. First, you can substitute a pin-compatible low-dropout voltage (LDO) linear voltage regulator for the 7805. Second, you can substitute a low-resistance *p*-channel power MOSFET for the 1N5817 diode.

Substituting an LM2940 or LP2954 for the 7805

The LM2940CT-5.0 ("dash" 5.0, not "negative" 5.0) and the LP2954IT are drop-in pin compatible replacements for the 7805 in the circuits of this book (see Figure 7-5). No kidding! Pull out the 7805 from the circuit and put in either an LM2940 or an LP2954.

 NOTE *That's a bit of a trick because I designed the first circuit with enough capacitance to meet the requirements of the other components. Still, they're compatible in this circuit. There's nothing wrong with designing a power supply or any circuit to accept a variety of components. In fact, flexible circuit designs are quite valuable if you run out of a particular part.*

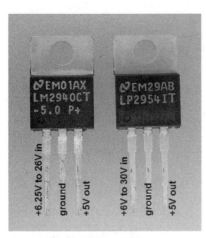

Figure 7-5. Either the LM2940CT-5.0 (left) or the LP2954IT (right) can replace the 7805.

Like the 7805, the LM2940CT-5.0 is a 5 V linear voltage regulator in a TO-220 package capable of up to 1 amp output ($1.29 to $1.65; #LM2940CT-5.0 at Digi-Key and #107182 at Jameco). The LM2940 automatically protects against reverse batteries, so diode D1 isn't necessary to protect regulated circuits or the voltage regulator itself. (However, the robot's motor driver chips and other unregulated chips are at risk without D1.)

The LP2954IT is also a 5 V linear voltage regulator in a TO-220 package. It's available from Digi-Key, #LP2954IT, for $3.98 (ouch!). Unlike the other two regulators, the LP2954IT is only capable of 250 mA of output. Like the LM2940, the LP2954 has reverse-battery protection.

Both the LM2940 and LP2954 have a lower minimum input voltage than the 7805. These kinds of regulators are called *low dropout* (LDO). Comparing Figure 7-1 to Figure 7-5, it appears that these low-dropout regulators provide only a 0.75 V to 1 V improvement in the minimum input voltage. But, as you'll soon see, under room temperatures and reasonably low current draws (250 mA), these devices perform much better than the manufacturers' specifications and much better than the 7805.

Substituting a Power MOSFET for the 1N5817

The other improvement you can make to lower the minimum input voltage is to replace the 1N5817 diode with another component that can provide the same reverse-battery protection for the entire robot. But the replacement component is a transistor, not a diode, so the "extra" lead needs to be connected to something, which in this case is ground (see Figure 7-6).

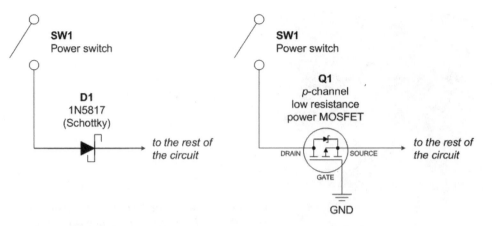

Figure 7-6. Most of the power supply circuit remains unchanged. Remove diode D1 (left), and replace it with MOSFET Q1 (right).

Switching On and Off the Robot Based on the Battery Connection

A metal oxide semiconductor field effect transistor (MOSFET) is a transistor switch, which, just like a regular physical switch, can be turned on and off. A *p*-channel enhancement MOSFET switch turns on when the voltage at the gate lead is lower (by an amount specified by the manufacturer) than the voltage at the drain lead.

In this circuit, the MOSFET's gate lead connects to the lowest possible voltage, 0 V, and the MOSFET's drain lead connects to the highest possible voltage, 6 V to 20 V. Because the gate lead has a lower voltage than the drain lead, the *p*-channel MOSFET switches on and power flows into the rest of the circuit.

What if someone reverses the battery?

In that case, the MOSFET's gate lead connects to the highest possible voltage, 6 V to 20 V, and the MOSFET's drain lead connects to the lowest possible voltage, 0 V. Because the gate lead now has a higher voltage than the drain lead, the *p*-channel MOSFET switches off, cutting power flow from the rest of the circuit. Thus, the circuit is protected.

Powering a Full Circuit Requires a Power MOSFET

One of the key words in the description of Q1 is that it must be a "power" MOSFET. Unlike a regular MOSFET, a power MOSFET is designed to handle large amounts of current. To protect all of the parts from a reverse battery, all the power (including motor power) is going to flow through this MOSFET. Therefore, a power MOSFET is appropriate.

Of course, the word *power* is subject to interpretation. What's important is to check the manufacturer's datasheet to see how much current the particular MOSFET can handle to determine if that's enough for your robot.

Saving Voltage Drop Through Low Resistance

Inherent to its internal structure, a MOSFET contains a built-in diode. Therefore, you're really replacing diode D1 with both a transistor and a diode.

To save on voltage drop, Q1 must be a low-resistance MOSFET. For example, the one I selected has a resistance of 0.11 Ω (⅛ of an ohm). Recall that the voltage drop of the 1N5817 diode is about 0.3 V at 50 mA and about 0.45 V at 1000 mA.

To compare the diode's efficiency to the MOSFET's efficiency, a little math is required to convert the MOSFET's resistance into a voltage drop:

```
voltage drop in volts = current in amps × resistance in ohms
```

Example 1 (50 mA):
```
voltage drop in volts = 0.050 A × 0.11 Ω
voltage drop = 0.0055 V
```

Example 2 (1 A):
```
voltage drop in volts = 1 A × 0.11 Ω
voltage drop = 0.11 V
```

Fantastic! The example MOSFET's consumes virtually no voltage at 50 mA and one-fourth the voltage of the 1N5817 diode at 1 amp.

Increasing Resistance at Lower Voltages

According to the datasheet, the example MOSFET achieves a 0.11 Ω resistance only when the gate is at least 10 V less than the drain. That's an industry-standard voltage for comparison purposes. MOSFETs increase in resistance as the voltage difference is lowered.

Unfortunately, you need a low resistance to occur at 6 V or even 5 V, not 10 V. If you had all that extra voltage to throw away, you could just use a regular diode in the first place.

In practice, I measured the voltage drop of the example MOSFET to be 0.028 V at 170 mA when the gate was 5.7 V lower than the drain. This computes to be the following resistance:

```
resistance in ohms = voltage drop in volts ÷ current in amps
resistance in ohms = 0.028 V ÷ 0.170 A
resistance = 0.165 Ω
```

All that worry for nothing! As expected, the MOSFET's resistance increased from 0.11 Ω at 10 V to 0.165 Ω at 5.75 V. But the resistance is still very low.

Selecting a Low-Resistance P-Channel Power MOSFET

The MOSFET in the previous example is the International Rectifier IRFU5505 Ultra-Low On-Resistance P-Channel HEXFET Power MOSFET, or FU5505 for short (see Figure 7-7). HEXFET is just the brand name for this series of MOSFETs from International Rectifier (http://www.irf.com/).

Figure 7-7. The FU5505 MOSFET in an I-Pak through-hole package

I selected the FU5505 for the power supply circuit for many reasons:

- The datasheet specifies that the maximum permitted V_{GS} (which stands for *gate-to-source voltage*) can be ±20 V, which is important because, in the normal operation of this circuit, the gate could be 0 V and the source could be around 19.8 V. The 19.8 V value is the drain (up to 20 V) minus the voltage drop (calculated at less than a couple of tenths of a volt); 19.8 V is less than 20 V (or, actually, -19.8 V is less than -20 V), so this is within the specified limits.

- The datasheet specifies a maximum current of 18 amps; that's much higher than the 1-amp limit of the voltage regulator. Add a couple of 3-amp motors (which would be very high for a small robot), and this MOSFET still has lots of breathing room.

- The datasheet specifies an ultralow on-resistance of 0.11 Ω (the lower, the better). The resistance could be higher and still be acceptable, but the resistance translates into voltage drop, which you're trying to minimize.

- The datasheet specifies a $V_{GS(TH)}$ (which stands for *gate-to-source voltage threshold*) of between 2 V and 4 V; this indicates that the MOSFET begins turning on between 2 V and 4 V. That's important because this power supply should run at 6 V and maybe even 5 V—if the gate-to-source voltage threshold were, say, 7 V to 8 V, then the MOSFET wouldn't turn on for a 6 V power supply.

- The I-Pak through-hole package fits nicely in a solderless breadboard.

- The FU5505 is available from Digi-Key ($1.33, #IRFU5505) in single quantities. A great part isn't of much interest if the hobbyist can't get it or if the vendor requires a large-quantity purchase.

- The FU5505 is the same one I use in my custom H-bridge motor driver circuit (see Chapter 10). It saves money to buy in bulk and reuse the same part.

- Most important, I laugh every time I read the part number—it's like the part is trying to pick a fight with me. I suspect the designer was having a bad day when someone at the company asked him to give it a name.

Analyzing the Minimum Input Voltage of Various Linear Regulator Circuits

Recall that a linear voltage regulator must have an unregulated input voltage that's greater than the desired regulated output voltage. Five volts is the desired operating voltage for the regulated robot circuits presented in this book, but the parts in those circuits are specified to accept as little as 4.75 V without problems. Logically, the minimum input unregulated voltage must be somewhat higher than 4.75 V for the minimum output regulated voltage to be at or higher than 4.75 V.

You want to design the circuit to output 5 V while receiving the lowest possible unregulated input voltage because of the following:

- Extra voltage is wasted, which is inefficient.

- Extra voltage usually means a greater number of batteries. That requires extra space, costs money, and weighs down the robot.

As discussed earlier, manufacturers tend to be conservative in their datasheets when specifying the minimum unregulated voltage that's acceptable. Therefore, the following sections show how to test what the actual input and output voltages can be for each of the voltage regulators described so far.

Defining the Test Apparatus

You could drain a battery pack over time and observe the effect of the declining voltage on the various regulators. But that takes awhile and isn't quickly repeatable.

Instead, I hooked up my RadioShack AC power adaptor and set the output to +12 VDC. Then I attached that to an LM1117T ADJ variable-voltage regulator circuit with a potentiometer to output any voltage from 11 V down to 1.25 V. I then fed the output of the LM1117 to the voltage regulator circuit being tested.

I used two multimeters (see Figure 7-8). One multimeter displayed the output voltage of the LM1117 variable regulator to guide the precise adjustment of the "unregulated input voltage" being supplied to the voltage regulator under test. The second multimeter displayed the regulated output voltage of the voltage regulator under test.

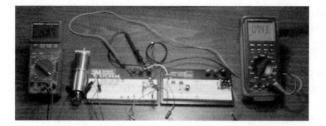

Figure 7-8. A multimeter displaying the output voltage of the regulator being tested (left), a high-quality motor (normally not a regulated load) and a group of LEDs to simulate a load (second to left), a solderless breadboard with the voltage regulator being tested (middle), a solderless breadboard with an LM1117 adjustable voltage regulator to simulate different "unregulated" input voltages (second from right), and a multimeter displaying the output voltage of the LM1117 to allow precise tuning (right)

Introducing the LM1117 Adjustable Voltage Regulator

The 1117 ($1.00 to $1.16; #LM1117T-ADJ at Digi-Key and #511-LD1117V at Mouser) is an 800 mA low-dropout, adjustable, positive, linear voltage regulator. The LM1117 has a lower maximum current rating than the 7805 and LM2940 voltage regulators being tested. However, this wasn't an issue because I wanted to compare those regulators against the LP2954, which has a 250 mA current limit.

Because the LM1117 is in a TO-220 package, it looks the same as the other voltage regulators presented thus far in this chapter. But don't be fooled. The pins aren't compatible (see Figure 7-9). By the way, I was fooled for about an hour.

Figure 7-9. Although it looks similar, the LM1117 adjustable voltage regulator doesn't have the same pin arrangement as the 7805, LM2940, or LP2954.

Setting Up the LM1117

The circuit for the adjustable voltage regulator (see Figure 7-10) includes similar parts as the fixed-voltage regulator circuits presented earlier. SW1, C1, C2, VR1, R1, and LED1 perform the same functions as before. However, the left-to-right placement of the components in the schematic is flipped because the pins on the regulator are flipped.

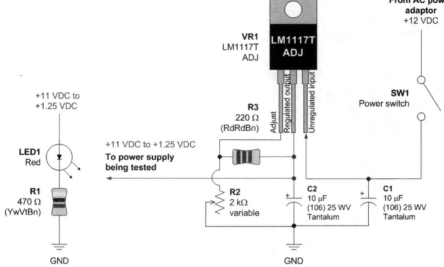

Figure 7-10. The LM1117 adjustable voltage regulator schematic

The values of C1 and C2 are 10 µF to generally comply with the example presented in the datasheet. If you plan on using the LM1117 for a robot, consider raising the value of C2 or supplementing it with a higher-value aluminum electrolytic capacitor (see the next chapter for details on bulk capacitors).

The construction of capacitors C1 and C2 is specified as tantalum in the datasheet. C1 and C2 must have a working voltage of 25 WV or better because they need to deal with maximum input and output voltages of 12 V and 11 V, respectively.

Ten µF 25 WV through-hole dipped tantalum capacitors ($0.50 to $0.93; #DT-1025 at All Electronics, #399-1418 at Digi-Key, and #94078CP at Jameco) are popular for power supplies and other circuits. You should select the same capacitor with 35 WV ($0.75 to $1.50; #N14TA03510U at Electronix Express, #399-1435 at Digi-Key, and #33689CP at Jameco) if your robot's battery pack exceeds 12 V. The same capacitor with 10 WV or 16 WV ($0.39 to $0.70; #DT-1016 at All Electronics, #399-1391 at Digi-Key, #N14TA01610U at Electronix Express, and #94060 at Jameco) is appropriate for 5 V (or lower) regulated voltages. To save money, consider purchasing any of these capacitors in lots of ten or more.

R2 and R3 are new to the voltage regulator circuit. They form a voltage divider that alters the output of the LM1117 by adjusting the value of R2. A multiturn potentiometer for R2 provides finer adjustments of the output voltage than a single-turn potentiometer provides, but either one will work.

You could add reverse-battery protection to this circuit the same way as in prior circuits using a diode or MOSFET. Because this was just for limited testing, I skipped the reverse-battery protection and crammed the circuit into the upper corner of a spare solderless breadboard (see Figure 7-11).

Figure 7-11. The LM1117 adjustable voltage regulator (without reverse-battery protection) implemented on a solderless breadboard

Presenting the Input/Output Voltage Results of Three 5 V Linear Voltage Regulators

I tested four circuits with two different loads (100 mA and 250 mA) for a total of eight trials. The LM1117 simulated "unregulated" voltages from 10 V down to 4.7 V in steps of 0.1 V.

I then plotted the results in the range of 7 V down to 4.8 V because that's where all the action is (see Figure 7-12). Above 7 V, all the regulators provided full output voltage. Below 4.8 V, all the regulators failed to provide an output voltage higher than 4.75 V, which is the minimum required by most 5 V chips and sensors.

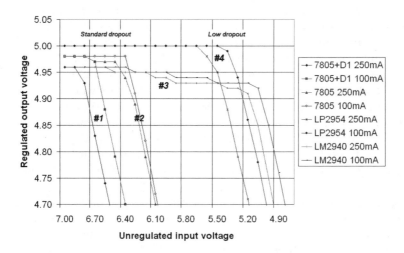

Figure 7-12. The results of the voltage regulator tests. As the input voltage (horizontal axis) drops below critical values, the output voltage of each regulator drops sharply.

Note that all of the regulators began with an output between 4.95 V and 5 V, which is superior to the range officially tolerated. If, for example, your voltage regulator is providing 4.92 V or 5.03 V output, it doesn't mean that there's something wrong with your circuit. The datasheets show that those values are within the accepted range.

For the purposes of these tests, each voltage regulator's minimum input voltage (horizontal axis) is scored at 0.1 V higher than the point at which the output voltage (vertical axis) finally drops *below* 4.75 V. Looking at the bottom left of Figure 7-12 and running across to the bottom right, the input voltage requirements of the voltage regulators with reverse-battery protection are, in order of increasing capability, the following:

- 7805 plus a 1N5817, at 250 mA, requires an input voltage of 6.7 V or more

- 7805 plus a 1N5817, at 100 mA, requires an input voltage of 6.5 V or more

- 7805 plus an FU5505, at 250 mA, requires an input voltage of 6.2 V or more

- 7805 plus an FU5505, at 100 mA, requires an input voltage of 6.2 V or more

- LP2954 plus an FU5505, at 250 mA, requires an input voltage of 5.3 V or more

- LP2954 plus an FU5505, at 100 mA, requires an input voltage of 5.1 V or more

- LM2940 plus an FU5505, at 250 mA, requires an input voltage of 5.0 V or more

- LM2940 plus an FU5505, at 100 mA, requires an input voltage of 4.9 V or more

Current Loads Affecting the Minimum Required Voltage

Each regulator was tested while supplying 100 mA to a simulated load (a bunch of LEDs). Then, each test was repeated with a 250 mA load (a bunch of LEDs plus a motor).

Referring to item #1 in Figure 7-12, the line to the left of #1 is a 7805 regulator with a 1N5817 diode supplying 250 mA. To the right of #1 is the same circuit supplying 100 mA. The lines follow each other down with a gap of about 0.14 V. Most of the gap is caused by the differences in voltage drops across the diode at 100 mA and 250 mA.

In fact, in each pair of lines across the graph, the minimum required voltage for each regulator is always lower for lighter loads. That's an important thing to remember when building your robot. If you've loaded up the circuit board with LEDs and goodies, plan on providing a higher voltage to your linear regulator. If your battery pack can't quite supply enough voltage, try pulling out some LEDs.

Item #2 in Figure 7-12 is interesting in that a 7805 with an FU5055 doesn't show that much of a difference between supplying a 250 mA load and a 100 mA load. Comparing item #1 (7805 with 1N5817) to item #2 (7805 with FU5505) illustrates that using an FU5505 MOSFET instead of a 1N5817 diode makes a considerable difference (about 0.3 V) in the minimum input voltage for a 7805 under both loads.

Low-Dropout Voltage Regulators Make a Difference

Notice the gap in the bottom middle of Figure 7-12. There's a 0.9 V difference between the best-case standard-dropout 7805 and the worst-case low-dropout LP2954 and LM2940. Comparing the best-case overall winner (LM2940) to the worst case (7805 + IN5817) is a difference of 1.6 V or better. That's equivalent to a whole AA alkaline battery!

Dropping Suddenly vs. Dropping Steadily

The LM2940 exhibits a strange phenomenon. Its output declines about 0.05 V (see item #3 in Figure 7-12) as the input declines about 1.2 V. The other regulators hold relatively steady (item #4) until a sudden and steep drop. Although I prefer that a regulator maintain a constant output voltage as long as possible, it doesn't matter much if the variation is only 0.05 V.

Considering Various Factors in Linear Voltage Regulators

As you've just read, the minimum input voltage could be a significant differentiator in selecting a particular linear voltage regulator. Price is another factor. Other factors are also worth considering.

Protecting Against a Reverse Battery

The LM2940 and LP2954 have built-in reverse-battery protection, but the 7805 doesn't. However, a regulator's reverse-battery protection doesn't do a lot of good in most small robots because the motor driver chips usually receive unregulated power, which isn't protected by the regulator. So, you'll probably need a component (either a diode or a MOSFET) for reverse-battery protection anyway.

Protecting Against Short Circuits

All of the regulators examined in this chapter provide protection against a short circuit (+5 VDC touching 0 VDC) or current overload in the regulated circuit. Without damaging themselves, the regulators limit the maximum current that can flow. This feature significantly reduces the chance of fires or battery damage.

Protecting Against Thermal Overload

All three voltage regulators examined in this chapter provide protection against the regulator overheating, also called *thermal overload*. Manufacturers don't specify how the regulator protects against thermal overload, but I suspect the regulator will jump out of the circuit and go get a glass of cold water.

Heating can be a problem because it increases the voltage drop (thus increasing the minimum input voltage required) and could potentially damage nearby capacitors. Consider adding a metal heat sink (see Figure 7-13) if any of these conditions are true:

- Your robot's circuit is drawing 250 mA or more from the regulator

- The regulator is exposed to temperatures greater than room temperature

- The input voltage is more than 10 V (because all of the voltage in excess of 5 V is converted into heat)

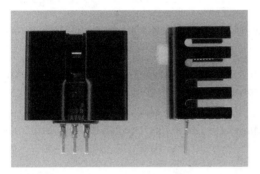

Figure 7-13. Two examples of metal heat sinks. A heat sink attaches to a chip or component to increase the exposed thermal surface area, providing better heat dissipation. Applying thermal grease between the component and the heat sink will further increase contact and thermal transfer.

During tests performed earlier, when the input voltage was 10 V and the current load was 250 mA, the regulators became hot enough for me to feel the difference with my finger. Admittedly, "Did it burn my finger?" isn't the wisest of tests.

Simplicity and Low Cost of a Complete Circuit

Some linear voltage regulators, such as the 7805, have the feature of not officially requiring capacitors. This makes for a very simple and low-cost circuit. On the other hand, the LM2940 demands a mix of tantalum and aluminum electrolytic capacitors for optimal performance (see the datasheet for details). Improved performance often has cost and complexity associated with it.

Consuming Quiescent Current

Besides consuming some voltage, linear voltage regulators also consume some current for their own purposes. This current, called *quiescent current*, is in addition to the current provided for the benefit of the circuit.

For example, the 7805 has a quiescent current of between 5 mA and 8 mA. With a 100 mA robot brain connected, if you measured the current going into the input pin on the 7805, it might read 105 mA. If you measured the current going out of the 7805's output pin and into the robot brain, it might read 100 mA. The "consumed" current of 5 mA is being sent into the ground pin.

The quiescent current of any component is lost or wasted in performing the function of that component. This represents the electrical cost of using that component.

....

Surprise! Surprise! The Trick of the Low-Dropout Regulators

The LM2940 provides a superior minimum input voltage over the lowly 7805. Unfortunately, in exchange, the LM2940 has a quiescent current of between 10 mA and 60 mA. Actually, the LM2940 has a maximum quiescent current of 130 mA (found lurking in the datasheet graphs) when the LM2940 is supplying 1 amp with an input voltage below 8 V.

Like the LM2940, the LP2954 also provides a superior minimum input voltage. In exchange, the LP2954 has a quiescent current of between 0.09 mA and 33 mA. The quiescent current increases with the load current. So, the 33 mA quiescent current occurs only when the LP2954 is putting out 250 mA.

....

Isolating Power and Noise

Almost all voltage regulators provide an important service that's usually not touted in individual datasheets because the feature isn't unique to a particular regulator. Voltage regulators tend to absorb or reduce electrical noise (spikes and dips) generated outside of the regulated circuit. Also, voltage regulators tend to separate out a local power source (stored in capacitor C2 in the circuits presented earlier) usable only by the regulated circuit.

The voltage regulator's ability to isolate a clean power supply is really important in robots. First, the delicate digital brains (logic chips and microcontrollers) aren't as easily upset by the electrically noisy motors because the noise is diminished or eliminated by the voltage regulator's input circuit. Second, the brains don't have to compete for battery power when the motors start moving, which is a notoriously heavy demand on the battery.

Avoiding Connecting Motors to Regulated Voltage

The noise and power isolation service provided by the voltage regulator would be sharply impacted if you connected the robot's motors to the regulated power supply instead of the unregulated power supply. The motor noise wouldn't have to go through the voltage regulators input filters; it'd be injected directly into the regulated circuit.

Also, the chips are going to have to compete with the motors for drawing power from C2.

You could create a robot with two voltage regulators, one for the brain circuit and another for the brawn (motor) circuit. That would be okay because you'd then have two partially isolated circuits.

In fact, in a really complicated robot, you could have a bunch of circuits, each with their own voltage regulator. That kind of design would keep electrical noise separate, as well as protect each circuit from damage caused by the other circuits (assuming all the communication connections between the circuits were properly protected). Think of it: One board could short out or overload, but the rest of the robot would remain alive!

There are two more reasons you don't want to connect motors or heavy current loads to a regulated supply. Both reasons have to do with a battery's ability to deliver the greatest amount of electrical power.

Producing Maximum Physical Power by Connecting Motors to Unregulated Electrical Power

First, motors have the greatest physical power (speed and torque) when connected to the highest voltage and least-resistant source of power. Because a linear voltage regulator must receive a higher input voltage than its output voltage, a motor connected to the higher unregulated input voltage always outperforms a motor connected to the lower-regulated output voltage.

Additionally, a voltage regulator can't deliver changes in current as quickly as a battery. Because a battery can provide a larger, less-resistant current flow when the motor starts, a motor connected to the battery always outperforms a motor connected to a regulated supply.

NOTE *In the previous two paragraphs, "always outperforms" assumes the motor is properly rated for the battery. Of course, if you connect a 3 V pager motor to a 12 V battery, "outperform" would translate into "outmelt." A dual-regulated supply (5 V for the brains, 3.3 V or less for the pager motor) might be an appropriate solution to supply power to a pager motor.*

Avoiding Burdening a Voltage Regulator with Motor Loads

The second reason not to connect a motor to the regulated power supply is that voltage regulator limits the total amount of current it can supply. For example, the 7805CT has a current limit of 1 amp. You don't want the current-hungry motors eating up most of that. In fact, if your digital circuits alone required only 75 mA, it'd make more sense to purchase the cheaper and smaller 78L05 rather than connecting motors to the more expensive and larger 7805CT.

Remember, too, that lighter loads require less input voltage and consume less quiescent current. Those are two more good reasons to connect motors to unregulated power, not regulated power.

NOTE *Why did I connect a motor to the voltage regulators during minimum voltage testing earlier in this chapter? I did that simply because I needed a heavy load for the 250 mA tests. I didn't care about injected electrical noise or motor power. And I did in fact want to burden the voltage regulators for testing purposes.*

Selecting a Linear Voltage Regulator for Your Robot

The best choice for a linear voltage regulator depends upon the choice of battery and the activity level (current draw) of the robot.

The 9 V Battery in a Moderately Active Robot

A typical alkaline 9 V battery has a factory-fresh voltage of 9.6 V that can decline to as low as 4.8 V with use. But, honestly, at less than 6 V the battery is reasonably exhausted.

TIP *You should measure battery voltage with the battery connected to the robot or other circuit and with the device powered on. A disconnected battery's voltage is much higher than when the battery is actually supplying current. For example, a 9 V alkaline battery that measures 6.2 V on its own is likely a dead battery. As soon as it tries to provide current to a circuit, the voltage drops like a rock. However, a 9 V alkaline battery that measures 6.2 V when supplying current may actually have some life left in it.*

A 9 V battery provides a lot of spare voltage for any type of 5 V linear voltage regulator. Therefore, the larger voltage drop of a standard-dropout regulator isn't a significant disadvantage.

A 9 V battery achieves higher voltage by connecting multiple small cells in series. However, small cells aren't physically capable of providing large currents, and they don't have large energy capacities. Therefore, any amount of current drawn from a 9 V battery is significant. As such, the regulator's quiescent current is worth considering in the selection process.

A 7805 is a good choice for a 9 V alkaline battery robot. With a 1N5817 diode, the circuit is inexpensive and protected but will fail at less than 6.7 V. With the more expensive FU5505 MOSFET, the regulator circuit can be supplied from a 9 V battery throughout its useful life (down to 6 V). The 7805 draws a maximum current of 8 mA for its own use, which is better than the maximums of 33 mA and 60 mA (or 130 mA) of the LP2954 and LM2940, respectively.

Rechargeable 9 V batteries routinely provide more than 6 V during their useful life. Nickel-metal hydride (NiMH) rechargeable batteries have even lower capacities than alkaline batteries. Therefore, the 7805 with FU5505 is an acceptable choice for rechargeable 9 V batteries.

The 9 V Battery in a Low-Draw Longevity Robot

A caveat applies to the 7805 recommendation for 9 V batteries when your robot is going to be drawing small amounts of current. For loads of 50 mA, the LP2954 typically uses only 1.1 mA as opposed to the 7805's typical 5 mA. With only a 1 mA load, the LP2954 consumes less than 0.1 mA.

If your robot sleeps often or is designed for a longevity contest, then the LP2954's low quiescent current and low-dropout voltage will extend battery life. Whereas the 7805 would cut out at 6 V, the LP2954 might actually be capable of draining a 9 V alkaline battery fairly near to the manufacturer's unrealistically low 4.8 V rating.

The Alkaline Four-Pack

A four-pack of alkaline AA or AAA batteries combines a convenient size with a reasonable capacity. The pack begins at 6.4 V and drops to 3.2 V (yeah, right) with use. Frankly, 1 V per cell is a more reasonable cut off, with the four-pack being at 4 V.

None of the voltage regulators are going to support voltages much below 4.9 V. The 7805 cuts out at 6 V, just when the cells in the battery pack have reached their nominal 1.5 V value. So, a 7805 is an inappropriate choice in this example.

The LP2954 is expensive and can't provide currents higher than 250 mA. However, the low-quiescent current at low-current loads could make the LP2954 a legitimate consideration.

Probably the best choice for an alkaline four-pack is the LM2940. The low-dropout voltage means the robot will get effective use of about half the life of the battery pack. The LM2940 can supply up to 1 amp of current. The LM2940's maximum quiescent current isn't significant to an alkaline pack already providing 1 amp.

The 12 V Winter Robot

A 12 V micro-snowplow robot is a slightly contrived example of a robot with a 12 V battery. It's intended to remind you that the voltage higher than 5 V is discarded by the linear voltage regulator as heat. With a 12 V battery and a decent current draw, the voltage regulator is going to need a heat sink. Perhaps the waste heat from the regulator could be put to good use to heat the battery to provide better performance in a micro-snowplow robot?

Changing Marketplace Is Limiting 5 V Linear Regulator Selection

There are several directions apparent in the linear voltage regulator market:

First, for voltages higher than 8 V, it's worth using a more efficient type of regulator, called a *switching regulator*. A switching regulator converts the extra voltage into current, instead of wasting it as heat. As such, the switching regulator runs cooler, and the battery lasts longer. The downside is that switching regulators are more expensive, are more complex, and are electrically noisier.

The second trend is that 5 V circuits have lost their dominance to lower voltage circuits, such as 3.3 V. It's getting harder to find factory-fixed 5 V linear regulators. In the future, you may simply choose an adjustable linear voltage regulator, such as the LM1117, and tune it to 5 V in your circuit.

The third trend is that surface-mount packages are now much more common than TO-220 through-hole packages. Surface-mount packages generally don't dissipate heat as well, which makes the inefficiency and heat generation of linear voltage regulators that much less desirable.

A hybrid solution is popular with some designers. A switching regulator in a central location is used to efficiently generate a voltage just greater than the minimum required by low-dropout regulators. Then, tiny low-dropout regulators (see Figure 7-14) are used in many isolated circuits to provide small, simple local power supplies. Because the input voltage is at the minimum required, the low-dropout regulators don't need to discard much voltage. Thus, they run cooler and much more efficiently.

*Figure 7-14. The Maxim (*http://www.maxim-ic.com/*) MAX8881EUT50 is a 200 mA maximum load, low-dropout, 5 V linear voltage regulator with a maximum quiescent current of only 3.7 µA! The regulator circuit for the MAX8881 is as simple as those presented in this chapter. However, this regulator isn't easy to prototype on a solderless breadboard because the chip is as small as the head of a pencil. The size comes in handy for size-constrained robots, such as a mini-sumo robot. This picture is from the circuit board of the mini-sumo robot Have a Nice Day.*

Heading into Optimizations

This chapter presented a simple, reliable, inexpensive voltage regulator that's appropriate for any robot whose battery voltage is more than 5 V. It compared a few interchangeable regulators to assist you in the selection process. Maximum current, voltage dropout, and quiescent current are usually the most significant factors to consider.

Reverse-battery protection can be built into the regulator itself, can be provided by a diode, or, better still, can be provided by a low-resistance power MOSFET. Most voltage regulators have other safety features built in, such as short-circuit protection and thermal overload protection.

All of the fixed-voltage regulators examples used the same capacitors. As you'll find out in the next chapter, you can improve the power supply by installing additional capacitors. A few other components can make any voltage-regulated power supply more suitable for a robot.

CHAPTER 8

Making Robot Power Supply Improvements

Covers Bulk Capacitors, Fast Off Switch, Exploding Tantalum, Bypass/Decoupling, Overcurrent Protection, and Overvoltage Protection

THE MANUFACTURERS' DESIGNS and schematics for power supplies, such as the 7805 linear voltage regulator presented in the previous chapter, are tailored for the average electronic device. However, robots are far from being average electronic devices.

Manufacturers of voltage regulators certify their products with the fewest number of components and the smallest values of capacitors possible. Larger-value capacitors cost more, and obviously each additional component adds to the material cost as well as to the labor cost. A high-volume manufacturer may decline to select a voltage regulator that appears to require too much extra expense in additional circuitry.

Yet robots place larger demands on the battery and regulators than do many other types of devices. After all, robots have motors, emitters, and buzzers. Because most homemade robots are one-time creations, adding a couple of dollars worth of larger capacitors and protective components is a small, one-time expense.

Whether you choose a linear voltage regulator, a switching voltage regulator, or even no regulator at all, this chapter presents some additional components and practices that are especially beneficial for robots:

- Bulk up the input and output capacitors to prevent voltage dips

- Add a variety of capacitor values and types to reduce noise

- Spread small capacitors throughout your regulated circuits to provide local power and to reduce circuit noise at its source

- Add a fuse or self-resetting device to prevent current overload because of short circuits

- Add a zener diode to the regulated circuit to restrain overvoltages

Bulking Up the Input and Output Capacitors

One of the differences between robots and other electronic projects is that robots have motors. Motors draw a significant amount of current during use. At peak times, a battery may struggle to provide enough current to the motors. This causes the battery's voltage to temporarily drop (*sag*).

Increasing the capacitance of the input and output capacitors (C1 and C2 in Figure 7-3 in the previous chapter) by 10 times or 100 times the original value can compensate for voltage sag. In addition, a large-value input capacitor can provide the burst of current needed by the motors when first starting. This can actually improve the responsiveness of "underfed" motors.

Large-value capacitors are referred to as *bulk* capacitors when used to supply extra current during periods of heavy demand. Instead of completely replacing C1 and C2 as they're listed in the voltage regulator manufacturer's datasheet, it's better to leave them as is and supplement them with bulk capacitors in parallel (see Figure 8-1). This is because, along with a larger capacitance, some other characteristics of the bulk capacitors differ unfavorably from the smaller, manufacturer-recommended capacitors.

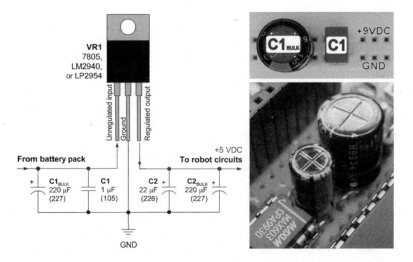

Figure 8-1. A schematic for a voltage regulator circuit with bulk capacitors added in parallel (left). A bulk capacitor in parallel with the standard-value capacitor on a solderless breadboard (top right). A standard capacitor and a bulk capacitor beside a low-dropout MAX603 voltage regulator on the mini-sumo robot Bugdozer (bottom right).

Note that an increase in either capacitance or working voltage (WV) usually results in a corresponding increase in the capacitor's physical size (see Figure 8-2). But don't be fooled by size alone. A capacitor could be physically larger to provide other benefits, such as improved temperature stability or lower equivalent series resistance (ESR). Check the capacitor's label for the capacitance value and working voltage. For the purposes of bulk capacitors, you're looking to increase the capacitance value.

Figure 8-2. Aluminum electrolytic capacitors of increasing capacitance and working voltage. Notice that physical size increases not only with working voltage (left to right) but also with capacitance (front to back). Front row: 22 μF 10 WV, 16 WV, 25 WV, 35 WV; middle row: 220 μF 10 WV, 16 WV, 25 WV, 35 WV; back row: 2200 μF 10 WV, 16 WV, 25 WV, 35 WV (left to right).

Increasing Battery Lifetime with Bulk Capacitors

The more current that's drawn from a battery, the shorter its total life span. For example, a 2.85 amp-hour (Ah) rated battery may be capable of supplying 0.1 amp for 28.5 hours (0.1 amp times 28.5 hour equals 2.85 amp hours). But that same battery might supply only 0.4 amp for four hours (0.4 amp times 4 hours equals only 1.6 amp hours) or 1.0 amp for one hour (1.0 amp times 1 hour equals 1.0 amp hours). So, a 2.85 Ah battery might be only a 1.0 Ah battery under greater current-draw conditions. If the battery sometimes has 0.1 amp drawn from it, sometimes has 0.4 amp drawn from it, and sometimes has 1 amp drawn from it, then the resulting capacity will be somewhere between 2.85 Ah and 1.0 Ah.

Studies have shown that bulk capacitors can increase the life span of a battery in devices that have intermittent high-drain surges by helping the battery supply those life span–draining bursts of power.

Delayed Power-Off Because of Bulk Capacitors

One of the downsides of adding bulk capacitors is that because they're capable of storing much more power, they can actually continue to supply power to the robot even after the power switch has been turned off. The most obvious symptom is that the power indicator LED slowly dims after shutting off power rather than being instantly extinguished. This is caused by the voltage decreasing relatively slowly as the bulk capacitors discharge.

The opposite also occurs at startup. The bulk capacitors are empty and require a heavier current flow from the battery to charge. The causes the circuit voltage level to increase a little more slowly after the power switch is turned on because the battery has to service both the circuits and the bulk capacitors.

You can see the turn-on and turn-off times with an oscilloscope if desired (see Figure 8-3). In my sample circuit, it took 5 milliseconds for a 9 V battery and 5 V voltage regulator to power up the circuit from 0 V to 4 V with a 220 µF capacitor installed. Power down took more than 900 milliseconds to drop from 5 V to 1 V.

 NOTE *The sample circuit received 5 V from a voltage regulator. Nevertheless, I chose to measure the amount of time it took for the voltage to change by 4 V because a capacitor doesn't fill or drain at a linear rate. The rate of change decreases as the capacitor's voltage approaches the final destination voltage. It was easier to determine exactly when a change of 4 V had occurred than guessing when the curved line had finally reached 5 V.*

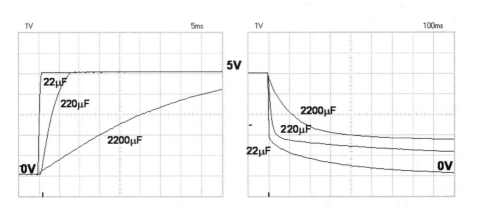

Figure 8-3. Startup and shutdown times with various values of bulk capacitors. Oscilloscope trace of a circuit powering up with different value capacitors (left). Oscilloscope trace of a circuit powering down with different value capacitors (right). Note that the horizontal scale of the power down trace is 20 times longer. The most important thing to learn from this figure is that a circuit doesn't power up or power down instantly. Also, the amount of time it takes to power up or power down increases as capacitance increases.

You don't really need an oscilloscope to measure your startup and shutdown times. Just watch the power indicator LED at power-on and power-off to get a sense for whether an obviously slow startup or shutdown is occurring with your robot.

A slowly rising or slowly falling voltage can be a real problem. The actions of most chips are undefined when operated below their minimum required voltage. For example, a microcontroller may start randomly flipping its outputs on and off, thus powering motors in unexpected ways. Or, the microcontroller may write garbage to various memory locations (even overwriting its own programming). The longer the chip is in a low-voltage situation, the more likely a problem will occur.

Ultimately, a microcontroller really ought to have a low-voltage detect circuit that suspends its operation during low-voltage conditions. Most modern microcontrollers have this feature built into them. Alternatively, separate low-voltage detection chips are available to disable the microcontroller via its reset pin, thus halting the microcontroller until it's safe to operate.

Using a DPDT Power Switch to Reduce Turn-Off Time

Low-voltage detection circuits are good for pausing microcontrollers. As for the rest of the robot, you can use a double-pole double-throw (DPDT) switch for the power switch (SW1 in Figure 7-2) to quickly discharge the capacitors at power-off. In the on position, the first pole of the power switch connects the battery to the unregulated parts (motors, motor drivers, C1, $C1_{BULK}$, voltage regulator input, and so on), and the second pole of the power switch connects the voltage regulator output to the regulated circuit (including C2 and $C2_{BULK}$) as usual (see Figure 8-4).

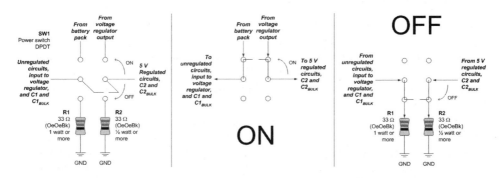

Figure 8-4. Utilizing a DPDT switch to connect the unregulated and regulated circuits to their normal connections (battery and voltage regulator, respectively) or to connect them to ground to quickly drain their capacitors

In the off position, the first pole of the power switch connects the C1 and $C1_{BULK}$ input capacitors (as well as the rest of the unregulated circuit) to a low-value resistor connected to ground. The second pole of the power switch connects the regulated circuit (including C2 and $C2_{BULK}$) to a different low-value resistor connected to ground. This provides paths to quickly drain the capacitors when the power switch is put into the off position, thus hastening the power-off time.

A low-value resistor is a better solution than shorting the circuits directly to ground. An extremely large current would flow if the capacitors were shorted directly to ground, causing damage to the capacitors and possibly the power switch.

Speaking of possible damage, for this circuit you should use metal-oxide film resistors rated for 1 watt ($0.24; #P33W-1BK at Digi-Key) or better. Although the resistors must dissipate a lot more instantaneous power than their continuous wattage rating would seem to permit, the total energy dissipated is limited to what's stored in the capacitors, and the discharge is nonrepetitive. Therefore, for power supplies of 20 V or less with a total capacitance of 1000 µF or less, these resistors are within their specified peak pulse overload and peak pulse overvoltage limits. For up to 5000 µF, use 3-watt resistors; for below 380 µF, ½-watt resistors will do.

The DPDT power-switch trick helps only to quickly turn off the robot; it doesn't improve the turn-on time. But if the batteries are properly rated and the bulk capacitors aren't obnoxiously large values, then the turn-on time shouldn't be a problem. Notice in Figure 8-2 that the turn-on time was roughly 16 times faster than turn-off time.

The other advantage of the power-switch trick is that it drops the voltage all the way down to ground (GND) more quickly than would the leakage through the power indicator LED. Some microcontrollers and other circuits benefit from the power line dropping below 100 mV fairly quickly.

Selecting Bulk Capacitors

Many robot builders choose a 2200 µF or 4700 µF capacitor for their unregulated bulk capacitor. This value seems high to me for a battery-powered robot (it's appropriate for solar-powered robots). For battery-powered robots, I prefer 220 µF to 330 µF. A quick survey of my robots revealed values of 22 µF, 220 µF, 330 µF, and 1000 µF. Seriously, if your battery-powered robot needs 4700 µF of capacitance to prevent mysterious resets, something else is happening.

You can calculate rise and fall times by measuring the resistance of your robot's circuit and then applying a resistor-capacitor (RC) time formula to calculate the maximum capacitance for the longest rise and fall times you're willing to accept. But it's not worth too much attention if you're using pull-up and pull-down resistors for default values (more on this in later chapters) and your microcontroller halts upon low-voltage detect.

I recommend 220 µF 35 WV aluminum electrolytic capacitors ($0.12 to $0.41; #220/35VR at All Electronics, #P5166-ND at Digi-Key, #N14ER035220U at Electronix Express, #93770 at Jameco, and #140-XRL35V220 at Mouser) as effective, low-cost, unregulated bulk capacitors. If you desire a smaller physical size, a 25 WV capacitor is acceptable for 12 V batteries and a 16 WV capacitor is acceptable for a 9 V battery. Because motors generate voltage spikes, I approximately double the applied voltage to calculate an appropriate WV rating for unregulated capacitors. Some electrical engineers might accept 20 percent derating for quieter circuits.

I recommend 220 µF 10 WV or 16 WV aluminum electrolytic capacitors ($0.06 to $0.36; #P964-ND at Digi-Key, #198871 at Jameco, and #140-XRL10V220 at Mouser) as effective, low-cost, and reasonably small for regulated 5 V bulk capacitors. And 6.3 WV aluminum electrolytic capacitors might be acceptable in a 5 V (or lower voltage) regulated circuit as long as the motors or other inductive components (chokes, relays, solenoids, transformers, or coiled wires) aren't connected to regulated power.

Implementing Higher Margins of Safety for Tantalum Capacitors

Although you don't always have to double the WV rating for aluminum electrolytic capacitors, never skimp on the WV rating for tantalum capacitors. Always choose a WV for tantalum capacitors that's *at least* double the maximum voltage to which you expect them to be exposed. The reason is that tantalum capacitors are much more sensitive to damage from overvoltage, and they tend to short out, catch fire, or explode when they fail (see Figure 8-5).

Figure 8-5. A bulk unregulated tantalum capacitor exploded and caught fire on the Soup robot.

In Figure 8-5, the unregulated voltage was 19.2 V, and the capacitor was rated at 35 WV. However, the motors were switching multiple amps on and off very quickly and were probably generating pretty severe voltage spikes. It's also possible that the exploded tantalum capacitor was defective.

A PPTC overcurrent-protection device (explained later in this chapter) safely disconnected battery power before I could even reach the robot's power switch. By replacing the damaged capacitors and lowering the unregulated voltage to 12 V, the robot works just fine to this day. However, the circuit board still smells weird.

Adding Voodoo Capacitors

When building circuits, I prefer to fully understand the reason for adding a component or making a connection. I'm usually willing to accept a manufacturer's suggested schematic as is, but I'd much rather it properly explain its component choices so I can make modifications appropriate to my intended uses.

That scientific philosophy extends to correcting defects or glitches. I'm not willing to throw stuff into my circuit or code to mask a problem. During experimentation, I may radically change a value on the board to see if it affects the outcome, but that's a test technique designed to isolate a problem and lead to a logical explanation. Ultimately, nothing gets permanently installed or removed from my robot unless I understand its purpose and it functions as designed and expected.

With that said, here's a shotgun approach to capacitor technology: Besides the capacitors you selected for definite reasons, throw a variety of moderate-value to low-value capacitors onto your circuit board. For each capacitor, simply connect one lead to the positive bus and one lead to the ground bus.

A 0.68 μF metallized polyester capacitor, a 10 μF tantalum capacitor, and a 220 μF aluminum electrolytic make for a nice, well-rounded power supply. Oooh! What's this? A 1 μF monolithic ceramic on the opposite end of the board? Nice choice!

That may sound strange, but different capacitor technologies have different attributes. Some capacitors radically change capacitance with temperature, and some don't. Some capacitors perform well at low frequencies, some capacitors perform well at midrange frequencies, and some perform well at high frequencies. Some capacitors respond quickly, and some don't. Some provide large capacitances cheaply, and some cost more than steak by the pound.

The shotgun approach of indiscriminately installing a variety of capacitor values and technologies might be called *voodoo capacitance*. It'll never fix a problem with your robot's code or circuit design, but it'll reduce hidden sources of noise. The prior paragraph explains that there's a legitimate scientific basis behind this approach, even if it isn't purposeful by the circuit designer.

The next time someone points to a particular group of capacitors on your robot's board and asks what the capacitors are for, tell them, "They're parallel capacitors whose individual resonant frequencies produce different bandpass filters, shunting unwanted electrical noise to ground. Also, I picked that particular one because it's blue and fits nicely in that location."

Sprinkling with Bypass/Decoupling Capacitors

As previously discussed, a *capacitor* is a component that can store and release electrical energy. It's not like a battery. A capacitor doesn't generate power—it just stores energy temporarily.

A drinking glass is like a small capacitor. It doesn't pump water; it just stores it for local use.

When you look at a circuit board filled with electronic parts, think of the integrated circuits (logic chips, op amps, microcontrollers, and so on) as your dinner guests. They should all have a drinking glass (or a beer mug, depending on your guests) with them. That way, if someone temporarily hogs the spigot, the remaining guests still have a reasonable short-term supply.

You'll find at least one 0.1 μF capacitor for each chip in all of my circuits (see Figure 8-6). This is a standard accepted practice in electrical engineering. Simply connect the positive pin on the chip to the positive lead of the 0.1 μF capacitor, and connect the other lead of the capacitor to ground. Alternatively, connect the ground pin on the chip to the ground lead of the 0.1 μF capacitor, and connect the other lead of the capacitor to positive power.

TIP *If you're using ceramic monolithic 0.1 µF capacitors (the most common and popular choice for that size), they're nonpolarized. Either capacitor lead can be connected to ground or positive power.*

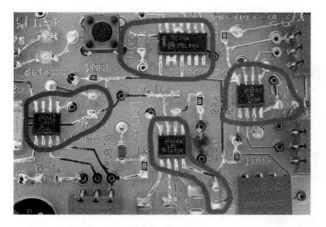

Figure 8-6. Four chips and four 0.1 µF bypass/decoupling capacitors on an alarm-detection circuit for a fire-fighting robot. The bypass effect of the 0.1 µF capacitors is that they act as low-impedance local power sources for each chip. The decoupling effect of the 0.1 µF capacitors is that they absorb chip-generated switching noise at the point of origin so the rest of the circuit isn't bothered.

 NOTE *The "home smoke-detector alarm tone" detection circuit in Figure 8-6 uses an LM386 audio amplifier to increase the signal from a tiny microphone. The amplified signal is fed into an LMC567 tone decoder that's set to trip at 3.5 kHz. When the LMC567 indicates (even briefly) that a fire alarm is detected, the 74HC74A flip-flop turns an output high (5 V) and leaves it on even if the LMC567 no longer hears the fire alarm. You can hook the flip-flop output to a power transistor or soft power-on button for the rest of the robot. This allows the robot to sleep in a "powered-off" state until there's a fire.*

Bypassing the Long Path to the Power Supply

As just described, a small-value capacitor employed to provide a local power source is called a *bypass* capacitor. It sidesteps the impedances (parasitic resistance and inductance) inherent in the paths from the relatively far-away power source.

Beware of long leads on through-hole capacitors (see Figure 8-7). In some cases, the inductance and resistance of the long leads themselves exceed that of the power supply that the capacitor was intended to bypass. In other words, the shortcut to the local power source may ironically be longer than just drawing from the original power supply itself. Therefore, datasheets always advise to connect a bypass capacitor as near to the chip as possible.

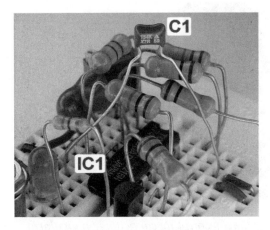

Figure 8-7. Worse than worthless? The long leads of capacitor C1 defeat the intended purpose of bypassing and decoupling IC1. Look at the leads on those resistors! This is going to be a noisy circuit.

Decoupling Noise at Each Source

Besides being called bypass capacitors, the 0.1 µF capacitors are also referred to as *decoupling* capacitors. Decoupling is the process of isolating, disconnecting, or separating one thing from another.

In this case, the 0.1 µF capacitors reduce electrical gate–switching noise at its originating source, the chip itself, thus isolating noises to individual subcircuits. The AC portion (noise) is separated from the DC portion (the 5 V power lines) by combining the capacitor with the resistance and inductance inherent to the components and traces to form frequency filters.

In fancier circuits, you can filter specific frequencies by purposely adding a mathematically determined resistor or inductor to create more targeted decoupling. Because you aren't physically adding a resistor or inductor in conjunction with a 0.1 µF capacitor, some people might argue that these 0.1 µF capacitors are simply bypass capacitors. Nonetheless, the decoupling effect clearly does exist and serves to benefit circuit operation.

Selecting Bypass/Decoupling Capacitors

In summary, 0.1 µF capacitors connected close to the power pins on chips provide both bypass (low-impedance local power source) and decoupling (noise reduction and isolation) effects. Using capacitors in this manner is beneficial to the smooth operation of your circuit.

Buy a large quantity of 0.1 µF capacitors, and sprinkle liberally throughout your circuit boards. Seriously, no fewer than one per chip! A 0.1 µF 50 WV ceramic monolithic bypass capacitor is a good choice ($0.06 to $0.08 in quantities of 100; #BC1127CT at Digi-Key, #N14MN050.1U at Electronix Express, #25523 at Jameco, and #80-C315C104M5U at Mouser).

Preventing Damage from Short Circuits or Overcurrent

Most voltage regulators provide some form of short-circuit (power and ground wires connected together) or overcurrent (current draw exceeding design or specifications) protection for the regulated circuits. However, that still leaves unprotected the unregulated components (such as the motor driver chips).

Deciding If Overcurrent Protection Is Required

Most solid-state (no moving parts) small consumer devices don't have unregulated components, so the overcurrent protection from the regulator is sufficient. Devices powered by alkaline consumer batteries are protected because alkaline batteries have a high internal resistance that prohibits them from putting out large currents.

If your robot has only regulated circuits, or if your robot uses only small alkaline consumer batteries (9 V, AA, AAA) in series, then your robot probably doesn't *require* additional overcurrent protection. However, if your robot has unregulated components (such as motor driver chips), or if your robot uses batteries capable of putting out multiple amps (alkaline in parallel, alkaline C and D cells, NiMH, NiCd, Li ion, Li poly, lead acid, and so on), then overcurrent protection is recommended.

Considering the amount of time and attention you're going to put into your robot, isn't it worth a few minutes of time and $0.50 to add short-circuit protection? Or, you could just allow your thin circuit board traces to melt in order to disconnect short circuits (see Figure 8-8).

Figure 8-8. Overcurrent protection, the hard way. This 0.040-inch circuit board trace (etched on a 1-ounce/foot-squared copper board) melted apart on one of my robots when a 7.4 V lithium polymer battery discharged through a short circuit. I can't tell you how many hours I spent replacing chips until I found this trace on the back of the board. An overcurrent protection device could have prevented this damage.

Protecting with a Fuse

A fuse is the most common, inexpensive method of protection for larger devices or for devices routinely exposed to unknown levels of current (such as a multimeter). A fuse contains a narrow section of wire (between the battery and the circuit) that overheats and melts apart when too much current passes through it, thus disconnecting the circuit from the power source.

The biggest problem with a fuse is that it's a one-time use device. Once it's blown, it needs to be replaced. This means you need to keep enough of the properly rated fuses in stock, and you'll probably have to disassemble the device to perform the actual replacement. In a robot, positioning the fuse holder in a convenient location in the device can reduce time and frustration.

On the plus side, fuses are inexpensive, widely available, and reasonably small.

Protecting with a Manually Reset Circuit Breaker

Circuit breakers overcome the one-time-use disadvantage of fuses. A circuit breaker provides some form of a switch that pops to an electrically disconnected state when too much current passes through it. After correcting the fault source, the user presses the circuit breaker switch to reconnect the circuit to the power source.

The primary disadvantages of circuit breakers are that they tend to be more expensive and larger than fuses. They also operate more slowly than most fuses. Finally, it's possible for a circuit breaker to become stuck in an on position and therefore fail to perform its protective duty.

Circuit breakers are common on higher-priced devices, AC devices, or devices that may be overtaxed by user, such as an AC outlet strip. You don't want a consumer opening an AC device to replace a fuse.

Circuit breakers are appropriate for larger or high-current robots (AC or DC).

Protecting Robots from Short Circuits and Overcurrents with a Solid-State Auto-Resetting PPTC Device

Polymeric positive temperature coefficient (PPTC) overcurrent-protection devices are excellent for protecting both the regulated and the unregulated portions of a medium or small robot. They are small, are relatively inexpensive (around $1 or cheaper), can be used repeatedly, have no moving parts, and automatically restore the current flow when the fault condition has been corrected.

Greatly Increasing Resistance to Greatly Reduce Current

Like a fuse or circuit breaker, a PPTC overcurrent-protection device overheats and trips when too much current passes through it. Unlike a fuse or circuit breaker, the PPTC works not by physically disconnecting the circuit but by the PPTC changing its resistance from a very low value (less than $1\ \Omega$) to a very high value (greater than a $1\ \text{M}\Omega$).

PPTC overcurrent protection devices are technically positive-coefficient nonlinear thermistors or semiconductors that can pass specified currents when in their normal state but when heated by excessive current can suddenly change resistance around a certain temperature.

As long as the faulty circuit has a very low resistance (say, because of a short circuit), the majority of voltage is dropped across the tripped PPTC in its high-resistance state. This causes the PPTC to stay heated, thereby maintaining a high resistance and thus reducing current flow from the power source to the fault. When the fault is removed from the circuit, the circuit's resistance increases to its normal value, thus dividing the voltage more evenly between itself and the high-resistance PPTC. This allows the PPTC to cool and return to its normal low-resistance state, thereby restoring normal current flow to the circuit.

The auto-resetting or self-resetting feature of the PPTC is one of its best features. Unlike a one-shot fuse or manually reset circuit breaker, you can bury the PPTC in a difficult-to-service location in the robot. Also, unlike a manual circuit breaker, the PPTC automatically restores power after the problem has been corrected. This can be useful in a robot entered into a contest, where the operator isn't permitted to physically touch the robot during competition. After a brief period of inoperation brought on by a temporary short or current surge, the robot may suddenly come alive again after the PPTC cools.

Cautions About PPTC Devices

Sometimes a fuse or manually reset circuit breaker can be safer than a self-resetting device. One manufacturer provided a vivid example: You don't want to use a self-resetting device in a garbage disposal. The disposal could resume operation at the moment a person clears the food jam with their hand (ouch!). This might also be a concern for a combat robot.

Another important note about a PPTC device is that, unlike a fuse, a small amount of current continues to flow while the PPTC is tripped. As such, the circuit continues to have some voltage across it.

Neither of these situations is likely to be a problem in a lunch-box-sized robot with 12 V supplied by alkaline batteries. But never forget to turn off the power switch and disconnect the power source before attempting to service any robot. Approach a stalled PPTC-enabled robot with the awareness that it could restart at any time.

Installing PPTC Overcurrent-Protection Devices

Most PPTC overcurrent-protection devices look like capacitors (see Figure 8-9) in that PPTC devices are thin, are slightly rounded, and have two leads. All of the PPTC devices I've encountered so far have been yellowish orange in color.

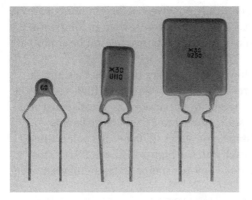

Figure 8-9. Several examples of PolySwitch PPTC self-resetting overcurrent-protection devices. RXE005 holds at up to 0.05 A and trips at 0.10 A, RUE110 holds at up to 1.1 A and trips at 2.2 A, and RUE250 holds at up to 2.5 A and trips at 5.0 A (left to right).

PPTC overcurrent-protection devices are extremely easy to install. Simply insert a PPTC between the unregulated power source and the rest of the circuit (see Figure 8-10). PPTC devices aren't polarized; either lead can be connected to the power source.

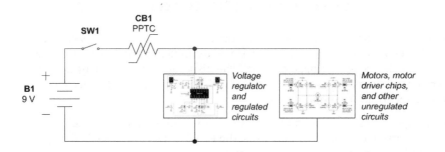

Figure 8-10. A schematic of a robot protected by a PPTC self-resetting overcurrent-protection device. The PPTC is labeled "CB1" because it performs the equivalent function of a circuit breaker. However, the schematic symbol looks like a resistor with a line graphing a rapid rise across it.

Selecting PPTC Overcurrent-Protection Devices

A PPTC overcurrent-protection device has a few parameters worth knowing about:

- Hold current
- Trip current
- Reaction time
- Effect of ambient temperature
- Normal operating resistance

Choosing a Rough Current Limit

A PPTC is specified with a (lower) maximum hold current that it'll carry indefinitely without tripping and with a (higher) minimum trip current at which the PPTC is guaranteed to trip. Like fuses and circuit breakers, PPTC overcurrent-protection devices come in different current ratings. You need to select a PPTC that's rated to reliably hold at the maximum current you want to permit in your robot.

Don't forget that motors draw a much larger current at startup than when running under medium or light loads. Be sure to take the maximum current of all motors into account. Fortunately, because of the bulk capacitor(s) and the relatively slow reaction time of a PPTC, it may be possible for the motors to briefly draw a surge of current without tripping the device. Also, as the motors begin to spin, even if the PPTC started to trip, the motors will draw less current and the PPTC will self-reset.

The reaction time of a PPTC depends on how much current is being drawn over its hold current. The more current is drawn, the faster the PPTC reacts. This means that drawing a current somewhat over the PPTC's hold current will cause the PPTC to take a long time to trip (a matter of seconds). However, the PPTC will react in milliseconds if the trip current is exceeded.

Because a PPTC is a thermally tripped device, please note that the actual current at which the PPTC will trip is going to vary based on ambient air temperature and thermal transfer to the PC board or mounting clip. If you place a PPTC beside a hot component (for example, a heavily loaded linear voltage regulator), the PPTC will trip at a lower current than if it were beside a cooling fan. In this sense, you can consider a PPTC overcurrent device to provide some over-temperature protection as well.

The lesson here is that you shouldn't rely on the PPTC for a specific current trip point. Instead, you should think of the PPTC as protection against a major fault, such as a short circuit.

Accepting Some Voltage Loss in Exchange for Protection

One of the downsides to PPTC overcurrent-protection devices is that they have a little bit of resistance during normal (nontripped) operation. Just like the low-resistance MOSFET presented in the previous chapter for reverse-battery protection, the resistance of the PPTC translates into a voltage drop (loss) from the battery. Therefore, you want to select a PPTC with the lowest initial resistance for the desired maximum anticipated hold current.

At hold currents below 300 mA (0.3 amp), it's not uncommon to see PPTC devices with an initial resistance of about 1 Ω. For hold currents over 1 amp, PPTC devices commonly have much better initial resistances of 0.1 Ω or less.

PPTC devices with lower maximum voltage ratings tend to be smaller and have lower initial resistances than devices rated for higher, maximum voltage. Because most robots tend to have battery packs lower than 30 V, it's worth selecting the PPTC device that's rated for lower voltage to receive the benefits of lower resistance and smaller physical size.

Purchasing PPTC Overcurrent-Protection Devices

Two popular brands of PPTC overcurrent-protection devices are the Bourns MultiFuse resettable overcurrent protectors (http://www.bourns.com/) and the Tyco/Raychem PolySwitch resettable devices (http://www.circuitprotection.com/). You can find the devices in the "Fuses" section of catalogs from suppliers such as Digi-Key and Mouser.

It isn't possible for me to recommend a single part number for a PPTC overcurrent-protection device because each robot requires a PPTC part whose hold current slightly exceeds the current draw for that particular robot. However, as an example of a part I might choose for a robot that isn't intended to draw more than 1 amp, a RUE110 from Digi-Key for $0.49 has a low initial resistance of between 0.05 and 0.10 Ω, is guaranteed to supply up to 1.1 amp indefinitely, and will trip within milliseconds if the current exceeds 2.2 amps. You can use it with supply voltages up to 30 V.

Preventing Damage from Overvoltage in a Regulated Circuit

A regulated circuit is supposed to have no greater than a specific voltage coming from the regulator, such as 5 V. However, an accidental connection between the regulated and unregulated wires can cause the regulated voltage (5 V, for example) to rise to the unregulated voltage (9 V, for example), destroying logic chips, microcontrollers, and some capacitors.

How likely is that to occur? Well, most robots have both regulated chips (such as a microcontroller) and unregulated chips (such as a motor driver) on the same board. As such, unregulated and regulated power lines are close to each other. An errant screwdriver (or screw or metal shaving) is all that it takes to make the connection.

Robots in metal cases are more vulnerable to this potential catastrophe. One time, I barely avoided disaster with my Sweet robot. A header pin from the motor power line touched the robot's metal body, and a phototransistor with a metal case also rubbed against the metal body (on a rough edge where the phototransistor was peeking out). The phototransistor was connected to the 5 V regulated power line, thus completing the connection between unregulated (motor) power and regulated (logic chip) power.

Introducing the Zener Diode

A zener diode looks like most other diodes, except that a zener diode is often in a metal case to dissipate heat (see Figure 8-11). *Zener* is pronounced like the word *wiener* but with a *z*.

Figure 8-11. A 1N5232B 5.6 V zener diode

When connected in the usual way for a diode (anode to +, cathode to -), a zener diode performs just like any other diode. It permits current flow in one direction while blocking current flow in the other direction.

However, a zener diode has a specifically tailored maximum reverse voltage that it can block. If the voltage is higher than that limit, a reverse current is permitted to flow. This is called the *breakdown voltage* or *avalanche point*. (Although *breakdown* and *avalanche* sound nasty, the zener diode isn't harmed when this voltage is exceeded as long as an appropriately sized resistor limits current.)

Of course, given enough voltage, any diode eventually permits a reverse current to flow. However, a zener diode is designed with a sharp on/off transition at a specific voltage (see Figure 8-12). Also, unlike a standard diode, a zener diode is intended to operate with a reverse current under ordinary use without becoming damaged. In fact, zener diodes are usually installed "backward" (reverse biased) to purposely exploit their voltage transition point.

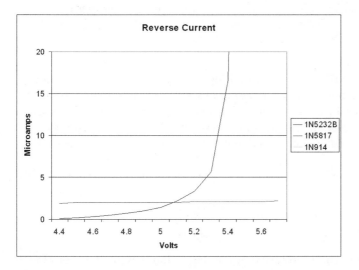

Figure 8-12. A graph of the reverse currents permitted by three different types of diodes. The 5.6 V 1N5232B zener diode shows a rapid change from blocking to conducting as it approaches 5.6 V. The 1N5817 Schottky diode shows a slowly rising leakage current around 0.000002 A or 2 μA (a very small number). The 1N914 general-purpose fast-switching small-signal diode has so little leakage that it doesn't even show up on the graph.

Using a Zener Diode to Short Circuit Power Upon Overvoltage

As installed in Figure 8-13, a 5.6 V zener diode blocks reverse current across it in a 5 V circuit. But if somehow the regulated voltage should rise higher than 5.6 V—for instance, if unregulated voltage accidentally gets connected to regulated voltage—then the zener diode turns on and permits current to flow through it.

Take careful note of the direction the zener diode is installed. It must have the band (cathode) toward the positive voltage. If the zener diode is installed with the band toward ground, then any voltage higher than approximately 1.1 V will flow through the zener to ground, likely destroying it unless the regulator shuts down in time.

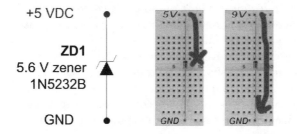

Figure 8-13. A schematic for overvoltage protection using a zener diode (left). A 5.6 V zener diode doesn't conduct when the regulated voltage is properly at 5 V (middle). A 5.6 V zener diode conducts when the regulated voltage becomes polluted by a 9 V battery's unregulated voltage (right).

Unlike an LED, I haven't put a current-limiting resistor in series with this zener diode. I want the zener diode path to have as low of a resistance as possible. Because electricity is "lazy" (seeks the easiest path), it'll choose to go through the low-resistance zener diode path rather than through the more resistant 5 V chips. I've purposely created a short circuit that denies current to the rest of the regulated circuit when the voltage exceeds 5.6 V.

This form of protection is called a *clamp*. It's a last ditch effort to save the circuit.

Tripping Overcurrent Protection with the Overvoltage Short Circuit

Although the rest of the circuit is protected by the clamp short circuit, the poor zener diode won't survive long with all that current flowing through it. If you've wisely installed a fuse or PPTC overcurrent-protection device, it'll trip and disconnect power from the circuit.

It's teamwork! It's the one-two combo! One device (the zener diode) detects an overvoltage and causes a short circuit. The second device (the fuse or PPTC) detects a short circuit and disconnects power. The circuit is saved!

The beauty of a zener diode and PPTC combination is that neither is harmed in the process. When the overvoltage fault is removed, the zener diode stops conducting and the PPTC self-resets. Note that there could be some power cycling (turning on and off) with this combination, but that's far less harmful than an unconstrained overvoltage.

Taking One for the Team: The Sacrificial Death of Mr. Zener

If the period of overvoltage is brief, such as a voltage spike or brief swipe from a screwdriver tip, then no harm is done. However, if the overvoltage is prolonged and no overcurrent protection is provided, then the zener diode can overheat and be destroyed.

I hope (I'm told it "always" happens), the zener diode will die in a conducting (shorted) state so that the zener diode's sacrifice continues to protect the other components. At that point, the zener is toast and will have to be desoldered and replaced.

Choosing an Appropriate Breakdown Voltage

Why not use a 5.1 V zener diode instead of a 5.6 V zener diode to prevent overvoltage in a 5 V circuit? There are several reasons:

- A voltage regulator is still within operating limits if it outputs 5.1 V. In fact, up to 5.25 V is usually within standard operating ranges of almost all 5 V chips.

- The breakdown voltage of zener diodes is affected by temperature. A 5.1 V zener diode might start conducting at less than 5 V if the temperature changes enough.

- Zener diodes leak a little bit of current (less than 1 mA) when blocking. A zener diode leaks more current as its breakdown voltage is approached. A 5.6 V zener diode still provides adequate protection for 5 V chips while leaking (wasting) less current than a 5.1 V zener diode.

By the way, you can use the zener-diode trick in a circuit with a different regulated voltage (3.3 V, for example). Of course, be sure to select a zener diode with a breakdown voltage slightly higher than the particular regulated voltage.

You can also use the zener-diode trick in unregulated circuits when you want only to provide protection against a maximum value but don't otherwise need voltage regulation. For example, high-speed CMOS chips (HC) operate with voltages between 2 V and 6 V. A four-pack of 1.2 V NiMH cells would work well for those chips, even without regulation. However, you could add a 6.2 V zener diode to short circuit higher voltages just in case someone attached the wrong battery pack. This also provides reverse-battery protection because the current would immediately flow through the then-forward-biased zener diode, resulting in a short circuit, tripping the PPTC or fuse.

Purchasing Zener Diodes

A couple of common 5.6 V zener diodes are appropriate for protecting a 5 V circuit against overvoltage.

The 1N5232B ($0.04 to $0.16; #1N5232BTRCT at Digi-Key and #179055 at Jameco) is rated for 0.5 watts. The 1N4734 ($0.09 to $0.25; #1N4734 at All Electronics, #1N4734AMSCT at Digi-Key, and #N11 1N4734 at Electronix Express) is rated for 1 watt. Because this is going to be used only for a last-ditch desperate measure, rather than for continual operation, either the 0.5 W or 1.0 W zener diode will do.

Putting It All Together for a Robust Robot Power Supply

In the beginning of the previous chapter, I presented a simple linear voltage regulator. Since then, I have suggested a number of improvements (see Figure 8-14).

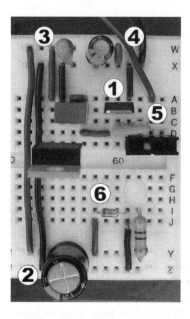

Figure 8-14. A linear voltage regulator with numerous simple improvements

Follow these steps to make the improvements:

1. Use a low-resistance, *p*-channel power MOSFET to prevent damage from a reverse battery.

2. Include the capacitors suggested by the manufacturer. After that, add a bulk capacitor to the regulated output and to the unregulated power (not illustrated) supply.

3. Add various low- and medium-value capacitors of different chemistries and technologies at various places on the circuit board to collectively benefit from their individual strengths.

4. Include at least one 0.1 μF capacitor for every chip to bypass board imped-
    ance (providing a "local" power supply) and to decouple (isolate and reduce)
    circuit noise. Put each capacitor as close as possible to its targeted chip, and
    keep the lead length of each capacitor as short as possible.

5. Add a PPTC overcurrent-protection device to limit the maximum current that
    can flow through the robot.

6. Add a 5.6 V zener diode to the 5 V regulated circuit to prevent damage from
    overvoltage.

All of these improvements are optional but highly recommended. You can build
the robots in this book using the simplest form of the linear voltage-regulator power
supply if you so choose. However, given the value of your time and the amount of hard
work you'll put into your robot, for cheaper than $10 of parts, you can gain a lot of pro-
tection and even possibly improve performance.

CHAPTER 9

Driving Miss Motor

Covers All Motor Modes, Single-Transistor Motor Drivers, Diode Protection, Bipolar H-Bridge, and Interfacing to Logic Chips and Microcontrollers

A *MOTOR DRIVER* **IS THE COMPONENT** or circuit in a robot that supplies electrical power to a motor. A motor driver can be as simple as a single transistor or as complicated as a set of chips with discrete components attached.

The first motor-driver circuit presented in this chapter is a single transistor that can only turn a motor on or off. From this humble beginning, the motor-driver circuit is built up to a classic H-bridge for full bidirectional motion, coasting, and electrical braking. This chapter finishes with a couple of methods of connecting an H-bridge motor-driving circuit to the logic chips or microcontroller that will command the motor.

All of the discrete transistors used in this chapter are bipolar technology. They're inexpensive, easy to hook up, and fairly hardy. The next chapter walks through the same motor-driver circuits using MOSFETs (a type of field-effect technology transistor). Additionally, the next chapter discusses motor-driver chips, which include nearly complete motor-driver circuits in a single component.

The robots in this book use reversible, permanent magnet, brush DC motors. These are the most common types of electric motors found in hobbyist robots. For more details on these types of motors, see Chapters 17 and 18 of *Robot Building for Beginners* (Apress, 2002). Although not discussed directly, the motor drivers described in this chapter are applicable to stepper motors, relays, LEDs, or even power control for other circuits.

Why a Motor Driver?

Why have a motor driver at all? Why not control a motor directly from the robot's brain—either a microcontroller or a logic chip?

Logic chips and microcontrollers are designed for data processing, which requires millions of tiny pathways and microscopic electronic switches. But motors are straightforward and power hungry. Motors need a few rugged switches and bigger wires to carry the current.

Because the internal structure needed for data processing (lots of skinny pathways) is different from the structure needed for power delivery (a few thick pathways), it turns out that almost all logic chips and microcontrollers lack the ability to supply enough voltage or current needed to run a motor directly.

This isn't a technological issue so much as an economic issue. Logic chips and microcontrollers could have thicker switches and pins appended to their packages. But because so many logic chips and microcontrollers are used for purposes other than robots and motor control, a combination microcontroller/motor-driver chip wouldn't be useful or cost-effective for most semiconductor customers.

A motor driver is simply one or more relatively large semiconductor arranged to deliver large amounts of power, usually under the control of a logic chip or microcontroller. Most motor drivers have four major attributes that a microcontroller doesn't have by itself:

- Motor drivers provide higher currents to the motor

- Motor drivers often provide higher voltages to the motor

- Motor drivers isolate the logic circuits from spikes and electrical noise generated by the motors during use

- Motor drivers usually supply the motors with unregulated power directly from the batteries, rather than regulated power from the power supply circuit

Running Motors at Higher Voltages Than Logic Chips Can Provide

Small DC motors generally require between 1.5 V and 24 V, with most targeted at 12 V. All other things being equal, higher voltages result in greater physical power output from a motor.

For most modern logic chips, the high-level outputs supply only between 1.8 V and 6 V, with 3.3 V and 5 V being the most common. If voltage were the only limitation, a 6 V motor could be run acceptably at 5 V from a microcontroller. But running a 12 V motor at 5 V would compromise performance.

Supplying More Current to Motors Than Logic Chips Can Provide

Small DC motors generally require between 20 mA and 2 amps (2,000 mA) of electrical current while running, with currents from 50 mA to 300 mA being common. Higher currents are drawn when the motor starts up, when the motor is heavily loaded, or when the motor is stalled.

Most modern microcontrollers and logic chips can supply up to 25 mA from a "high-current" pin but usually no more than 5 mA to 10 mA from standard pins. Some BiCMOS (bipolar combined with MOSFET technology) logic chips can provide currents up to 50 mA per pin. Still, that falls short of the electrical-current needs of nearly all motors.

Causing Logic Errors with Motor Noise

Besides requiring higher voltages and currents, motors also generate a lot of electrical disturbances. Electrical dips, spikes, and reverse voltages can be disturbing, if not downright destructive, to chips. Motors can stall or break down, and their wires can become disconnected or shorted together.

No one wants an unreliable robot. However, the electrical noises from a motor can drive microcontrollers and logic chips crazy. So, the motor driver acts as a protective electrical supplier by isolating the motors from the logic and microcontroller chips.

Supplying Motor Power from Unregulated vs. Regulated Power

In most cases, it's desirable to connect the robot's motors directly to an unregulated power source, such as a battery pack, rather than the regulated power source used by the robot's brain and logic circuits:

Because motors generally consume much more current than the rest of the robot, the regulator would need to be rated for much greater current if a motor were attached to the regulator. This results in a reduced selection of regulators, which tend to be larger and more expensive. Regulating higher currents also generates a lot more heat because even the best regulating conversion process isn't 100 percent efficient.

Motors are likely to be rated to run at a higher voltage than the regulated voltage supplied to logic circuits. So, assuming the unregulated power source is of a higher voltage than the regulated source, the motors would have a more powerful output if connected to the unregulated source.

The regulator provides some isolation from electrical noise. If the motors are on the same side of the circuit as the logic circuits, most of the isolation benefit is lost.

The rotational consistency that might be expected by applying a constant voltage to the motor (rather than the slowly declining voltage of an unregulated battery pack) isn't reliable in reality. The rotational consistency is altered by changes in frictional forces (wheel slippage, lubrication heating up in the gears, and so on) and environmental hiccups (bumps). For robots, there are more reliable ways to control distance or speed than a regulated voltage.

Based on these reasons, all of the circuits that follow supply unregulated power to the motors. However, technically, these circuits could be supplied regulated power, if desired.

Also worth noting is that there's nothing preventing these motor-driver circuits from being powered from a battery pack that's separate from the logic circuit's battery pack. If you're going to use two separate battery packs, be sure the ground wires from both battery packs are wired together (a common ground) and that the robot's power switch connects/disconnects the robot from both battery packs at the same time. For simplicity sake, I prefer a single battery pack for the entire robot.

Demonstrating the Four Modes of a Motor

A reversible, permanent magnet, brush DC motor has four fundamental modes: rotating clockwise, rotating counterclockwise, coasting freely, and braking/stopping. With a small motor and a 9 V battery, you can experience all four modes for yourself (see Figure 9-1).

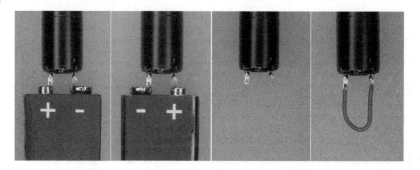

Figure 9-1. Power connected to motor terminals for clockwise rotation, power flipped for counterclockwise rotation, power disconnected for free rotation/coasting, and motor terminals connected together for braking/stopping (left to right)

Gearhead motors are better for observing clockwise versus counterclockwise motion because the speed of rotation is usually slowed down enough to make the direction of rotation visible to the human eye. Plain motors (no gears) are better for distinguishing between the coasting and braking states because the friction of the gears in a gearhead may be enough to make it seem like the motor is braking.

Rotating Clockwise

It's easiest to determine the direction of the rotation of a motor shaft if you attach a disc with markings (see Figure 9-2) to the motor shaft. For quick, temporary attachment, use tacky, reusable, moldable adhesive.

Most motors have a polarity indication near the motor terminals, such as a plus (+) sign. Alternately, some motors have a red or white wire, or a red or white stripe on a wire, to indicate positive. Some motors have a black wire or black stripe on a wire to indicate negative. If your motor doesn't provide any polarity indication of any kind, you can experiment with the motor connected to the battery both ways and then mark the polarity of the motor terminals when the motor shaft rotates clockwise.

Figure 9-2. Clockwise is the direction that clock hands travel, as viewed when the motor's shaft points toward you (left). Two example target discs for attaching to a motor shaft to observe direction of rotation (center). The top disc is more reliable for electronic tachometers or counters. The bottom disc is easier for humans to count rotations or detect the direction of rotation. Reusable, moldable adhesive (such as stretchy modeling clay) makes it easy to temporarily attach a disc to a motor shaft for testing (right).

Most motor shafts rotate clockwise when the positive terminal of the battery is connected to the positive terminal of the motor and the negative terminal of the battery is connected to the remaining terminal of the motor. I say *most* motors because, of the dozens of types of motors I tested from my collection, one gearhead motor shaft rotated counterclockwise when connected with proper polarity.

Why the lone holdout? For spur gearhead motors, the rotational direction of the gearhead output shaft is reversed from the rotational direction of the original motor output shaft if the number of gear stages is odd (as opposed to even). Planetary gearboxes retain the direction of rotation regardless of the number of stages.

Rotating Counterclockwise

In a reversible motor, simply flip the terminals of either the power source or the motor to reverse the direction from clockwise to counterclockwise. By the way, this is a good trick to remember if ever one or more of the wheels on your robot are rotating in the wrong direction. Simply flip the connections to the motor.

Reversible motors allow robots to move forward and backward by controlling the polarity (+/-) of the power provided to the motors.

Rotating Freely/Coasting (Slow Decay)

When the motor terminals are disconnected from everything, the motor shaft should spin freely. You can observe this effect by either twisting a plain motor shaft with your fingers or powering up a gearhead motor, disconnecting power, and then observing that the shaft continues to rotate for a brief time.

This mode is called *slow decay* because the energy in the motor is consumed gradually through friction. A robot with electrically disconnected motors can be more easily rolled and tends to coast to a stop rather than stop suddenly.

Braking/Stopping (Fast Decay)

The first three modes—clockwise, counterclockwise, and coasting—are fairly obvious. This last mode is a little less intuitive.

With the battery removed, electrically connect the motor terminals of a plain motor using a piece of bare wire (the rightmost image in Figure 9-1) or a screwdriver. Try spinning the shaft with your fingers. You'll find the motor to be more sluggish than with the wire or screwdriver removed. Another way to observe this effect is to get a motor going with a battery, remove the battery, and then quickly press a wire or screwdriver across the motor terminals. The motor stops fairly rapidly (although not instantly).

This mode is called *fast decay* because the energy in the motor is consumed not only through friction in the gears or shaft but also in the motor's electrical coil. A robot with its motor terminals electronically connected doesn't roll as easily and tends to stop suddenly rather than coast to a stop.

Using Up More Energy

Here's a fun experiment to help understand fast decay: Attach an LED directly to a plain motor and then spin the motor's shaft quickly with your fingers (see Figure 9-3). The LED flashes brightly with each finger twist. If the LED doesn't light, rotate the shaft in the opposite direction.

 CAUTION *An LED is usually accompanied by a current-limiting resistor. It's unnecessary here because you're unlikely to be able to generate enough electrical power with a twist of your fingers to melt the bond wire in the LED. However, if it makes you nervous for your LED to go naked, add a 1 kΩ resistor in series with it. Frankly, I can't guarantee that voltage spikes aren't pitting the LED die, so I wouldn't recommend using your great-grandmother's heirloom Nichia blue LED for this experiment.*

Figure 9-3. A plain (nongearhead) motor with an LED across the terminals to demonstrate where the energy is going in a fast-decay setup

Think about this: Assume you inject generally the same amount of energy each time you spin the motor shaft with your fingers. The more things that consume that energy, the faster the energy will be used up and the sooner the motor shaft will stop spinning. The LED emits energy as light. So, the motor stops spinning sooner when the LED is attached because not only is the motor doing all the things it was before as a bare motor (making noise, generating heat through friction), but also it's now emitting light.

Connecting (shorting) the motor terminals causes the energy to be consumed even more rapidly than with an LED or other load. For comparison, imagine how quickly the energy in a battery would be consumed if the battery's terminals were shorted together.

Braking by Fast Decay

Fast decay provides a useful feature on a robot: electronic brakes. They're not as powerful as physical brakes, but they still help a robot pivot in turns and prevent itself from rolling down a gently sloped hill.

Driving Simply with a Single Transistor

Now that you've observed the four fundamental modes of a motor (clockwise, counterclockwise, coast, and brake), you'll learn about motor-driver circuits that can place a motor in one or more of those modes. Depending on your robot, you may not need all four modes, in which case you can choose one of the simpler circuits.

The most basic motor driver is a single transistor switch. With the transistor switch turned on, the motor is connected to the power source, usually a battery. With only a single transistor, the motor can be turned on in one direction only, either clockwise or counterclockwise, depending on how the motor is wired to the circuit. When the transistor is turned off, the motor is turned off (coasts).

A single transistor switch circuit doesn't permit the motor to reverse directions and the motor to be electronically braked. But the single-transistor circuit is simple and cheap. It's perfectly effective for, say, dropping a scoop at the beginning of a robot sumo match (see Figure 9-4).

Have a Nice Day begins a mini-sumo robot match with its scoop in an upright position to meet the strict width and depth requirements of the contest. Then, when the action begins, a transistor switches on power to the motor connected to the scoop arms (see Figure 9-5). The scoop drops forcefully into position. The transistor switch is then turned off to conserve power and prevent the motor from overheating in the stalled (scoop pushed down completely) position. Every few seconds, the transistor switch is briefly pulsed on in order to push the scoop back down, should it somehow have become raised.

Figure 9-4. A composite image of Have a Nice Day dropping its scoop from a raised position. Only a single transistor is used to drive the scoop's motor.

Figure 9-5. Installed horizontally within Have a Nice Day, a small gearhead motor with LEGO gears rotates a LEGO cross axle connected to scoop arms on both sides

Have a Nice Day is unable to lift up its scoop even though the gearhead motor is strong enough to do so. A single-transistor motor driver can drive the motor in only one direction, so the scoop can only be lowered. A more complex motor-driver circuit could have been installed in Have a Nice Day, but that was unnecessary because you can restore the scoop by hand to the upright position after a mini-sumo match is complete.

Introducing the NPN Bipolar Single-Transistor Motor-Driver Circuit

The single-transistor motor-driver circuit is simple (see Figure 9-6). In this first example, you'll use an ordinary 2222A, which is an NPN bipolar general-purpose transistor. To break it down, "2222A" is the part number, "NPN" is the internal arrangement of the semiconductor layers, and "bipolar" is a type of transistor technology.

NOTE *The bipolar transistors used in this chapter are inexpensive, commonly available, and popular in the hobbyist robotic community. Consider these transistors good for learning about motor drivers. However, these particular transistors aren't very powerful. You'll be disappointed with these experiments if you try driving a motor that requires much more than 300 mA.*

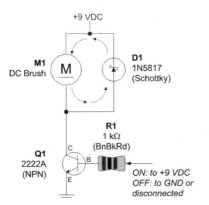

Figure 9-6. Schematic for a 2222A NPN bipolar single-transistor motor-driver circuit. The letters surrounding Q1 refer to the transistor's collector (C), base (B), and emitter (E) leads.

Switching with a Transistor

In Figure 9-6, transistor Q1 acts as the power switch for the motor. Imagine a physical switch was there instead of a transistor. If the switch were turned on, the motor would be connected to 9 V and ground and would spin. If the switch were turned off, the motor would be disconnected from ground and wouldn't spin.

Bipolar transistors switch off when no current is applied to the base (B) lead. You can accomplish this either by physically disconnecting the wire leading to the transistor's base lead (so obviously no current will flow) or by connecting the base lead of an NPN transistor to ground (0 V).

Bipolar transistors turn on when current flows through the base lead. For the 2222A, a voltage of approximately 0.6 V or higher is necessary to allow current to begin flowing through the base. However, under the heaviest loads, the 2222A transistor could theoretically require up to 2.0 V at the base, according to the manufacturer's datasheet. That's still a low enough voltage that most modern 5 V logic chips have enough output power to turn on this transistor.

Because you're not using any chips to control this circuit at this time, Figure 9-6 says "ON: to +9 VDC." This was simply convenient for testing the circuit with a 9 V battery. However, don't be fooled into thinking that this transistor actually needs 9 V to turn on. Resistor R1 consumes any extra voltage applied beyond the 0.6 V to 2.0 V required by the transistor's base.

Using Transistors As Off/On Switches, Not Amplifiers, in Motor-Driver Circuits

Like a dining-room dimmer switch, transistors can operate between full off and full on by applying a current to the base lead that's somewhere between fully switched on (saturated) and fully switched off. However, motor-driver circuits are designed to avoid this feature of transistors because the power levels associated with driving motors could cause a partially enabled transistor to overheat. Therefore, all of the motor-driver circuits in this book are designed to turn transistors fully on or fully off.

Limiting Base Current with a Resistor

Resistor R1 protects the transistor's base lead against too much voltage or too much current. R1 is a low enough value to ensure that enough current flows into the base lead when 9 V (in this example) is applied to R1 to fully switch on Q1. At the same time, resistor R1 is a high enough value to prevent Q1's base lead from receiving so much current that it could become damaged. In this role, resistor R1 is called a *current-limiting* resistor. Current-limiting resistors are connected to LEDs for the same purpose.

With an ideal 5 V logic chip controlling R1, you can calculate the maximum amount of current that can flow into Q1's base lead:

```
base current in amps = (logic chip voltage - transistor base voltage)
 ÷ current limiting resistor in ohms
base current in amps = (5 V - 0.6 V) ÷ 1000 Ω
base current in amps = 0.0044 A or 4.4 mA
```

The previous calculation shows that an ideal 5 V logic chip need only supply 4.4 mA to begin turning on Q1. However, the current draw is reduced when the base is at the maximum voltage (heavily loaded motor):

```
base current in amps = (5 V - 2.0 V) ÷ 1000 Ω
base current in amps = 0.003 A or 3.0 mA
```

According to the datasheets, a 2222A transistor can theoretically provide up to 500 mA of continuous current (and peaks of up to 1000 mA) when fully turned on. To convert 3 mA of base current into 500 mA of collector-emitter current, the gain must be greater than the following:

```
minimum gain required = current desired ÷ base current
minimum gain required = 500 mA ÷ 3.0 mA
minimum gain required = 166.7
```

The 2222A datasheet indicates the guaranteed minimum gains are only about 30 · times the base current. Because your minimum gain required (166.7) is greater than the minimum gain guaranteed (30), the transistor is unlikely to be able to provide enough current to drive 500 mA motors with a 5 V logic chip and 1,000 Ω resistor (R1).

You can use a smaller-value resistor (such as 470 Ω) for R1 in this circuit to provide greater power output. However, it's wiser to use a higher-rated transistor rather than push the 2222A to its limit.

The benefits of this single-transistor motor driver should now be apparent. A 5 V logic chip that can supply only a few milliamps by itself is now capable of controlling a higher-voltage (9 V or whatever) motor with several hundred milliamps of current.

Protecting the Transistor with a Diode

Like resistor R1, diode D1 protects transistor Q1. A spinning motor has quite a lot of energy in it. When transistor Q1 switches off, the voltage in the motor actually increases and reverses polarity as the electromagnetic field collapses. Diode D1 provides a rugged path for any high voltages to return to the battery or circulate in the motor. If D1 weren't there, the motor voltage might be high enough to force itself through Q1 to ground, damaging Q1 in the process. When used in this manner, a diode is called a *flyback diode*.

Implementing the NPN Bipolar Single-Transistor Motor-Driver Circuit

The single-transistor motor driver is easy to implement on a solderless breadboard (see Figure 9-7). The motor (M1) can be any brand of small DC brush motor, as long as the start-up current doesn't exceed 500 mA and the loaded (running) current doesn't exceed 300 mA.

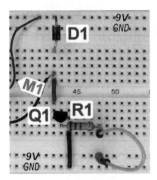

Figure 9-7. 2222A NPN bipolar single-transistor motor-driver circuit implemented on a solderless breadboard

The Schottky 1N5817 diode (D1) is the same component introduced in Chapter 7. It's installed with the cathode end (the one with a band) connected to positive voltage so that battery power *won't* normally flow through it. If you mistakenly install the diode the wrong way, the motor won't spin when the transistor turns on.

In Figure 9-7, pay close attention to the flat side of Q1. The transistor's label faces away from the front of the board. The left side of Figure 9-8 shows the leads of the 2222A transistor.

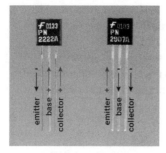

Figure 9-8. The leads of a 2222A NPN transistor (left).
The leads of a 2907A PNP transistor (right)

The 2222A is a widely available general-purpose transistor. For solderless bread-board experiments, purchase transistors in a TO-92 through-hole package ($0.09 to $0.26; #PN2222A at Digi-Key, #178511 at Jameco, #512-PN2222A at Mouser, and #TR2222 at Solarbotics).

A jumper wire appears at the bottom-right corner of Figure 9-7. One end of the wire connects to the current-limiting resistor (R1). The other end of the wire can be connected to the 9 V bus to turn the motor on, or the wire can be connected to the ground bus to turn the motor off.

In a robot, an output pin of a chip would take the place of the jumper wire. When the chip's output pin goes high (5 V), the motor spins. When the chip's output pin goes low (0 V), the motor stops. Transistor Q1 drives the motor based on the signal from the chip.

Introducing the PNP Bipolar Single-Transistor Motor-Driver Circuit

The PNP bipolar circuit (see Figure 9-9) is similar to the NPN circuit. In this case, a 2907A transistor is used instead of a 2222A.

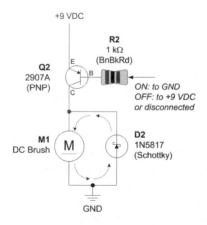

Figure 9-9. A 2907A PNP bipolar single-transistor motor-driver circuit

The motor and diode are in the same orientation as before, but now they're wired to ground, as opposed to positive voltage. The transistor and resistor have moved to the top of the circuit to switch the motor connection to positive voltage, as opposed to ground. The current-limiting resistor R2 performs the same function as R1 in the prior circuit—the resistor protects the base lead of the transistor (Q2) from having too much current pass through it.

The big difference in the PNP motor-driver circuit is that this circuit turns on when the transistor's base is connected to ground. That's the opposite of the NPN transistor. Actually, the base of transistor Q2 needs only to be brought to 0.6 V below positive voltage (9 V minus 0.6 V equals 8.4 V) to allow current to start flowing. The connection to the base resistor doesn't actually need to be brought all the way to ground. However, bringing it all the way to ground increases current flow to the transistor's base, which allows the transistor to turn all the way on (saturate) with heavier motor loads.

To turn the motor off, the base of the PNP transistor needs to be disconnected or brought up to positive voltage. Therefore, this circuit isn't quite as immediately practical as the NPN version because the output of a 5 V chip would be unable to bring the PNP base lead up to 9 V. However, some chips, such as the LM393 comparator used in Sandwich (from *Robot Building for Beginners*) have no problem disconnecting the base lead to turn the motor off. (Sandwich's motors are in fact driven by 2907A PNP transistors.)

Implementing the PNP Bipolar Single-Transistor Motor-Driver Circuit

The PNP motor driver (see Figure 9-10) is as easy to implement as the NPN motor driver. In this case, the flat (labeled) side of the transistor faces toward the front of the board. Refer to the right side of Figure 9-8 to see the leads on a 2907A transistor.

When the jumper wire (the top-right corner of Figure 9-10) is connected to ground, the motor spins. When the jumper wire is connected to 9 V (or is disconnected), the motor is turned off.

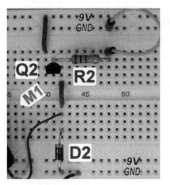

Figure 9-10. The 2907A PNP bipolar single-transistor motor-driver circuit on a solderless breadboard

Like the 2222A, the 2907A is a popular and highly available bipolar transistor. Purchase it in a TO-92 package ($0.09 to $0.26; #PN2907A at Digi-Key, #178520 at

Jameco, #512-PN2907A at Mouser, and #TR2907 at Solarbotics) for prototyping on a solderless breadboard.

Putting the NPN and PNP Motor Drivers Together

This next circuit combines the NPN and PNP motor drivers (see Figure 9-11). It may look complicated at first glance, but it's really not. It's the same parts in the same places from the prior circuits. The only difference is that one motor wire connects in the middle of the circuit, and the other motor wire connects to ground. This arrangement is sometimes called a *totem pole* or *half bridge*.

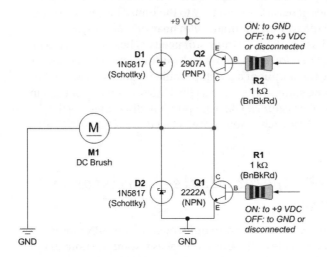

Figure 9-11. The previously presented NPN and PNP circuits connected

Implementing the Combination NPN and PNP Motor-Driver Circuit

With the exception of the motor wires, Figure 9-12 shows the components installed on a solderless breadboard in the same positions as they were in Figure 9-7 and Figure 9-10.

Figure 9-12. NPN and PNP circuits put together on the same solderless breadboard

Notice that only one jumper wire (in the top-right corner) is used. Trust me for a moment here and use only one jumper wire.

When the jumper wire is connected to R2 and GND, transistor Q2 switches on. Thus, the motor wire in the middle of the board becomes connected to 9 V, so the motor spins. This is exactly how the PNP bipolar single-transistor motor-driver circuit worked.

When the jumper wire is pulled out and connected to R1 and 9 V, transistor Q1 switches on. The motor wire in the middle of the board becomes connected to ground through transistor Q1. At first glance, this doesn't seem to do much because the other wire of the motor is also connected to ground. However, the motor is now actually in brake mode (recall the far-right side of Figure 9-1).

This two-transistor motor driver is a minor improvement over a single-transistor motor driver because the two-transistor motor driver can make the motor spin in one direction or brake. This circuit is actually half of the final circuit you're heading toward, thus the name *half bridge*.

Avoiding a Short Circuit

By combining the NPN and PNP circuits, the motor wire in the middle of the board can now receive either 9 V or ground. Unfortunately, if you're not careful, by switching on both Q1 and Q2 at the same time, the middle of the board will receive *both* 9 V and ground (see Figure 9-13).

Figure 9-13. Don't do this. With two jumper wires, both transistors are turned on at the same time, causing battery power to shoot from 9 V, through Q2, through Q1, and into ground.

That's a short circuit! That's not good!

Because motor-driver components are usually connected to higher, unregulated voltages and because motor-driver components are capable of carrying higher currents than logic chips, a short circuit in a motor driver can cause a lot of damage. The most likely damaged components will be the motor-driver transistors; they'll overheat and burn out. Also, the breadboard can melt, and the battery can be harmed from the large surge of current. The motor, resistors, and diodes are unlikely to be damaged because they aren't in the short-circuit path.

When building a motor-driver circuit, always be on the lookout for a configuration of the switches (transistors) that would allow current to flow from positive to ground without passing through the motor. Motor-driver designers go to a lot of trouble to make sure that errant commands from chips aren't permitted to set the switches into a shorting state. For this experiment, having only one jumper wire prevents more than one transistor from being turned on at the same time.

The Classic Bipolar H-Bridge

Doubling the previous circuit gets you the classic H-bridge (see Figure 9-14). This circuit is called an *H-bridge* because it kind of looks like a capital letter *H*.

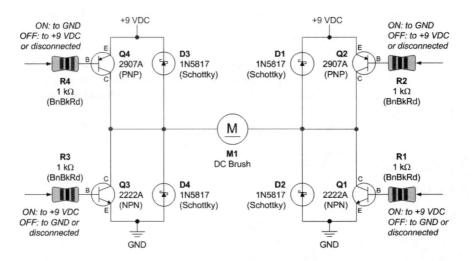

Figure 9-14. A classic bipolar NPN and PNP H-bridge motor driver

It looks tortuous, but it's really just four transistor switches (two PNPs on top and two NPNs on the bottom) in the same configuration as the circuits already presented so far in this chapter. The right half of Figure 9-14 is the same as Figure 9-11. The left half of Figure 9-14 is the same circuit mirrored from the right half.

Drum roll, please! An H-bridge provides all four motor modes: spin clockwise, spin counterclockwise, coast, and brake.

Spinning Clockwise with an H-Bridge

When resistor R2 is connected to ground, then PNP transistor Q2 is switched on. When resistor R3 is connected to 9 V, then NPN transistor Q3 is switched on. This provides a path for current to flow from 9 V, through Q2, through the motor, through Q3, and to ground (see Figure 9-15). Assuming you have the positive lead of the motor connected to the side of the H-bridge with Q2 on it, then the motor spins clockwise.

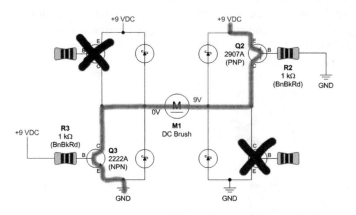

Figure 9-15. The motor spins clockwise with Q2 and Q3 switched on.

Spinning Counterclockwise with an H-Bridge

When resistor R4 is connected to ground, then PNP transistor Q4 is switched on. When resistor R1 is connected to 9 V, then NPN transistor Q1 is switched on. This provides a path for current to flow from 9 V, through Q4, through the motor, through Q1, and to ground (see Figure 9-16). Assuming you have the positive lead of the motor connected to the side of the H-bridge with Q1 on it, then the motor spins counterclockwise.

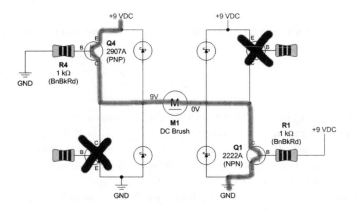

Figure 9-16. The motor spins counterclockwise with Q4 and Q1 switched on.

Slowing Down with an H-Bridge Electronic Brake

When resistor R3 is connected to 9 V, then NPN transistor Q3 is switched on. When resistor R1 is connected to 9 V, then NPN transistor Q1 is switched on. Both wires of the motor are connected to ground, and ground connects to itself, so the motor wires are effectively connected (see Figure 9-17). This results in a fast dissipation of motor energy, just like the LED experiment earlier in this chapter.

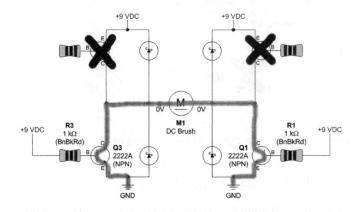

Figure 9-17. The motor brakes with Q1 and Q3 switched on (low side). The high-lighted path shows that both leads of the motor connect to ground. (Furthermore, one or the other associated diodes is also going to provide an additional one-way electrical path depending on which direction the current is flowing through the motor.)

An electronic brake isn't as effective as a physical brake. But, still, a speeding robot will slow down quickly with the electronic brakes turned on.

Braking High

There's another way to electronically brake with an H-bridge. When resistor R4 is connected to ground, then PNP transistor Q4 is switched on. When resistor R2 is connected to ground, then PNP transistor Q2 is switched on. This connects both ends of the motor to 9 V, and both 9 Vs are connected; thus, both motor wires are connected (see Figure 9-18). So, again, the motor is electronically braked.

Braking with the PNP switches (high side) and braking with the NPN switch (low side) are both legitimate, effective methods of electronic braking. A reason why a builder might choose to brake with the low-side transistors is that the type of transistors (NPN) often used on the low side tend to be less resistant. A less resistant path can drain away the motor's energy faster.

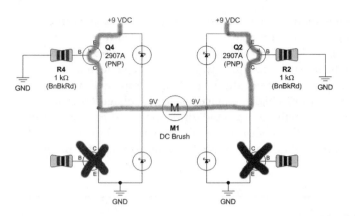

Figure 9-18. The motor brakes with Q4 and Q2 switched on (high side). The high-lighted path shows that both leads of the motor connect to 9 V. (Again, one diode or the other diode will also carry current.)

However, there are perfectly acceptable reasons to brake with the high side. Perhaps your microcontroller or logic chip starts up with 0 V outputs, which is ideal for pulling all the resistors to ground (thus enabling Q2 and Q4 for braking) at power-up. Or, some fancy H-bridge chips allow current to be measured on only the high side switches, and therefore enabling the high-side transistors allows the robot to detect when the motor is still spinning down or something is trying to push the robot.

Either method of electronic braking is fine.

Coasting with an H-Bridge

Last, but not least, if none of the resistors are connected to anything, then none of the transistor switches are turned on. The motor is able to spin freely because neither of the motor leads is electronically connected to anything (see Figure 9-19).

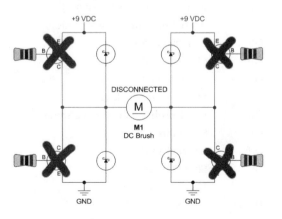

Figure 9-19. The motor rotates freely (coasts) with all switches turned off.

With all of those wires and diodes, you might think there must be some sort of electrical path to something, even with the transistors turned off. However, for current flow to occur, the electricity must be able to complete a full path from one motor wire to the other motor wire. In the previous examples, two transistors (or, technically, one transistor and one diode on the opposite side during braking) completed a path.

Conventional current flows from a higher voltage to a lower voltage. Can you draw a path from either motor lead, down through ground (through the battery), down from 9 V, to the other motor lead? Nope, the diodes are pointing the wrong direction, and the switches are disabled. No path. No flow. Any power in the motor stays in the motor until it gradually decays through heat, friction, vibration, and noise.

NOTE *Please don't draw in this book.*

Enumerating the Other H-Bridge Combinations

An H-bridge consists of four transistor switches with two states each (on and off). That means there are 16 (2^4) possible states. Five have already been listed as being useful. Of the remaining eleven, four provide braking in one direction only, and the other seven result in nasty short circuits (see Table 9-1).

Table 9-1. H-Bridge Motor-Driver Combinations

#	Q4	Q3	Q2	Q1	Result
1	Off	Off	Off	Off	Coast
2	Off	Off	Off	On	Brake clockwise only
3	Off	Off	On	Off	Brake counterclockwise only
4	Off	Off	**On**	**On**	**Short circuit**
5	Off	On	Off	Off	Brake counterclockwise only
6	Off	On	Off	On	Brake both directions (low side)
7	Off	On	On	Off	Spin clockwise
8	Off	On	**On**	**On**	**Short circuit**
9	On	Off	Off	Off	Brake clockwise only
10	On	Off	Off	On	Spin counterclockwise
11	On	Off	On	Off	Brake both directions (high side)
12	On	Off	**On**	**On**	**Short circuit**
13	**On**	**On**	Off	Off	**Short circuit**
14	**On**	**On**	Off	On	**Short circuit**
15	**On**	**On**	On	Off	**Short circuit**
16	**On**	**On**	**On**	**On**	**Double short circuit**

Notice that a short circuit can occur only if Q4 and Q3 are on at the same time or if Q2 and Q1 are on at the same time.

Implementing the Classic Bipolar H-Bridge

The H-bridge circuit (see Figure 9-20) is implemented with only four transistors, four resistors, and four diodes. Notice that only one jumper appears on each side of the board, thus eliminating the possibility of a short circuit. Compare Figure 9-20 to the schematic shown in Figure 9-14.

Figure 9-20. H-bridge motor driver implemented on a solderless breadboard

Take some time to play with the H-bridge. It's satisfying to see the motor spin forward and backward and to feel the effects of coasting and braking. It's valuable to understand how an H-bridge works because all of the motor-driver chips evolve from this basic design.

Interfacing with the High Side

So far, the transistors have been turned on and off using jumper wires to connect the base resistors to the power buses on a solderless breadboard. Ultimately, you want the H-bridge to be controllable by your robot's brain (chips), not by you (jumper wires).

You can switch off the low-side transistors (NPN Q3 and Q1) with 0 V and switch them on with a couple of volts. There's no problem connecting the NPN transistors to a 5 V or even a 3.3 V logic chip or microcontroller, as long as the motor doesn't draw more than a couple hundred milliamps. You can switch on the high-side transistors (PNP Q4 and Q2) with 0 V (okay so far) and switch them off by bringing the base resistor input up to approximately the same as the emitter, which is 9 V in the example case (uh-oh). That's a problem. A 5 V logic chip can't directly generate 9 V.

You need some sort of circuitry to permit a logic-level (standard voltage) chip to control the high side of the H-bridge. This type of circuitry is usually called a *level shifter* or *interface*.

Avoiding an Interface by Not Regulating the Logic Chips

Most high-speed CMOS (HC) chips operate from 2 V to 6 V. Let's say you build a robot completely out of those types of chips, and you don't bother with voltage regulation. Now let's say the power source was four nickel-metal hydride (NiMH) batteries that ranged from 4.8 V (nominally charged) to 4 V (exhausted). The robot would work fine without needing to alter the bipolar NPN/PNP H-bridge shown in Figure 9-14.

Instead of receiving 9 V, the H-bridge would receive 4.8 V. Because the chips are also receiving 4.8 V, they'd have no problem raising the base of the PNP transistors up to emitter voltage (4.8 V) to turn the PNP transistors off. No interface is necessary.

Avoiding an Interface by Regulating the H-Bridge

Another option to allow the chips to interface with the PNP transistors is to regulate the H-bridge to the same voltage as the chips. For example, by putting a 5 V regulator on the H-bridge, then 5 V chips could raise the base of the PNP transistors up to emitter voltage (5 V). No interface would be necessary.

For small, low-current motors and a fairly low-voltage battery pack (6 V to 8 V), a regulated H-bridge wouldn't be such an awful idea. Of course, you're throwing away voltage that could otherwise go to the motors.

Interfacing a PNP via an NPN

I've already established that a standard chip can control an NPN transistor. Also, I've established that an NPN transistor is good for switching something to ground or for disconnecting something. Furthermore, I've established that a PNP transistor turns on when connected to ground and turns off when disconnected.

Ah-ha! A logic chip can control an NPN transistor, and an NPN transistor can control a PNP transistor (see Figure 9-21).

The circuit in Figure 9-21 is identical to the single-transistor circuit originally presented in Figure 9-9 except that Q5 and R5 have been added. Q5 now performs the function of connecting R2 to ground or disconnecting R2, instead of using a jumper. R5 is just the current-limiting resistor for Q5.

When R5 is connected to ground, Q5 turns off, which causes R2 to disconnect, which causes Q2 to turn off, which prevents the motor from receiving current, so the motor doesn't spin. When R5 receives more than 0.6 V, then current begins flowing into the base of Q5, turning it on. When Q5 turns on, it connects R2 to ground. With R2 connected to ground, the base of Q2 is more than 0.6 V below the emitter, causing current to flow, causing Q2 to turn on. When Q2 turns on, the motor (M1) receives current and begins to spin.

You're using one switch to turn on another switch. That's a textbook use of transistors!

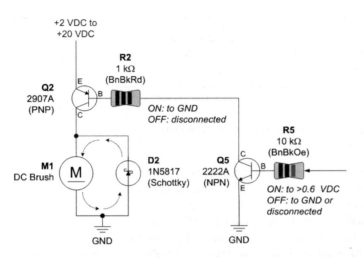

Figure 9-21. A 2907A PNP bipolar single-transistor motor-driver circuit with a 2222A NPN bipolar interface for control compatibility with a standard logic chip

Flipping the Switch

There's a subtle change in the way this circuit is now controlled. With the PNP transistor, you had to apply 0 V to turn the motor on and 9 V to turn it off. That's a little weird. After adding the NPN transistor, the motor now turns on when 9 V (or 5 V) is applied and turns off when 0 V is applied. It's mentally easier for a human to program and debug a circuit when positive voltage turns it on and ground turns it off.

Selecting a Resistor Value for R5

The NPN transistor isn't switching much current to turn on Q2. Even at 20 V, ignoring the voltage drops along the way, the maximum current flowing through R2 is only going to be as follows:

```
20 V ÷ 1000 Ω = 0.02 A = 20 mA maximum
```

Q5 barely has to turn on to supply 20 mA. So, to save on current, Q5 receives a current-limiting resistor (R5) that's ten times as resistive as R2. Not only does this save a tiny bit of battery life, but also it has the added benefit of requiring less current from the logic chip controlling it. Remember this transistor-controlling-another-transistor trick if you ever need to drive a final transistor that requires too much current for your particular logic chip.

TIP *There's nothing wrong with using a 1 kΩ resistor for R5 if you don't care about saving current, if your chip can drive up to 20 mA, and if you prefer to buy 1 kΩ resistors in bulk.*

Specifying the Voltage Range for the Bipolar Motor-Driver Circuits

The schematics previously presented in this chapter are labeled as receiving 9 V. I did this for the simplicity of experimenting with a 9 V battery. All of the circuits presented in this chapter should function well from 2 V through 20 V.

Below 2 V, the limited amount of current flowing at the base of the transistors can begin preventing the transistors from fully switching on (saturating). That being said, I found that the circuit in Figure 9-21 continued to drive a high-efficiency motor with only 0.8 V.

Don't use these circuits greater than 20 V because the 1N5817 diode isn't rated for more than 20 V. Theoretically, you could replace the 1N5817 with a 1N914 or 1N4001 and increase the voltage to 40 V. However, the 2907A and 2222A transistors shouldn't be used to supply more than 500 mA. I question how common it is to find a motor that consumes less than 500 mA under load with a voltage greater than 20 V. But, if necessary, you can always replace the example transistors with more power bipolar transistors, such as those in the TIP family.

Now that the motor-driver circuit has an NPN interface transistor, the logic chip voltage can be either lower or higher than the motor-driver circuit. But don't raise the base voltage of a PNP bipolar transistor more than 5 V higher than the emitter voltage. In other words, the robot brain shouldn't be given a voltage that's 5 V more than the motor-driver circuit is receiving. That's a little silly anyway. But if you decide to run a 1 V pager motor with a bipolar transistor H-bridge controlled from a 13.5 V CMOS chip, you're on your own.

Implementing a PNP Single-Transistor Bipolar Motor Driver with an NPN Interface

The PNP motor driver with NPN interface is fairly easy to implement on a solderless breadboard (see Figure 9-22). The only trick is that the flat, labeled side of the 2907A PNP transistor faces forward, and the flat, labeled side of the 2222A NPN transistor faces toward the back of the board.

Figure 9-22. 2907A PNP motor driver with a 2222A NPN interface implemented on a solderless breadboard

Finishing the Bipolar H-Bridge

With the addition of NPN transistors to interface to the PNP transistors (see Figure 9-23), the bipolar H-bridge circuit is finally ready for a robot. A microcontroller or logic chip can now apply a couple of volts to R1, R3, R5, or R6 to turn on the switches and drive the motor forward, backward, coast, or brake.

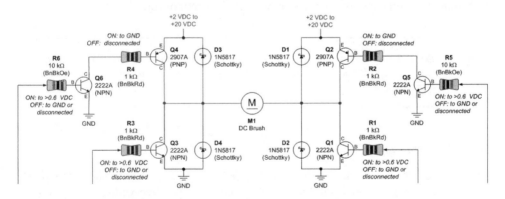

Figure 9-23. The bipolar H-bridge with two additional resistors and NPN transistors to interface the high-side PNP transistors to logic-level chips

This is a perfectly good and complete H-bridge that you should be proud to use in any of your smaller robots. It's inexpensive, has widely available parts, and performed about middle-of-the-pack in performance testing (see the next chapter).

On the downside, it's limited to providing approximately 300 mA of continuous current or 500 mA peak current to a motor. That should be more than adequate for a lunch-box-sized robot. As mentioned earlier, you can replace the transistors in this H-bridge with power bipolar transistors to provide a higher amount of continuous current, if desired.

TIP *Instead of using power bipolar transistors to achieve greater current delivery, I recommend this same H-bridge circuit implemented with MOSFETs, as described in the next chapter.*

Using an Interface Chip

Besides NPN transistors, another option for interfacing with the high side of an H-bridge is to use a chip specifically designed for converting a lower input voltage into a higher output voltage.

One approach is to select a chip with an open-collector output. An open-collector output either connects the output to ground or disconnects it. That's really no different from an NPN transistor. For example, the CD74AC05E provides six logic-level inputs with six open-collector (ground or disconnect) outputs. So, it's a little like a six-pack of NPN transistors on a chip but with a more limited current output.

NOTE *The AC series of chips is a combination of bipolar and CMOS transistors. So, although it doesn't technically contain just "six NPN transistors," the analogy is legitimate.*

Choosing the 4427

A more potent level-shifting chip is the 4427 (see Figure 9-24). It has the added feature of converting a logic-level input into either a ground or a positive-voltage (not disconnected) output.

The 4427 has two inputs and two outputs. The inputs require 2.4 V or greater to turn on but only 10 μA or less of current. The outputs can drive up to 1.5 A, which far exceeds the current requirements of the base of almost any common bipolar transistor.

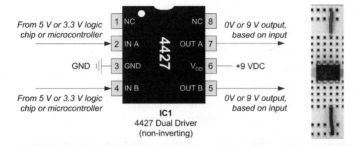

Figure 9-24. Schematic where 0 V to 5 V inputs are converted into outputs of either 0 V or 9 V (left). Pins 1 and 8 are labeled "NC" for no connection. Just leave those pins unconnected. Notice that the ground and positive voltage (9 V in this example) power supply isn't attached to the corner pins as it would be on most chips. The TC4427A driver chip in an 8-pin DIP package on a solderless breadboard (right).

Interfacing the 4427 to the H-Bridge

Instead of using NPN transistors to drive the high-side PNP transistors, you could use the outputs of the 4427. Alternatively, a more interesting circuit drives both the high and low side transistors of the original H-bridge circuit (see Figure 9-25).

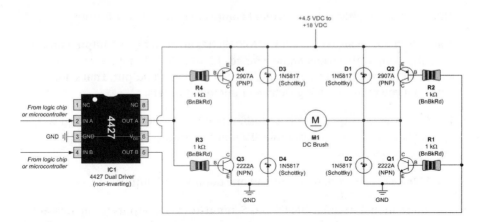

Figure 9-25. With the 4427, you can now control the motor with only two lines instead of four. The H-bridge can't be short circuited anymore (good); however, coast mode is no longer available.

When input A of the 4427 is 5 V, output A is 9 V (or whatever voltage is supplying the H-bridge). As such, transistor Q4 turns off, and transistor Q3 turns on. When input A is 0 V, output A is 0 V. As such, transistor Q4 turns on and transistor Q3 turns off. Input B and output B have the same effect on transistors Q2 and Q1. Thus, you can control all four transistors (and therefore the motor) with only two lines from a logic chip or microcontroller (see Table 9-2).

Table 9-2. Motor Modes with a 4427 Driver Chip

Input B	Input A	Result
0 V	0 V	Brake both directions (high side)
0 V	5 V	Spin clockwise
5 V	0 V	Spin counterclockwise
5 V	5 V	Brake both directions (low side)

This arrangement is almost perfect. The H-bridge can't be short circuited anymore (see the next chapter for information about shoot-through), even if the microcontroller runs amok and outputs randomly. Unfortunately, the transistors can't all be turned off at the same time, so coast mode is no longer available. But, for most robots, coast mode isn't necessary.

The 4427 requires a power supply of at least 4.5 V and permits no more than 18 V, so the H-bridge range is no longer 2 V to 20 V. But that's not a huge loss.

Selecting the 4427 or a Close Family Member

The 4427 chip is an improved version of the original 427 buffer/driver chip. Many 4427 pin-compatible chips are available:

- The 4424 has a higher output current (3 amps) than the 4427 (1.5 amps).

- The IXYS (http://www.ixys.com/) IXDN404PI has an even higher output current (4 amps) along with a wider voltage range (4.5 V to 25 V), but it does require at least a 3.5 V input rather than a 2.4 V input to turn on an output. That's not significant if you're using 5 V logic chips or microcontrollers.

- The 4426 is an inverter instead of a buffer; that is, the outputs are the logical opposite of the inputs. For example, 0 V input produces 9 V output, and 5 V input produces 0 V output.

- The 4428 has one inverted output and one noninverted output.

- The International Rectifier IR4427 has Schmitt-triggered inputs (more tolerant of electrical noise or slowly changing input control signals) and built-in pull-down resistors.

- The Texas Instruments (http://www.ti.com/) TPS2812P drives voltages up to 40 V when pin 1 is hooked up to power (pin 1 isn't connected on any of the other chips).

Just like the 7805/LM2940/LP2954 pin-compatible voltage regulators in Chapter 7, you can generally mix and match pin-compatible components based on price, desired features, and availability. There are different manufacturers of the same chip, such as the Microchip (http://www.microchip.com/) TC4427 or the Maxim MAX4427. Compare and contrast the datasheets to spot any significant differences. My favorite is the IXDN404PI.

The IXDN404PI ($1.68; #IXDN404PI at Digi-Key), TC4427ACPA ($1.46; #TC4427ACPA at Digi-Key), IR4427 ($1.80; #IR4427 at Digi-Key), and TC4424CPA ($2.63; #TC4424CPA at Digi-Key) are all available in an eight-pin DIP appropriate for solderless breadboards. The eight-pin DIP provides the advantage of being able to be socketed on a robot. That way if the motor-driver chip is damaged (or you suspect it of being damaged), you can swap in a replacement chip quickly.

The 4427 is officially designed for driving power MOSFETs. I'll use the chip for doing just that in the next chapter. However, the 4427 (and the members of that family) can drive the bipolar H-bridge just fine. In fact, with the 4427 you can lower the resistor values and drive power bipolar transistors to provide more current to a motor, if desired.

You can even connect LEDs in parallel to the output of the 4427 to add a little flash to your robot. The outputs of most logic chips and microcontrollers would be unable to provide enough power for both an LED and a transistor H-bridge, but the 4427 has plenty of power to spare.

Mastering Motor Control

You now have the knowledge to add full motor control to your homemade robots. This chapter described the most important reasons for needing a motor driver, which are providing higher voltages to a motor, providing higher current to a motor, protecting the logic chips from motor noise and spikes, and supplying a motor with the full power of plentiful unregulated voltage.

A simple single-transistor motor driver is fine for single-direction control. With four transistors, complete motor control is available but only at logic-level voltages. With six transistors, complete motor control is available up to 20 V or higher, controllable by a standard logic chip or microcontroller.

By adding a level shifter or interface chip, not only can the logic-level chips control the high-side transistors, but you can also reduce the number of control lines. In doing so, you can avoid the undesirable transistor combinations, thus eliminating short circuits.

The next chapter explores a more powerful transistor technology: power MOS-FETs. The chapter also discusses complete H-bridge chips with interfaces and other features. Finally, the motor-driving portion of this book concludes with a head-to-head comparison of some motor-driving circuits and chips.

CHAPTER 10

Driving Mister Motor

Includes Power MOSFET Motor Drivers, Pull-Up and Pull-Down Resistors, Shoot-Through, Parallel MOSFET for Serious Motors, and Motor-Driver Chip Match-Up Including the 4427 Family, the SN754410, and the Feature-Rich MC33887

THE PREVIOUS CHAPTER CONCENTRATED on using discrete bipolar transistors to drive motors. The most elemental usage is a single transistor that can turn on a motor in a single direction. More complex arrangements, such as an H-bridge, provide full motor control.

This chapter begins by re-creating the previously presented circuits, this time using metal oxide semiconductor field effect transistors (MOSFETs) instead of bipolar transistors. MOSFETs are much more efficient and can provide more power to the motor. However, unlike bipolar transistors, MOSFETs must always be connected to a voltage source. They can't be left disconnected.

You don't always have to build your own H-bridge. In fact, modular H-bridge chips can save a lot of time and mental energy when building a robot, and most chips offer safety, control, and monitoring features that wouldn't be worth the trouble of building yourself. This chapter discusses three motor-driver chips.

At the end of this chapter, the chapter compares a few motor drivers head to head for power delivery and efficiency.

Driving Motors with MOSFETs

For the purposes of driving motors, I'll limit the discussion to a particular type of field-effect transistor, the enhancement-mode power MOSFET. A power MOSFET delivers large amounts of current, unlike a digital logic MOSFET present in most modern chips, which is optimized for high switching speeds and lower voltages.

Introducing the N-Channel Power MOSFET Single-Transistor Motor-Driver Circuit

The single-transistor *n*-channel MOSFET motor-driver circuit (see Figure 10-1) is similar to the single-transistor NPN bipolar circuit presented in the previous chapter. Applying ground to the gate lead of Q1 turns the transistor off, which electrically disconnects the motor. Applying 9 V to the gate lead of Q1 turns the transistor on, which electrically connects the motor, causing the motor to spin.

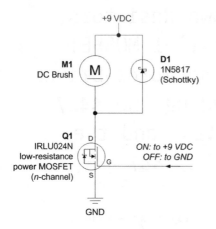

Figure 10-1. Schematic of a single-transistor n-channel power MOSFET motor driver. The letters surrounding Q1 refer to the transistor's drain (D), gate (G), and source (S) leads.

Controlling the Transistor Switch with Voltage, Not Current

Because MOSFETs are controlled with a voltage, not a continuous current flow, a gate current-limiting resistor is usually not necessary. If fact, because no significant current flows into a MOSFET's gate (the equivalent control pin to a bipolar transistor's base) during a steady state, the MOSFET circuit is incredibly efficient. That is, almost no power is expended in keeping the transistor turned on.

However, most MOSFETs require the application of a greater voltage to turn on than do most bipolar transistors. Older generations of power MOSFETs usually required the gate to be at least 10 V more positive than the source (for *n*-channel transistors) to fully turn on. However, the most recent generation of power MOSFETs that are labeled "logic-level" can turn on with as little as 3 V.

With about 3 V, the IRLU024N power MOSFET can switch an equivalent amount of current—500 mA, for example—as can the 2222A bipolar transistor. With about 5 V, the IRLU024N can easily provide ten times that amount of current to the motor. That doesn't mean the motor has to consume that much current, just that the MOSFET is capable of providing it.

Always Connecting the Gate of a MOSFET

Bipolar transistors require base current to provide current to the motor. Disconnect the wire from the base of a bipolar transistor, and the control current flow stops; thus, the transistor turns off.

Conversely, MOSFETs are controlled by the voltage present at their gate. In fact, a MOSFET's gate acts like a tiny capacitor. After the MOSFET is charged up to a voltage (say, 9 V), disconnecting the wire initially causes the charge to remain where it is. Where is it going to go?

A MOSFET that's turned on won't necessarily turn off when disconnected. Instead, the MOSFET gate must be connected to a different voltage (say, 0 V) to reduce the charge at the gate to the voltage level required to turn the MOSFET off.

There are plenty of sources of trivial (and not so trivial) electrical leakage in the air and on circuit boards. So, if you disconnect a MOSFET gate from a deliberate power source, such as a battery, then you're leaving the gate charge accessible and vulnerable to unknown stray voltages. The gate could just as easily trickle charge up as it could discharge down or even stay unchanged. Therefore, it's unreliable to leave a MOSFET gate disconnected. The MOSFET could switch on, switch off, oscillate (switch back and forth), or partially switch on.

This rule of never leaving a MOSFET gate disconnected holds true for all components made out of MOSFETs, such as complementary MOSFETs (CMOS) chips. CMOS-based chips usually contain the letters C, HC, VHC, or AC in their chip number, such as "74AC14."

If you've ever heard someone say "Don't leave the input floating," they're referring to this phenomenon. The input on a CMOS chip is a MOSFET gate. By leaving the input disconnected, the charge on the gate of the MOSFET in the chip can float up or down. Any circuit attached to that MOSFET might behave erratically as stray charges switch it off, switch it on, or switch it somewhat on. This generates electrical noise, uses power, and may interfere with the desired operation of the device.

Will all disconnected gates eventually cause trouble? Will the MOSFET explode? Will it kill you to leave an input floating? No. It's just that you're leaving the transistor essentially uncontrolled.

 CAUTION *Then again, this could kill you. Consider what would happen if you left the gate input of your power MOSFET motor driver disconnected and the MOSFET randomly switched the motor on. Is that motor large and heavy? Is it connected to a buzz saw?*

Because MOSFETs use virtually no power to maintain a state, there's almost no electrical cost in making sure the gate is connected to some known voltage. If you have extra input pins on a CMOS chip, simply connect them to ground if you don't have any better thoughts of what to do with them.

One final way of thinking about this is "Don't leave the gate open."

Implementing the N-Channel Power MOSFET Single-Transistor Motor-Driver Circuit

The leads on the IRLU024N power MOSFET (see Figure 10-2) are different from the leads on the 2222A bipolar transistor. Rather than a TO-92 package, the IRLU024N comes in an I-Pak ($1.11; #IRLU024N at Digi-Key) that's also compatible with a solder-less breadboard. However, if you're making your own printed circuit boards, plan on using slightly larger holes (0.046 inches) to accommodate the I-Pak instead of a TO-92 package.

Figure 10-2. IRLU024N low-resistance n-channel power MOSFET in an I-Pak package

The MOSFET circuit is implemented on a solderless breadboard (see Figure 10-3) in much the same way as the bipolar version of the circuit. The jumper wire can be connected to 9 V to turn on the motor or connected to ground (0 V) to turn off the motor.

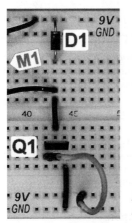

Figure 10-3. IRLU024N implemented as a motor driver on a solderless breadboard

If the jumper wire were to be disconnected, the transistor (Q1) would be left in an indeterminate state. During testing of this circuit, the gate is going to be disconnected briefly as you move one end of the jumper wire from 9 V to 0 V. There's very little consequence to doing so with a small motor and small power source. However, there's a way to avoid this situation by providing a default input value when the jumper is disconnected.

Providing a Default Input Value with a Resistor

As discussed, a MOSFET is uncontrolled if the gate is disconnected. Although a current-limiting resistor is unnecessary, you can attach a pull-up or pull-down resistor to the gate to provide a default voltage when the official control signal is disconnected.

A pull-up or pull-down resistor is just an ordinary resistor connected in a way to provide a default value. Just like you won't find "current-limiting" resistors in a parts catalog, you won't find "pull-up" or "pull-down" resistors in a parts catalog. They're just named that way to describe the function that an ordinary resistor is performing in a particular arrangement in a circuit.

Setting the Input High by Default with a Pull-Up Resistor

A pull-up resistor is a high-resistance resistor connected from the MOSFET's gate to positive voltage (see the left side of Figure 10-4). If nothing else other than the resistor is connected to the MOSFET's gate, it's easy to see that the gate receives the voltage level (say, 9 V) provided through the pull-up resistor. Therefore, the pull-up resistor is doing its job to maintain an electrical connection between the gate and some voltage, even when no other connection or signal exists.

There's no conflict if a jumper wire connects the gate to the same voltage (say, 9 V) as does the pull-up resistor. The voltage level remains unchanged (see the middle of Figure 10-4).

However, if a jumper wire provides a different voltage (say, 0 V), then the pull-up resistor's relatively weak signal is overridden (see the right of Figure 10-4). Instead of providing a 9 V signal to the gate of the transistor, current flows through the pull-up resistor into ground. The gate capacitor is also discharged to ground (0 V), turning off the MOSFET.

After a MOSFET's gate reaches the input voltage, virtually no more current flows with the pull-up resistor connected. When the jumper wire is also connected to 9 V, again no current flows. This is because conventional current flows from a higher voltage to a lower voltage. Both the pull-up resistor and jumper wire are connected to the same voltage, not a higher or lower voltage, so no current flows between them.

In these first two situations, the MOSFET motor driver remains as power efficient as when no pull-up resistor was used at all.

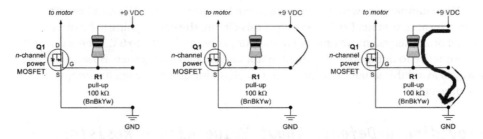

Figure 10-4. A 100 kΩ resistor connected to 9 V provides a default on signal to the n-channel transistor, even without a jumper wire or other signal being present (left). Both the pull-up resistor and jumper wire agree that the transistor should be on (middle). The jumper wire overrides the default value provided by the pull-up resistor (right). Both the gate charge and the current from the pull-up resistor flow to ground. A very small current will continuously flow from 9 V, through the pull-up resistor, into ground.

However, when the jumper wire is connected to ground, current does continually flow from 9 V, through the resistor, to ground. It's not very much current, though:

```
9 V ÷ 100,000 Ω = 0.00009 A = 0.09 mA = 90 µA
```

Therefore, using a pull-up resistor is only a little less power-efficient than not using a pull-up resistor when the control signal connects to ground.

Setting the Input Low by Default with a Pull-Down Resistor

As shown in Figure 10-5, a pull-down resistor is just like a pull-up resistor except that a pull-down resistor connects from the MOSFET's gate to ground instead of to positive voltage. The only functional difference is that it provides the opposite default signal.

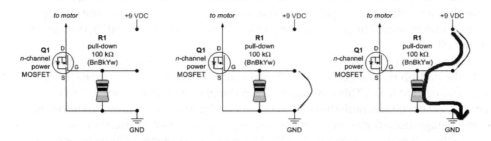

Figure 10-5. A 100 kΩ resistor connected to ground (0 V) provides a default off signal to the n-channel transistor even without a jumper wire or other control signal being present (left). Both the pull-down resistor and jumper wire agree that the transistor should be off (middle). The jumper wire overrides the default value provided by the pull-down resistor (right). The gate capacitor charges to 9 V, turning on the n-channel MOSFET. Note that a tiny current will continuously flow from 9 V, through the pull-down resistor, to ground.

Because power MOSFET's usually control heavy loads (such as motors, buzz saws, and so on), the preferred default condition is off. Therefore, a pull-down resistor would usually be the most appropriate choice for an *n*-channel power MOSFET because it'd connect the gate to ground, turning the *n*-channel MOSFET off by default.

Choosing a Value for a Pull-Up or Pull-Down Resistor

The higher the resistance of the pull-up or pull-down resistor, the less power it uses when the control signal (represented by a jumper wire) is a different voltage. Then why not make the resistor value 1 MΩ (1,000,000 Ω) and really save power?

There are several reasons to avoid choosing a really high resistance pull-up/pull-down resistor:

- The resistor must be more influential than the air, circuit board, component, and other leakages. The higher the resistance value, the less able the pull-up/pull-down resistor is in overwhelming electrical noise and leakages.

- The higher the resistance, the less current flows through the resistor. The gate of a MOSFET is a tiny capacitor. The less current that can flow through the resistor, the more time it's going to take to charge/discharge the voltage of the gate's capacitor. As the gate charge changes, the MOSFET is going to go from a fully switched on (or off) state, through a partially turned on state, to a fully switched off (or on) state. Partially turned-on MOSFETs are unsuitable in digital circuits and motor drivers. You'd like the pull-up resistor to be able to provide a reasonable current flow to set the gate charge of the transistor in a fairly short amount of time.

- *Experts only:* If you're going to use the pull-up resistor to provide the on signal and only use an open-collector chip or transistor to provide the off signal, then the pull-up resistance affects the maximum pulse-width modulation (PWM) rate (used for motor speed control) that can be achieved. At a high enough frequency, the resistor won't have had enough time to fill up the gate before the next pulse pulls the signal back down. The MOSFET will never fully turn on, and maximum power will not be achieved. My advice is to use push-pull drivers, such as the 4427, for high PWM speeds and frequencies.

- Again, as the PWM frequency increases, the time available to charge or discharge the gate capacitor decreases. To complete the charging and discharging process in a shorter time period, and to make the MOSFET transition between on and off states as quickly as possible, large currents must be able to flow into and out of the gate capacitor. Although this capacitor is typically tiny (for example, 480 pF), high-speed push-pull drivers such as the 4427 are designed to deliver up to 1.5 amps during the charge/discharge cycle.

There are several reasons to avoid choosing a really low resistance pull-up or pull-down resistor:

- The lower the resistance, the more current flows when the control signal is a different voltage than the pull-up/pull-down resistor. This is wasted power.

- Although a jumper wire is being used in these examples, the control signal is usually generated by a logic chip or microcontroller in the robot's brain circuit. The lower the resistance of the pull-up/pull-down resistor, the harder it is for the control signal to override it. In fact, if the resistor's value was really low—say, 100 Ω—few chips could override it. If the current provided by the resistor were equal to the current that the chip could provide, the MOSFET's gate would see a voltage halfway between the two voltages.

All of that being said, robot builders commonly use pull-up and pull-down resistors with resistance values between 10 kΩ and 220 kΩ. Many manufacturers use a value of 47 kΩ. I tend to use 100 kΩ. Industrial applications tend to use 10 kΩ because the cost of wasted electrical power is much cheaper than the cost of an accident in an electrically noisy industrial environment.

Because pull-up and pull-down resistors have very little current flowing through them (because of their high resistance), they can be rated for ⅛ watt or even less. Of course, ¼-watt and ½-watt (and so on) resistors work perfectly well.

The following calculations show the power wasted by a pull-up or pull-down resistor under a variety of circumstances:

```
power wasted in watts = voltage² ÷ resistance
Worst case example: power wasted in watts = 20 V² ÷ 10,000 Ω = 0.04 W
Ordinary case example: power wasted in watts = 12 V² ÷ 100,000 Ω = 0.00144 W
Best case example: power wasted in watts = 9 V² ÷ 220,000 Ω = 0.000368 W
Logic chip example: power wasted in watts = 5 V² ÷ 100,000 Ω = 0.00025 W
```

As you can see by the previous calculations, a ⅛-watt resistor (0.125 W) is more than adequately rated for these pull-up/pull-down usages.

Choosing Between No Resistor, a Pull-Up Resistor, or a Pull-Down Resistor

If the transistor's gate is never going to be electrically disconnected from the control signal, then there's no reason to use a pull-up or pull-down resistor.

Note, however, that most microcontrollers take longer to power up than the rest of the circuit and that most microcontrollers' pins are in a "disconnected" state (input, high-z, or tri-state) until the software has had a chance to initialize the pins. Therefore, if the motor driver connects to a microcontroller, then use pull-up/pull-down resistors on the motor driver inputs to set the desired default values.

Stabilizing Motors at Power-Up

Choose pull-up and pull-down resistors that set the H-bridge into either brake mode or coast mode by default. Obviously, avoid a default setting that places the H-bridge into a short circuit (either the robot won't power up or it'll have a smoky power-up) or that provides power to the motors (runaway robot).

I've seen plenty of robots that jerk a little bit when the power switch is first turned on. This is usually because of the builder choosing either no default values (random or essentially uncontrolled motor driver because of the lack of pull-up or pull-down resistors) or the wrong default values for the motor driver. Then, a few microseconds after power-up, the microcontroller wakes up and sets the motor driver to the correct idle state.

Throughout this book, I've selected a pull-up or pull-down resistor wherever appropriate to provide either a coast mode or a brake mode for the motor driver.

Safeguarding Subcircuits, Cables, Connectors, and Daughter Boards

Another good location for pull-up and pull-down resistors is anywhere an input cable or input connector attaches. That way, if the cable should become disconnected or shake loose intermittently because of vibrations, then the pull-up/pull-down resistors will assert safe input values automatically. This also allows a board to be separated from the rest of the robot for independent testing.

Reducing Noise and Power Consumption on Unused Inputs

Another good place for pull-up and pull-down resistors is on any unused inputs on a chip. Because the pull-up/pull-down resistors keep the gate in a steady state, the chip's internal MOSFET transistors associated with those unused inputs will consume almost no power. And because the transistors aren't switching back and forth (oscillating), less electrical noise is generated.

It's no big deal if you should decide to use those inputs later. The newly attached control signals will override the default values provided by the pull-up or pull-down resistors.

Revising the N-Channel Power MOSFET Single-Transistor Motor-Driver Circuit to Include a Pull-Down Resistor

Adding a pull-down resistor (R1) to the *n*-channel power MOSFET motor-driver circuit (see Figure 10-6) ensures that the motor stays off until a control signal turns it on. When turned on, this version of the circuit is only slightly less efficient because of the current that drains through R1 to ground, but, as noted previously, it's not significant.

Updating the earlier circuit on the solderless breadboard is as easy as adding a single 100 kΩ resistor from the transistor's gate to ground (look ahead to Figure 10-7). Now the motor automatically turns off when the jumper wire (representing the control signal) is removed.

One important thing to note in Figure 10-6 is that although the positive voltage connected to the motor can be up to 20 V (no more because of the limit of the 1N5817 diode), the maximum voltage that can be applied to the gate of Q1 is only 16 V because of the limits of IRLU024N. If you'd prefer a circuit with higher limits, you can replace D1 (in the datasheets, look for the maximum reverse voltage) and Q1 (in the datasheets, look for maximum V_{GS} or gate-source voltage) with higher-rated components.

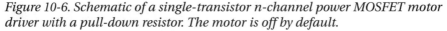

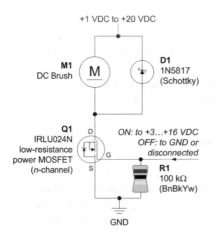

Figure 10-6. Schematic of a single-transistor n-channel power MOSFET motor driver with a pull-down resistor. The motor is off by default.

Notice also that the motor voltage can be as low as 1 V, but the gate of Q1 still requires at least 3 V to turn on. This isn't an error in the schematic. The MOSFET's gate simply requires a particular minimum voltage to reasonably turn on (about 3 V for a logic-level MOSFET or 5 V to 10 V for a standard MOSFET). For example, this circuit would work fine for a pager motor that's receiving 1.5 V from a single-cell battery, driven by a logic-level *n*-channel power MOSFET connected to a 3.3 V or 5 V logic circuit.

Implementing the N-Channel Power MOSFET Single-Transistor Motor-Driver Circuit with a Pull-Down Resistor

If you placed your components on a solder breadboard as shown in the earlier example, a pull-down resistor (R1) fits nicely in the lower left corner (see Figure 10-7).

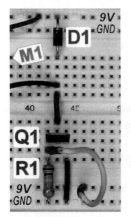

Figure 10-7. As implemented on a solderless breadboard, this single-transistor n-channel power MOSFET motor driver has a pull-down resistor (R1 is a 100 kΩ resistor connected from the transistor's gate to ground) so that the motor is off by default. However, in this figure, the jumper wire (in the lower-right corner) is connected to 9 V and is overriding the pull-down resistor, so the motor is turned on.

Introducing the P-Channel Power MOSFET Single-Transistor Motor-Driver Circuit

There are two types of simple bipolar transistors, the NPN and the PNP. Therefore, it shouldn't come as too much of a surprise that the *n*-channel MOSFET is complemented by the *p*-channel MOSFET. Just like the bipolar PNP, the *p*-channel MOSFET can be used on the high side of a motor (see Figure 10-8).

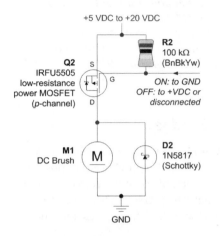

Figure 10-8. *Schematic of a single-transistor p-channel power MOSFET motor driver with pull-up resistor so that the motor is off by default*

A pull-up resistor (R2) is included in the circuit so that the transistor (and thus the motor) is turned off by default. You can simply remove the resistor if a control signal will always be driving the transistor's gate voltage high or low.

Keep the resistor in the circuit if you're going to use an NPN bipolar transistor, an open-collector chip, or an *n*-channel MOSFET to interface Q2 to logic-level voltages (recall Figure 9-21 in the previous chapter). That's because each of those interface methods disconnects the control signal to enter an off state. Disconnection works fine for turning off a bipolar transistor, but a pull-up resistor is required for a MOSFET to bring the *p*-channel transistor's gate up to the proper voltage level to turn it off.

Implementing the P-Channel Power MOSFET Single-Transistor Motor-Driver Circuit

Chapter 7 introduced the IRFU5505 for reverse-battery protection. You'll reuse that part here as a motor driver.

When the *p*-channel MOSFET motor-driver circuit (see Figure 10-9) receives only 5 V and the gate is grounded, the IRFU5505 can easily provide as much current as the 2907A. However, at 6.5 V, the IRFU5505 can easily provide ten times the amount of current as the 2907A. With a 9 V battery and a grounded gate, the IRFU5505 is almost fully turned on.

Figure 10-9. As implemented on a solderless breadboard, this single-transistor p-channel power MOSFET motor driver has a pull-up resistor (R2 is a 100 kΩ resistor connected from the gate to 9 V) so that the motor is off by default. However, in this figure, the jumper wire (in the upper-left corner) is connected to ground (0 V) and is overriding the pull-up resistor, so the motor is turned on.

Introducing the Power MOSFET H-Bridge

The power MOSFET H-bridge (see Figure 10-10) is similar to the bipolar H-bridge. A *p*-channel (high side) and *n*-channel (low side) power MOSFET provide either positive voltage or ground to one motor terminal, and another pair of MOSFETs provides either positive voltage or ground to the other motor terminal. The MOSFET H-bridge provides the same motor modes (clockwise, counterclockwise, brake, coast) as does the bipolar H-bridge.

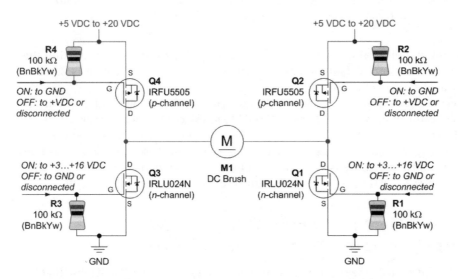

Figure 10-10. Schematic of an H-bridge consisting of p-channel and n-channel power MOSFETs. Pull-up (R2 and R4) and pull-down (R1 and R3) resistors turn all of the transistors off by default so that the motor is in coast mode.

Adding Schottky Diodes Is Optional but Recommended

Unlike the bipolar H-bridge, discrete *flyback* diodes aren't absolutely required in a power MOSFET H-bridge because the power MOSFETs include diodes as part of their semiconductor structure. The diodes within the power MOSFETs are called *body diodes* and are shown in the schematic symbols (see Figure 10-11).

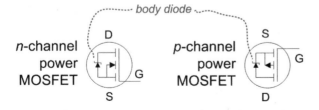

Figure 10-11. Both the n-channel (left) and p-channel (right) power MOSFETs include a diode intrinsic to their internal structure.

Because the MOSFET's body diodes are in the same location and the same orientation as the Schottky diodes in the bipolar version of the H-bridge, the Schottky diodes are no longer required to handle reverse motor currents.

You can still add Schottky diodes back into the circuit if you so desire. Schottky diodes require approximately half the voltage to turn on than do MOSFET body diodes. Because the Schottky diodes will consume all or nearly all of the reverse motor current, the MOSFETs will not heat up as much. All in all, the addition of Schottky diodes will result in less energy loss and a slight improvement in performance.

Having built-in diodes means you need to be careful about how you insert or wire a power MOSFET in a circuit. In Figure 10-11, note the opposite locations of source (S) and drain (D) in relation to the body diode in *n*-channel versus *p*-channel MOSFETs. If you insert or wire a power MOSFET backward, the power will rush through the body diode. Such a mistake would seriously mess up a motor-driver circuit. Conversely, the forward-biased body diode is beneficially employed in the reverse-battery protection circuit (shown way back in Figure 7-6).

Implementing the Power MOSFET H-Bridge

The IRLU024N and IRFU5505 power MOSFET H-bridge can be fairly compact on a solderless breadboard (see Figure 10-12). Notice that only one jumper wire is used on each side of the H-bridge to prevent short circuits. The pull-up and pull-down resistors turn off any transistors not connected to a jumper wire.

Figure 10-12. H-bridge implemented on solderless breadboard with IRLU024N n-channel and IRFU5505 p-channel power MOSFETs

Interfacing to a Power MOSFET H-Bridge

Just like the PNP transistors in the bipolar H-bridge, the high-side (*p*-channel) transistors in the power MOSFET H-bridge must be brought up to the positive power voltage to be turned off. Just like with a bipolar H-bridge, you can use an open-collector chip, NPN bipolar transistors, or *n*-channel MOSFETs to drive the high-side gates of the MOSFET H-bridge from logic-level voltages. However, I prefer the 4427 chip for this purpose (see Figure 10-13).

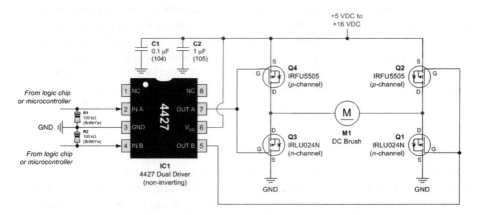

Figure 10-13. Schematic of a power MOSFET H-bridge interfaced via a 4427. This circuit has a shoot-through problem.

Notice that the pull-up and pull-down resistors have been removed from the gates of the transistors in this circuit. That's because the 4427 is always active and connected to the gates of the transistors, so no default values are necessary. However, two pull-down resistors have been added to the inputs of the 4427, so the motor-driver circuit will be in brake mode by default at power-up. If the microcontroller dawdles a bit in asserting its outputs, the motor driver and motors will be waiting patiently in an "idle" state.

Also worth noting is that the maximum voltage that this circuit can handle is now only 16 V because the 4427 provides this voltage to the gates of the transistors, and the gates of the IRLU024Ns (Q1 and Q3) can handle only 16 V.

Adding Capacitors to Support Rapid Charging and Discharging of the Power MOSFETs Gates

The tiny capacitors at the gates of the power MOSFETs can have a large enough capacitance that they can't be entirely ignored or dismissed. In this case, the capacitance is equivalent to about 1 nF per side of the H-bridge. The 4427 has to charge and discharge those capacitors every time the H-bridge changes motor modes. As such, it's helpful to have some power-supply capacitors nearby to provide bursts of power.

C1 is the standard one-per-chip-recommended 0.1 μF monolithic ceramic bypass/decoupling capacitor. C2 is a higher-value, 1 μF capacitor to provide power for charging and discharging the gates. Something fast such as a plastic film capacitor would be a good choice. Also, if your robot isn't using a large value (greater than or equal to 220 μF) bulk capacitor on the input to the voltage regulator, then be sure to add a bulk capacitor near this motor circuit.

Exposing a Flaw: Shoot-Through

There's a flaw in the circuit in Figure 10-13. Because both a high-side (*p*-channel) gate and a low-side (*n*-channel) gate are driven by a single signal voltage from the 4427, there's a short period of time that the *p*-channel and *n*-channel transistors are active at the same time.

For example, with a 16 V power supply there will be a moment when both the *p*-channel gate and the *n*-channel gate reach 8 V at approximately the same time. Eight-volt gates with a 16 V power supply is an on condition for both transistors. When both transistors on one side of an H-bridge are enabled, that's a short circuit! This condition is called *shoot-through*.

The shoot-through could be present for 1 to 25 nanoseconds, depending on a lot of variables. Replacing the 4427 chip with an IXDF404PI chip (1.5 Ω of resistance) decreases the shoot-through time because of the superior current output of the IXDNF404PI. Selecting MOSFETs with lower gate capacitances will also reduce shoot-through time.

The shoot-through problem isn't the kiss of death. In practice, connecting the gates of an *n*-channel and *p*-channel MOSFET usually functions adequately, despite brief moments of shoot-through. However, if the motor state is changed often (such as with PWM or a robot that changes directions a lot), use a design such as Figure 10-15 to avoid shoot-through.

Implementing the Power MOSFET H-Bridge with a Single 4427 Interface

In less active robots, I've actually implemented H-bridges with the gates of an
n-channel MOSFET and a *p*-channel MOSFET tied together (see Figure 10-14). This
simplified the circuitry, reduced cost, and reduced board space. Shoot-through wasn't
a significant enough factor in these types of robots to be concerned.

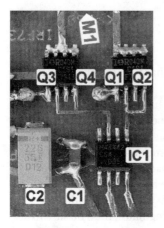

*Figure 10-14. The surface-mount version of the
Maxim MAX4427 interfacing to a pair of combination
n-channel/p-channel chips (IRF7343) on a robot. Each
IRF7343 chip contains an independent n-channel
and p-channel power MOSFET, packaged together for
convenience.*

Using Two Interface Chips Eliminates Shoot-Through and Adds Complete Motor Control

You can eliminate shoot-through by using a pair of 4427 chips (see Figure 10-15). You
can now control each gate of the H-bridge individually. This has an additional advantage of being able to select motor coast mode by turning off all of the transistors at the
same time.

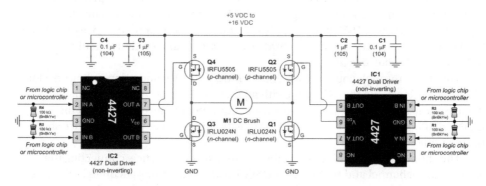

*Figure 10-15. A discrete complementary power MOSFET H-bridge driven by two
4427 MOSFET driver interface chips*

By turning off one transistor before turning on the other, no shoot-through can
occur. Furthermore, a pause (*dead time*) can be programmed to occur between

switching off one transistor and switching on the other transistor. This allows all of the switching transients from the motor to be discharged through the diodes. There-fore, current flow completely stops before a reverse voltage is supplied through the opposite two transistors.

There are some downsides to using a pair of 4427s besides price and added circuit complexity. First, you now need to control four lines per motor instead of two. That's bothersome because typically a robot builder is always running out of spare output pins on their microcontrollers. Second, the short-circuit combinations of enabled transistors are no longer prevented by the interface chip. That means all of the H-bridge short-circuit combinations must be avoided by the microcontroller. A PPTC current-limiting device on the power supply (see Chapter 8) and pull-down resistors on the 4427 inputs make the circuit safer.

Selecting Power MOSFETs

Power MOSFET technology is improving rapidly. Prices are decreasing, and capabilities are increasing. You should consider a number of factors when selecting a power MOSFET for your motor driver:

Price: Power MOSFETs aren't inexpensive. They can range from about $0.40 to $3 each. That can make a homemade discrete H-bridge fairly expensive.

Package: Power MOSFETs are available in many varieties of through-hole and surface-mount packages. Through-hole packages tend to dissipate heat much better than surface-mount packages. But if your robot's motors aren't drawing much current, a surface-mount package is just fine.

V_{DS} (also called $V_{(BR)DSS}$ or V_{DSS}): Drain-to-source breakdown voltage is the maximum power-supply voltage that the transistor permits. Obviously, a V_{DS} of 20 V wouldn't be acceptable for a robot whose motors are powered by 24 V. But a V_{DS} of 20 V for a 9 V robot is fine. Although silly, a V_{DS} of 100 V would work for a 12 V robot, but you could probably select a MOSFET with other superior characteristics in exchange for a lower V_{DS} in this example.

V_{GS}: The voltage at which the transistor starts to turn on. Generally speaking, the lower, the better. Power MOSFETs labeled "logic-level" can be controlled by voltage levels of standard logic chips. In exchange for being "logic-level," the maximum voltage the gate can accept is usually lower. For a robot with a power supply of less than 10 V, logic-level power MOSFETs are a good choice. Otherwise, standard power MOSFETs are a better choice because they permit the use of higher operating voltages.

C_{ISS}: This is input gate capacitance. The lower, the better. The lower the gate capacitance and inductance, the faster the power MOSFET can be switched on and off, with lower power expenditures. If your robot doesn't use a pulsing method of controlling motor speed and shoot-through isn't a problem, then gate capacitance doesn't matter that much. *Experts*: Capacitance isn't the only factor that limits pulse speed. Inductance also plays a significant role.

I_D **and** I_{DM}: These are maximum continuous current and maximum pulsed current, respectively. The higher, the better. This is the theoretical maximum amount of current that can be supplied to the motor through the transistor. Be careful when looking at a datasheet to not mentally transpose the two values. Your design limits should be based on I_D. These numbers are fine for comparison purposes, but it's likely your circuit board and the transistors will melt from heat build-up if you attempt to supply this current continuously. Use the maximum current rating for only brief surges. Use parallel MOSFETs (explained a little later in this chapter) and heat reduction techniques (fans and heat sinks) to increase the maximum current your motor driver can safely handle.

$R_{DS(on)}$: This is the resistance of the transistor in ohms (or milliohms) when turned on. The lower, the better. Assuming the transistor meets the first three requirements (price, package, and maximum voltage), the on resistance of the transistor is the most important characteristic.

Reducing Switch Resistance Is Desirable

An ideal motor-driver switch would have no resistance whatsoever when turned on. In that case, all of the voltage from one end of the battery to the other end of the battery would be provided to the motor.

On the other hand, if you were to place a resistor between the battery and one end of the motor, the voltage would be divided between the motor and the resistor. The higher the resistance of the resistor, the more voltage it'll get and the less voltage the motor will receive. Recall that motors produce greater physical power with greater voltage. So, having resistance between the battery and the motor is undesirable.

In addition, resistors limit current. This means a resistor between the battery and the motor would limit the maximum current that the motor could draw. If the motor doesn't require much current and the resistor value is small (thus not limiting current too much), then the current-limiting effect of the resistor wouldn't be significant. However, if the resistor's value is large enough, the motor may not start (recall that a motor consumes the largest current at start-up and stall), or the motor may not continue to turn, even if started by hand.

Lastly, a resistor transforms current into heat. The more current that flows through a resistor, or the more voltage that drops across it, the hotter it's going to get. If you double the current through a resistor (or double the voltage drop across it), the resistor produces *four* times as much heat (wasting four times as much power).

Recognizing That MOSFETs Have Resistance

Getting back to MOSFETs, one of the most important specifications to examine when selecting a power MOSFET for motor driving is the amount of resistance between the drain and source leads. This resistance is called R_{DS}. R stands for *resistance*, D stands for *drain*, and S stands for *source*. This resistance is just like having a resistor between the motor and the battery.

Within the operating limits of the transistor, the higher the voltage applied between the gate and source of the power MOSFET, the lower the resistance of the switched path between the drain and source. So, even if it's possible to turn on a logic-level power MOSFET with only 2 V, it's preferable to drive the MOSFET with a higher voltage because the resistance (R_{DS}) decreases and more current will be available for the motor to convert to mechanical power.

Heating Up Increases a MOSFET's Resistance

A resistor expends power as heat. Because a MOSFET has some resistance (R_{DS}), the current flowing through the MOSFET generates heat within the MOSFET itself. If the MOSFET's package is unable to dissipate heat (through the air or through circuit board traces) as quickly as the heat is being generated, the MOSFET's temperature rises. Of course, the lower the resistance of the MOSFET, the less heat is generated in the first place.

And now for the maddening twist: As a MOSFET heats up, its resistance increases! That means even less power is delivered to the motor. So, keep heavily loaded MOSFETs cool with heat sinks, plenty of space, and air flow (fans). Such measures are unnecessary with relatively small motors because the MOSFET's package will likely be able to dissipate heat as quickly as it builds up. (The MOSFET remains cool to the touch.)

CAUTION *Always use extreme care when touching a potentially hot surface. ChiBots guru Don Kerste says, "My granny always wet the tip of her finger just before tapping an iron to see if it was hot."*

Paralleling MOSFETs Decreases Resistance

A popular trick with MOSFETs is to place more than one at each switch point. For example, in the single-transistor *n*-channel power MOSFET motor driver, you could add a second *n*-channel power MOSFET with the identical connections (drain, source, and gate) as the first power MOSFET (see Figure 10-16).

NOTE *For low-power hobbyist applications, this section on paralleling MOSFETs is adequate. But be aware that you must master many other factors and details to truly derive the full theoretical benefits of parallel MOSFETs, especially in higher-power situations.*

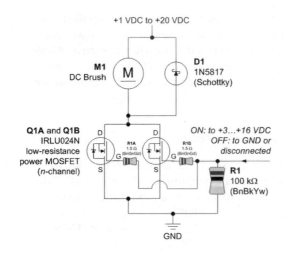

Figure 10-16. An n-channel power MOSFET motor driver with parallel MOSFETs resulting in about half the resistance. This results in approximately half the heat build-up in each MOSFET, or a total current-carrying capability of almost double. Resistors R1A and R1B (1.5 Ω) are optional to ensure the control current is shared.

TIP *A resistor between 1.5 Ω and 3 Ω is commonly added at the gate of each paralleled MOSFET to ensure they share the control current as they're switched on and off. Otherwise, one MOSFET will likely engage earlier than the other, thus not producing the intended compound capabilities at a critical time (motor start-up).*

Just like with parallel resistors, the resistance of two equal MOSFETs is half the original value:

```
equivalent resistance in ohms = R_DS ÷ 2
equivalent resistance in ohms = 0.11 Ω [maximum for IRLU024N] ÷ 2
equivalent resistance in ohms = 0.055 Ω
```

A lower resistance results in more power delivered to the motor!

An additional advantage of parallel MOSFETs is that each MOSFET has to carry only a portion of the current. So, parallel MOSFETs can supply a greater maximum current than a single MOSFET (assuming all of the MOSFETs are the same part).

Because each parallel MOSFET is providing only a portion of the power, each MOSFET has to dissipate only a portion of the heat. Because each MOSFET stays cooler, their resistance stays lower.

Of course, you can add even more power MOSFETs in parallel to further decrease resistance, increase maximum current capability, and reduce heat build-up. Theoretically, you can extend this setup infinitely:

```
equivalent resistance in ohms = 1 ÷ ( (1 ÷ R_DS Q1A) + (1 ÷ R_DS Q1B) + (1 ÷ R_DS Q1C)
                        + and so on )
```

As you can see, the effective resistance of parallel MOSFETs decreases with each additional MOSFET. In fact, sometimes it's cheaper to buy a bunch of inexpensive power MOSFETs that have a relatively high R_{DS} and place them in parallel than to buy a single expensive power MOSFET with a very low R_{DS}.

Adding parallel MOSFETs isn't just limited to the "single-transistor" circuit. For example, you can build an H-bridge with four power MOSFETs with eight power MOSFETs (two in each location). For technological reasons, *n*-channel MOSFETs are available with lower resistances than *p*-channel MOSFETs at the same price. Therefore, you might decide to parallel only the *p*-channel transistors in an H-bridge if the *n*-channel transistors already have a decent enough R_{DS}. In that case, you could build an H-bridge with six power MOSFETs: two single low-side (*n*-channel) transistors and two pairs of parallel high-side (*p*-channel) transistors. Or, you might even choose to parallel only the transistors that are turned on when the robot is driving forward, figuring reverse is less often used and can be less efficient.

The downsides of using parallel MOSFETs are the following: The cost is higher, more space is needed, and the total gate capacitance is increased because all the little gate capacitors need to be driven. The increase in gate capacitance decreases the maximum switching rate and increases power consumption during switching. I recommend adding a C1 and C2 power-supply capacitor to each 4427 driver chip per each added parallel power MOSFET.

Contrasting Parallel MOSFET Transistors with Parallel Bipolar Transistors

The positive temperature coefficient (resistance increases with temperature) of MOSFETs is the reason you can place MOSFETs in parallel. Because the first MOSFET heats up more than the second MOSFET, the resistance of the first MOSFET increases. This causes less current to flow through the first (more resistant) MOSFET and more current to flow through the second (less resistant) MOSFET. Now the second MOSFET begins to increase in resistance because of the heat of the increased current load, and the first MOSFET begins to decrease in resistance because of the reduced heat from the decreased load. The MOSFETs self-balance their resistance and current load. In this way, they share the load automatically.

On the other hand, as a bipolar transistor heats up, its resistance decreases (negative temperature coefficient). As such, a pair of bipolar transistors can't share the load. Whichever bipolar transistor starts with a slightly lower resistance will receive a slightly higher current flow. This higher current flow leads to greater heating, which leads to a lower resistance, which leads to a higher current flow, and so on, until that transistor is performing all of the work. This is called *thermal runaway*. Therefore, you can't parallel bipolar transistors to increase the maximum current delivery.

Driving Motors with Chips

About half of my robots have custom-designed H-bridges made out of individual discrete transistors. Sometimes I built the discrete H-bridges for fun. Other times I built them to meet a specific need of an unusual robot, such as a low voltage (such as less than 3 V) for which commercial motor-driver chips weren't readily available.

Many times it's easier to use a complete manufactured motor-driver chip rather than build your own H-bridge. Commercial motor-driver chips have more complex features (sometimes), have simpler controls (sometimes), take up less space (sometimes), cost less (sometimes), and are faster to design and solder into a robot. If you prefer not to build your own H-bridge, then commercial motor-driver chips are a good choice.

If you're really not interested in motor-driving technology at all, you can even find modules with motor connectors and motor chips installed and ready to run. That is, someone takes a motor-driver chip, designs a circuit board around it, adds any necessary remaining parts (such as capacitors and connectors), and solders it all together; all you need to do is plug it into your robot.

Unfortunately, many motor-driver chips and motor-driver boards seem to come and go over the years, so it isn't worth recommending specific part numbers in a book. Instead, I've decided to present three totally different motor-driver chips as examples of the types of choices available, along with some criteria for evaluating any motor driver you run across. I'll concentrate on an altered-use chip (4427), a simple bipolar chip (SN754410), and an integrated MOSFET chip with all the bells and whistles (MC33887).

Dreaming of the Ideal

Because there are many different kinds of motors for many different kinds of tasks, there are many kinds of motor drivers for those many kinds of motors. Which motor driver you choose depends upon the motor and the task.

In a perfect world, a motor driver would do the following:

- Accept inputs from the robot's brain at the low voltages and currents common to logic chips and microcontrollers.

- Allow the robot to command the motor in all four modes: clockwise, counterclockwise, brake, and coast.

- Provide speed control.

- Control multiple motors.

- Provide outputs up to the highest voltages and currents needed by the motor.

- Isolate the robot's brain from electrical noise and motor faults.

- Protect the motor and motor driver from overheating and self-destruction.

- Optionally allow use of a heavy-duty power source separate from the one being used for the logic chips (such as a separate motor battery pack).

- Provide feedback to the robot's brain on motor power consumption and operation, including any fault conditions.

- Independently revert to a safe mode when the robot's brain isn't in control, such as during power-up, during shutdown, during resets, or in case of a communication disconnect.

- Consume very little power for its own operations.

- Generate very little heat.

- Be in the smallest, least complicated packaging. Sometimes the small, surface-mount packages are more complicated than an old-fashioned DIP.

- Require few, if any, additional components.

- Be inexpensive, in production, and readily available.

Ha, ha, ha! Few commercial motor-driver chips come close to matching this wish list. You'll have to compromise.

Using the 4427-Family As a Stand-Alone Motor Driver

Interestingly, you can use many chips as low-current motor drivers even if that wasn't their intended purpose. In fact, a 74AC240 inverting buffer chip powers many BEAM robots.

TIP *CMOS chips contain MOSFET transistors, which can be used in parallel. The outputs of MOSFET transistors in a chip can be tied together to drive a load in parallel. For example, in the eight-inverter 74AC240 chip, half of the inverter inputs could be wired together, and their associated outputs could be wired together. The other half of the inverter inputs could be wired together, and the other half of the outputs could be wired together. This would create two inputs and two outputs, with the two outputs being able to drive 100 mA each. The two tri-state (enable) pins disconnect the outputs so that coast mode would also be available. It's now a miniature H-bridge.*

Even though it wasn't their intended purpose, the chips in the 4427 MOSFET driver family (4427A, 4424, IXDN404PI, IR4427, TPS2812P, and so on) can be used as stand-alone motor drivers without any additional discrete transistors. For example, the 4427A has two logic-level inputs, outputs up to 18 V, pulsed output currents up to 1.5 amps (but can't drive motor currents that high), and provides two outputs that can go high or low like two halves of an H-bridge (see Figure 10-17).

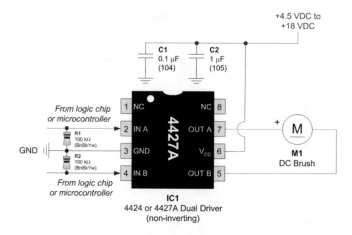

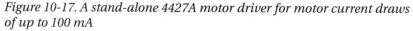

Figure 10-17. A stand-alone 4427A motor driver for motor current draws of up to 100 mA

The body diodes in the MOSFET outputs of the 4427A can handle the reverse currents of a small DC motor, so no Schottky diodes are necessary. However, avoid the plain 4427 chip; you should use the 4427A (or one of the other chips) in the circuit shown in Figure 10-17 to prevent reverse motor voltages from damaging the chip.

For motors that draw less than 100 mA of current, the 4427A works just fine. But the 4424 chip is better, and the IXDN404PI is the best in that same circuit. Remember, they're all pin-compatible, so you can test performance yourself. The reason for the difference in performance is because of the differences in output resistance.

The 4427A has a relatively high resistance of between 7 Ω and 10 Ω per output. Because a pair of outputs are needed to drive a motor, that's like having a 20 Ω resistor between the motor and the battery. Compare that with the combined resistance of an IRLU024N (0.065 Ω to 0.11 Ω) and an IRFU5505 (0.11 Ω) power MOSFET, and you'll see the 4427A has approximately 100 times the resistance. You're trading excellent performance (power MOSFETs) for simplicity (4427A by itself) and lower cost.

The relatively high resistance (R_{DS}) of the 4427A outputs (10 Ω) means that at some point, with a motor that draws enough current, the chip will dissipate more power itself than will reach the motor. The motor won't start, and the chip will overheat. Also, because higher-current motors generate higher-reverse currents when stopped or switched, the lack of discrete diodes in Figure 10-17 starts becoming more worrisome.

With optional Schottky diodes and an IXDN404PI chip, Figure 10-18 is a superior circuit for motors drawing less than 1 amp at up to 25 V. However, the circuit remains fairly simple and inexpensive.

The stand-alone IXDN404PI provides a decent, easy-to-control motor driver in a small amount of space with a reasonably small number of parts. In fact, Figure 10-19 is from the board of Roundabout, the robot presented in detail starting in Chapter 13. This particular implementation didn't need pull-down resistors on the controller inputs because it's always connected directly to the outputs of a logic chip.

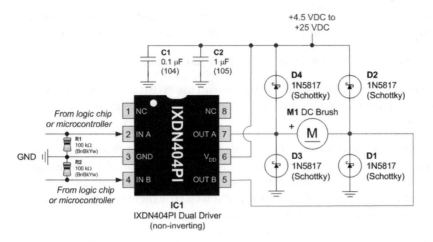

Figure 10-18. A stand-alone IXDN404PI motor driver with optional Schottky diodes

Figure 10-19. Implementation of a stand-alone IXDN404PI motor driver with optional Schottky diodes. The motor connects to the motor-driver board with a removable Molex connector (M1).

Getting the Classic Bipolar H-Bridge on a Chip

Instead of hacking a CMOS logic chip or a MOSFET driver chip, perhaps you'd prefer a chip purposefully designed for driving motors. Let's start with a bipolar motor-driver chip.

There's nothing wrong with a robot that uses the discrete bipolar H-bridge circuit presented back in Figure 9-14. It's a perfectly usable motor driver. But you could make a couple of desirable improvements:

- You could integrate the whole circuit into a single chip to save time, to reduce space, and to avoid wiring mistakes. Actually, why not put two H-bridges onto the same chip so that two motors can be controlled because most robots have at least two motors?

- You could reduce the number of inputs required to control the H-bridge to three or two lines instead of four, and the short-circuit states could be prevented.

- You could increase the maximum current beyond 500 mA.

- You could reduce the voltage needed to turn off the PNP transistors from 9 V to something more compatible with 5 V chips (one solution was presented in Figure 9-23).

The Texas Instruments SN754410 Quadruple Half-H Driver ($2.70 to $5; #R6-754410 at Acroname and #296-9911-5 at Digi-Key) chip includes all of the features just mentioned. It's the pin-compatible successor of the classic L293 and L293D. You can use the four half-H drivers independently, or you can use them in pairs to make two full H-bridges to drive two motors (see Figure 10-20).

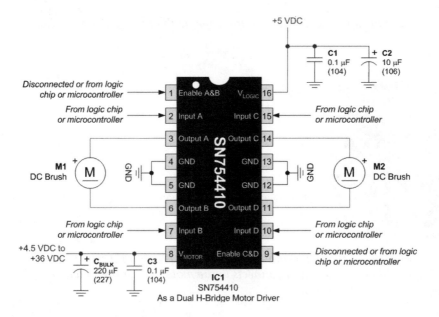

Figure 10-20. Driving two motors using the SN754410. The 220µF bulk capacitor (C_{BULK}) isn't necessary if there's already an unregulated bulk capacitor at the input of the voltage regulator circuit. As always, I tend to add more capacitors than the manufacturer officially requires.

NOTE *I've taken the liberty to slightly rename some of the pins on the SN754410 chip for clarity because the datasheet has unintuitive labels.*

With the SN754410, you get *two* complete motor drivers in a convenient 16-pin DIP that run from 4.5 V up to 36 V. Between that and the low price, this chip is popular in the amateur robotics community.

The SN754410 provides access to all four motor modes (see Table 10-1) and avoids short circuits. It has built-in diodes at the outputs and thermal-overload protection.

Table 10-1. SN754410 H-Bridge Motor-Driver Combinations

Enable A&B	Input A	Input B	Result
0 V	0 V	0 V	Coast
0 V	0 V	5 V	Coast
0 V	5 V	0 V	Coast
0 V	5 V	5 V	Coast (I found this to be the lowest power usage—about 11mA)
5 V	0 V	0 V	Brake both directions (low side)
5 V	0 V	5 V	Spin counterclockwise
5 V	5 V	0 V	Spin clockwise
5 V	5 V	5 V	Brake both directions (high side)

Unfortunately, as you'll see in the head-to-head competition later in "Evaluating Motor Drivers," the SN754410 doesn't provide maximum power output to the motors. Additionally, the SN754410 consumes up to 100 mA of current for its own use (quiescent current). So, it's not particularly efficient.

Neither of these issues should dissuade you from using the SN754410 chip in a robot. Just plan your battery pack and motor power accordingly.

Introducing the MC33887: A Feature-Rich MOSFET H-Bridge Motor Driver

In contrast to the simple motor drivers presented so far, the Motorola (http://e-www.motorola.com/) MC33887 is all that and the kitchen sink!

The MC33887 runs from 5 V to 28 V, with logic-compatible inputs. It can continuously deliver up to 5.2 amps with an R_{DS} typically of only 0.12 Ω. It provides motor current usage and fault feedback information. It protects against overcurrent, overtemperature, undervoltage, and disconnected inputs. It can enter a sleep mode that consumes less than 50 μA. It provides all motor modes (clockwise, counterclockwise, brake, and coast) while preventing shoot-through and short circuits. It can even run motors off a completely different battery pack than the logic circuits, if desired.

No discrete Schottky diodes are necessary, but you could add them to slightly improve performance.

If the MC33887 can be faulted for anything, it's that it can't be pulsed (PWM) at more than 10 kHz, it controls only one motor, and it isn't available in a through-hole package. Looking at the schematic (see Figure 10-21), you may consider the complexity to be a fault. In all fairness, most of the pins can be connected to 5 V, ground (GND), or left disconnected if their associated features are unnecessary for your particular robot.

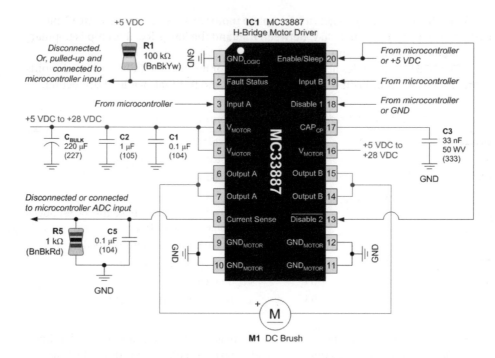

Figure 10-21. Driving a motor with the MC33887 with all of the features. To save space in the schematic, instead of saying "From logic chips or microcontroller," it just says "From microcontroller." However, don't misundertand—logic chips can control this motor-driver chip just fine.

If you wanted a simple setup without motor feedback, sleep, or fast pulsing, you could do the following:

- **No sleep**: Connect Enable (pin 20) and Disable 2 (pin 13) to 5 V. The chip will always use 20 mA or less while running or idle. The chip will no longer be able to be powered down to less than 50 µA.

- **No feedback**: Disconnect Fault Status (pin 2) and Current Sense (pin 8). This also eliminates the need for R1, R5, and C5.

- **No fast pulsing**: C3 isn't necessary if you don't plan to pulse the motor rapidly.

- **Bulk capacitor**: C_{BULK} isn't necessary if you already have a large, unregulated capacitor connected to the input of the voltage regulator.

The previous changes result in Figure 10-22. Only three control lines are needed to fully control a motor. You can even make the circuit simpler if you don't need motor coast mode by connecting Disable 1 (pin 18) to ground. Then, only two control lines are needed.

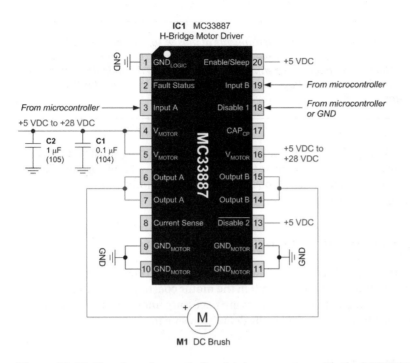

Figure 10-22. Simpler schematic for driving a motor with the MC33887 without feedback, sleep, or fast pulsing

Understanding the Pins

The MC33887 comes in a 20-pin heat-sinked small outline package (HSOP) surface-mount package ($6.73; #MC33887DH at Digi-Key) that has large enough pins to hand solder. The pins on the 54-pin SOIC package are just a little too skinny for me.

Built into the 20-pin HSOP package is a large heat sink on the underside of the chip. You can place a matching trace on the printed circuit board to assist in wicking away heat. None of my robots need 5.2 amps of continuous power. As such, I would've preferred that the underside of the chip package had remained nonconductive so that I could've run logic traces underneath. Of course, you can paint the bottom of the chip or insert an insulating sheet if you desire to run traces directly underneath the chip.

Twenty pins seems like a lot. It can be overwhelming. However, pins 1, 9, 10, 11, and 12 all connect to ground. Pins 4, 5, and 16 all connect to the motor's power supply. And pins 6 and 7 and pins 14 and 15 are pairs connected to the motor. So, after eliminating duplicates, this is more like a 12-pin chip, without eliminating any of the features.

TIP *Actually, pin 1 isn't exactly a duplicate of pins 9, 10, 11, and 12. Pin 1 can be connected to a different battery pack ground for the logic circuits if you want truly isolated logic and motor power supplies. Also notice that this chip doesn't have or need a pin for the logic voltage (usually 5 V) power supply. It has a built-in 5 V regulator.*

If the MC33887 could have been made into a 12-pin (or 14-pin industry standard) package, then why the extra pins? Because this chip can handle a lot of current! Therefore, the power supplying pins (ground, positive voltage, and motor connections) are all duplicated to provide thicker paths for the power to flow.

Disconnecting Inputs Results in Protective Reaction

The MC33887 handles any disconnected input pins gracefully. Except for Input A and Input B, all other disconnected inputs result in the motor coasting or braking. Thus, no external input pull-up/pull-down resistors are necessary under ordinary circumstances because the MC33887 automatically defaults to safe modes.

Controlling the Motor Modes

The MC33887 provides access to all useful motor modes. The datasheet includes a lengthy listing of all the possible input conditions. Table 10-2 contains the most important combinations. (This table assumes Disable 2 is always 5 V.)

Table 10-2. MC33887 H-Bridge Motor-Driver Control Combinations

Enable	Disable 1	Input A	Input B	Result
0 V	Doesn't matter	Doesn't matter	Doesn't matter	Coast (low power sleep; less than 50 µA)
5 V	5 V	Doesn't matter	Doesn't matter	Coast
5 V	0 V	0 V	0 V	Brake both directions (low side)
5 V	0 V	0 V	5 V	Spin counterclockwise
5 V	0 V	5 V	0 V	Spin clockwise
5 V	0 V	5 V	5 V	Brake both directions (high side)

Implementing the MC33887 H-Bridge Motor Driver

Because of the surface-mount package, the MC33887 can't be experimented with directly on a solderless breadboard. I chose to make a printed circuit board that could hold three MC33887DH chips along with the necessary capacitors and connectors, as well as some test points for experimentation. A complete portion of the board appears in Figure 10-23.

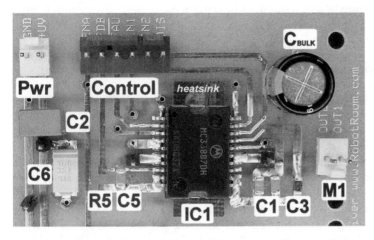

Figure 10-23. An MC33887DH MOSFET H-bridge motor driver fully implemented on a printed circuit board

The following are some things worth noting about the photograph of the printed circuit board:

- I added a second 0.1 μF capacitor at C1 simply because I had space on the board.

- C6 is an added 10 μF tantalum capacitor. Again, this is simply because I had space on the board. This is a voodoo capacitor.

- A very wide, electrically isolated trace on the printed circuit board underneath the MC33887 acts as a heat sink. You can see it sticking out at the top and bottom of IC1. Use a blob of heat sink grease to make sure the bottom of the chip actually makes contact with the trace. (Heat sink grease is a thermal conductor.)

- The enable pin on the control connector has a trace that extends to the rest of the MC33887 chips on the board. It's likely that if one motor chip is going to be put into sleep mode, then they all are going to be put to sleep. This saves a control line. If separate control over the sleep mode of each chip is necessary for a particular robot, then the trace can be cut before it reaches the next connector on the board.

- R1 is missing from the motor-driver board because it's pulled up on the control board.

- R5, the current sense feedback resistor, isn't yet soldered onto the board because I hadn't decided on a value for it.

Sensing Motor Current

The ability to sense the amount of current a motor is drawing provides uniquely valuable input for a robot. In fact, a multiwheeled robot could negotiate a room with obstacles and drop offs (such as stairs) using current sense alone.

Sensing Obstacles or Dangerous Conditions Through Motor Current Sensing

When a motor stalls (doesn't rotate even when power is applied), it draws its maximum amount of current. A stalled motor can overheat and become permanently damaged, may overload a homemade motor-driver circuit, and quickly drains the battery. During prototyping, many designers encounter motor stall because of selecting a nongear-head motor or selecting a motor that has too little torque for the robot's mass. However, operating robots most often stall their motors when the robot has run up against an obstacle.

If the motor-driver circuit has the ability to measure motor current, then the robot can be programmed to recognize a high current (stalled condition) and take action. The robot can try backing up and turning different directions to free itself from an undetected obstacle. Or, at the least, the robot can turn off power (coast mode) to the stalled motor and perhaps signal for assistance.

Sensing Motor Disconnection, Potential Falls, Being Turned Over, or Being Picked Up

A disconnected motor consumes no current. A bare motor consumes a small amount of current. After adding gears, a wheel, and perhaps a slightly askew motor mount assembly, the motor consumes a bit more current. When placed on the ground with the mass of the robot's body weighing down the motor, the motor consumes even more current.

These differences in current draw permit the robot to detect certain conditions. For example, if a motor became disconnected, it wouldn't draw any current. The robot could then alert its master of the error condition. Or, even better, the robot could alter its behavior to limp over to a repair station (yeah, right).

A robot with many wheels spaced far enough apart would permit one or two wheels to go over a ledge without the whole robot falling. As some of the wheels lost contact with the floor, the robot would see a dramatic reduction in current draw (less than the usual amount of current for plain driving around) for the motors that drive those wheels. The robot could then back up or change direction.

If a robot somehow became tipped over or if a robot were picked up, then all of the motors would draw less current than normal. The robot could turn itself off, call out for aid, or could right itself with the aid of an arm or flipping mechanism. Any of these reactions would certainly be more dignified than the robot helplessly spinning its wheels.

Converting Motor Current to a Voltage in the Motor Driver

You can design a discrete H-bridge with a very low-resistance (usually 0.1 Ω or less) resistor between the low-side transistors and ground to measure motor current. As the motor consumes additional current, the voltage increases across the fixed resistor.

A comparator or microcontroller analog-to-digital converter (ADC) can read the voltage directly. However, usually the voltage is pretty low, such as less than 0.5 V. So, you can employ an op-amp to amplify the current sense voltage up to the maximum regulated voltage of the logic circuit, such as 5 V, before the comparator or microcontroller reads the value. This provides a wider range of values. The other advantage of using an op-amp in this situation is that you can design a circuit to isolate the logic circuits from electrical motor noise and voltage spikes that exceed the maximum regulated voltage.

The big problem with using a resistor in the H-bridge for current sensing is that you're trying hard to avoid any resistance between the battery and the motor. Any resistance represents lost power.

The MC33887 uses a nonintrusive technique for motor current sensing. Instead of connecting a resistor in series with the entire motor power path, it disconnects a small portion of the total MOSFET from the motor path and uses a sympathetic effect to mirror a reduced version of the total current. For the MC33887, the current coming out of the Current Sense (pin 8) feedback pin is equal to $\frac{1}{375}$ of the current passing through the high-side power MOSFETs. The current sensing doesn't work if both high-side MOSFETs are turned off, so it's best to brake the motor with the high-side MOSFETs if current sensing is important during that period. The following discussion applies to Figure 10-21.

You can calculate the appropriate resistor value for R5 based on the maximum current you expect the motors to draw. Use a motor's datasheet (accurate) or an ohmmeter (approximate because of other resistances in the motor) to determine the winding resistance, which can then be used to calculate stall current:

```
maximum current in amps = maximum voltage from unregulated battery pack ÷
    motor winding resistance in ohms
example maximum current in amps = 9.6 V ÷ 13 Ω
example maximum current in amps = 0.739 A (round up for safety)
```

Now you can calculate the proper R5 resistor to use with the example motors:

```
R5 current resistor in ohms = regulated logic voltage maximum ÷
    (maximum current in amps × percentage coming through current sense pin)
example R5 current resistor in ohms = 5 V ÷ (0.739 A × (1 ÷ 375))
example R5 current resistor in ohms = about 2537 Ω (round down for safety)
```

You'll now double-check that. In a stalled condition, if 0.738 amp is pouring through the motor, only $\frac{1}{375}$ of that current is going to be pouring out the current sense feedback pin. That fractional current will flow through resistor R5 to ground.

```
voltage across R5 in volts = current through R5 in amps ×
    resistance of R5 in ohms
example R5 voltage = (0.739 A × (1 ÷ 375)) × 2537 Ω
example R5 voltage = 0.0019707 × 2537 Ω
example R5 voltage = about 5 V
```

You won't be able to find a 2537 Ω resistor. Err on the side of decreasing the resistance to prevent the voltage from significantly exceeding the regulated logic maximum. In this example, a 2.5 kΩ resistance would be a marginal choice because the tolerance of resistors can be ±5 percent. A 2.2 kΩ resistance would be a better choice because it provides a margin of error, but the expected maximum voltage will no longer make it all the way to 5 V.

Evaluating Motor Drivers

This chapter and the previous chapter have presented several motor drivers. Also, new motor drivers appear on the market all the time. How do you choose one to use? Assuming price, availability, and package are all acceptable, there are a lot of criteria to consider.

First, you should decide which of the motor modes (clockwise, counterclockwise, brake, and coast) your robot *really* requires. If you need the motor to spin in only one direction, then a simple single-transistor motor driver may be all you need. If you don't need coast, then a number of simple H-bridges with logic interfaces may be appropriate. If you need all motor modes and protection against selecting a short-circuit mode, then a full-fledged H-bridge motor-driver chip may be required.

Second, you must determine if the motor driver is rated for the maximum current and maximum voltage required by your robot. For voltages between 5 V and 18 V and for currents less than 1 amp, you have a wide range of choices. Outside of that range the choices become slimmer. If your robot's voltage or current needs are unusual, then a homebuilt discrete H-bridge may be your best choice.

Third, you should decide if your robot requires any special features (such as current sense), fewer control lines, or any safety features (such as overcurrent protection). That may reduce your selection to just a few motor-driver choices.

Two other important factors are worth considering. How much power does the motor driver deliver to the motors as compared to the amount a direct connection to the battery would provide (power delivery)? And, how much power does the motor driver use for itself (efficiency)?

I tested five different motor drivers and a direct connection for power delivery and efficiency from 5.5 V to 10 V using the variable regulated power supply presented in Chapter 7. The motor drivers tested are as follows:

- Discrete 2222A and 2907A bipolar H-bridge (Figure 9-14)

- Discrete IRLU024N and IRFU5505N power MOSFET H-bridge (Figure 10-10)

- Standalone 4427A (Figure 10-17)

- SN754410 (Figure 10-20)

- Motorola MC33887 (Figure 10-21)

Evaluating Motor-Driver Power Delivery

When a motor is connected directly to a battery, the motor receives the maximum voltage and the maximum current that the battery can supply. This is considered 100 percent power delivery for that particular battery.

Power equals voltage times current. The current drawn by the motor varies with the amount of load placed on the motor. However, unless the motor attempts to draw too much current from the battery, the voltage provided across the motor leads of a running motor stays more or less constant. So, it turns out that just by measuring the voltage between both motor leads of a running motor, you can determine how good that motor driver is at supplying power to that motor.

Ignoring voltage drop in the wires and other minor sources, every bit of voltage not provided to the motor is wasted by the motor driver as heat. If you've gone to the expense of purchasing extremely high-quality, high-efficiency motors, such as a Maxon or Portescap, or you've gone to the trouble to build a competitive robot (such as mini-sumo or a line-follower), you want the motor supplied with every drop of power it can use.

Evaluating Motor-Driver Voltage Output with a Very Light Load

For the first test, I selected an unloaded high-efficiency motor (drawing only 10 mA at 5.5 V) to provide the best-case scenario for a motor driver to be able to provide the maximum amount of power. The lighter the current load, the easier it is to deliver full voltage.

Using a high-impedance digital multimeter, I simply measured the voltage across the motor while it was running with each motor driver. Therefore, you can easily re-create this experiment with any motor driver and motor you have lying around.

By definition, the direct power connection provides 100 percent voltage delivery. So, at 5.5 V, the motor received all 5.5 V. At 10 V, the motor received all 10 V.

The labeled lines in Figure 10-24 show the results of the motor drivers in the order of highest voltage delivery to lowest voltage delivery. All but the SN754410 were able to provide 95 percent or better of the battery voltage to the motor. The Motorola MC33887 and discrete power MOSFET H-bridge (IRLU024N and FU5505—either stand-alone or driven by a 4427 interface) provided 100 percent voltage as far as the multimeter could detect.

The discrete bipolar H-bridge (2222A and 2907A) performed very well (99 percent to 100 percent) with a light load, as did the 4427A (96 percent to 98 percent). However, the SN754410 didn't perform well, even though it's based on the same basic transistor technology. The SN754410 datasheet clearly indicates it has a significant voltage drop in the V_{OL} and V_{OH} specifications.

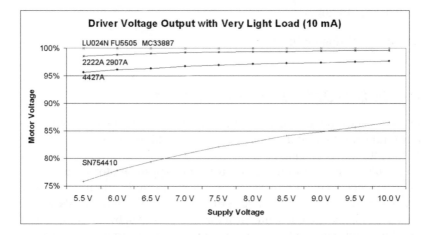

Figure 10-24. Voltage delivered by various motor drivers with a very light motor load (10 mA at 5.5 V)

Evaluating Motor-Driver Voltage Output with a Moderate Load

For the next test, I selected a motor that simulated a significantly loaded condition for a lunch-box-sized robot. With the bulkier motor (275 mA at 5.5 V), this test was intended to be difficult for the motor drivers to provide maximum voltage.

The labeled lines in Figure 10-25 show the results of the motor drivers in the order of highest voltage delivery to lowest voltage delivery. The power MOSFET–based devices once again command the lead, but they show a slight dip at lower gate voltages (around the 5.5 V range). Still, 98 percent to 99 percent voltage delivery is wonderful.

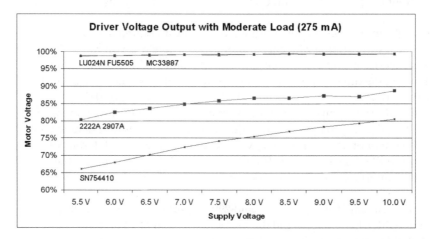

Figure 10-25. Voltage delivered by various motor drivers with a moderate motor load (275 mA at 5.5 V)

The discrete bipolar transistor H-bridge (2222A and 2907A) has increased its voltage drop considerably, even at about only half of its official rated current capability. An 80 percent voltage output doesn't automatically rule out this H-bridge as a legitimate motor driver at these current levels, considering how inexpensive it is to build.

The SN754410's voltage output has also dropped considerably, hitting lows of 65 percent voltage delivery. To put that in perspective, that's only 3.6 V delivered from a 5.5 V power supply. Heavy loading isn't an excuse because the SN754410 is being used at less than one-third of its rated current capacity.

Hold on! There's a chip missing from the list! The 4427A acting stand-alone (not driving discrete power MOSFETs) overheated and failed to drive the motor at all. Just a reminder: For currents greater than 100mA, step up to a 4424 or an IXDN404PI. For currents greater than 250 mA, properly use that chip family to drive discrete power MOSFETs.

Evaluating Motor-Driver Efficiency

Besides the ability to provide maximum power to the motor, another factor to consider in a motor driver is how much power it uses for itself. For example, in a bipolar transistor H-bridge, a lot of current goes into the transistor base leads. That current doesn't get supplied to the motor, so that current is essentially wasted.

The efficiency of the motor driver is calculated as follows:

```
power delivered to motor in watts = current in amps through the motor ✕
    voltage across the motor leads in volts
total power in watts = (unregulated current in amps through the motor driver ✕
    unregulated voltage in volts) + (regulated current in amps through the
    motor driver ✕ regulated voltage in volts)
efficiency (in %) = power delivered to motor in watts ÷ total power in watts ✕ 100
```

For the purposes of the following tests, sleep mode isn't considered for efficiency testing because the motor must be running.

Evaluating Motor-Driver Efficiency with a Very Light Load

For this third motor-driver test, I returned to the unloaded high-efficiency motor to provide the worst-case efficiency scenario for a motor driver. After all, if the motor driver consumes 10 mA for chip operations (quiescent current) out of the box, it's going to equal or be less than 50 percent efficiency when driving a 10 mA load. This test should magnify any overhead or fixed current consumption by the motor driver.

As expected, the graph in Figure 10-26 tells a frightful (if slightly unfair) tale. The exception is the discrete power MOSFETs, which show off their relative lack of current usage in a steady state, operating at 100 percent efficiency. The 4427A is fairly efficient as well, sipping less than 1 mA for its own purposes.

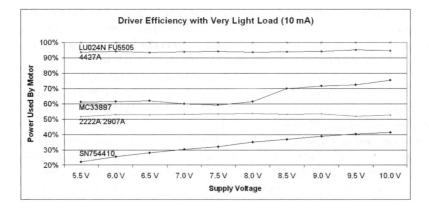

Figure 10-26. Motor-driver efficiency by various motor drivers with a very light load (10 mA at 5.5 V)

The MC33887 has enough quiescent current to have its results dragged down. Because it scored 100 percent in the voltage delivery test, this demonstrates that a motor driver is capable of providing maximum output voltage (probably the most important attribute) while not guaranteeing 100 percent power-usage efficiency in doing so.

The SN754410 is pathetic under these conditions.

Evaluating Motor-Driver Efficiency with a Moderate Load

For this last motor-driver test, I stepped up to the moderately loaded (275 mA at 5.5 V) case. This provides a fairer test of motor-driver efficiency because the fixed (out-of-the-box) quiescent current can be overshadowed by the more significant amount of power being drawn by the motor.

Figure 10-27 shows that the MC33887 has risen quite a bit in efficiency. That suggests that the amount of power consumed by the MC33887 doesn't increase significantly depending upon the amount of power being provided.

The discrete bipolar transistor H-bridge (2222A and 2907A) doesn't rise as much in efficiency with an increase in voltage, as do the other motor drivers. This is because of the ever-increasing current flow through the fixed-value resistors connected to the transistor base leads. You could improve the efficiency of this circuit at higher voltages by choosing slightly higher value current-limiting resistors.

At 10 V, the SN754410 is looking usable. The efficiency trend is definitely climbing. Perhaps the SN754410's performance in these tests would've been better if the tests had continued through higher voltages, such 20 V.

One last note on efficiency: These tests were performed on motors running in a steady state. MOSFETs are best at providing steady power. However, if the motor driver had been switched off and on a lot, as occurs in a PWM speed control, the constant charging and discharging of the MOSFET gates would've caused a decline in efficiency.

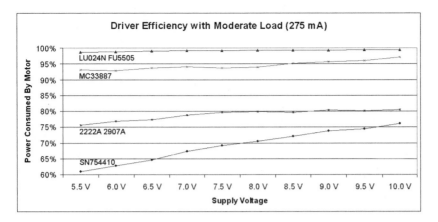

Figure 10-27. Motor-driver efficiency by various motor drivers with a moderate load (275 mA at 5.5 V)

Summary

I hope that this chapter and the previous one have introduced you to a lot of interesting possibilities in driving motors. Although motor control can seem overwhelming, any time you invest in selecting a motor driver will be time well spent. After all, motion is one of the most important parts of a robot. Then again, there's nothing wrong with selecting the very simplest motor driver because building an actual robot is more imperative than dwelling on minute details to the point of inaction.

With the circuits and chips presented in this book, you should have no trouble finding an H-bridge circuit or motor-driver chip roughly appropriate for either basic or full motor control. If you should find customization necessary, the concepts of logic interfacing, parallel transistors, pull-up and pull-down resistors, voltage limits, and current limits should be well enough understood by now to provide a sense of where to start and what to change.

I happen to prefer discrete power MOSFET H-bridges or MOSFET-based chips for my robots. To me, the ability to deliver full power to the robot's motors with fairly high efficiency outweighs the increased cost and complexity.

In the next two chapters, you'll switch gears a little and look at an infrared obstacle sensor. But, after that, you'll actually put the motor driver to good use in building a robot.

CHAPTER 11

Creating an Infrared Modulated Obstacle, Opponent, and Wall Detector

Covers the Panasonic PNA4602M 38 kHz Infrared Detector; Covers the 74AC14 Bicolor LED Driver; Shows How to Select Infrared Emitters, Select Trimpots, Reduce Cross Talk, and Select Capacitors

FROM AN ELECTRONICS PERSPECTIVE, the easiest method of detecting a wall, obstacle, or object is with a physical contact switch. However, because stand-alone switches provide small contact areas, robot builders resort to bumper schemes to increase coverage area. Unfortunately, even then there are blind spots (especially above and below the bumper), and obstacles can get caught and hung up on the robot's bumpers. An additional deficiency of physical switches is that it's more desirable to look farther ahead so that either an obstacle can be avoided in the first place or a sought-after object can be optimally targeted.

A vision system—say, a camera—would be a great solution because of the wide field of view. However, interfacing a microcontroller to a camera tends to be complicated. For simplification, you can make a 1-pixel vision system with a single photoconductor, such as a cadmium-sulfide photoresistor. Although that works fairly well for avoiding walls or objects because of the change in brightness from shadows, it isn't useful for targeting specific objects at a distance.

In this chapter and the next chapter, you'll learn how to build a popular reflective detection system. This system is based upon transmitting a modulated infrared wave and receiving the wave's reflection if it bounces off an object or wall (see Figure 11-1).

This detector is fairly inexpensive, can be tailored to provide adequate detection up to 1 meter away, and performs well in a variety of indoor lighting conditions. This chapter also includes information about bicolor LED indicators, electrical noise, and capacitors.

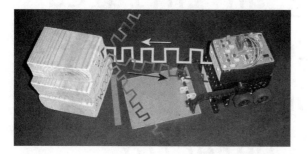

Figure 11-1. The Have a Nice Day robot detecting a mini-sumo opponent by emitting an infrared 38 kHz square wave and detecting part of the signal bouncing back

Detecting Modulated Infrared with a Popular Module, or, Another Reason to Hog the Remote Control

Most consumer remote controls communicate using infrared light. On the receiving end, inside the stereo, TV, or VCR is an electronic circuit that must be able to discriminate between natural infrared light and infrared light that's generated by the remote control. To make the distinction, most remote controls blink on and off in a regular, repeating square wave, thousands of times per second. When this regular pattern of infrared light is received, the TV recognizes it as an incoming command signal.

At first, a blinking pattern may not seem unusual enough to provide reliable distinction from background lighting. However, consider the effectiveness of a person waving to you in a crowd. Even if other people are moving their hands for other purposes, a regular hand wave *usually* provides enough of a pattern to distinguish it from the crowd.

Robot hobbyists can take advantage of remote-control infrared technology, not only for its ability to perform reliably in a variety of indoor lighting conditions but also in the availability of low-price remote-control components. In fact, Panasonic and Sharp manufacture components that include the receiver circuit and the phototransistor in a single, stand-alone, inexpensive part.

Introducing the Panasonic PNA4602M Photo IC

The infrared receiver module used in this book is the Panasonic PNA4602M Photo IC (see Figure 11-2). It's available from Digi-Key for about $1.28.

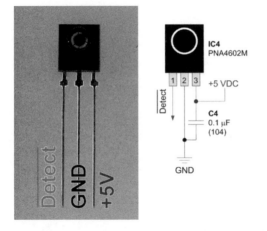

Figure 11-2. The Panasonic PNA4602M infrared photo IC (left) along with wiring diagram (right)

Hooking Up the PNA4602M Photo IC

The PNA4602M is easy to hook up and use. Pin 2 connects to ground (GND). Pin 3 connects to 5 V. Because this is a bipolar part, not CMOS, the voltage supply must truly be between 4.7 V and 5.3 V, not the flexible range of 2 V to 6 V associated with CMOS parts. Also, because PNA4602M contains a chip, not just a phototransistor, a good robot builder places a 0.1 μF capacitor across the voltage supply lines to reduce noise and ensure glitch-free operation.

The only pin remaining, pin 1, indicates when an infrared signal is detected. In the case of this chip, it looks for a 940 nm infrared beam turning on and off 38,000 times a second, also known as 38 kHz. There's some leeway; for example, a 980 nm infrared beam at 37 kHz is also detectable, but the range and reliability is reduced.

The chip doesn't care how bright the infrared beam is, and the chip doesn't purposely provide any sense of signal strength. Either a 38 kHz signal is detected or it isn't.

The detect pin (pin 1) is a little peculiar in that it outputs 5 V when no signal is detected and outputs 0 V when a signal is detected. That's sort of the opposite of what you might expect. To call attention to this, in a schematic or writing diagram, a line or bar is drawn over the pin label "Detect" to indicate that detection is represented by a low (0 V) output. In the robot's brain (microcontroller software), you can always flip the value immediately after the robot reads the output if it makes things easier for you to understand and debug.

Testing the PNA4602M Photo IC

The PNA4602M is easy to experiment with on a solderless breadboard. Simply follow the wiring diagram in Figure 11-2. With power turned on, measure the voltage of the detect pin (pin 1) with a multimeter (see Figure 11-3). Normally, the meter should display about 5 V.

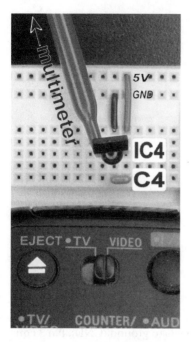

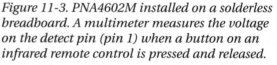

Figure 11-3. PNA4602M installed on a solderless breadboard. A multimeter measures the voltage on the detect pin (pin 1) when a button on an infrared remote control is pressed and released.

Aim a remote control (Sony remotes usually work well) at the rounded portion of the PNA4602M, and press and hold a button on the remote. Assuming your remote control emits a 38 kHz carrier wave at around 940 nm, the meter should display the voltage dropping to about 3.5 V on the detect pin.

Why doesn't the voltage drop all the way to 0 V? The remote control isn't continuously sending 38 kHz. The remote control encodes command data by sending 38 kHz bursts. Depending on the length of time a burst appears and goes away, a 1 bit or a 0 bit is represented. Over a short period of time, a full group of bits representing a command are transmitted. As such, a 38 kHz signal isn't active long enough for the voltage to drop all the way to 0 V on the multimeter display.

Looking Closely at the Modulated Signal

If you connect the detect pin (pin 1) of the PNA4602M to an oscilloscope, you can observe the command data bits transmitted by the remote control. Because the PNA4602M strips away the 38 kHz signal, the only way to observe the 38 kHz wave is by attaching a photodiode or phototransistor nearby. The top of Figure 11-4 shows the voltage across an ordinary phototransistor; the bottom of Figure 11-4 shows the voltage at the detect pin of a PNA4602M.

NOTE *While using a PNA4602M, a separate phototransistor isn't necessary because the robot isn't going to be interested in seeing the actual 38 kHz wave. This is merely for illustrative purposes.*

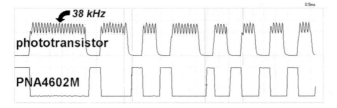

Figure 11-4. An oscilloscope trace of the voltages of an ordinary phototransistor (top) and the PNA4602M photo IC (bottom). This shows the PNA4602M output dropping low whenever a 38 kHz signal is detected.

A robot's microcontroller could listen to the PNA4602M's detect pin and time the spacing between detections to decode the bits from a remote control. In doing so, it's possible to add remote control to a robot. Or, the robot could emit data as well as receive data, creating a communication channel. However, that's a subject for another book. For now, you'll concentrate on using the remote-control receiver technology for object detection.

Simpler, bare sensors, such as plain photoresistors, are affected by changes in lighting conditions. But bright light, dim light, shadows, reflections, and everyday background noise won't cause the PNA4602M to falsely indicate detection. As shown in the oscilloscope trace, the PNA4602M is interested only in whether a 38 kHz modulated signal is present.

Looking Even More Closely to See the Detection Delay

There's a slight lag in detection because the PNA4602M needs to see a full wave or two at 38 kHz before it knows it's a real signal (see Figure 11-5). In practice, this delay isn't significant.

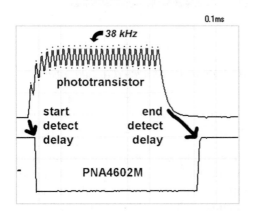

Figure 11-5. A closer view of the oscilloscope trace, which shows that the PNA4602M takes little time to start detecting the 38 kHz signal and a lot more time to give up and raise pin 1 to indicate the 38 kHz signal has gone away

Expanding the Detection Circuit to Include an LED Indicator

It would be nice to connect an LED directly to the detect pin (pin 1) of the PNA4602M to indicate when a 38 kHz signal is being received. Unfortunately, the PNA4602M isn't capable of directly supplying enough power to light the LED.

Adding a 74AC14 Inverter Chip to Drive the LED

Instead of driving an LED directly from the detect pin, another component can read the signal and drive the LED. A single transistor, a logic chip, or even a microcontroller would work fine for this purpose. For this circuit, I chose to route the detect signal into a 74AC14 inverter logic chip, which buffers (copies) the signal and then supplies power to an LED (see Figure 11-6).

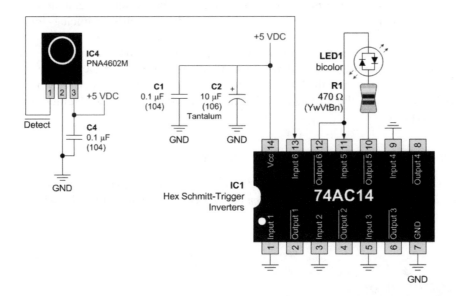

Figure 11-6. The detect pin of a PNA4602M photo IC is connected to two inverters in a 74AC14 chip to power a bicolor LED.

Examining the Indicator Circuit

At first sight, the circuit in Figure 11-6 may seem awfully fancy to simply turn on an LED. But the remainder of the pins on the 74AC14 chip will be put to good use later in the chapter. The schematic is a little less complicated than it might initially appear when you see that the setup of IC4 and C4 remains unchanged from Figure 11-2.

Cleaning the Power Supply with Local Capacitors

C1 is a standard 0.1 µF 10 V (or better) monolithic ceramic bypass capacitor (see Chapter 8 for part numbers). Per good practice, one capacitor is included for each chip. C4 is for IC4, and C1 is for IC1.

C2 is a 10 µF 10 V (or better) tantalum capacitor (see Chapter 7 for part numbers) used as a bypass capacitor that steadies the local power supply when switching the LED on and off. Although not absolutely necessary for the circuit in Figure 11-6, C2 becomes more and more vital in preventing false detections as additional components are added to this circuit. You'll learn more about this later in the "Reducing Cross Talk with a Tantalum Capacitor" section.

Powering the LED with an Advanced CMOS Logic Chip

IC1 is an Advanced CMOS (AC) chip. That's not the name of a manufacturer or brand; it's the name of the underlying technology. Don't try substituting an HC, LS, ALS, or other technology. A 74AC14 ($0.25 to $0.75; #296-4301-5 at Digi-Key, #211844 at Jameco, #511-74AC14B at Mouser, and #74AC14 at Solarbotics) is required because it can supply up to 24 mA per individual output pin. LED1 is going to require the following:

```
(5 V (power supply) - 1.6 V (LED voltage drop)) / 470 Ω (resistor R1) = 7.2 mA
```

An output current of 7.2 mA is just on the edge of being too much for a high-speed CMOS (HC) chip to supply. If you want to make LED1 brighter by lowering the resistance of R1, then an HC chip will disappoint.

IC1, a 74AC14 chip, is labeled as a "Hex Schmitt-Trigger Inverter." The "Schmitt-Trigger" functionality isn't necessary for this experiment but is necessary later and will be described in Chapter 12. The "Hex" portion of the label signifies that there are six inverters in this chip (*dual* means two, *quad* means four, and *hex* means six). Because only two of the inverters are being used for this experiment, the remaining four inputs (pins 1, 3, 5, and 9) are connected to GND (0 V). Unused inputs should never be left unconnected on CMOS chips.

The "Inverter" portion of IC1's label signifies that a signal on an input pin is flipped on an output pin. So, a 5 V input becomes a 0 V output, and a 0 V input becomes a 5 V output. This makes the chip versatile because it can flip a signal if desired, or you can run the signal through a second set of pins and flip it back.

Showing Both Detect and No-Detect States with a Bicolor LED

LED1 is a bicolor LED. When one lead has a higher voltage, the LED lights up with one color (usually red), and when the other lead has a higher voltage, the LED lights up with another color (usually green). The voltage across the leads must be higher by about 1.6 V to 2.0 V (or greater), depending on the color emitted by the LED.

R1 is a 470 Ω resistor that limits the amount of current passing through LED1. If R1 wasn't there, the skinny bond wire inside of LED1 could melt because of too much current passing through it. R1 can be reduced all the way to 140 Ω to make the LED brighter. A resistance much less than that would cause the current to exceed 24 mA, which is the limit of the chip and about the limit of the LED. On the other hand, the resistance of R1 can be increased as much as desired to lower power consumption, but brightness of the LED will be decreased proportionately.

When experimenting on a solderless breadboard, it's helpful to solder a resistor to a lead of a T1 (3 mm) bicolor LED (see Figure 11-7). This makes it a lot easier to simply insert the LED anywhere you want. Otherwise, you'll need to hunt for a spare column on the breadboard where the resistor and LED lead can connect.

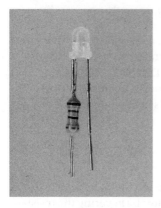

Figure 11-7. A bicolor LED ($0.22; #94060 at Jameco) with a resistor soldered on by hand

For my test circuit, I chose for LED1 to turn green when no signal is detected ("All clear") and to turn red when a signal is detected ("Something is there!"). If your circuit displays the opposite colors, simply remove the bicolor LED, flip it around so that the LED leads swap breadboard holes, and reinsert.

Illustrating LED and Logic Chip Current Flow When Nothing Is Detected

Figure 11-8 shows the LED circuit in action when the PNA4602 *doesn't* detect a signal. Pin 1 of IC4 (PNA4602M) outputs 5 V to pin 13 of IC1 (74AC14). Pin 12 is always the inverse of pin 13, so it switches to 0 V. Pin 11 is connected to pin 12, so it receives 0 V. Pin 10 is always the inverse of pin 11, so it switches to 5 V.

To light the LED, current flows from pin 10 (5 V), through R1, through the green LED in LED1, and into pin 12 (0 V).

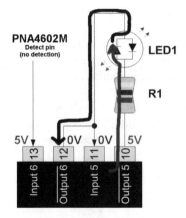

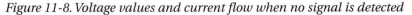

Figure 11-8. Voltage values and current flow when no signal is detected

Illustrating LED and Logic Chip Current Flow When Something Is Detected

Figure 11-9 shows the LED circuit in action when the PNA4602 *does* detect a signal. Pin 1 of IC4 (PNA4602M) outputs 0 V to pin 13 of IC1 (74AC14). Pin 12 is always the inverse of pin 13, so it switches to 5 V. Pin 11 is connected to pin 12, so it receives 5 V. Pin 10 is always the inverse of pin 11, so it switches to 0 V.

To light the LED, current flows from pin 12 (5 V), through the red LED in LED1, through R1, and into pin 10 (0 V).

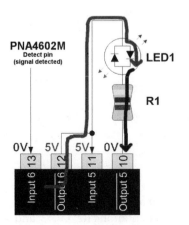

Figure 11-9. Voltage values and current flow when a signal is detected

A remote control aimed at this circuit changes the LED from green (no detect) to a mix of green and red (detect). The LED won't change to solid red because the remote control doesn't emit a continuous 38 kHz wave.

Completing the Reflector Detector Circuit

At this point, you may be waiting to see how you can use a remote-control receiver to detect obstacles. Instead of just passively listening for a signal (such as from a remote control), the robot can emit a 38 kHz wave and detect if the signal bounces back. This is known as an *active reflective sensor system*.

The circuit in Figure 11-10 includes two detectors (IC3 and IC4), two detection LED indicators (LED1 and LED2), two infrared emitters (IED3 and IED4), and a 38 kHz wave generator. By having a pair of emitters and detectors, the robot receives more information, thus improving navigation.

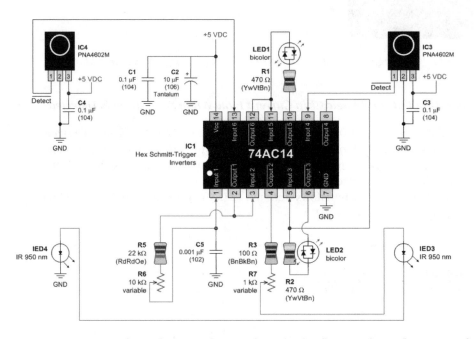

Figure 11-10. Complete schematic for a 38 kHz dual reflective object detector with bicolor LED indicators

Examining the Complete Reflector Detector Schematic

Don't panic! You've already seen the IC4 portion of the circuit and most of the top half of IC1. IC3 is merely a copy of IC4. The portion of the circuit containing R2, LED2, and pins 9, 8, 6, and 5 of IC1 is merely a copy of the portion of the circuit containing R1, LED1, and pins 13, 12, 11, and 10 of IC1. In fact, the only really new stuff is connected to pins 1, 2, 3, and 4 of IC1. That is, only IED4, R5, R6, C5, R3, R7, and IED3 are novel.

Generating the 38 kHz Wave

R5, R6, C5, and pins 1 and 2 of IC1 create a voltage-controlled oscillator (VCO). Not surprisingly, the values of the parts were chosen to generate a 38 kHz square wave.

R5 and R6 combine a fixed 22 kΩ resistor with a variable 10 kΩ resistor (a poten-tiometer) in series. When R6 is dialed down to 0 Ω, they act like a 22 kΩ resistor. When R6 is dialed up to 10 kΩ, they act like a 32 kΩ resistor. R6 can also be dialed to any resistance between 0 kΩ and 10 kΩ. So, R5 and R6 can take the place of a resistor with any value from 22 kΩ to 32 kΩ.

C5 is a 0.001 µF (1 nF) capacitor. When pin 2 of IC1 outputs 5 V, current is going to charge capacitor C5 through resistors R5 and R6. When pin 2 of IC1 outputs 0 V, current is going to flow from capacitor C5 through resistors R5 and R6. The amount of time it takes to charge and discharge C5 depends upon the dial setting of potentiometer R6. Lower resistance allows the charging/discharging process to occur faster.

Now here's the trick: C5 is also connected to input pin 1 of IC1. Input pin 1 controls the output of pin 2 (it's the inverse of pin 1). When C5 charges enough, input pin 1 sees a "high" voltage and switches pin 2 to 0 V. That causes C5 to begin discharging. When it discharges enough, input pin 1 sees a "low" voltage and switches pin 2 to 5 V. The process of filling and draining occurs over an over again.

What you'd like to do is to dial potentiometer R6 to a resistance that causes C5 to cycle 38,000 times a second (38 kHz). My R6 setting ended up measuring about 3.3 kΩ. However, differences in R5, C5, and IC1 prevent a single resistance value from being consistent from board to board. Instructions for fine-tuning the timing appear in the next chapter.

Emitting the 38 kHz Wave

Back in Figure 11-10, notice that output pin 2 of IC1 is connected to input pin 3. Input pin 3 controls output pin 4. Therefore, as output pin 2 switches from 5 V to 0 V to 5 V to 0 V (and so on), output pin 4 also switches. Because this is an inverter chip, output pin 4 will be the inverse of output pin 2, but that doesn't matter. The important point is that output pin 4 switches back and forth as often as output pin 2, thus producing a 38 kHz copy.

Connected to output pin 4 is a fixed resistor (R3) followed by a variable resistor (R7). R3 and R7 form a combined resistor that can vary from 100 Ω to 1100 Ω. Infrared LEDs (IED3 and IED4) are connected to R7. By changing the dial on R7, you can con-trol the brightness of the infrared LEDs. The fixed resistor (R3) is there for safety. Even if you turn the variable resistor down to 0 Ω, the fixed resistor continues to limit current to the LEDs.

If the robot sees too far (such as backing away from a wall that's actually across the room), you can turn down the brightness on the infrared LEDs by increasing the resistance of R7. If the robot doesn't see far enough (such as not seeing a nearby oppo-nent on a robot sumo ring), you can turn up the brightness on the infrared LEDs by decreasing the resistance of R7. Because IC3 and IC4 detect the signal emitted by IED3 and IED4 as it bounces off of objects, it's important to have control over the brightness of the signal.

R7 doesn't change the frequency of the signal. The infrared LEDs are turned on and off by output pin 4 of IC1, which copies the oscillator frequency of pin 2 of IC1. The frequency at pin 2 is set by R6.

Why bother making a copy of the signal coming from pin 2? Why not connect the infrared LEDs (and resistors) directly to pin 2? Although it's technically possible, any current diverted from pin 2 will alter the rate at which C5 charges and discharges. As the infrared LEDs and resistor heat up, the amount of current they divert changes, again affecting C5's cycle rate. Changes to C5's cycle rate alter the frequency output. It's preferable to tune the rate to 38 kHz once and not have to touch it after that. Therefore, it's advantageous to make a copy (*buffer*) of the signal through pins 3 and 4 and attach output loads to pin 4.

Implementing the 38 kHz Reflector Detector on a Solderless Breadboard

You can implement the complete circuit on half of an 840 tie-point solderless breadboard (see Figure 11-11). However, what isn't shown is the 5 V power source. See Chapters 7 and 8 for instructions on how to build and implement a 5 V power source.

Figure 11-11. This is a 38 kHz dual reflective object detector with indicators implemented on a solderless breadboard.

The labels for R1 and R2 are missing from Figure 11-11. Let me assure you that the resistors are on the breadboard. They're actually built into the legs of LED1 and LED2 (as illustrated in Figure 11-7).

Selecting an Infrared LED for the PNA4602M

IED3 and IED4 are infrared with a peak emission wavelength that should be around 940 nm. You can think of the wavelength as the equivalent of the LED's color in the infrared portion of the light spectrum. If you had a receiver that was good at picking up blinking green lights, you'd want a green LED rather than a blue LED. In this case, the PNA4602M is good at picking up blinking 940 nm lights, so you'll prefer a 940 nm LED.

Besides wavelength, you should consider five other characteristics when purchasing infrared LEDs:

Size/package: Standard T1¾ (5 mm) and smaller T1 (3 mm) look like normal LEDs. Infrared LEDs are also available in flat side-emission and double-emitter packages. This is mainly a question of style and personal choice. The T1¾ package is the most commonly available.

Output power: This is usually 3 mW to 10 mW (average about 5 mW) but can be as high as 33 mW. This is the sum of all the energy emitted as infrared light. This makes it easier to compare the efficiency and light output of one LED versus another.

Maximum continuous and pulse current rating: Infrared LEDs usually allow much higher currents than standard LEDs. Continuous (nonpulsed) current is ordinarily about 100 mA maximum, and pulses can be as high as 1 amp (but the LED requires time between pulses to cool). Don't believe me? Open your remote control, and check the current-limiting resistor (see Figure 11-12).

Figure 11-12. The inside of a standard consumer remote control. Resistor R2 is labeled "2R2," which is a resistance of 2.2 Ω. With two fresh AA batteries supplying 3.2 V, assuming a 1.2 V drop across IED1 and a 0.2 V drop across the bipolar transistor driver, the infrared LED receives current pulses of 0.81 amp.

Half-beam angle: This is usually ±20 degrees to ±45 degrees but not unheard of to be as low as ±5 degrees and as high as ±100 degrees. A narrower beam is better for spotting objects farther away or for interrupter break-beam pairs. A wider beam is better for implementing a virtual bumper to avoid running into nearby objects.

Price: They cost $0.20 to $3.50 (and average under $1) depending on the wavelength, package, and power output.

Purchasing an Appropriate Infrared LED

For the breadboard implementation of the circuit, I chose a pair of 940 nm wavelength, 5-mm metal package, 5.4 mW power output, 100 mA continuous/10-amp pulse, ±10-degree half-beam angle ($1.85; #N08 LED55C at Electronix Express). The 10-amp pulse rating with metal case is overkill, considering I'm only sending 3 mA through the pair.

However, it was the narrowest beam I had in my infrared LED box. I'm not wasting 10-amp $1.85 LEDs on the final soldered circuit, though.

Less expensive infrared LEDs are equally appropriate. The key is to choose one that emits from 925 nm to 955 nm (for 98 percent of maximum sensitivity) and has a beam angle that you desire for a particular purpose. When shopping for infrared LEDs to use with the PNA4602M detector, first eliminate any infrared LEDs that aren't from 910 nm to 985 nm (90 percent maximum sensitivity). Then, eliminate any that aren't within your budget. Next, select an LED of the size (T1¾ or T1) and beam angle you desire for a particular application. I find that the emitted energy (mW) rating isn't that helpful for selection purposes except in differentiating an infrared LED that has a value less than or greater than the average of the group.

At 10 mW, ±30 degrees, and 940 nm, the N08L5013IRAB from Electronix Express provides a nice compromise for $0.50. Digi-Key features a couple of good choices: the LN66F 13 mW/sr, ±15 degrees, 940 nm for $0.61 or the LNA2903L 9 mW/sr, ±25 degrees, 950 nm for $0.45.

Selecting Trimpots for R7 and R6

R7 determines the brightness of the infrared LEDs. After installing the completed circuit in a robot, it may be desirable to adjust the brightness to tweak performance. But you probably won't alter the brightness setting much after that. Additionally, if the brightness changes slightly, performance won't be greatly affected. Therefore, you can use a small, relatively imprecise (and therefore less expensive) trimmer potentiometer (also known as a *trimpot*). See the left side of Figure 11-13.

R6 controls the frequency of the wave being emitted. The closer the wave is to 38 kHz, the easier it is for the PNA4602M to detect the wave. However, like R7, after being fine-tuned, R6 isn't going to be altered very often. So, a large "finger-friendly" potentiometer is unnecessary. Therefore, you should use a small, relatively precise (and therefore more expensive) multiturn trimmer (see the right side of Figure 11-13).

Figure 11-13. A less expensive Bourns 3386W series single-turn trimming potentiometer (left) and a more expensive Bourns 3296W series multiturn potentiometer (right)

Another advantage of a multiturn potentiometer is that the value is less likely to change significantly once correctly adjusted. Any minor change of the adjustment screw (say, because of vibration) results in less of a change in resistance. So, a multiturn trimpot not only facilitates fine frequency adjustments but also helps keep the frequency rock-steady at 38 kHz with minimal drift. This means a more consistent performance by the robot over time.

Purchasing Trimpots

Digi-Key has 1 kΩ 3386W (R7) available for $1.29 as #3386W-102. Digi-Key has 10 kΩ 3296W (R5) available for $2.50 as #3296W-103.

To save money, you could substitute a single-turn potentiometer for R5, #3386W-103, for $1.29. However, that will make it more difficult to perfectly tune 38 kHz. It's not really a huge deal if you don't plan on stretching the maximum detection range.

Adding Trimpots to the Circuit

Before adding any trimpot to a circuit, always try to adjust the trimpot to the general center of its range to avoid any radically high or low values when the circuit first powers up. It's easy to see when a single-turn trimpot's dial is in the center; just look at the arrow or flathead screwdriver notch. For a multiturn trimpot, it's better to connect an outer lead (first or third) and the middle lead to a multimeter and turn the dial until the meter reads about half the trimpot's labeled resistance.

Selecting Capacitors

Not counting the capacitors in the 5 V power supply, there are five capacitors in the reflector detector circuit. C1, C3, and C4 are ordinary 0.1 μF monolithic ceramic bypass capacitors included for noise reduction and local power benefits for each chip: IC1, IC3, and IC4. However, C2 and C5 are a little more interesting.

Reducing Cross Talk with a Tantalum Capacitor

One of the biggest complaints about solderless breadboards is the relatively large amount of electrical noise generated. The largest sources of electrical noise are the wire leads of components because they tend to retain a longer length than they'd have on a finished soldered circuit. Additionally, the solderless breadboard itself has columns of unterminated and ungrounded metal contacts that act like miniature antennas.

Some of this electrical noise leaks into otherwise unconnected circuit paths—an effect called *cross talk*. There are a number of techniques for reducing cross talk, but the most effective method is to transfer the circuit from a solderless breadboard to a printed circuit board. That's unacceptable here because it eliminates the purpose of using solderless breadboards in the first place, which is ease of experimentation. So, you'll try a less radical approach, even if it isn't as effective.

The side effect of cross talk in the reflector detector circuit is that the PNA4602M detectors will occasionally falsely detect a signal that isn't being reflected from anything. In fact, a really nasty solderless breadboard circuit can cause an almost continual "detection" even with the infrared LEDs removed!

There are two bad things about these false detections. First, they reduce the maximum range of the detector because you'll probably have to turn down the brightness of the emitters to reduce the amount of electrical noise. Second, a rare false detection isn't noticed by a casual human observer but is almost always noticed by the quick-thinking digital robot brain. To achieve maximum usefulness from the reflector detector, you must program the robot's software so that random, brief changes in detection state are either ignored completely or have little effect (for example, the robot nudges a little to one direction every once in a while and then nudges a little to the other direction every once in a while).

Software can be written to easily ignore transitory spikes, as illustrated in the oscilloscope trace on the left side of Figure 11-14. However, software can't overcome constant false detections, as illustrated in the oscilloscope trace on the right side of Figure 11-14. In fact, the sensor would be downright useless.

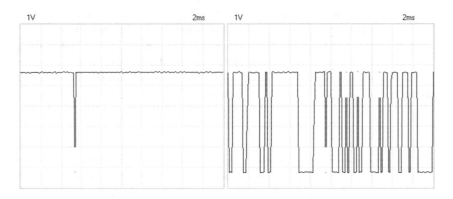

Figure 11-14. Sporadic false detection spikes can be disregarded in software (left). Incessant false detections make sensor data unusable (right).

Selecting the Correct Capacitor to Reduce False Detections

When I first assembled the circuit on my solderless breadboard, C2 was originally a 10 µF aluminum electrolytic capacitor. Being disappointed with the performance, I turned to the old trick of adding multiple parallel capacitors to decrease the effective series resistance (ESR). Even after adding four additional 10 µF aluminum electrolytic capacitors in key locations throughout the board, the detect pin still showed the noise illustrated on the right side of Figure 11-14. This noise was so noticeable that looking closely at the bicolor indicator LED showed both the red and green lighting up at the same time (to the human eye).

Pulling all five aluminum electrolytic capacitors and replacing them with a single 10 µF tantalum capacitor changed the detect pin output into what you see on the left side of Figure 11-14. Occasionally you could still see a hint of red in the bicolor indicator LED. So, I added another 10 µF tantalum capacitor, and the spikes disappeared almost entirely. In fact, you can spot the additional unlabeled tantalum capacitor at the bottom of the solderless breadboard in Figure 11-11. This second capacitor hasn't been included in the schematic because it was only needed on the solderless breadboard, not in the final soldered circuit.

Tantalum capacitors aren't magical. Other types of capacitors might have provided the same result. However, I didn't have the time or desire to search for the true cause. The lesson here is that if you're experiencing spurious signals, unstable outputs, or other electrical noise problems, a simple solution can sometimes be to switch or add different types of capacitors to obtain the best attributes of each type. As consolation to advocates of aluminum electrolytic capacitors, they're used in my power supply for this breadboard, which might explain why adding more of them didn't reduce the source of this particular noise problem.

Inserting Polarized Capacitors in the Correct Orientation

Tantalum and aluminum electrolytic capacitors are generally polarized components. This means a polarized capacitor has a positive lead (the anode) and a negative lead (the cathode). If inserted incorrectly, the capacitor won't perform its function and will likely become damaged.

To demonstrate the rivalry between aluminum electrolytic and tantalum capacitors, on the package they stripe the opposite lead as the other. Aluminum electrolytic capacitors usually have a stripe on their package indicating the negative lead (see the first two capacitors in Figure 11-15). Tantalum capacitors usually have a stripe on their package indicating the positive lead (see the last two capacitors in Figure 11-15). Will these two chemistries ever get along?

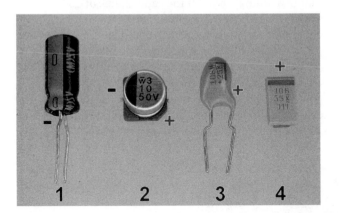

Figure 11-15. ① *Aluminum electrolytic radial through-hole capacitor with a stripe and a minus (-) sign indicating the negative lead.* ② *Aluminum electrolytic surface-mount capacitor with a stripe indicating the negative lead and a notch indicating the positive lead.* ③ *Tantalum radial through-hole capacitor with a stripe and a plus (+) sign indicating the positive lead.* ④ *Tantalum surface-mount capacitor with a stripe/bar indicating the positive lead.*

NOTE *I'm somewhat joking about this whole rivalry thing. But because of recent shortages, tantalum prices have risen significantly. Also, there are social, environmental, and political issues surrounding tantalum's sourcing. Multilayer ceramics are taking aim at the low end of the classic sweet spot for tantalum capacitors (1 μF to 100 μF). At less than 1 μF, ceramics and plastics rule. At greater than 100 μF, aluminum electrolytic capacitors win out because of low cost. I plan to sit on the sidelines until someone wins, and then I'll go around claiming I preferred that kind of capacitor all along ("Oh, yes! I've been using organics for years!")*

Selecting a Timing Capacitor

The capacitance of most capacitors isn't manufactured to strict tolerances. It isn't uncommon for a capacitor to be specified at +80/-20 percent value. That is, if you order a 68 μF capacitor and measure it with a multimeter, the capacitor might be 122 μF or it might be 54 μF, but it will still be considered within specifications. In practice, modern capacitors, like modern resistors, actually tend to be much closer to their intended value than the manufacturer officially guarantees. Even so, capacitance does change with age and temperature.

Usually a variation in capacitance isn't significant to most circuits. When selecting C2, I found significant noise reduction at 4.7 μF, doubled the value, and rounded up to the nearest available capacitor value to provide some margin. So, if the 10 μF capacitor happens to be 18 μF or 8 μF, it still meets the needs of the circuit.

Although such variations don't matter much for bypassing and noise reduction, such variations aren't insignificant to a timing circuit. If the capacitance of C5 is doubled, the frequency of the wave is halved. With the value specified, variable resistor R6 can only compensate for some minor variation in C5's capacitance.

For capacitance tolerance, temperature stability, small size, and low cost, a polyester (also known as Mylar) film capacitor is a good choice for C5 (about $0.10; #RMC-102 .001 at All Electronics, #P4551 at Digi-Key, and #14MR100.001U at Electronix Express), as shown in Figure 11-16. Metallized polyester, polypropylene, polycarbonate, and silver mica are also acceptable substitutes. In fact, the last three are superior for timing operations although larger and more expensive than polyester film.

Figure 11-16. A selection of radial-lead capacitors, all rated 1 nF. Polyester (Mylar) film capacitor, metallized polyester, silver mica, and ceramic disc (left to right). (But don't use a ceramic disc for the timing circuit.)

Making It Work

In this chapter, you learned about the component parts in a sensor system that relies on a reflected infrared signal for object and wall detection. The chapter covered the 38 kHz detector (PNA4602M) in some detail. (You'll never look at a remote control the same way again.) The chapter also covered primary attributes to consider in selecting an infrared LED.

This chapter also discussed some choices in capacitor technology. The next time you encounter erratic circuit behavior, consider adding a variety of capacitors across the board. Capacitors won't fix a bad circuit design or incorrect wiring, but they can reduce electrical noise that interferes with sensitive readings.

Finally, the chapter touched on a few reasons you might choose to select a multiturn trimpot instead of a single-turn trimpot. But the considerable worth of a multiturn trimpot will be covered in greater detail in the next chapter, where you'll fine-tune the emitter's output frequency.

Fine-Tuning the Reflector Detector

Covers Hand Tuning, Plugging Infrared Leaks, Tuning with a **Multimeter** with Frequency Mode, Tuning with an Oscilloscope, Infrared Limitations, and Comparing Distance Detection with Various Materials

AFTER PUTTING TOGETHER the reflector detector, whether on a solderless breadboard or a printed circuit board, you'll need to tune the frequency of the emitted wave to 38 kHz. Along the way, you'll likely encounter common problems that this chapter explains how to test for and correct.

This chapter also describes and demonstrates some of the weaknesses of infrared reflective detection, even when the circuit is operating optimally. If you're aware of these limitations in advance, you can better plan for placement of the sensors on the robot, as well as avoid relying too heavily on things that the sensor can't do well. In the end, you'll understand both the popularity and complaints surrounding this technology.

Tuning In 38 kHz

Recall that you can't specify a specific fixed resistor value for R6 because the actual resistor capacitor (RC) timing depends on the actual (rather than labeled) resistor (R5 and R6) values and actual capacitor (C5) values on that particular board. In addition, the inputs of the 74AC14 (pins 1 and 3 of IC1) consume some current, and the board itself has inherent resistance, capacitance, and leakage. As such, you use a potentiometer (in this case, a multiturn trimpot) to adjust the resistance until the charging/discharging cycle of C5 occurs 38,000 times a second.

You have several ways to tune the circuit: by detection, by multimeter, and by oscilloscope. It's worth reading about all three methods because some of the information and debugging techniques overlap.

Selecting Halfway Between the Start of Detection and End of Detection

The most practical way to tune the circuit is simply to place your hand a few centimeters over the emitters and detectors (see Figure 12-1) and slowly turn the adjustment screw on trimpot R6 until the bicolor LEDs (LED1 and LED2) change color to indicate detection. Mentally note the position of the screw and then continue to slowly turn it until detection ceases. It's likely 38 kHz in the middle of the range of when detection started and when detection ended.

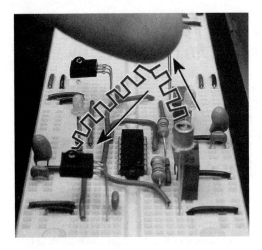

Figure 12-1. Tuning the circuit by turning the trimpot until a hand or other reflective object is detected

Never Indicating Detection Suggests Something Is Wrong with the Emitters

Recall in the previous chapter that you can test the detectors with an ordinary Sony remote control. At this point, I assume you've performed that testing on the current circuit and that you can rule out the detectors as being at fault.

After trimming, if the circuit never detects your hand, make sure R7's resistance is turned down enough to allow enough current to flow through IED3 and IED4. If necessary, use a video camera or digital camera to view the infrared LEDs to be sure they're emitting (infrared appears as pinkish or purple through most electronic camera view screens). Check that one or both LEDs aren't inserted with the wrong polarity.

If you get desperate, you can temporarily substitute high-brightness red LEDs to make sure the emitter portion of the circuit is functioning. However, the detectors won't work with the red LEDs installed because the red LEDs emit at a wavelength from approximately 630 nm to 700 nm, not the 940 nm needed for operation by the detectors.

Always Indicating Detection Suggests Signal Leakage

The PNA4602Ms may always indicate detection even when a hand or an object isn't in range of the sensors. Assuming the circuit is wired correctly, the most common causes of false detection are that the circuit is too noisy, too much infrared light is being emitted from the infrared LEDs, and infrared light is leaking from the sides of the infrared LEDs.

Checking for Circuit Noise Signal Leakage

On a solderless breadboard, you can quickly diagnose whether the 38 kHz signal is leaking into IC3 and IC4 via circuit noise either by removing IED3 and IED4 or by replacing them with yellow-green (2 V or less) LEDs. By doing so, neither IED3 nor IED4 emit infrared light. Replacing them with yellow-green LEDs has the advantage of permitting current to flow through those pathways as usual, thus emitting electrical noise to somewhat the same extent as when the infrared LEDs were in place.

If pin 1 of either IC3 or IC4 remains at less than 2.5 V (as opposed to 5 V, which represents "no signal detected") with yellow-green LEDs in place, then noise from the circuit is likely the cause of the false detections. The infrared LEDs can't be the signal source because they've been removed. To correct an electrical noise problem, try adding capacitors (see "Cleaning the Power Supply with Local Capacitors" in Chapter 11), shortening wires and leads, or moving IC3 and IC4 farther away from the rest of the circuit. However, believe me, if you have a messy board with long wires crossing all over the place, this circuit isn't going to work well for you.

Shooting the Messenger

When discussing circuit noise and false detection, some builders make the mistake of blaming the quality of the detector. They overlook that these photodetection ICs are built for inclusion in devices that are only detecting, not transmitting. For example, the DVD, TV, and CD player receive signals from a remote control, whose transmission circuit is electrically separate and physically distant.

Furthermore, the whole purpose of these detectors is to communicate the signal, not ignore it. It's to their benefit that the detectors are really sensitive. Speaking of which, the PNA4602M has an even more sensitive sibling part, the PNA4612M00YB. But even with its metal shielding, that part is far too sensitive to electrical noise to use in a reflective detector circuit.

Admittedly, sometimes detectors are included in the same circuit as a transmitter for the purpose of sending and receiving data. However, infrared exchanges are half-duplex communications: One device talks while the other device listens. Therefore, the unit transmitting can ignore its detection circuit during transmission. Self-generated circuit noise is usually not a problem as long as it can disable its 38 kHz generator while listening. That's not possible in the reflective detector because the 38 kHz signal must be generated and emitted while listening for the reflection.

Checking for Infrared LEDs Being Too "Bright"

Another common source of signal leakage, in an otherwise correctly wired circuit, is too much light being emitted from the infrared LEDs. Try turning the dial on R7 to increase its resistance. At lower resistances, enough current flows for some infrared LEDs to bounce light off of white or otherwise reflective ceilings and nearby objects. At higher resistances, even nearby objects can go undetected.

You'll find that adjusting R7 is one of the most valuable techniques in altering the sensitivity of the reflector detector circuit, especially after installing the circuit in a robot. Depending on the robot's reliance on this particular circuit, adjustments to the total infrared output can significantly alter the behavior of the robot. A robot spooked by a far-away wall needs the light output turned down. A robot that smacks into a black (less reflective) wall needs the light output turned up.

Leaking Signal from the Sides of the Infrared LEDs

The final most common source of signal leakage is infrared light being emitted from the sides or bottoms of the infrared LEDs. Although a half-beam angle may be specified as ±20 degrees (for example), a small amount of light is still emitted at broader angles. In fact, the best datasheets usually have a graph showing how much light is emitted at each angle. It's not uncommon for a relative (normalized) 1 percent of the infrared light to be emitted at ±90 degrees, even in a ±20-degree half-beam angle infrared LED.

Depending on the location and direction of the infrared LEDs in a circuit, the light escaping from the sides of the infrared LEDs can proceed directly to the PNA4602M detectors without being reflected off a nearby object. Therefore, you must eliminate side leakage almost completely for this circuit to be useful as a reflective detector.

Try placing a thick, infrared-opaque object (sheet metal, for example) between the infrared LEDs and the PNA4602Ms so that only reflected light could possibly be detected. If that eliminates the false detections, then you know that side leakage is a concern. *Side leakage from a "bare" (unaltered) LED is almost always an issue!*

Fortunately, there are many simple ways to reduce or solve the problem:

- Choose an infrared LED with a narrower beam angle.

- Cover the sides and bottoms (not the tops, please) of the infrared LEDs with black paint (see Figure 12-2). I've successfully used a single coat of Testors Flat Black Enamel #1149.

- Cover the sides and bottoms (again, not the tops) of the infrared LEDs with black heat-shrink tubing. Be warned, however, that depending on the type and thickness of the heat-shrink material, some heat-shrink tubing may be somewhat transparent to infrared light. I find heat-shrink tubing slightly less effective than black paint.

- Glue a metal tube around the sides of the infrared LEDs. Specifically, ¼-inch outer-diameter (inner diameter is reduced by 0.014-inch thick walls) aluminum or brass telescoping tubing works well for T1¾ package LEDs, except that the bottom portion of the LED is exposed. You can sand the bottom edges of the LED to allow the tube to extend lower. Painting the insides of the tubing black (before gluing to the LED) can further reduce photons at stray angles.

- Purchase an infrared LED with a metal case. This has the added benefit of more rapid heat dispersion. But that's not a concern with LEDs being driven at less than 20 mA.

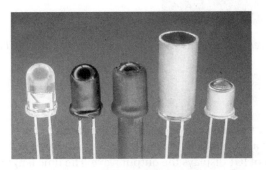

Figure 12-2. Standard infrared LED, sides painted black, covered with heat-shrink tubing, brass tube placed over the infrared LED, and an LED with a metal case (left to right)

I often choose a combination of the previous techniques. For example, I select an LED with a narrow beam angle, paint the sides and bottom black, and then add either heat-shrink or metal tubing to it. That's probably overkill. The important point is to avoid bare infrared LEDs because enough light leaks from the sides to cause direct false detections.

Using a Multimeter with Frequency Detection

With the manual tuning technique just described, you should be able to tune and test the reflector detector circuit. A more precise way to tune the circuit is with a multimeter that has frequency measurement.

Although you should refer to your multimeter manual for specific instructions, most often you'll attach the multimeter's ground/negative probe to GND on the reflector detector circuit and the multimeter's positive probe to pin 4 of IC1. Pin 4 is a better choice than pin 2 because even a high-impedance multimeter would otherwise drain some current from pin 2, thus affecting the charge/discharge timing cycle of capacitor C5. You'd end up with a circuit perfectly timed only when a multimeter is attached.

With the multimeter attached, simply adjust R6 until the frequency reads 38 kHz on the multimeter (see Figure 12-3). Note that the multimeter probes have IC hook adaptors connected to jumper wire connected to the solderless breadboard. That's a lot easier than using one hand to hold the positive probe in place, the other hand to hold the ground probe in place, and the third hand to turn the trimpot.

Figure 12-3. A multimeter with a frequency measurement mode is probably the best way to tune the circuit.

Using an Oscilloscope

Although an oscilloscope is probably the most complex way to tune the circuit, it does give you the opportunity to get a close look at the quality of the output wave. Connecting an oscilloscope to pin 4 of IC1 displays the output wave. The time length of one rising edge to the next rising edge should be $\frac{1}{38000}$ of a second, which is about 0.0000263 seconds or 26.3 μs (microseconds); see Figure 12-4.

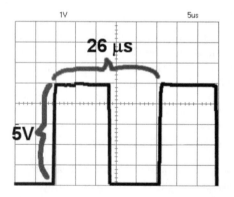

Figure 12-4. The grid in the oscilloscope trace represents 1 V for each step vertically and 5 μs for each step horizontally. The wave is about 5 grid units tall, or about 5 V. The wave is more than 5 grid units wide peak to peak, or a little more than 26 μs. Mr. Oscilloscope says, "It's a nice, clean, 38 kHz square wave at output pin 4 of IC1."

Revealing the Purpose of a Schmitt-Trigger Inverter

If you're going to the trouble of hooking up the reflector detector circuit to an oscilloscope, then sneak a peek at pin 1 (yes, it'll slow down the timing for the moment). The voltage wave at pin 1 isn't a square wave; it's a triangle wave with slight curves to the sides of the triangle (see Figure 12-5). The up slope is the capacitor charging, and the down slope is the capacitor discharging.

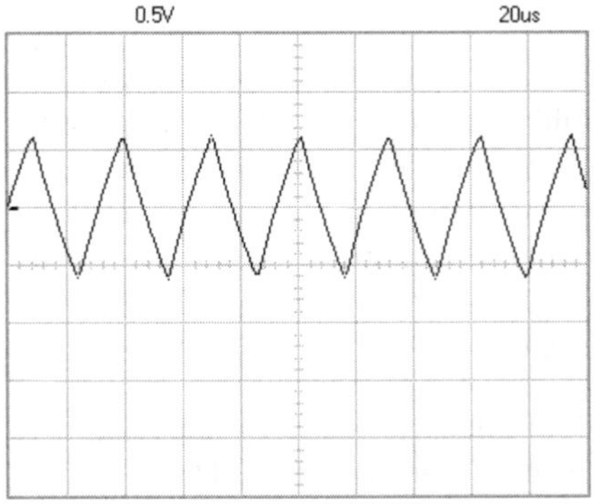

Figure 12-5. The classic triangular wave with slight arcs is the heart of an RC circuit as the capacitor charges and discharges repeatedly.

Standard logic chips despise slow rise and fall times. A standard chip uses a lot of power, changing its mind as to whether a 2.5 V signal is high (5 V) or low (0 V) or high (5 V) or low (0 V). After all, this is supposed to be an on/off digital logic chip, not an "any-value-in-between" analog chip. A Schmitt-trigger input is specifically designed to accept a noisy digital signal, a slow moving analog signal, or an otherwise messy nondigital signal and convert it into a clean digital signal.

A Schmitt trigger works through a process called *hysteresis*. Instead of having fixed high and low trip points, it has one moving trip point. It lowers the trip point when the signal is interpreted as high, and it raises the trip point when the signal is interpreted as low. In doing so, an input can't vibrate between 49 percent and 51 percent of the supply voltage and change the output. The input has to go up to 66 percent and then all the way down to 33 percent. (The actual voltages and percentages vary based on the chip.)

For example, let's say the input is 2.5 V in a 0 V to 5 V circuit. Let's say the starting trip point is set at 3 V. When the input reaches 3.01 V, the Schmitt trigger declares the input "high" and then lowers the trip point to 2 V. Well, 3.01 V is still higher than 2 V, so the input still qualifies as "high." In fact, now it's clearly very high compared to 2 V. If this noisy input briefly drops down to 2.99 V, who cares? The fact is that 2.99 V is still higher than 2 V, and the input is still declared "high." Finally, the input makes its way down to 1.99 V and is declared "low." The Schmitt trigger then changes the trip point up to 3 V. Well, 1.99 V is still low compared to 3 V. In fact, now it's clearly very low. There's no middle line to straddle. As soon as you pass the line, the line moves away.

Diagnosing Problems Encountered in Circuit Tuning

If you can't tune the reflector detector circuit to 38 kHz, then there are a number of potential solutions:

- Check the voltage being delivered to the circuit. If it isn't between 4.7 V and 5.3 V, check your power supply. The voltage should be steady. If not, try adding some bulk (10 µF or better) capacitors or swapping out the existing capacitors. My power supply provides a voltage that doesn't vary much more than from 4.97 V to 5 V over the course of five minutes. Not only will an out-of-range power supply prevent the PNA4602Ms from working, but also it'll definitely affect the frequency generated because VCO stands for *voltage*-controlled oscillator.

- Check the wiring to make sure the circuit looks like the schematic (see Figure 11-10) and the solderless breadboard example (see Figure 11-11).

- If, after turning the trimpot R6 to its minimum and maximum, the frequency is still too *low* (less than 38 kHz), reduce the resistance value of R5. For example, substitute a 13 kΩ resistor. Then try adjusting the trimpot again.

- If, after turning the trimpot R6 to its minimum and maximum, the frequency is still too *high* (more than 38 kHz), increase the resistance value of R5. For example, substitute a 30 kΩ resistor. Then try adjusting the trimpot again.

- If you still can't get the frequency in range, double-check the actual capacitance of C5 using a multimeter. If it's 1 nF, then replace R5 with a piece of wire and replace R6 with a single-turn large-value trimpot, such as 500 kΩ. After roughly tuning in the approximate frequency, pull R6 and measure the resistance using a multimeter. That should give you an idea of the resistance to shoot for in your circuit.

Targeting Reasonable Frequency Accuracy

Don't be too concerned if you can't achieve exactly 38 kHz. My circuit's frequency tends to float between 37.93 kHz and 38.07 kHz. Anything between 37 kHz and 39 kHz works great. You can even get reasonable detection from 35 kHz to 43 kHz. By the way, an interesting trick for reducing cross talk (circuit noise) or to limit the range of detection is to purposely detune the circuit.

Stretching for Unreasonable Frequency Accuracy

If you really want to achieve a finely tuned frequency, you can narrow R6 to a smaller resistance trimpot so that each turn of the adjustment screw affects a smaller change in resistance. Follow these steps:

1. First tune the circuit as best as you can with the standard values of R5 and R6.

2. Pull out R5 and R6 and measure their resistances. Mine ended at 21.66 kΩ and 3.3 kΩ for a total of 24.96 kΩ.

3. Find a smaller resistance multiturn trimpot, say, 1 kΩ instead of 10 kΩ.

4. Subtract half the value of the new trimpot (1 kΩ divided by 2 equals 0.5 kΩ) from the prior total (24.96 kΩ minus 0.5 kΩ equals 24.46 kΩ). This is new desired value for R5. You're not likely to find a resistor of this value, but you can connect two in series—say, a 24 kΩ resistor connected to a 0.470 kΩ resistor.

5. Place the new R5 (24.47 Ω) and new R6 (0 Ω to 1000 Ω) into the circuit.

6. Now when you turn the screw on the multiturn trimpot (R6), each turn makes a much smaller change in the frequency.

This explains the purpose of R5. It could be eliminated, and R6 could simply be a single 50 kΩ trimpot. However, each little nudge of the trimpot's screw would cause a fairly large change in frequency. Even vibration caused by movement of the robot might cause shifts in frequency. By including R5 as a base, R6 can have a smaller range and therefore more finely tune the frequency.

Accepting the Limited Accuracy and Stability of the Oscillator Circuit

The oscillator portion of the circuit is fairly simple and uses few components. The downside is that this circuit isn't that accurate or stable. A crystal-based circuit would improve accuracy and stability but is really unnecessary because the PNA4602M is fairly tolerant. The following are some of the known limitations of the oscillator circuit:

*   As the components age, the oscillator circuit may need retuning from time to time. That's easily enough accomplished.

*   The supply voltage affects the oscillator's frequency. However, most modern regulators do a fine job of staying within a half percent of the desired voltage.

*   The oscillator's wave may become erratic if placed near noisy sources such as motors. Increasing the capacitance of C5 while decreasing the resistances of R5 and R6 would improve noise immunity at the expense of increased power usage.

*   The oscillator isn't temperature stable. After tuning the oscillator to approximately 38.02 kHz, I placed the board in the freezer. This was a bit risky for two reasons: First, the bulk capacitors might be damaged below 0° C. And second, my wife might have wanted some ice for her drink. After about 20 minutes, I removed the slightly frosted board and powered it up. The frequency had dropped to 37.83 kHz. That's not bad (99.5 percent of the original frequency). The frequency returned to 38.01 kHz after the board warmed up to room temperature. The biggest problem with the cold ended up being the reduction in capacitance of tantalum capacitor C2, causing false detections to reappear until the board warmed up.

Limitations of the Reflector Detector

A 38 kHz infrared reflective detector works well for many tasks and thus finds itself in many robot designs. However, there are environmental circumstances that a robot might encounter that limit the usefulness of any light-based reflective detector.

Failing to Work Outdoors or Under Bright Lights

Detection is impossible or the detection range is severely reduced in sunny conditions or with really bright indoor lights. This is caused by the large amount of ambient lighting producing such a large amount of current in the photodiode (built into the photodetector IC) that the relatively weak amount of light from the 38 kHz infrared beam becomes insignificant by comparison. Either the photodiode is fully saturated (all the way turned on already) by the bright ambient lighting or the peaks and valleys of the noise (shadows, output fluctuations) of the bright ambient lighting are greater than the peaks and valleys of the 38 kHz square wave coming from the infrared LEDs.

The following are a couple of potential solutions:

- Block the direct rays of overhead ambient lighting by adding a roof or cover on top of the emitter, the detector, and the object to be detected. Of course, this doesn't work for wall detection.

- Add a transistor to the emitter circuit (see the next chapter) so that 1 amp or more can be poured through properly rated infrared LEDs. The problem with this, besides power consumption, is that the emitters would then be too powerful for indoor or nighttime use, where the lack of background light noise would permit detectable reflections from even across the room.

- Change from light-based detection to sound-based detection (such as the clicking sonar of a Polaroid camera), capacitance detection (such as a stud finder), or physical detection (such as a touch switch).

Failing to Detect Certain Kinds of Objects

Another potential problem area for an infrared reflective detector is that the detector can't see objects that either readily absorb infrared light or are mostly transparent to infrared light. This is because the detector relies on the infrared pattern being reflected off the object. Obviously, if the object absorbs that light or the light simply passes through the object, then this detector isn't going to work very well on that object.

Because many sumo robots use light-based detectors of some kind or another, many sumo robots have adopted a defense against detection: They're painted black (see Figure 12-6). Most black paint absorbs infrared light as well as visible light, making the robot difficult for an opponent to detect.

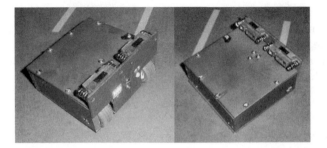

Figure 12-6. Hard2C is a mini-sumo robot that relies on stealth for an edge. The robot is painted flat black, which is the same as the color of the sumo ring itself. Additionally, the robot is only 4 cm tall (the rear column is 6 cm tall). Therefore, as the robot's name indicates, this robot is "hard to see."

Truly infrared-transparent objects are simply not going to be detectable with infrared light. However, objects that absorb infrared light can be detected by rearranging the physical positions of the emitters and detectors. By aiming the infrared LEDs directly at the detectors, with a gap between them, an object that absorbs infrared light can be detected when it comes between the LED and the detector. This is called an *interrupter* or a *break-beam sensor*, as opposed to a reflective sensor.

The break-beam sensor inverts the voltage value that indicates object detection. Because the LED is now aimed at the detector, a 0 V (signal detected) appears at pin 1 when no object is present. When a nontransparent (absorbing or reflecting) object comes between the LED and the detector, a 5 V (no signal detected) appears at pin 1 because the signal has been interrupted.

Failing to Detect Objects Far Away or Really, Really Close

Another deficiency of the infrared reflective detector is true of all active (emitting) sensors: They have a minimum and maximum range. The reflective detector requires the emitted signal to bounce off of an object and return to be detected. If the object is too close, the beam won't have spread out enough from the emitter to be reflected back into the detector. Conversely, if the object is too far away, the signal will have spread out too much, thus dimming too much to be detected when it reflects back.

You can tailor the infrared LED's beam angle to suit particular purposes either by choosing a different LED or by employing lenses. A narrower beam angle supports greater distances at the cost of less coverage area. A wider beam angle can support short distances at the cost of less focused targeting.

Before proceeding with angle tweaking, you need to determine whether your robot really needs to see up that close or see that far away. Of what value is it for the robot to detect the existence of something somewhere between 2 millimeters and 2 meters away? If the sensors provided distance data, then it might be of value, but this circuit indicates only that something exists in that direction.

Also, think three-dimensionally for a minute: The infrared beam spreads out from the LED like a cone with a spherical top. At some distance, depending on the height of the sensors on the robot, the beam eventually starts reflecting off the floor. Being given a digital indication that a floor, wall, or object is somewhere in the distance is of little practical value (I mean, other than for cliff detection). So, ease up on trying to stretch the detection distance.

Comparing Your Distances to Mine

If you're concerned that your reflector detector is performing poorly, you can compare your results to mine. I performed these barely scientific tests in a somewhat dimly lit room (between 40 and 60 lux). Remember that the greater the amount of ambient lighting, the poorer the signal to noise ratio and therefore the lower the detection range and reliability.

On the solderless breadboard, I installed a pair of Jameco 106526 infrared LEDs ($0.50 each, 940 nm, 20 degrees, 8 mW/cm^2, T1¾ package hand-painted black on the sides) for IED3 and IED4. The tests were performed with 3.5 mA of current flowing through the infrared LEDs with virtually no false detections when no target objects were present. (By the way, 50 percent false detections occurred when infrared LED current was increased to around 7.5 mA, and 100 percent false detections occurred at around 10 mA.)

I raised and lowered target objects to determine when there was no detection (almost no red in the bicolor LEDs), about half detection (equal mix of red and green in the bicolor LEDs), and full detection (almost no green in the bicolor LEDs). All objects were held parallel to the breadboard surface unless noted. Distances were measured from the top of the infrared LEDs to the bottommost point on the target (see Table 12-1).

Analyzing the Distance Results

Table 12-1 reveals a number of noteworthy pieces of information.

Line 1 shows that bare aluminum can be detected the farthest away of all objects targeted. If you want to build a sumo robot that can be quickly spotted by an opponent, build it out of bare aluminum.

Lines 3, 8, and 11 demonstrate the effect of transparent materials at different angles and shapes. Line 3 shows that holding the transparent material at just the correct angle (parallel to the emitter and detector) to give off that annoying reflection makes the material obvious to the sensors—nearly as detectable as white paper (line 2). Line 11 shows that the same transparent material, but now held at 45 degrees to avoid reflection, can't be detected by the sensors at all, regardless of distance. Line 8 shows a similar material in the shape of a cube no longer remains invisible to the sensors, even at 45 degrees. (Although not documented, polycarbonate sheet showed similar results to acrylic sheet in the other tests.)

Table 12-1. Sample Distance Measurements of the Reflector Detector Circuit

Line	Target Description	No Detection	Half Detection	Full Detection
1	Aluminum sheet. 1/16-inch thick, 20 cm × 30 cm, shiny but diffused (not like a mirror)	Greater than 195 cm	Approximately 185 cm	Less than 172 cm
2	White office paper. 1 cm thick stack, 8½ inches × 11 inches	Greater than 106 cm	Approximately 91 cm	Less than 81 cm
3	Clear acrylic sheet. 1/16-inch thick, 15 cm × 15 cm, optical-quality transparent, held parallel to the breadboard plane	Greater than 101 cm	Approximately 86 cm	Less than 78 cm
4	Hard2C robot. 6 cm thick, 10 cm × 10 cm, painted flat black, aluminum	Greater than 44 cm	Approximately 34 cm	Less than 27 cm
5	Pencil. 0.75 cm diameter, 19 cm long, yellow-orange, #2 lead, held with shiny aluminum eraser band covered	Greater than 32 cm	Approximately 28 cm	Less than 24 cm
6	Plastic egg. 2½-inch long, green, styrene, hung lengthwise from a string	Greater than 27 cm	Approximately 22 cm	Less than 17 cm
7	Hard2C robot. 6 cm thick, 10 cm × 10 cm, painted flat black, aluminum, held 45 degrees out of alignment from breadboard plane	Greater than 26 cm	Approximately 17 cm	Less than 13 cm
8	Clear cube. 15 cm × 15 cm, transparent, polycarbonate, hollow, held 45 degrees out of alignment from breadboard plane	Greater than 25 cm	Approximately 17 cm	Less than 11 cm
9	Wire, #22 AWG, white insulation, stranded copper	Greater than 23 cm	Approximately 17 cm	Less than 14 cm
10	Black conductive foam. ¼-inch thick, 1 foot × 2 feet, antistatic for ICs	Greater than 18 cm	Approximately 15 cm	Less than 11 cm
11	Clear acrylic sheet. 1/16-inch thick, 15 cm × 15 cm, optical-quality transparent, held 45 degrees out of alignment from breadboard plane	No detect	No detect	No detect

Therefore, building a flat shield from acrylic would avoid detection most of the time except when parallel to the opponent's infrared reflective sensors. However, a sumo robot whose entire body is acrylic is unlikely to enjoy the complete benefits. Transparent cube results are slightly better than can be achieved with flat black paint (line 7) except that a transparently housed robot is going to be showing off its highly reflective guts. Perhaps a robot coated with black antistatic foam (line 10) would be best of all at avoiding detection. In fact, the foam might also absorb sonar.

As for the results for smaller objects, a pencil (line 5) was noticeable ¼ meter away, which is impressive. A semi-infrared transparent styrene egg was detectable (line 6), as was a very skinny wire (line 9).

The most significant piece of information revealed in the distance table is that the reflector detector's detection distance varies greatly based on the size and color of the target material. Don't despair because most robots employing this sensor perform quite well under a variety of surroundings. However, under untested conditions, be prepared to tweak R7 to alter the detection distance.

Failing to Provide a Range Value

The PNA4602M is designed to output a digital signal (5 V or 0 V) to indicate detection. It doesn't provide a range value. It would be more useful if the detector provided a signal strength or distance to the object.

One potential way to extract more than a single bit of information from the detector is to pay attention to the noise. For example, a microcontroller could add ten consecutive inverted readings from the detector and call that signal strength. A 50 percent noisy signal would result in a 50 percent distance reading. Unfortunately, as you can see in Table 12-1, the difference between no detection and full detection isn't very much. Also, the reflectivity of the object completely alters the detection distance.

Getting Ready for a Practical Robot Application

In this chapter, you've tuned, tested, corrected, and validated the reflector detector circuit. Although it has some limitations, it's useful both as a short-distance, wide-angle bumper and as a longer-range, narrow-beam detector.

In the prior chapter, you learned about using bicolor LEDs in combination with a 74AC14 chip to indicate a digital value. That's practical not only for this particular detector but for anything else that provides a high or low output. Furthermore, you now know that because of the Schmitt-trigger inputs, the input signal can even be noisy and slow moving, and the 74AC14 will convert it to a clean, digital output.

In the next chapter, you'll combine the reflector detector with the circuits and machining techniques presented earlier in the book to create a functional robot that navigates with a virtual, wide-angle, contactless bumper.

CHAPTER 13

Roundabout Robot!

Build the Mindless Room Explorer, Connect Modules, Control with a Logic Chip, Reuse Sandwich, Build Body-Part Templates, Use Space-Saving Parallel Offset Motors, Swap Gears, Drill a Stack of Motor Mounts, Select Glides

THIS CHAPTER PUTS TOGETHER the robot-building blocks presented so far in this book to create a functional, wall-avoiding, obstacle-avoiding robot (see Figure 13-1). Roundabout is a simple robot that usually drives forward but can turn left, turn right, and reverse to avoid walls and obstacles it detects with its infrared sensors.

Figure 13-1. Roundabout, an obstacle-avoiding robot in a five-frame composite photograph showing it negotiate its way through the center of some box obstacles using onboard infrared sensors

Roundabout performs all of its actions without a microcontroller, so no programming is required. Unfortunately, with only a primitive logic chip for a brain, Roundabout inevitably encounters situations in which it gets stuck. Later chapters describe these situations and show how to add a microcontroller to improve the robot's autonomy.

This chapter includes details for re-creating Roundabout's custom body. However, there's no reason why you can't substitute different body parts to create a unique-looking robot with nearly identical behavior.

 NOTE *Sandwich, the line-following robot from my first book,* Robot Building for Beginners *(Apress, 2002), provides an excellent model to compare to Roundabout. If you don't know anything about Sandwich, remember that descriptions, images, and a movie are available online at* http://www.robotroom.com/Sandwich.html *(this address is case-sensitive).*

Examining Roundabout

Roundabout contains a single circuit board located atop the robot (see Figure 13-2). The front of the circuit board contains two infrared sensors for detecting walls and obstacles. A circular platform in the middle of the robot's body holds the robot together. Underneath, Roundabout contains two motors, two couplers, four gears, and two wheels with axles. A 9 V battery, located underneath in the rear, provides power.

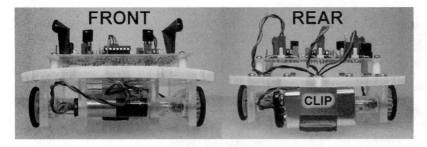

Figure 13-2. Front and rear views of Roundabout

Viewing Roundabout from the Side

Roundabout's wheels are on the outside of the robot, centered equidistant between the front and the rear of the robot (see Figure 13-3). This wheel location allows the robot to rotate in place (zero turning radius).

When accelerating forward, the robot tips backward and drags on the bottom rear of the body. When driving in reverse, the robot tips forward, dragging the front of the body. If the mass of the rear battery prevents your robot from tipping forward when driving in reverse, it may be necessary to taper the rear body corners to prevent them from snagging on carpet or gaps in the floor.

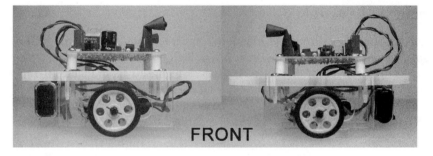

Figure 13-3. Right and left side views of Roundabout

Differential steering controls the direction that the robot travels. That is, the differences between the direction of each motor's spin (clockwise or counterclockwise) and the differences between the amounts of power delivered to each motor dictate the direction that the robot goes. Unlike a car, Roundabout doesn't steer by changing the angle of the wheels; the wheels always remain parallel to the robot's sides.

Viewing Roundabout from Above and Beneath

Roundabout's perimeter is completely encompassed by the circular midsection of the body. The motor and battery wires pass through the center of the platform (see "PASSTHRU" in the middle of the right side of Figure 13-4). The gears and wheels are within the circumference of the circular platform. As such, Roundabout can rotate freely in place without becoming locked against or snagged on any protuberance (look it up!).

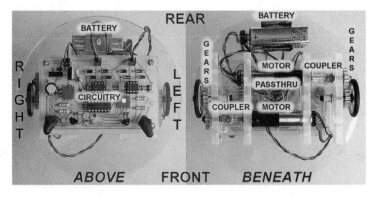

Figure 13-4. Views above and beneath Roundabout

On the left side of Figure 13-4, notice that the robot's sides are labeled "LEFT" and "RIGHT" to correspond with what would be your left and right sides if you were inside the robot facing forward. Additional information about Roundabout's body, motors, and gears appears in the "Examining Roundabout's Motor Mechanism" section later in this chapter.

Roundabout's Circuitry

Roundabout's circuitry consists of three modules: a linear 5 V voltage-regulator power supply (from Chapter 7, see Figure 7-2, Figure 7-3, or Figure 7-3 with Figure 7-6), a pair of motor drivers (from Chapter 9 or 10, see Figure 9-25, Figure 10-17, or Figure 10-18), and the infrared reflector detector (from Chapter 11, see Figure 11-10). The modules are connected as illustrated in Figure 13-5. Notice that Roundabout doesn't require any additional electronic parts beyond those already described in these modules.

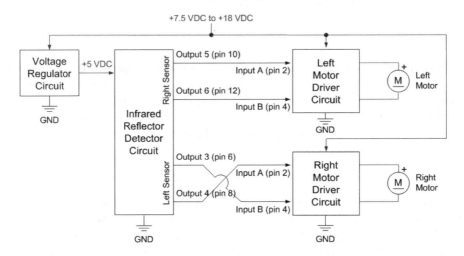

Figure 13-5. Block schematic of Roundabout's circuit. As is common to most robots, there's a voltage regulator, a brain (in this case, the 74AC14 of the infrared reflector detector), and motor drivers with motors.

Roundabout's circuitry can be implemented on a 3.8 inches by 2.5 inches circuit board using through-hole components (see Figure 13-6). Section 1 consists of a voltage regulator circuit. Section 2 consists of a pair of motor driver circuits. Section 3 consists of the infrared emitter detector circuit. Some renumbering of the part labels present in the original schematics for section 1 and section 2 was necessary so that no duplicate part labels appear on the aggregate board.

Supplying Power

The unregulated power source can be from 7.5 V to 18 V. Therefore, an alkaline 9 V battery or an 8.4 V NiMH Rayovac 9 V battery is adequate.

If a low-dropout linear regulator (LM2940, LP2954) and power MOSFET reverse-battery protection is installed instead of a 7805 with diode reverse-battery protection, then the minimum unregulated voltage can be as low as 5.5 V without significantly affecting the 5 V regulation. In that case, the robot can use a 7.2 V NiMH Energizer 9 V battery, a AA or AAA NiMH six-pack, or even a fresh AA or AAA alkaline four-pack.

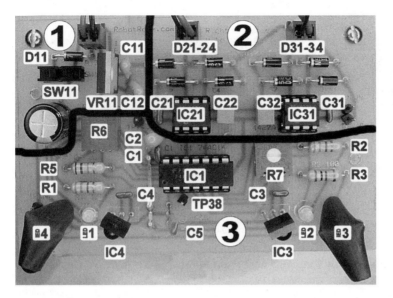

Figure 13-6. Implementation of Roundabout's circuitry on a homemade circuit board

The voltage regulator supplies 5 V to the infrared reflector detector circuit. Depending on how bright you set the infrared emitters and the bicolor LEDs, the infrared reflector detector circuit uses as little as 15 mA or up to 40 mA. Therefore, any of the 7805-compatible regulators would be perfectly adequate (even the 78L05) for providing enough current. However, if you plan on upgrading your robot with additional regulated circuits, such as a microcontroller, you might want to consider selecting a higher-current regulator such as the 7805C or LM2940.

Controlling Direction with Simple Logic

As you know, the infrared reflector detector circuit turns a bicolor LED red when an object is detected and green when no object is detected. The infrared reflector detector does so by setting one 74AC14 output high (5 V) and the other 74AC14 output low (0 V) to provide power to the red portion of the bicolor LED. To enable green, the outputs are reversed, with one 74AC14 output being set low (0 V) and the other 74AC14 output being set high (5 V). Well, surprise, surprise! Those are just the kind of control signals that a motor-driver circuit needs on input A and input B for clockwise and counter-clockwise control of a motor.

When both PNA4602M (IC4 and IC3) detectors don't see an obstacle, both motor drivers are controlled by the green signals (low and high), and the robot drives forward (see the left side of Figure 13-7). When both PNA4602M detectors see an obstacle, both motor drivers are controlled by the red signals (high and low), and the robot drives backward (see the right side of Figure 13-7).

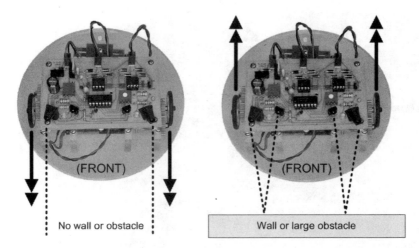

Figure 13-7. Roundabout moving forward when no obstacle is detected (left). Roundabout moving backward when an obstacle is detected by both sensors (right)

There's a bit of a trick here, which is common to almost all robots. Because each motor is physically facing the opposite direction with respect to each other, one motor has to spin in the opposite direction from the other motor for their attached wheels to move the robot in the same direction. To correct this condition, the control signals to the right motor drivers are simply flipped (see the crossover lines in Figure 13-5). Or you could flip the right motor-driver outputs instead. Or you could flip the wires on the right motor itself. Nevertheless, somewhere along the way, one motor has to have flipped wires to compensate for facing the opposite direction as the other motor.

Turning Left and Turning Right

The forward and reverse movements are fairly obvious and understandable. However, the left and right movements have a slight twist to them. Back in Figure 13-5, note that outputs 5 and 6 of the 74AC14 are associated with the *right* infrared sensor (IC4), but those outputs are connected to the *left* motor driver. Each sensor controls the motor on the opposite side of the robot's body so that the robot turns the opposite direction from a detected obstacle.

For example, when the left sensor detects an obstacle but the right sensor doesn't, the left sensor switches the right motor into reverse, but the right sensor tells the left motor to drive forward (see the left side of Figure 13-8). This causes the robot to rotate in place to the right, away from the obstacle located on the left. The opposite situation occurs when an obstacle is detected on the right side (see the right side of Figure 13-8).

When the robot has rotated far enough that the obstacle is no longer detected, then the robot stops rotating and proceeds to move forward again. Note that the crossover from left sensor to right motor and right sensor to left motor has no effect on full forward or full reverse movements because the signals coming from both sensors are the same (both "no detect" or both "detect").

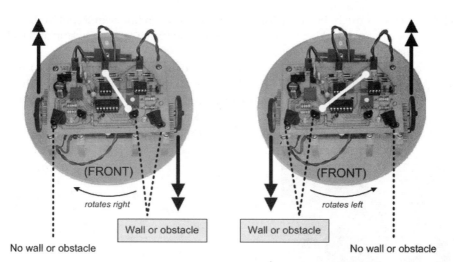

Figure 13-8. Roundabout rotates right when an obstacle is detected on the left side (left). Roundabout rotates left when an obstacle is detected on the right side (right).

The flipped wires and crossed-over controls may seem rather confusing. However, all robots that use differential steering have such an arrangement. That's just how motor rotations are translated into the motions of the robot. This isn't some contrived arrangement that you're using to make up for Roundabout's limited brain.

Gradually Heading Left and Gradually Heading Right

One of the most interesting behaviors of the Roundabout robot is when the PNA4602M doesn't completely detect an obstacle. Under those conditions, the PNA4602M tends to switch between detect (0 V) and no-detect (5 V) very quickly. Recall from the previous chapter that "partial" detection is indicated by seeing some red and some green at the same time in the bicolor LED.

If the robot is driving beside an obstacle, the PNA4602M may pick up reflections only once in a while so it briefly indicates a detection (0 V). When that occurs, the power supplied to the opposite motor is briefly reversed. It happens so quickly and so rarely that the robot doesn't appear to rotate in place. In fact, the slight starvation of the one motor results in a gradual arcing away from the obstacle, as opposed to a hard turn.

At 50 percent detection, the motor is switched between forward and reverse so much that it stops. That results in the robot pivoting around one stationary wheel rather than rotating in place.

Avoiding Infrared Leaks

When Roundabout was first built, it would sporadically stray left as though there were a ghost object on the right side. A visual inspection didn't indicate anything, but an oscilloscope trace of the right sensor revealed random detections. At first I thought the

PNA4602M detector might be faulty. But it turned out that an uncovered spot in the right emitter's paint was leaking enough infrared for the PNA4602M to pick up and lock onto intermittently.

Before you solder any infrared emitters to your board, hold each emitter up to an ultrabright, narrowly focused color LED. Select a color LED that most contrasts with the infrared emitter's lens and paint (or other covering). Position the infrared emitter with respect to the color LED so that the light enters the front of the infrared emitter and pours out of any uncovered locations (see Figure 13-9).

Figure 13-9. An ultrabright red LED (hidden in this photograph), sitting on a bread-board, illuminates an infrared emitter held by needle-nose pliers. A bare spot glows on the infrared emitter.

After careful inspection and a second coat of paint, I added black heat-shrink tubing to further cover the sides and rears of the infrared emitters. I decided not to shrink the tubing, which would have rendered it less flexible, so that, in the future, I could experiment with adjusting the angle of the emitters.

Building Roundabout's Body

I chose to make Roundabout's body by hand using a drill press/milling machine with a rotary table. However, you can use a plastic kitchen container or even a rectangular project box if you want. In fact, you can even put Roundabout's circuitry inside Sandwich from *Robot Building for Beginners* (see Figure 13-10).

Figure 13-10. Two different ways to add Roundabout's circuit to a sandwich-container body. Roundwich? You can save time and money by swapping Roundabout's circuit board into Sandwich's body (left). Notice the front eyeholes. A sandwich container with Roundabout's board mounted on top, a centered axle, and slightly different wheels (right)

If you're going to mount Roundabout's board inside of Sandwich, consider these tips:

- Drill some eyeholes for the emitters. Otherwise the plastic container may internally reflect enough infrared to cause false detections.

- Aim the emitters a bit upward and decrease the amount of current (R7) they're provided; otherwise, the low profile and downward angle of Sandwich's body may cause the floor to be detected. If this occurs, the robot constantly drives around backward (backing away from the floor), which is hilarious but not valuable.

- Replace Roundabout's onboard power switch with a two-pin Molex connector to connect it with Sandwich's rear power switch.

- Sandwich's light/dark line-following switch and tube LEDs aren't used by the stock Roundabout printed circuit board. Either leave those connectors detached or customize your homemade board to use those extra parts.

Declaring Caveats Because of Gearmotor Availability

In a perfect world, a robot builder would be able design a robot to the exact purpose and specifications as dreamed up in the robot builder's mind. In reality, most robots are built from whatever base can accommodate the gearmotors that the robot builder has on hand. Roundabout fits that description because I started modeling a base around a batch of gearmotors I was fortunate enough to obtain at an online auction.

Generally speaking, reasonably inexpensive high-quality gearmotors aren't readily available. Many builders must rely on odds and ends found in surplus catalogs. Sure, you can pay $75 or more per gearmotor and get exactly what you want from the manufacturer, but that's outside most hobbyists' budgets.

One option for top-of-the-line miniature gearmotors is auction Web sites. At eBay, try searching for the seller "thesequoiagroup." This seller offers new, overstocked motors from one of the highest-quality manufacturers (Maxon) at prices about one-third the price of retail. Of course, there's a limited supply, and you can't specify custom parameters like you can when you purchase directly from the manufacturer. I've purchased many motors from the Sequoia Group, and I've been very happy with them.

Another option for obtaining motors is the retail market, whose situation is improving with the growth of robotics as a hobby. You can find inexpensive gearmotors regularly stocked at Solarbotics. Also, Jameco and Lynxmotion routinely carry a supply of appropriate gearmotors. However, almost no motors are available from multiple sources. For example, whenever Jameco runs out of Sandwich's recommended motors, I'm inundated with emails requesting the name of another supplier (I'm not aware of another supplier of those exact motors).

Therefore, in fairness to readers, this book tries to avoid tying a robot's design specifically to one type of motor or one type of body. Instead, this book details the general attributes of a robot's motors and body so that you can select an appropriate choice from the motors and materials available to you.

Using Precision Escap Gearmotors in Roundabout

With all of the disclaimers mentioned, Roundabout uses 13 mm diameter, 12 V, 13N88-110 Escap motors (see Figure 13-11). These motors are reasonably efficient for their small size, which means battery life is extended.

Figure 13-11. Small-diameter Escap motors drive Roundabout.

These particular motors have a gearhead ratio of 352:1. That's too high. It results in only 25 RPM at 9 V. With 3 cm diameter LEGO wheels, Roundabout moves at approximately the following calculation:

```
linear speed in cm/s = wheel diameter in cm X π X (RPM ÷ 60 seconds in a minute)
linear speed in cm/s = 3 cm X 3.14159 X (25 RPM ÷ 60)
linear speed in cm/s = 3.927 cm/s
```

Roundabout is very slow. For comparison, Sandwich has a stock speed of approximately 26 cm/s. A lower gear ratio would improve performance, but the 352:1 ratio was the only gearhead available in these surplus motors. Of course, your Roundabout robot can be faster, depending upon the motors you select.

Leaning Toward Particular Attributes

It's preferable, but not required, that Roundabout's body has the following characteristics:

Small: It should be fairly small so that the robot can drive through narrow openings.

Light: It should be lightweight so the motors aren't overloaded. A 9 V battery may not be able to supply enough power to overloaded motors. Additionally, overloaded motors tend to stall when pulsed at less than maximum power, in which case the robot won't turn gradually when it partially detects an obstacle.

Two wheels: It should have two wheels located in the center of the robot so that the robot can rotate in place. If the wheels are located in the front of the robot, the rear side of the robot may collide with an obstacle while turning. If the wheels are located in the rear of the robot, the front side of the robot may strike an obstacle while trying to turn away.

Circular: It should be circular, if possible, for the same collision reasons stated in the previous point.

It's *required* that Roundabout's body provide an unobstructed forward view for the infrared sensors. If either infrared emitter is obscured, the signal could bounce off the obstruction and directly into an infrared detector, thus falsely indicating obstacle detection. If the detectors themselves are obscured, they may fail to receive a signal bouncing off an obstacle, thus falsely indicating a clear path ahead.

These are some attributes and measurements of my homemade Roundabout:

- A body diameter of 14 cm and a total height of 8 cm (including all wires and sensors)

- A mass of 266 grams without a battery and 314 grams with a 9 V battery

- Wheels located in the center

- Handmade circular body

I made three Roundabout robots out of ¼-inch thick acrylic sheet in fluorescent green, red, and orange ($6.57; #63389837, #63390033, and #63389936, respectively, at MSC Industrial Supply for 12-inch by 12-inch square sheets). You can also obtain 0.236-inch thick, cast acrylic sheets in fluorescent green, red, amber, and blue ($12.83; #85635K524, #85635K525, #85635K522, and #85635K523, respectively, at McMaster-Carr). Lots of opaque colors are also available, such as black, blue, green, red, white, and yellow, in addition to clear, gray-tinted, and bronze-tinted.

Acrylic is inexpensive, lightweight, and relatively easy to machine. Acrylic has some shortcomings—it's brittle, meaning it can crack and is moderately prone to scratches. But ¼ inch provides enough thickness for excellent body strength and for #4-40 screws to be drilled and tapped that hold the robot together.

Designing a Robot Body

When modeling a new robot, I usually have some desired parts in mind, such as motors, sensors, and raw body materials. I like to pile them on a desk and play around with overall shapes and orientations. Then I'll drag out a massive box of LEGO parts and build a rough frame.

For quick robots, I'll glue together the weight-bearing or structural LEGO bricks and drill some holes, and the robot's body is complete. However, for most of my robots, I prefer to make a more significant investment in machining to achieve specific shapes and body characteristics.

Over the years, I've gone from dreading machining to actually finding it a relaxing diversion from everyday life. The change of attitude was all a matter of practicing and obtaining the correct tools.

Creating a Template

After constructing a rough body from LEGO bricks or simply a loose collection of parts on the workbench, I create two-dimensional paper templates with a drawing program on my computer. Some builders choose to create elaborate three-dimensional models. That may be appropriate for production manufacturing or complex designs, but I'm interested only in making sure the parts are the correct size and that the holes align.

I use Microsoft Visio to combine lines, rectangles, and circles to produce precise two-dimensional representations of the parts that need to be machined (see Figure 13-12). Unlike a raster paint program, a vector-drawing program such as Visio permits you to select each element and resize or move them at any time.

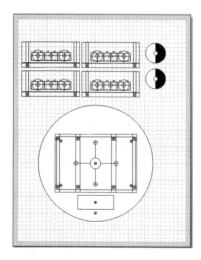

Figure 13-12. A paper template for the motor mounts and circular platform for Roundabout

After roughly sizing and positioning a drawing element with the mouse, you can type the dimensions and position desired. An alignment tool makes it easy to center or arrange shapes in relation to each other.

For example, you can create a circle that's exactly ⅛-inch diameter by typing that amount into the Size & Position window (see Figure 13-13). Then, drawing two lines and centering them within the circle using the alignment tool can create a crosshair to aid in centering the drill. Instead of a crosshair, you can use a centered dot if you prefer.

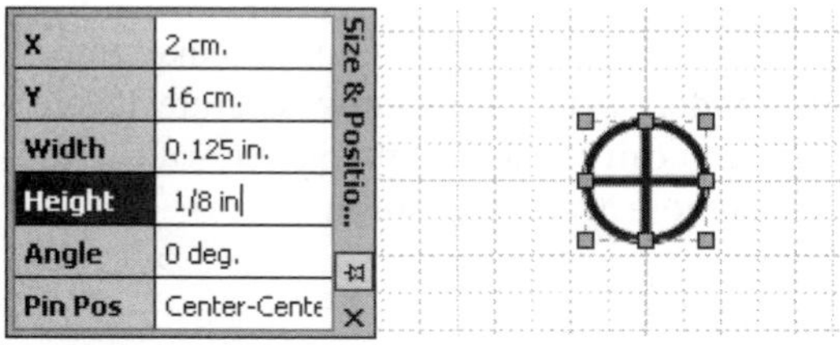

X	2 cm.	
Y	16 cm.	
Width	0.125 in.	
Height	1/8 in|	
Angle	0 deg.	
Pin Pos	Center-Cente	

Figure 13-13. Typing the desired dimensions for an unthreaded #4-40 hole with a crosshair

It's best to refer to the manufacturers' datasheets to obtain official measurements of motors or other parts that include certain size holes in specific locations. For everything else, a caliper (digital, preferably) can supply fairly accurate measurements.

After typing the dimensions and locations for all of the critical elements for a stand-alone part, you can group the drawing elements to move the part around as if a single piece. Place the pieces on top of each other where they'll meet in the final robot to make sure they fit and that the holes line up as you expect.

Using a drawing program has many advantages over drawing templates by hand:

- You can enter exact dimensions, angles, alignments, and positions

- Alterations are simple—not only to correct mistakes but also to upgrade the design for future generations of the robot

- You can duplicate elements and reuse them throughout a robot's body or for other robots

- You can quickly position parts on top of other parts to check for proper mating and then move them to separate locations in the document for printing

If you've never used a drawing program to design robot parts before, it may sound like a lot of work. But believe me, it actually saves a lot of time and produces more accurate results. Also, you're more likely to attempt a creative change if all it takes is dragging a mouse versus erasing, remeasuring, and redrawing lines by hand.

Printing a Template

When the template is ready, print it onto a piece of paper, a sticker, or a clear transparency (such as those used for overhead projectors). One problem with stickers is that they "gum up" cutting tools. Transparencies are nice because you can see the workpiece through them, and transparencies stretch less than paper. The downsides to transparencies are that they're more expensive than plain paper, and they won't provide any contrast between black ink and a dark workpiece. Then again, if you have a color printer, you can print the template in a different color on a transparency to improve contrast.

After printing, use a ruler to check a few of the longer dimensions to make sure they printed to the intended lengths. Most modern printers are fairly accurate. If you find the printout is off by 1 percent or more, you can reduce or enlarge the scale in the Page Setup or Printer dialog box to produce a more accurate printout.

Attaching a Template

Attach the printed template to the raw material to guide cutting and drilling. Low-adhesion masking tape (such as Scotch #2090 1-inch Painters' Safe-Release) works well for taping a template to the workpiece. Contact cement (rubber cement) and water-soluble glues are less successful—the ends of the paper tend to curl up.

NOTE *I'm sure many professional machinists cringe at the thought of relying on pliant paper marks during machining. After all, paper can easily slip, compress, twist, or rip during machining, thus misaligning subsequent machining operations. However, I've found paper templates to be more accurate than the marks I can produce by hand and more precise than my hobbyist power tools.*

Squaring the Template with the Workpiece

If the workpiece has a straight side, it may be beneficial to begin by lightly taping a pair of corners on the template and aligning the template to the workpiece's straight side using a machinist's square (see Figure 13-14). On a milling/drilling machine, you can then square the straight side of the workpiece with the milling table, which results in the template being squared with the milling table. With an aligned template, it's easier to line up parallel or perpendicular holes or cuts by simply rotating either the x-axis or the y-axis handwheel.

After aligning, rub down the taped corners to keep the template from moving. Add tape on the other corners of the template or anywhere the paper lifts up.

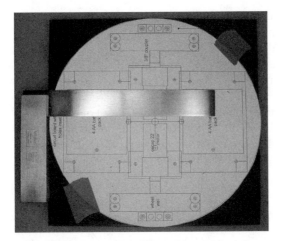

Figure 13-14. Using a machinist's square to align long lines on the paper template to a straight side of the raw workpiece

Punching Holes for Better Centering

Some builders find it beneficial to use a center punch to place a small indentation in the center of locations to be drilled (see Figure 13-15). During drilling, if the drill is slightly off the mark, it rolls into the indentation and drills in the intended location. Always wear safety goggles when using a punch and during drilling.

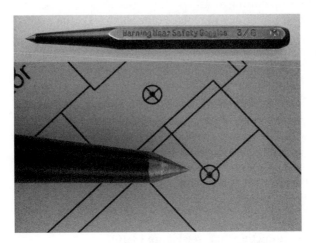

Figure 13-15. A center punch (top). The pointy tip of the punch marks the center of each hole to be drilled (bottom).

One advantage of using a center punch with a paper template is that even if the template shifts slightly during machining, the indentations in the workpiece continue to draw the drill to the originally intended location.

I don't find center punches to be helpful on a combination drilling/milling machine. The fine adjustments on the milling table provide better precision than my hand with a center punch.

Avoid center punching the locations of deep holes. If the drill is out of alignment with the punched indentation, it'll be drawn into the indentation and will then be drilling at a slight angle. For shallow holes, this isn't a significant problem. However, for deep holes, this runs the risk of damaging the drill and creating a conspicuously angled hole.

Removing Tape Before Machining Sides

The first step in preparing raw material to become a robot body part is to roughly cut the material down to slightly oversize with a hacksaw or other tool. After that, you have a couple of ways to approach finishing the outer edges of a workpiece.

You could measure the final dimensions by hand and finish the outer dimensions with a precision tool (such as a milling machine) before securing the template. For example, if you need to make a bunch of uncomplicated rectangular pieces, it's probably easiest to mark across a strip of material and cut them all to size.

Another approach is to secure the template to the rough-cut material by some internal means (glue or screws) and use the template as the outer guide. This works well for more complex shapes. Just make sure not to use tape on the outer edges that are to be cut because the tape gums up cutting tools.

The following is an example of using screws to replace tape when securing a template in anticipation of cutting the outer edge. In this example, more than one board is produced at the same time. However, this example works equally well for securing the template to just a single board. Follow these steps:

1. Roughly cut a pair of boards to slightly larger than the desired size.

2. Place the boards back to back.

3. Tape the boards together along with a paper template on top.

4. Drill a few holes throughout the template.

5. Tap the holes with threads for machine screws (not wood screws).

6. Attach screws to hold everything together (see Figure 13-16).

7. Remove the outer edge tape (which is no longer needed because the screws are holding everything together).

8. Machine the outer edges.

If you've placed multiple boards together for this process, you'll have created multiple matching boards. This saves time and produces excellent alignment.

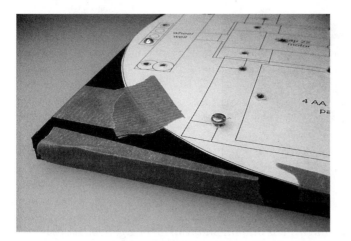

Figure 13-16. Two boards and a paper template originally held together with low-adhesive tape. After drilling and tapping, screws hold the boards together so that tape is no longer necessary. You should then remove the tape before machining the outer edges.

Constructing the Center Platform of Roundabout

Roundabout's circular center platform holds the robot together. The circuit board, battery, and motor mounts all attach to the center platform of the robot.

Milling or Purchasing a Disc

The disc that makes up the center platform of the robot was cut with a milling machine and a rotary table using the same technique as described for making wheels in Chapter 5:

1. Start with a piece of stock sheet of plastic or aluminum.

2. Using a hacksaw, jigsaw, or router, rough cut the workpiece to slighter larger than the diameter desired.

3. Drill one hole roughly in the center of the workpiece, or drill four holes around the center, to secure the workpiece to the rotary table.

4. Bolt the workpiece to the rotary table (see Figure 13-17).

5. Bring the cutting surface of the mill closer to the workpiece while rotating the rotary table. This produces a circular workpiece, centered around the securing hole(s).

Alternatively, you can purchase a pre-cut 6-inch diameter, 0.236-inch thick, clear acrylic disc for $5.58 from McMaster-Carr, #8581 K37. This saves a lot of labor, but, of course, you don't get your choice of colors, materials, or sizes.

Figure 13-17. A robot body roughly cut into the shape of an octagon will subsequently have its outer edges finished into a circle using a mill and a rotary table. Notice that four bolts with large washers hold the workpiece securely so that it won't unscrew as the workpiece rotates against the end mill.

Placing and Tapping Screw Holes in Roundabout's Center Platform

Roundabout's center platform requires many tapped and untapped holes for screws to hold the circuit board, battery, and motor mounts. Where to place these holes is based upon the size of your circuit board and your motors. It isn't unusual to go back and add holes to a robot base later to include new sensors, swap out parts, or make other upgrades.

You should drill a large hole in the center of the platform for passing motor and battery cables from underneath the robot to the circuit board mounted on top. To avoid the frustration of trying to force-feed connectors and wires through a narrow hole, try to lean toward oversizing the pass-through hole.

A ½-inch pass-through hole is adequate for the two-pin Molex connectors and the three cables used in Roundabout. In fact, ½ inch is about the maximum drill shank size that's going to fit in most hobbyist drill presses (some permit up to ⅝ inch). Remember, you can step up to a Silver & Deming drill for larger holes if necessary.

Examining Roundabout's Motor Mechanism

Roundabout's motors are mounted parallel to one another to reduce the width of the robot (see Figure 13-18). The robot would have been fairly wide had the motors been placed end to end.

Even though Roundabout's motors are 33 percent longer than Sandwich's motors, this motor arrangement permits Roundabout's total width to be 33 percent less than Sandwich's total width. The skinny tires help a lot, too.

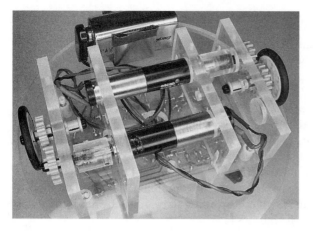

Figure 13-18. Parallel offset motors is a common arrangement to reduce a robot's width.

Using Matching Rectangular Motor Mounts

Roundabout's motor mounts are the four rectangular pieces to which the motors and gears are attached. Although they may look complicated at first, it turns out that the motor mounts are all alike. The motor mounts are all made at the same time by drilling three holes through a stack of four workpieces clamped together. As such, they're virtually identical, which keeps all of the parts neatly aligned.

In Roundabout, the wheel is supported only on the interior side. That's okay because Roundabout is fairly lightweight. However, if you prefer, the wheels of heavier robots can be supported on both sides by using six mounts (see Figure 13-19).

Figure 13-19. Soup, a much larger robot, also has parallel offset motors. By using two additional rectangular mounts (one on each end), Soup's wheel axles and external gears have greater protection against damage because the axles are supported on both sides.

Choosing Between Friction-Fit Motors and Using Mounting Screws

Roundabout exerts so little torque that you can simply insert the motors into the motor-mounting holes without bothering with screws. A tight fit between the motor casing and the mounting hole is possible by using plastic motor mounts. Like most plastics, acrylic compresses a little during drilling. After drilling, the plastic expands inward, thus slightly shrinking the resulting hole size. The final fit is tight enough that the motors are held in place by friction, which is called *friction fit*.

If for some reason the motor-mounting hole turns out large enough that the motor is loose, apply a drop or two of adhesive in the mounting hole. But don't use too much adhesive because you want to be able to twist the motor out for future servicing.

Friction-fit motors should only be attempted for very small robots. Although it's a neat trick, it's more appropriate to attach motors using screws and the mounting holes provided by the manufacturer on the motor's face.

Mounting Motors with Screws

Because Soup is a larger robot, screws attach the motors to the mounts. This means Soup's motor mounts are a little more complicated than Roundabout's motor mounts.

The outer two mounts of both sides of Soup (four total) are identical, just like Roundabout. However, Soup's two innermost mounts are different from the other mounts. The innermost mounts mirror each other. This is because one end of the mount encompasses the larger-diameter rear of the motor, and the other end of the mount has screws to hold the motor in place (see Figure 13-20).

Figure 13-20. The inner motor mount for Soup has two different hole sizes. The smaller of the two holes is surrounded by screws to hold the motor in place.

Connecting to LEGO Gears and Wheels

Roundabout uses ½-inch diameter couplers (see Figure 13-21) to connect the motors to LEGO gears and wheels. The coupler is made from a solid rod of the same color acrylic as the rest of the robot's body. Refer to Chapters 2 through 4 for instructions on making couplers.

Be sure to select a long enough cross axle for the coupler used in Roundabout because the coupler passes through a ¼-inch thick acrylic motor mount before meeting up with the LEGO gear. Mock assemble the body pieces, and try different lengths of axle before gluing the axle into the coupler.

Figure 13-21. A ½-inch diameter, solid-rod, fluorescent, acrylic coupler with flush setscrew and LEGO cross axle

Selecting LEGO Gears

As mentioned before, I prefer LEGO gears and wheels because of the high quality, relatively low cost, and common availability. One of the most important features of LEGO parts is their rapid interchangeability. Not only does this encourage experimentation, but also it permits alterations that can transform a dud robot into a contender.

The distance between the holes in each motor mount was selected to match the distance of two LEGO studs. Commonly referred to as LEGO unit (LU), the distance from LEGO stud to stud is ⁵⁄₁₆ inch. Therefore, the 2 LU distance between holes on each of Roundabout's motor mounts is ¹⁰⁄₁₆ inch (⅝ inch).

Centering Wheels with Idler Gears

At a distance of 2 LU, two 16-tooth LEGO gears mesh perfectly (see Figure 13-22). Equal tooth gears don't directly alter RPM or torque, but instead they deliver motor power from one location to another. With a 1:1 ratio, these are called *idler* gears. Again, they don't do much other than deliver motor power to a different location and, as a side effect, reverse the direction of rotation.

In this case, the idler gears shift the output of the offset motors to the center of the robot's body. Thus, even though the motors are offset, the final output (the wheels) are centered, which allows the robot to turn in place.

Figure 13-22. Two 16-tooth LEGO gears spaced 2 LU apart

It's generally preferable to try to design a robot without idler gears because each added gear increases inefficiency because of friction. However, they're appropriate in Roundabout's design because they permit a compact body to be combined with a zero-turning radius. Additionally, the LEGO gears isolate the gearmotors from bumps and other forces on the main axle (recall the beginning of Chapter 5). These external LEGO gears are easier and cheaper to replace than the tiny gears inside of the gearhead of the gearmotor.

Slowing Down the Speed and Increasing the Torque

An 8-tooth gear and a 24-tooth gear (see Figure 13-23) also mesh perfectly at a distance of 2 LU. By placing the 8-tooth gear on the motor output (via the coupler) and the 24-tooth gear on the wheel axle, the wheel rotates only 8/24 or ⅓ of the way for every rotation of the motor shaft. Thus, the robot slows down to about ⅓ speed.

Figure 13-23. An 8-tooth LEGO gear located on the motor output and a 24-tooth LEGO gear located on the wheel axle results in the robot slowing down but gaining pushing strength.

Of course, with a gearhead ratio of 352:1, my Roundabout robot doesn't need to be slowed down more than it already is. However, if your Roundabout robot's motors are too fast, try swapping in these 8-tooth and 24-tooth gears.

In exchange for slowing the robot down, the amount of torque (or pushing force) is increased by the same ratio. If your robot has a hard time getting moving or if your robot stops moving (stalls) on hills or obstacles, then try these higher ratio gears.

Increasing Speed in Exchange for Torque

What happens if you swap the gears? A 24-tooth gear on the motor and an 8-tooth gear on the wheel axle (see Figure 13-24) causes the wheel to turn three times for every turn of the motor shaft. The robot speeds up approximately three times.

Figure 13-24. A 24-tooth LEGO gear located on the motor output and an 8-tooth LEGO gear located on the wheel axle result in speeding up the robot.

This gear change has merit for my Roundabout robot! The 352:1 ratio effectively becomes approximately 117:1. The linear speed changes from 3.927 cm/s to the hectic pace of almost 11.8 cm/s. Okay, that's still pretty slow.

It's not very efficient to gear up in the gearhead and then gear down with external gears. But if you're stuck with a particular gearmotor, then external gear alterations can legitimately adjust performance.

Altering Speed and Torque with Pulleys Instead of Gears

LEGO also makes pulleys and belts that can be substituted for gears. You can arrange the parts with larger or smaller pulleys (see Figure 13-25) to provide an exchange of speed and torque.

Two equally sized pulleys can transfer power over long distances via a belt. This can be a much more efficient delivery system than a long series of gears.

Unlike gears, belt-driven systems provide greater flexibility in positioning each pulley at almost any reasonable distance desired. This assumes you can make or locate the correct length of belt. If the belt length is too short, the belt will be too tense and can break or load down the motor. If the belt length is too long, the belt will be too loose and can fall off or slip. Adjusting belt tension is part of the art of belt and pulley systems.

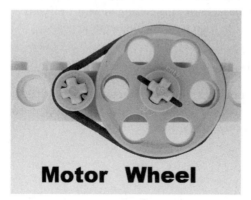

Figure 13-25. A smaller pulley connected via a belt to a larger pulley provides the ability to convert speed and torque, just as gears do.

The upside and downside to pulleys and belts is that belts can slip. If planned correctly, the belt can be designed to slip rather than allowing the motor to stall if the load becomes too great. Also, a slipping belt is far less injurious than broken teeth on a gear. However, as the belt wears and stretches, it begins to slip unintentionally, resulting in a loss of mechanical power.

TIP *An idler pulley can compensate for wear and help retain belt tension.*

Reaching the Physical Limits of LEGO Moving Parts

The proceeding pages provided examples of the wonderful interchangeability of LEGO parts. Rather than machining new body parts for each alteration, it's pleasant to be able to just pop off a couple of parts and pop on new ones. It answers a lot of "what if" questions very quickly.

That being said, LEGO parts have their limits. Being made out of low-density plastic, they're designed for a playful consumer market rather than mechanically demanding situations, temperature extremes, or long-term wear.

Case in point: When first built, Soup had a mass of about 1625 grams (about 3½ pounds) and two 6-watt motors. Soup mercilessly jammed the motors forward and backward to whip around corners and to hastily change directions. It didn't take too long for a crunching noise to emanate from Soup, followed by the robot sadly limping around one dead side. A shattered gear was the culprit (see the left side of Figure 13-26).

At first I thought it was a defective gear. Shortly after replacement, another gear lost a tooth (see the right side of Figure 13-26).

Figure 13-26. Shattered LEGO gear (left). LEGO gear with a broken tooth (right)

The microcontroller was then reprogrammed to gradually step down the speed of the motor when changing direction or braking. Also, the mass was lowered to 1,350 grams, and the voltage was reduced from 16 V to around 10 V. This combination of changes put Soup within the stress limits of the LEGO gears, avoiding any further damage.

Making Roundabout's Motor Mounts

Roundabout's motor mounts are made from the same thickness (¼ inch) and color acrylic as Roundabout's circular center platform. The thickness is important because #4-40 screws are going to go into or through each motor-mount piece to attach them to the center platform.

Defining Motor-Mount Dimensions

The actual motor-mount dimensions will depend on the size of the motors and the size of the wheels you choose. The key to using LEGO gears is having the motor and axle holes spaced the same distance as LEGO bricks. Figure 13-27 includes a two-dimensional representation of a LEGO brick beam superimposed over the motor and axle holes to demonstrate that they're the correct distance apart.

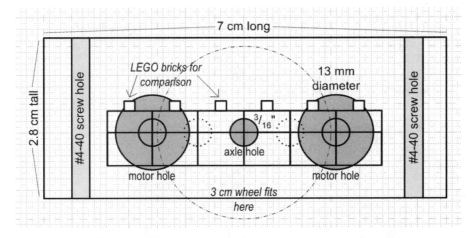

Figure 13-27. Dimensions and relative positions of holes in Roundabout's motor mounts. You may need to size your template differently, depending on the motors and wheels you choose.

If you're going to friction fit your motors, then the motor holes should be the same diameter as the motor (in this case, 13 mm). Otherwise, reduce the size of either the left or right motor hole to be slightly larger than the motor shaft (refer to Figure 13-20), and add screw holes as indicated in the motor's datasheet.

Notice that the axle hole is horizontally centered but not vertically centered. You need to position the axle hole vertically so that the wheel doesn't run into the center platform of the robot. Also, the wheel must clear the bottom of the motor mount to make contact with the ground.

Admittedly, the example motor mount doesn't leave much clearance for the wheel. Unfortunately, that means Roundabout has difficulty driving over small objects and uneven flooring, such as tile or door thresholds. However, because the bottom of the motor mount is close to the ground, the robot can slide on the heads of the screws or corners of the motor mounts without tipping very much.

Preparing the Raw Material

If the raw material comes with a protective film or lining, leave that in place during machining unless instructed otherwise by the manufacturer. Some plastics, especially acrylic, come with a paper covering that protects the material from scratches and molten chips during machining.

Using a hacksaw, I cut four rectangular pieces from a larger acrylic sheet. I then used a milling machine to cut flat, squared edges. Finally, I placed all four pieces into the vise of a milling machine and milled them all to the same height at the same time using an oversized end mill. A fly cutter would also have been a good choice.

Selecting Ready-Made Material Instead of Milling

It's only critical that the top edge, and perhaps the bottom edge, of the motor mounts be flat and perpendicular to the sides. Conversely, the left and right sides can be rough and even too long without affecting performance. This means that if you don't have a milling machine, simply purchase a strip of raw material already manufactured to the desired height. It'll come with a decent top and bottom edge. Then, just cut it to approximately the correct length (err on being too long, not too short) with a hacksaw. No milling necessary!

McMaster-Carr has ¼-inch thick, 1½-inch (3.81 cm) wide, 2-foot long black nylon for $6.98, #8674 K21. Translucent-white ultra-high molecular weight (UHMW) polyethylene strips are available with the same dimensions in 5-foot lengths for $5.85, #8702 K64. Both of these strips are wider than desired for 13 mm motors but may be ideal for larger motors.

Although neither nylon nor polyethylene is available in exciting fluorescent colors, they're both very slippery materials, which is useful for a robot that slides along the ends of the motor mounts. That same slipperiness can make the materials more difficult to secure during machining and can cause the drill to slide around. So be careful.

Drilling All of the Motor Mounts at the Same Time

Tape all of the motor-mount rectangular pieces together in a stack and tape a template on top (see Figure 13-28). In the following sections, you'll drill all of the motor mounts at the same time in a stack to save time and improve the overall fit; this will also make the holes come as close to parallel as possible. If the drill is slightly off for one hole, the same error will repeat throughout the stack, at least keeping the motor parallel and all the associated holes in alignment.

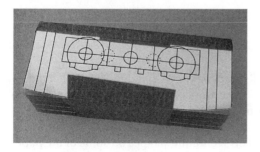

Figure 13-28. A stack of motor-mount pieces with a template, ready to be drilled

You might want to run a permanent pen line across one side of the stack so you can assemble the motor mounts on the robot in the same order and orientation that they were drilled. If that visually offends you, try numbering them in a corner with a pencil or light scratch.

Placing the Stack in the Vise, with Room to Spare

Place the motor-mount stack in a vise on the drilling machine. Place a parallel block or a *flat* scrap piece underneath the stack so the drill can penetrate through the stack without damaging the vise (see Figure 13-29). Beware: If the scrap piece isn't flat, the holes will be drilled at an angle with respect to the motor-mount material, and the motors may not fit in across two pieces.

Figure 13-29. Placing a flat scrap piece underneath the motor-mount stack to lift the stack up so that the vise won't be damaged as the drill exits the bottom of the stack

Insert a ¾₆-inch diameter drill into the drill chuck. Move the drill to the side of the stack and lower it until the body of the drill would fully breach the bottom of the stack (refer to Figure 13-29). Set the limit block to prevent the drill from being lowered any farther.

Positioning the Drill

Depending on the type of point on the drill, it can be somewhat difficult to tell if the drill is centered over the target. One method that works well with a paper template is to gently lower a spinning drill just to the point that it brushes against ("kisses") the template but not so far that it actually starts cutting into the workpiece itself. Then bring the drill up slightly to see where it landed. This technique scrapes off some of the paper and ink (see Figure 13-30), showing exactly where the drill is positioned with respect to the template.

If the drill is off the mark, reposition the drill relative to where it landed and try scraping the template again. This provides several opportunities for adjustment until that section of the template is too worn to provide more feedback. Of course, as long as the paper hasn't been completely breached, you can restore the crosshair with a pen and ruler to allow for additional positioning attempts.

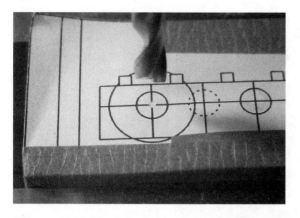

Figure 13-30. The ink at the center of the crosshair on the template has been worn off by the drill, indicating that the drill is positioned accurately.

Drilling Three Holes

Position and drill a 3/16-inch diameter hole for both motors and the center axle. Because this is a deep hole (four pieces of 1/4-inch material stacked together equals a 1-inch deep hole) for such a narrow-diameter drill, it's important that the drill is removed from the hole periodically to prevent the drill flutes from becoming clogged. With plastics, a parabolic drill ejects chips (cut-up material) better than a standard drill.

Although the axle hole is now finished, the motor holes aren't going to remain at a 3/16-inch diameter. These 3/16-inch holes act as pilot holes for the wider-diameter drill. Then again, if you have a powerful enough drill press, some people may choose not to drill pilot holes for the motor holes and instead rely on the stiffness of the wider drill to resist bending, thus avoiding angling the resulting hole.

Preparing to Drill Larger Motor Holes

Insert a wider-diameter drill that's equal to the diameter of your motors. In my case, I inserted a 13-mm drill for the 13-mm diameter Escap motors. If you can't locate a drill that's wide enough to accommodate your motors, perhaps you need to select smaller motors? Or perhaps a different method of mounting the motors (such as L-brackets, discussed in Chapter 18) would be more appropriate.

Move the drill to one side of the stack, and lower it until the body would fully breach the stack (see Figure 13-31). Set the limit block. These steps are necessary because wider-diameter drills are almost always longer than narrower-diameter drills; thus, the previous setting of the limit block would've permitted the wider-diameter drill to penetrate into the vise.

Figure 13-31. Setting the limit block for the new depth of the longer drill to avoid drilling into the vise. Notice that in this picture the stack has three ³⁄₁₆-inch diameter holes drilled in it as described in the prior instructions. Also notice that although tape is being used to hold the paper template onto the top of the stack, each work-piece is being held firmly in place by the vise (not merely by tape).

Positioning the Wider Diameter Drill

Because the center of the crosshair has been removed by the pilot hole, the template scratching technique can't be used to position the wider diameter drill. Instead, follow these steps:

1. Turn the drilling machine off. It was already turned off when you switched drills, right?

2. Lower the drill until it's fairly close to the workpiece but not actually touching the workpiece or the template.

3. Roughly center the drill over the circle on the template.

4. Visually select a cutting edge on the drill that appears to be the widest part of the drill.

5. Manually rotate the drill by hand until the selected cutting edge lines up with the circumference of the circle on the template (see the left side of Figure 13-32). If the drill isn't on target, reposition it until the drill edge meets the circle on one side.

6. Continue to rotate the drill by hand until that same selected cutting edge meets the other side of the circle (see the right side of Figure 13-32). If you

need to reposition the drill, then after repositioning slightly, go back to step 5 and repeat until the selected edge is equally close to both sides of the template circle. The drill is now horizontally centered.

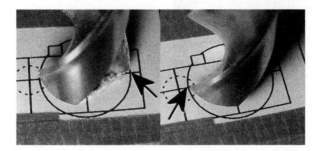

Figure 13-32. Horizontally aligning a wide diameter drill by first lining up one cutting edge and then rotating around and lining up that same cutting edge on the other side

7. Repeat steps 5 and 6, targeting the top and bottom of the template circle, to vertically center the drill.

When you become proficient at this method of positioning a drill, it takes only a few seconds to perform.

Drilling the Motor Holes

After positioning the drill, turn on the drilling machine and drill the hole. Go slowly and occasionally withdraw the drill from the hole to remove chips. Drilling a wider-diameter hole requires more work and places more stress on the drilling machine. The required torque is increased for wider drills, just as a large-diameter wheel increases the torque demands on a robot's motor.

If the plastic begins to melt, then one of the following is true:

- The drill is being fed into the hole too slowly, causing more friction than cutting.

- The drill is dull.

- The drill is clogged.

- The material and the drill are too hot; withdraw the drill, and let the drill and workpiece cool before proceeding. Plastic dissipates heat much more slowly than aluminum, making plastic more prone to heat build-up.

When the first motor hole is finished, reposition the drill over the second motor hole and drill it out. The stack should then look like Figure 13-33.

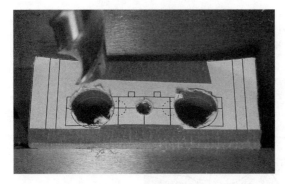

Figure 13-33. The stack of motor mounts with holes drilled for the motors and center axle

Making Holes to Secure the Motor Mounts to the Center Platform

You have a couple of options for securing the motor mounts to the robot's circular center platform. Adhesive is one option, but I prefer to be able to dismantle the individual body parts in case of errors, damage, or upgrades.

A better choice is to use screws. With screws, you need to decide between either drilling partially into the motor mounts or drilling all the way through the motor mounts.

Selecting Partially Drilled Motor-Mount Screw Holes with Threads

For partially drilled motor-mount screw holes, the holes are drilled to a depth of only 1 cm, more or less. The motor-mount screw holes are then tapped with threads (see Figure 13-34), and the center platform screw holes are untapped and slightly larger (recall the mating of tapped and untapped holes in Chapter 5). The screw is inserted from above, through the untapped platform screw hole, and into the threads in the motor-mount screw hole.

Figure 13-34. These motor mounts are drilled only partway and then tapped with screw threads. The screw is inserted from above the robot's center platform to secure the motor mounts.

For partially drilled motor-mount screw holes, use a #43 drill and #4-40 tap for the motor-mount holes. Use a ⅛-inch diameter drill for the mating holes in the robot's center platform.

For partially drilled motor-mount screw holes, the depth of the hole is much less, which avoids the drill bending and introducing angular errors. However, because these are blind holes (they don't go all the way through), they tend to "gum up" with chips during tapping. For acrylic or other brittle plastics, it's important to flush the threads clean of residue (mild soap and water and a narrow cleaning tool work well) or else the motor mounts can crack from stress after being screwed in place (recall tapping acrylic couplers in Chapter 4).

Selecting Fully Drilled, Unthreaded, Motor-Mount Screw Holes

Another option is to drill all the way through the motor mounts (see Figure 13-35). Use a ⅛-inch drill because the motor-mount screw hole will remain unthreaded. Then make the center platform holes with a #43 drill and tap them with threads from a #4-40 tap. Insert a much longer screw from below the robot, through the motor mounts, and into the threads of the center platform.

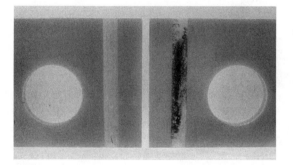

Figure 13-35. These motor mounts are fully drilled through and remain untapped. The screw is inserted from below and screwed into the robot's platform to secure the motor mounts. One motor-mount hole aesthetically ruined because of a poor choice of scrap material underneath the stack during drilling (right).

Fully drilled motor-mount screw holes have a couple of disadvantages. First, 2.8 cm is a deep hole for such a narrow-diameter drill. It's likely that the drill will bend and have some angular error. Second, long #4-40 screws are more expensive and are less available from suppliers.

One advantage of long holes and screws is that they look pretty cool.

Be careful of the type of flat scrap material you place underneath the stack during drilling. In my case, the flat scrap material was black ABS plastic. During drilling, the black plastic melted and was drawn up into the hole as the drill was removed. The melted black plastic mixed with the melted acrylic, forming an ugly screw hole. I could have avoided this problem by choosing clear plastic scrap material, wood, or parallels positioned away from the drilling locations.

Gliding Along

Having a screw head at the bottom of the motor mount permits the robot to glide on the screw head rather than the corner of the motor mount. Unfortunately, the screw head can become caught on carpeting or cracks. On the plus side, metal wears better than plastic corners, and it's easier to replace the screw than the motor mount.

An alternative for larger robots is to machine a replaceable block of slippery plastic to slide on, such as PTFE (Teflon), UHMW polyethylene ("the poor man's Teflon"), nylon, acetal (Delrin), or even polypropylene. Soup has Teflon slides in the rear for driving forward and erasers in the front for braking or cornering (see Figure 13-36).

Figure 13-36. Soup, which uses the same type of motor mounts as Roundabout, has chamfered slick Teflon slides in the rear and high-friction erasers in the front. Notice the screw holes in the center of the eraser (lower right) for securing the eraser to the robot's body with screws and washers.

Drilling the Motor-Mount Screw Holes

After choosing whether your motor-mount holes will be partial or all the way through, it's time to drill:

1. Reposition the stack in the vise to drill the screw holes, placing parallels or flat scrap underneath if you plan on drilling all the way.

2. Insert the desired diameter drill into the chuck.

3. Position the drill to the side of the stack, and set the limit block.

4. Position the drill in front of the template, and center it by using the template as a guide (see Figure 13-37). On a combination drilling/milling machine, lock the x-axis.

Figure 13-37. Centering the drill by using the template as a guide. Aside: Can you tell that the various motor-mount pieces don't exactly line up on the left side of the stack? That's too bad. If this happens to you at this point in the process, don't remove the tape and attempt to realign the pieces! It's important that the already drilled holes stay aligned relative to each other. It doesn't matter if the left and right edges line up. If it's really that important to you, completely finish drilling all the holes and then mill the ends of the stack.

5. Raise the drill, and center it over the width of each motor mount, drilling one hole at a time.

6. When finished with one end, the stack should look like Figure 13-38.

Figure 13-38. One end of the motor-mount stack is finished.

7. Unlock the x-axis (if necessary), and repeat steps 4 through 6 for the other end of the motor-mount stack.

8. Remove the motor-mount stack from the vise.

Congratulations! You now have four reasonably identical motor mounts. You can remove the tape and separate the pieces from the stack.

Tapping Partially Drilled Motor-Mount Holes

If you've chosen partially drilled motor-mount holes, tap them with a #4-40 tap. Don't forget to clean out the debris from the holes.

Revealing the Finished Motor Mounts

Try putting the motor body together. The LEGO axle holes aren't used in the middle two motor mounts (refer to Figure 13-18). Likewise, one motor hole is unused on the outside motor mounts. They're just artifacts of the manufacturing process. The other motor hole on the outside motor mounts leaves plenty of room for the coupler and gear to rotate without rubbing against the motor mount.

When you've determined that everything fits well and that no additional machining is required, you can peel off the protective film or paper (if your raw material came with it), as shown in Figure 13-39.

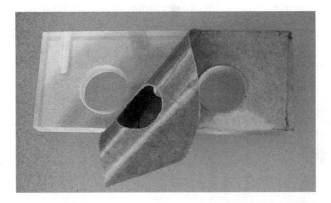

Figure 13-39. Peeling off the protective covering on an acrylic motor mount to reveal a beautiful finished piece

Summarizing Roundabout

Roundabout is a compact, obstacle-avoiding robot. The compactness comes from a parallel offset motor design with gears that center the wheels to enable the robot to turn in place. The unique motor mounts contribute precision alignment to the drive mechanism while not being overly arduous for a hobbyist to build.

Roundabout's simple modular electronic design is a combination of modules presented earlier in this book. Building robots from modules allows the designer to choose where to spend time, effort, and money on a robot. Modules also make it easier to diagnose and upgrade a portion of the robot at a time, which permits time-tested modules to be substituted or employed where desired.

In the next chapter, you'll test-drive Roundabout to demonstrate the abilities and weaknesses of the simple circuitry and body.

CHAPTER 14

Test Driving Roundabout

Perform Safety Checks, Drain Power, Measure Circuit Resistance, Monitor Current and Common Problems and Solutions, Create Obstacle Courses, Avoid Deadly Stall, Understand High-Beam Hysteresis, and Use Short Jumpers

THIS CHAPTER BEGINS BY DESCRIBING some tests and procedures that you should perform on any newly built circuits or robots to reduce errors and detect significant faults. After that, you'll prepare and launch Roundabout. In case of difficulties, this chapter includes a list of common problems and potential solutions.

Later in this chapter, you'll put Roundabout through a challenge to see what it does well and where it has weaknesses. Some changes are suggested and tried, but, ultimately, exploring the limitations of a simple logic gate brain paves the road to a microcontroller upgrade.

Preparing for the Test Drive

After soldering the robot together, but before powering up, you should perform a few simple procedures to prevent and check for faults.

Setting All Controls to Safe or Moderate Positions

Adjustable controls and switches may be in unknown states when first installed. Before testing a circuit board, do the following:

- Set the power switch to off.

- Flip all switches (including DIP switches) to their least active or safest positions. Nothing is more embarrassing than spending hours troubleshooting a "faulty" circuit only to find that you set the switches incorrectly.

- Dial all potentiometers to the middle of their ranges or to whatever makes sense for that circuit. This step simply provides moderate behavior values. This shouldn't be necessary to avoid electrical faults because a good circuit design includes a series resistor to establish a minimum resistance (if necessary) even when the potentiometer is turned to zero resistance. Likewise, you should design the maximum resistance value of the selected potentiometer so you don't cause any electrical damage.

Testing One Module at a Time

If the robot is modular, it's best to test boards individually prior to assembly. The same holds true for any removable components, such as motors. Not only does this decrease the number of variables when attempting to locate a fault, but it also reduces the number of components exposed to damage, should an all-encompassing fault exist (such as overvoltage).

Roundabout consists of only a single board. However, you may find it valuable to assemble and solder only the power supply (9 V batter snap, power connector, power switch, voltage regulator, and capacitors) to start. That way, you can test the power supply to make sure it provides a 5 V output before attaching and exposing any additional pieces.

If each module checks out as functional by itself, build up slowly by adding one module, connection, or board at a time. Of course, always turn the power off during assembly and disassembly and make sure that the robot's design allows for powering up with certain items disconnected. (Try to design boards with pull-up or pull-down resistors to provide default values because this practice permits isolated testing.)

Measuring the Resistance of the Complete Circuit

A quick measurement of the total resistance of a circuit board detects whether a short circuit or open circuit exists. This simple test replaces the power source (usually a battery) with an ohmmeter (usually a multimeter in resistance-measurement mode) to measure the effective total passive resistance that the battery will encounter.

Of course, when the robot is actually operating, it may switch on certain transistors or relays that provide different electrical paths than the paths that exist in the start-up state. Also, the low voltage provided by the majority of ohmmeters won't activate most semiconductors. Therefore, although this test can reveal some faults, it can't reveal all short-circuit or open-circuit conditions.

The following sections describe how to test the total resistance of a circuit.

Draining Power

It's important to remove and drain all power from the circuit before measuring resistance so the ohmmeter (or multimeter) won't be damaged and won't provide a false reading. To drain the power, follow these steps:

1. Remove all batteries and power sources from the robot or circuit board being tested. Leave those power sources disconnected throughout resistance testing.

2. Slide the robot's power switch to the on position.

3. Place a high-wattage (1 W, 2 W, 3 W, or greater—the higher the better), low-value resistor (10 Ω to 50 Ω—use a higher value for a lower-wattage resistor) across the circuit board's battery connector (not the battery!) for a couple of seconds (see Figure 14-1).

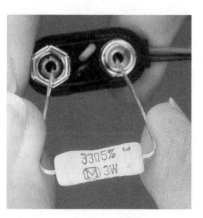

Figure 14-1. A 3 W, 33 Ω, metal-oxide resistor ($0.51, #P33W-3BK-ND at Digi-Key) discharging the robot's capacitors through the robot's 9 V battery snap

The resistor discharges any existing power from the circuit board's capacitors. For circuits with combined capacitances at less than 5000 μF, a 3 W, 33 Ω, metal-oxide resistor can safely discharge 20 V to less than 0.1 V in quicker than a second.

NOTE *A simple calculation of initial wattage (20 V times 20 V divided by 33 Ω equals 12.12 W) makes it appear that this exceeds the 3 W rating of the resistor. However, the voltage in the capacitor drops rapidly as the capacitor discharges. Therefore, the 12.12 W calculation indicates only the initial instantaneous peak wattage, not the ever-decreasing amount of energy that the resistor must dissipate. The resistor's label of 3 W is a rating of continuous wattage. (The formulas for calculating the resistor's peak wattage rating were too complex to include in this book.)*

Of course, shorting the power connector with the metal blade of a screwdriver also performs the same function, but it results in high enough current that circuitry could be damaged. As an alternative to a high-wattage resistor, a small DC motor can be effective in draining power and providing voltage-level feedback (by declining speed).

For circuits with very large capacitances, such as those with 1 F battery backup capacitors, use the highest-wattage resistor you can find, place multiple resistors in parallel, and/or use a higher resistance value. The resistor will need to stay in place for more than a few seconds. Use a voltmeter (or multimeter in voltage-measurement mode) to observe the declining voltage level.

Measuring Resistance

After all power has been drained from the circuit, attach an ohmmeter to the circuit board's battery connector. (Follow the instructions in the multimeter manual for measuring resistance.)

The measured resistance should begin at a very low value, perhaps less than 100 Ω, increasing rapidly. After a few seconds, the resistance should be fairly high, perhaps more than 5,000 Ω (5 kΩ), increasing more slowly. Finally, after about 30 seconds, the measured resistance should level off. The resistance of my Roundabout robot settled at about 35,000 Ω (35 kΩ). Of course, some robots may end up with a much higher or lower resistance.

The reason for the change in resistance is that the ohmmeter is applying a small voltage to measure the circuitry's resistance, and the circuit board's capacitors are charging up to that voltage. As the capacitors get closer and closer to the full voltage applied, the capacitors draw less and less current, thus the apparent resistance of the circuit increases.

Getting Too Low of a Resistance

Something is wrong if a robot's circuitry continues to have a very low resistance, such as less than 500 Ω, after 30 seconds of measuring. If the resistance is about zero, then there's a short circuit somewhere, such as crossed wires or a sloppy bit of solder splattered beyond its desired joint. It could also be that there's a bad component (less likely, but possible).

Check to see that all of the LEDs and diodes are installed in the correct orientation. If the circuit utilizes a zener diode for overvoltage protection, remember that it dies (needs replacing) in a shorted state. If you can't find the cause after visually examining the circuit board, try eliminating some variables by unplugging all connectors and removing all socketed components. Also, try adjusting the potentiometers and flipping the switches.

Whatever you do, don't connect the robot or circuit board to a power source if the circuit shows a very low resistance! If there's something wrong with the circuit, the low resistance will allow a high current draw, potentially resulting in permanent damage.

Getting Too High of a Resistance

On the other hand, something is likely wrong if the robot's circuitry has a very high resistance, such as more than 1,000,000 Ω (1 MΩ). Make sure the robot's power switch is turned on and that the ohmmeter is connected with the correct polarity to the battery snap.

Faults that could result in a high resistance include a broken wire, a broken circuit board trace, a loose connector, a loose part, a joint that isn't properly soldered, or a bad component. Examine the voltage regulator and reverse-battery protection to make sure they're in the correct orientation. Touching a low-value resistor (100 Ω) across a component's leads provides an alternate electrical path that can route around a component for diagnostic purposes.

Placing the Robot on Blocks

After determining that the robot or circuit board has a resistance within an appropriate range, you should take other steps before powering up. If the robot or circuit board includes motion components (motors or actuators), then secure those parts so that an out-of-control circuit wouldn't cause physical harm.

For most robots, this means simply placing blocks under the robot's body to lift the wheels or legs off of the ground. Alternatively, it's pretty easy to remove LEGO press-on wheels. In any case, you don't want a robot to run into you, to tangle itself up, or to fall off of the laboratory bench (your desk or kitchen table).

For robots with arms, be sure the surrounding area is free from obstructions and people. For larger robots or robots with projectiles, weapons, higher voltages, pressure systems, or other hazards, please take the necessary precautions to protect yourself and those around you during testing.

Checking Battery Voltage and Polarity

Turn your attention to the battery for a moment. Measure the battery's voltage with a voltmeter (or a multimeter in voltage-measurement mode) before connecting the battery to the robot. If the voltage is low on a disconnected battery, the battery's voltage is really going to be low when supplying power to a load, such as a robot with motors.

Check that the battery is installed with the proper polarity.

If the battery's voltage appears to be sufficient, don't forget that the voltage of a dying battery can appear high enough when disconnected but drops quickly when powering a load. Double-check the actual voltage supplied when the robot is finally powered on. When in doubt, test the battery and voltage on a robot that's known to be functioning correctly.

Make sure the maximum and minimum voltage range of the battery, as well as the maximum current the battery can provide, is within the limits and demands of the circuit that the battery is expected to power. Electronic devices can have odd behaviors (or no behavior) when underpowered and can overheat or become damaged if exposed to higher voltages than allowed.

Watching Current Usage During Power-Up

The following summarizes the status before powering up:

- Dials and switches in appropriate positions

- Individual modules tested

- Total circuit resistance not too low or too high

- Robot up on blocks and motions safely limited

- Battery appropriate, fresh, and installed correctly

One last test can indicate significant faults and possibly limit damage. Insert the probes of an ammeter (or a multimeter in current-measurement mode) between one terminal of the battery and the robot's battery connector to measure voltage during power-up. Note that when measuring current, the red probe always goes to the most positive voltage source. Be sure to begin measurements using the highest current range. Finally, the other terminal of the battery must be connected to the other terminal of the robot's battery connector to complete the circuit (see Figure 14-2).

Figure 14-2. Connecting a multimeter between one battery terminal and the battery snap to measure current

If current draw seems excessive after turning on the robot's power switch, quickly turn off the robot's power switch. Because overheating causes most component damage, it may be possible to terminate the condition quickly enough to avoid permanent harm.

Up on blocks, using a fresh alkaline 9 V battery (measuring 9.5 V), my Roundabout robot draws 32 mA with motors disconnected and 80 mA with Escap motors connected. Your results will differ based on battery voltage and the motors selected. For example, when that same circuit is placed into Sandwich's body with Hsiang Neng motors, the current draw is 130 mA. When either robot is placed on the ground, current draw increases further because the motors are working to push the robot.

Preparing the Robot and Correcting Minor Glitches

After fault checking, the following sections prepare Roundabout and test the robot's basic functionality.

Fine-Tuning the Infrared Reflector Detector

With the power on, tune the frequency of the infrared reflector detector circuit by adjusting R6. I used a multimeter connected to a 38 kHz test point (which connects to pin 4 of the 74AC14) to measure the frequency. See Chapter 12 for other techniques to adjust the frequency.

Next, with nothing in front of Roundabout, adjust R7 until the detector LEDs show only green (no hint of red). Try turning R7 up until red appears or a mix of red and green appears, and then turn R7 back down until only green appears. This results in the maximum sensing distance without false detections because of noise.

Flipping Bicolor LEDs

The fine-tuning step is when I discovered the first fault on my board. The detector LEDs showed red for no detection and green for detection. That's the opposite of what I expected! On bicolor LEDs, it seems that the relationship of the colors to the flat side of the LED package isn't consistent between manufacturers or part numbers. I had to desolder the LEDs and put them in "backward."

To avoid this problem, you can leave off the bicolor LEDs until you finish the rest of the circuit. Then, gently insert one bicolor LED without soldering. Hold the LED in place while powering up the robot. If the color is correct (depending on whether your hand or body is now being detected), then power down the robot and solder the LED in that orientation.

Normally, I don't recommend powering up a robot with a loose part. But the LED's electrical path is straightforward, and the associated current-limiting resistor limits maximum current draw. However, if your bicolor LED has long leads, you might want to trim the leads so they don't accidentally brush up against anything during orientation testing.

Testing the Sensors

The infrared reflector detector circuit should now be tuned to the correct frequency, and the emitters should be at their maximum value without generating false detections. Move your hand slowly from left to right and back again (repeat as necessary) in front of the robot to test the left and right sensors.

It may be necessary to nudge and bend the angle of the emitters and detectors toward the sides (see Figure 14-3) so the robot can sense obstacles on the left (left sensor only), right (right sensor only), and straight ahead (both sensors at the same time). If both sensors are incorrectly looking straightforward, they'll tend to detect the same obstacles rather than being stereoscopic. If you add Roundabout's circuit into Sandwich's body, it may also be necessary to bend the emitters and detectors upward so the floor won't be detected.

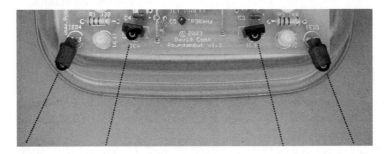

Figure 14-3. Emitters and detectors angled toward the sides to improve independent detection of flanking obstacles. Adding a baffle (opaque piece of material) in the center or shrouding the top, rear, and center side of each detector would further improve the stereoscopic abilities of the sensors.

The PNA4062M detectors can have serious false-positive and false-negative detection problems with fluorescent lighting. In such an environment, it's necessary to cover the top and rear of the detectors with an opaque material, such as aluminum. At my office, Roundabout fails miserably unless it's under a desk.

Mixing Up Motor Connections

Motor connections can be confusing. Instead of logically tracing each path, sometimes it's easier to plug the motors in and observe the direction of spin. During this test, make sure the robot is up on blocks and then power up:

1. When you hold your hand in front of the left sensors, the left LED changes colors, and the right motor should change directions. If, instead, the left motor changes direction, then swap the left and right motor connectors. Don't perform the next step until you've established that each motor is controlled by the sensor on the opposite side of the robot.

2. With no obstacles in front of the robot (both bicolor LEDs are green), both wheels should be rotating toward the front of the robot. That is, the left motor rotates counterclockwise, and the right motor rotates clockwise. For any motor that rotates in the wrong direction, swap the motor's wires on the connector.

   These motor-testing steps are when I discovered the second fault on my robot. The motor sides were flipped, and one of the motors had its wires reversed. Oh, well! It was easily enough corrected.

3. Using a permanent marker, label the motor connectors with an "L" and an "R" to avoid a future mix-up during servicing or disassembly.

Evaluating Roundabout's Performance

After building Roundabout, checking for fault conditions, and preparing for launch, it's finally time for some fun. Initially, you should subject the robot to informal testing and casual observations ("Fly! Be free, little robot!"). A few minor problems may crop up. Eventually, you can concentrate on analyzing and improving performance.

For Roundabout's maiden voyage, place the robot on a smooth level surface, cordoned off from any drop-offs. Turn on the power switch, and enjoy!

Encountering Problems with the Test Drive

A number of problems can become immediately apparent when you place the robot on the ground. What follows are a number of common ailments and suggestions for possible corrective actions.

Encountering a Reversing Robot

If the robot's bicolor LEDs turn red and the robot constantly reverses, then perhaps the following is happening:

- The robot has too much detection range and is detecting walls or far-away obstacles. Turn down R7.

- Something in the robot's body is reflecting infrared light into the detectors. Check for obstructions.

- Infrared light is escaping from both of the emitters and directly entering the detectors. Check for leakage (see the previous chapter) and build up the side and rear covering.

- The robot detects the floor. Bend the sensors upward.

- You didn't perform the earlier tests and corrections of the sensors and motors.

Encountering a Stalling Robot

If the robot has trouble starting to move and needs a push, or if the robot stalls even with pure red or pure green detections, then perhaps the following is happening:

- The motors aren't geared down enough. Try an 8-tooth LEGO gear on the motor shaft and a 24-tooth LEGO on the wheel.

- The properly geared motors are too weak to move the robot's mass. Did you make Roundabout out of ½-inch thick stainless-steel plate? (I don't believe body armor is called for here.) Reduce the robot's mass or replace the motors with more powerful motors.

- The battery may be exhausted. Recharge or replace.

- The motor requires too much current from the battery; 9 V batteries should be expected to supply a maximum of only about 300 mA total, including motors and the circuits. Lithium 9 V batteries supply even less; step up to AA or AAA NiMH batteries or more efficient motors.

- The motors are rated for a higher voltage than is being provided; for example, 24 VDC motors being driven at 9 V will either stall or operate at about one-third of their nominal speed. Because Roundabout uses a linear voltage regulator, it's better to replace the motors with motors rated for 9 V to 12 V, rather than increase the battery pack voltage.

- The motor driver chips are underrated for the selected motors. If you're using a 4427A motor driver by itself (without discrete transistors), then step up to a 4424 or IXDN404PI.

Encountering a Slow-Motion Robot

If the robot has no trouble getting moving or changing directions but moves at a slow, constant pace, then perhaps the following is happening:

- The motors are geared up too much. Try a 24-tooth LEGO gear on the motor shaft and an 8-tooth LEGO on the wheel. Or, replace the motors with ones that have a lower gear ratio.

- The motors are rated for a higher voltage than is being provided. Replace the motors with motors rated for 9 V to 12 V.

- The battery's voltage is too low. Currently available 9 V NiMH rechargeable batteries produce only nominal voltages of 7.2 V or 8.4 V; try installing a multi-cell AA or AAA battery pack.

- Accept the robot as is, taking advantage of the slow speed for easier scientific observations.

Encountering a Speeding Robot

If the robot moves too fast, then perhaps the following is happening:

- The motors aren't geared down enough. Some beginners attempt to use plain motors (without gearheads) to save money, which doesn't work; adding mass to slow down the robot results in a stall, so try an 8-tooth LEGO gear on the motor shaft and a 24-tooth LEGO on the wheel or replace the motors with geared motors.

- The battery has too high of a voltage for the selected motors. Try a 7.2 V Energizer NiMH rechargeable 9 V battery.

- The motor's nominal voltage is rated lower than the voltage being supplied. For example, some gearhead motors are wound for 6 V, 4.5 V, 3 V, or even 1.5 V. Running a motor at a higher voltage than rated will reduce the motor's life span and can quickly damage the motor or gears. A 6 V motor on a 7.2 V robot isn't too worrisome. However, it's preferable to avoid voltages exceeding 150 percent of the motor's rating.

Encountering a Rotating Robot

Assuming the room has plenty of space for the robot to explore, if the robot moves around in a circle or tends to veer to one side, then perhaps the following is happening:

- There's an electrical fault, such as a motor connection that's loose or broken. Try disconnecting the motors and reconnecting them. If that doesn't work, try swapping the motor connectors to see if the robot rotates in the opposite direction. If the robot subsequently rotates around the opposite wheel (not just rotating around the same wheel but backward), the problem is with the connectors or circuit, not with the motor or mechanics. Check the voltages with a multimeter to troubleshoot the failure. Try swapping the motor driver chips as well.

- The coupler setscrew has come loose on one of the motors. Tighten the screw.

- The coupler LEGO cross axle has come loose. To verify, try twisting the cross axle while holding the coupler body. It may be necessary to reglue the cross axle into the coupler.

- The wheel axle has come loose. Make sure the gears are meshing properly.

- A press-fit or friction-fit motor is rotating in place. Try twisting the motor body to see if it rotates. If so, a little glue may correct the problem. If the motors are too powerful, they should be held in place with screws rather than with friction or glue (or tape).

- A screw, 24-tooth gear, or the bottom of a motor mount is stuck on a gap on the floor or is dragging on the ground. Check the underside of the robot for debris. Move the robot to a different surface to see if the same behavior occurs.

- The wheel axle hole is too large, causing camber in the wheels. The amount of up/down movement in the wheel axle should be small, equivalent to the amount present if LEGO bricks were used.

- The wheel axle or motor coupler axle hole is too small, causing too much friction. With the gearmotor removed, the wheel, gears, and axles should spin freely by hand. Gradually enlarge tight holes, a little bit at a time, until the parts spin freely. Some fine grit sandpaper (facing outward) wrapped around a LEGO axle or a nontapered rotary-tool grinding stone (spun by hand) may help enlarge a hole. Try not to use a reamer or other tapered tool because the axle holes should be straight, not conical.

- The gears or the wheels are gunked up. Check for hair (gross!), stickiness, dirt, or broken gear teeth.

- Infrared light is escaping from one of the emitters and directly entering a detector. Check for leakage (see the previous chapter), and increase the side and rear coverings.

- Or, lastly, perhaps one of the motors is defective. Try disconnecting the motor from the robot and powering the motor directly from a battery.

Exercising All of the Robot's Maneuvers

When Roundabout is operating normally, it can perform four primary maneuvers. You can easily test these maneuvers using your hand or placing a bright object (piece of paper) in front of one, both, or neither sensor:

- The robot drives forward when no obstacles are detected. Both wheels rotate forward.

- The robot drives backward when both sensors detect an obstacle at the same time. Both wheels rotate backward.

- The robot rotates left when the right sensor detects an obstacle. The left wheel rotates backward, and the right wheel rotates forward.

- The robot rotates right when the left sensor detects an obstacle. The right wheel rotates backward, and the left wheel rotates forward.

Roundabout has four useful secondary maneuvers that are subtler. These maneuvers are made possible by the rapid switching of the PNA4602M detectors during states of partial detection:

- The robot gradually veers left when an obstacle is mostly detected on the right side. The left wheel turns more slowly than the right wheel.

- The robot pivots left when an obstacle is about 50 percent detected on the right side. The left wheel stops while the right wheel continues to rotate forward.

- The robot gradually veers right when an obstacle is mostly detected on the left side. The right wheel turns more slowly than the left wheel.

- The robot pivots right when an obstacle is about 50 percent detected on the left side. The right wheel stops while the left wheel continues to rotate forward.

Roundabout has one last "maneuver," which is highly undesirable. This is discussed in more detail later in the "Getting Stuck" section. The robot stops or wiggles in place when obstacles are about 50 percent detected by both sensors. Neither wheel rotates much at all. Except for slippage or a change in environment, Roundabout gets stuck in this state. This situation is indicated by both the green and red within each bicolor LED appearing to be lit up at the same time (see Figure 14-4).

Figure 14-4. A two-lead bicolor LED with both dies illuminated "simultaneously" by rapidly switching the polarity back and forth

Challenging Roundabout

After correcting minor problems, my Roundabout works pretty well. I hope this is true for your Roundabout robot.

Roundabout can get stuck on carpet and tile because of the robot's low clearance. However, larger-diameter wheels and a rear castor should conquer that problem.

Roundabout sees most obstacles. Dark-colored objects tend to invoke the dreaded 50 percent detection stop condition. Light-colored objects (such as white walls and doors) tend to be seen too far away, resulting in premature turning and avoidance.

Avoiding Toilet Paper Alley

The problem with light-colored objects became especially acute when I tried to create an artificial environment for the robot, made out of ordinary household items. In particular, I wanted to build a maze out of objects that were readily available in any home and that were inexpensive, safe, stackable, and consistent in appearance. My solution was "rolls of toilet paper."

Well, Roundabout was having none of that!

White toilet paper is highly reflective of infrared. When I built a corridor out of the stuff (never mind the preceding conversation with my wife), the robot could see it so far away that all it wanted to do was back up. After turning R7 down to the lowest emission level, the robot barely agreed to enter Toilet Paper Alley (see Figure 14-5).

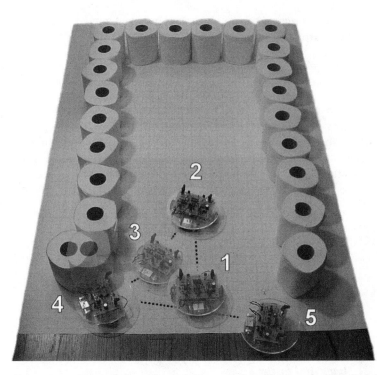

Figure 14-5. Roundabout hesitantly entering about one-third of the way into Toilet Paper Alley as shown by positions ① and ②. The robot subsequently backed out ③ until it struck a roll with its sensorless rear ④. After rotating in place, the robot sped out ⑤, barely escaping with its life.

One of the more serious issues raised by this test is that Roundabout backs up blindly. Perhaps the addition of a single rear sensor would allow a future model of Roundabout to choose to rotate in place to look for a new direction when the rear path is blocked.

Switching to Blocks of Wood

Testing the robot's behavior in a dead end was finally accomplished by switching from toilet paper to blocks of wood. As long as the corridor is wide enough, Roundabout performs the feat fabulously for a logic-gate robot (see Figure 14-6).

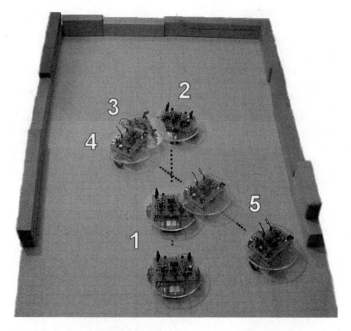

Figure 14-6. Roundabout proceeds about halfway into the wooden dead end as shown by positions ① and ②. The robot rotates slightly and backs up ③. When the robot is far enough away from the wall that only one sensor detects the wall, the robot rotates again ④ until the sensors spot the opening. Finally, the robot exits, gradually turning a bit more away from the rear wall as it approaches ⑤.

Ringing Around the Robot

Like most robots, Roundabout has trouble with narrow chair legs or objects raised off the ground just enough to get jammed under. Sometimes an obstacle will be just outside the peripheral range of the sensors, causing the robot to brush up against it.

I chose to make Roundabout's body circular because so many other robot builders seem to select that shape. I hadn't experimented with circular robots before, and being that they're so popular, I was expecting some incredible advantages.

With centered wheels, a circular body clearly provides the ability to rotate in place without getting hung up on corners or obstructions. This benefit alone is worth the hassle of cutting circular platforms.

I thought a circular body would also guide the robot past obstacles or thread the robot through appropriately sized openings, even if the robot were slightly off target. However, in each case, I found that the robot actually turned toward the obstacle instead of away from it (see Figure 14-7).

Figure 14-7. A black lamp base with a narrow center pole isn't detected by Roundabout's infrared sensors. Without the aid of additional types of sensors, the robot must rely on the shape of its body to help guide the robot away from the obstacle. In this example, the opposite occurs. Even when the robot barely brushes against the side of the lamp base, the added friction on the obstacle side causes a turn toward the obstacle, eventually getting the robot completely stuck.

I doubt my choice of materials contributes to the problem because acrylic is pretty slick. Being made on a milling machine with a rotating table and an eight-flute end mill, the shape is close to a true circle, with no apparent coarseness. More experiments are necessary to determine if a shape can be found that permits a differentially steered robot with centered wheels to consistently glance off of an obstacle.

Getting Stuck

You can arrange an environment to accentuate the robot's abilities and reduce the opportunities for failure. A flat, clean floor with moderately reflective, medium-to-large walls and obstacles can permit Roundabout to have a full run from a fresh battery.

Unfortunately, Roundabout has an end state that, given enough time, it's destined to enter.

Evaluating a Drunkard's Walk

I first read about a paradigm called the "drunkard's walk" in the book *Full House* by Stephen Jay Gould (Harmony Books, 1996). A large portion of the book is dedicated to the argument that the ultimate result of evolution is diversity, not a singularly "best" creature. It's a thought-provoking book that I highly recommend to anyone considering an evolutionary path to improving his or her robotic creations.

The situation is this: A drunken man walks out of a bar. He randomly staggers down the sidewalk. On one side of the sidewalk is an impenetrable wall. On the other side of the sidewalk is the gutter. Given an infinitely long walk and a nonsober man, what are the chances that the man will reach the gutter?

It's mathematically possible that the man will never reach the gutter because a true random walk could always be toward the wall. However, with each step, it's more and more mathematically probable that the man will fall into the gutter.

This wouldn't be the case if the man had his wits about him. In that case, he'd purposely steer clear of the gutter, but then the walk would no longer be random.

Because there's only one end state to this scenario (the gutter) and because there's no state that can be entered that prevents reaching the gutter state (the man never reaches home), the ending to this paradigm is inevitably the gutter.

Another way of phrasing this paradigm is this: Because this scenario ends only when the man ends up in the gutter, the man always ends up in the gutter—just as your car keys are always in the last place you look for them because after you find them, you stop looking.

Evaluating Roundabout's Walk

Imagine that Roundabout is placed in a circular room with a flat floor and no obstacles and with an infinite battery and infinite lifespan. Assuming slip, imperfect sensing, electrical noise, and wall reflectivity, Roundabout's motions eventually produce a generally random pattern of movement.

If both of Roundabout's sensors *can* enter a 50 percent detection state (stopping both motors with rapid switching between forward and reverse), given random activity, then the sensors eventually *will* enter a 50 percent detection state.

In a normal room, you can easily imagine a few situations where Roundabout's sensors both produce 50 percent detection. For example, if the robot is heading directly toward a wall at some angle (perpendicular, if the sensors are aimed identically and have identical sensitivity), then the sensors will reach a 50 percent detection point at the same time. A less obvious situation is where two objects of differing reflectivity cause the robot to gradually veer into the 50 percent detection situation (see Figure 14-8).

As soon as one wheel stops at 50 percent detection, it becomes more likely that Roundabout will pivot the other wheel until it stops at 50 percent detection. The gradual turning that makes performance eerily smooth also leads (methodically, not randomly) to the end state.

Interestingly, faster robots, such as Roundabout with Sandwich's motors, reach the end state less often because the robot's momentum causes the robot to continue to roll a little after the motor stops. Thus, the robot tends to roll past 50 percent detection states.

Figure 14-8. A lighter-colored object (in this case, red) on the left side reflects an equal amount of infrared light as does the nearer but darker-colored object (in this case, blue) on the right side. In this figure, Roundabout isn't moving because it senses 50 percent detection on both sensors. Therefore, both motors are driven backward and forward very quickly, resulting in no overall movement.

Reducing Detection Ambiguity

Perhaps you could design a circuit to reduce the rapidly switching detection signal from the PNA4602M, thus eliminating the stopped motors? You'll now explore a couple of approaches you could take.

Attempting to Use a Resistor-Capacitor Circuit

The most obvious solution is to add a resistor and capacitor to the detection signal, just like the circuit used in Chapter 6 to clean up (*debounce*) a signal from a push button or a switch. Figure 14-9 shows two components inserted between the PNA4602M and the 74AC14 chip.

The switching of the original signal (see the left side of Figure 14-10) is reduced significantly (middle) by the addition of the resistor and capacitor. Unfortunately, this results in a signal that's neither 5 V nor 0 V during periods of heavy fluctuation. Normally, it wouldn't be acceptable to input a middle-of-the-range voltage into a digital CMOS chip. However, the 74AC14 has Schmitt-trigger inputs that are specifically designed to accept such voltages.

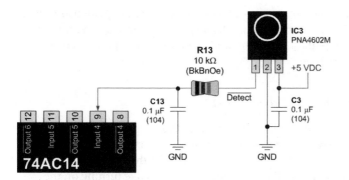

Figure 14-9. C13 begins charge when the detect pin is 5 V and begins to discharge when the detect pin is 0 V. Resistor R13 reduces the amount of current that the detect pin can supply, thereby increasing the time needed for voltage across C13 to change. Combined, R13 and C13 slow the rate of change seen by input 4 (pin 9) on the 74AC14 chip.

Now comes the kicker. Although this revised circuit effectively eliminates rapid 50 percent switching from the detector to the 74AC14 input, it still produces a voltage that's about 50 percent (about 2.5 V). As the voltage rises and falls (say, between 40 percent and 60 percent) with the changing detection signal, it rises above and falls below the hysteresis of the Schmitt-trigger inputs. Therefore, ironically, the 74AC14 still generates a wave between 40 percent and 60 percent, just over a longer period of time than before.

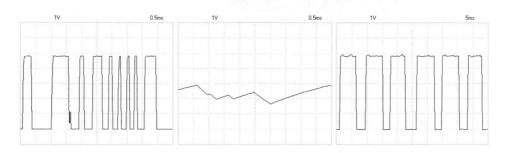

Figure 14-10. Unadulterated PNA4602M detect signal switching back and forth at approximately 50 percent detection (left). Applying an RC circuit does indeed reduce voltage swings because of detection fluctuations (middle). However, over time (ten times the scale), the output of the 74AC14 still outputs a roughly symmetrical wave (right).

NOTE *Unfortunately, the three traces in Figure 14-10 couldn't be taken at the same time from the same signal, so they don't quite match up. They're independent examples.*

Interestingly, the circuit now converts a digital signal to an analog signal and then back to a digital signal. This results in retaining the 50 percent stopped condition but eliminates the gradual (0 percent to 25 percent and 75 percent to 99 percent) turning ability. That's not what you wanted.

Attempting to Use High-Beam Hysteresis

My next idea was to eliminate the problem at its source. That is, prevent the PNA4602M from receiving a signal that wasn't consistently detectable. The concept is simple: When the PNA4602M indicates detection, even briefly, the output of the associated infrared LED is boosted to retain the detection. (It's sort of like turning on the high-beam headlight on a car when you see something by the side of the road.) Then, when the signal is no longer detected (even with the high beam turned on), the high beam is turned off.

Figure 14-11 shows the changes to the infrared reflector detector circuit. All other portions of the circuit remain as they were originally presented in Figure 11-10. The failed resistor-capacitor modification shown in Figure 14-9 has been discarded.

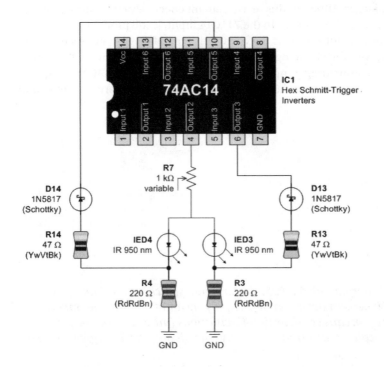

Figure 14-11. Schematic containing only the changes made to the infrared reflector detector circuit. Emitters IED3 and IED4 no longer completely share current, so pins 6 and 10 may provide extra current paths independently to the individual emitters when obstacles are detected.

Analyzing the High-Beam Circuit

For the moment, concentrate on the right side of the robot's emitter and detector circuit. The left side is a mirror image of the right side of the circuit and performs in an identical manner.

When detection occurs on the right side of the robot, PNA4602M goes low (0 V). That's connected to pin 13 (0 V), which inverts pin 12 (5 V), which is connected to pin 11 (5 V), which inverts pin 10 (0 V). So pin 10 is nothing more than a copy of the output from PNA4602M.

Normally, current flows through R7 (adjustable brightness), through IED4 (the infrared emitter), through R4 (current-limiting resistor), and to ground (0 V). However, when pin 10 goes low, current can also go through R7, through IED4, through R14 (another current-limiting resistor), through D14 (one-way valve with a low voltage drop), and into pin 10 (0 V). More current can flow through IED4 with two paths than just with one path. IED4 is a current-controlled device; the more current flowing through it, the brighter it gets. High beams on!

R14 is necessary to prevent too much current from flowing through the new path, which might damage IED4. It isn't possible to move R4 above IED4 and eliminate R14 because all of the current would proceed directly to ground without bothering to go through the voltage drop at D14. You'd have only the original path then, so brightness wouldn't increase.

When pin 10 goes high (5 V), diode D14 blocks the flow that would otherwise pass through R14 and R4. High beams off!

If diode D14 weren't included, then the emitter's output would decline further than normal when no object was detected. Also, a lot of current (5 V divided by (47 Ω plus 220 Ω) equals 18.7 mA) would be wasted going from pin 10, through R14, through R4, and into ground.

Implementing the High-Beam Circuit

I stretched Roundabout's circuit board (see Figure 14-12) to add the high-beam components. While I was at it, I made room in the center of the circuit board for the battery cable and the motor cables to pass through a hole rather than around the rear. (It ended up seeming like this was a waste of valuable circuit board space, and it was a pain to route all of the signals around the hole.)

Figure 14-12. Roundabout's stretched circuit board contains a hole in the center for wires ①, high-beam paths of diodes and resistors ②, headers to allow emitter current measurement ③, and a split between the brain and the brawn ④.

Measuring Current with Two-Pin Male Square Headers and Shorting Jumpers

Because the stretched circuit board was an experimental model of the Roundabout robot, I placed a two-pin male square header (see Figure 14-13) in series with each infrared emitter. With a shorting jumper (also called a *shunt*) in place, the electrical path is connected normally, and the emitter receives power.

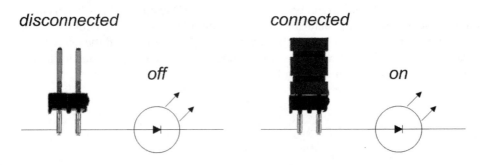

Figure 14-13. A two-pin header electrically interrupts the current path to the infrared emitter. The black insulating plastic that holds the header pins together doesn't pass electricity from pin to pin (left). A shorting jumper contains a strip of metal to electrically connect the pins of the header, thus completing the path (right).

With the jumper removed, you can connect the probes of an ammeter (or multi-meter in current-measuring mode) to measure the amount of current flowing through the emitter (see Figure 14-14). This allowed me to verify that more current does indeed pass through the correct emitter when an object is detected (high beams on).

Figure 14-14. A two-pin male square header in the path leading to the infrared emitter (left). A shorting jumper electrically connects both header pins together, completing the path during normal operation (middle). By removing the jumper and attaching ammeter probes, current goes through one probe to be measured and then out the other probe to continue on to the infrared emitter (right).

Square-pin headers are commonly available. The pins are available with tin or gold plating. Either is fine. Look for 0.1-inch (2.54 mm) center-to-center spacing between pins because that's the most popular standard. The most common height of the pin above the insulator is from 0.230 to 0.240 inches although you can find heights as much as 0.910 inches.

A variety of arrangements are available, with either straight pins or right angles and either single or double rows. The most appropriate choice depends on the amount of space available and the layout of your board.

Although pre-cut lengths, such as two pins, are available, it's more economical to purchase a long strip and snap (or cut) the strip down to the desired length. These strips are sometimes called *breakaway* or *snappable* headers. The other advantage of a strip is that you don't need to stock a bunch of different pre-cut lengths.

The prices vary from $0.24 to $1.09, depending on the plating and the number of pins. Here are some examples of single-row straight-pin headers from Digi-Key: the two-pin tin-plated WM6402, the 36-pin tin-plated S1012-36, and the 40-pin gold-plated A26512.

Shorting jumpers usually cost from $0.09 to $0.33 each, depending on the style and plating. The minimum quantity order is usually ten pieces. Jumpers come in a variety of colors. Some examples from Digi-Key are the tin-plate S9000; the red, plastic, gold-plate A26230; the blue, plastic, gold-plate A26226; and the top-of-the-line gold-plate 929957-08.

Rerouting Signals and Controls with a Multipin Header

An especially nice feature of the stretched Roundabout circuit board is a dual-row multipin male square header (see ④ in Figure 14-12) that separates all connections between the brain (74AC14) and the brawn (motor drivers). You can disconnect the motor control signals from the 74AC14 (pins 6, 8, 10, and 12; see Figure 13-5) from the motor drivers by removing the jumpers. You can place an add-on circuit board containing a microcontroller or other logic circuit onto the header to read the original motor control signals but provide different control signals to the motors.

The header also includes pins with unregulated voltage, regulated voltage (5 V), and ground to supply power to the add-on circuit board. Two additional pins lead to spare holes on the stretched circuit board for future expansion, such as adding floor sensors.

The outermost pins on the header are in the middle of the high-beam paths. Removing the jumpers from the pins interrupts the paths, which disables high beams, and the robot behaves like the original Roundabout. Or, with the add-on circuit board attached, the microcontroller can turn the high beams on and off as it desires.

Looking for Improved Performance

The high-beam paths definitely increased/decreased the brightness of the infrared emitters, as they were designed to do. Unfortunately, the stretched Roundabout still got stuck in some 50 percent detection situations. Perhaps resistors R13 and R14 should have been reduced further to provide an even stronger infrared light source during unstable detection situations.

Running Out of Simple Ideas

I can just imagine the quantity of solutions I'm going to receive from readers when this book is published. I welcome all suggestions. I'll post the best simple circuits on my Web site.

Believe me, I've come up with some functional but complicated solutions. For example, I've developed an RC circuit attached to a window comparator with a logic gate to force all signals between 40 percent and 60 percent but pass through all other signals to permit gradual turning.

But then it struck me. This problem is so easily solved by a microcontroller that it provides the perfect transition point to explain why robot builders use microcontrollers in addition to, or even in place of, logic-gate chips.

CHAPTER 15

If I Only Had a Brain

Covers the Motorola MC68HC908KX8 Microcontroller, the Microcontroller vs. the Logic Chip, How to Program a Microcontroller, A Simple LED Example, Heartbeat, Seven-Segment LED Display, Inputs (Digital, Analog, Interrupts, Reset, Pull-Up and Pull-Down), Outputs (Avoiding Glitches, High Current, Pulse-Width Modulated, Serial Communication), Single Infrared Detector, Memory, Speed, Clocks, Timers, Watchdogs, and Microcontroller Selection Criteria

MANY VIABLE ROBOT BRAINS are built from discrete semiconductors, interface chips, and/or logic chips. Sandwich, Roundabout, and most BEAM robots are classic examples of robots that operate without microcontrollers. These robots are simple enough to reproduce using off-the-shelf parts and don't require programming or special development tools.

It's possible to increase the behavioral complexity of a simple robot by adding logic chips and other components. However, beyond a certain point, it becomes easier, faster, and cheaper to add rules and behaviors through software, rather than hardware.

This chapter introduces the microcontroller. The chapter begins with a brief overview of how a microcontroller is programmed and debugged. Then, it covers the common features available in most microcontrollers. Finally, this chapter concludes with some criteria you might want to consider when selecting a microcontroller.

Considering the Motorola KX8 Microcontroller As an Example

The example microcontroller selected for this book is the Motorola MC68HC908KX8 (or simply, the KX8). The KX8 chip exemplifies the features commonly available in a wide variety of microcontrollers, regardless of manufacturer. The KX8 comes in a small, nonthreatening 16-pin DIP package (see Figure 15-1) and requires no additional special components.

Figure 15-1. The Motorola KX8 microcontroller comes in an easy-to-use, standalone 16-pin DIP package, similar to logic chips. Other than the power, ground, and interrupt input (leave disconnected if unused) pins, all of the remaining pins are user-configurable as inputs, outputs, or specialized functions.

By focusing on a single microcontroller, the KX8, the examples in this book are consistent and less confusing. However, I'm aware of the strong loyalty that builders have to their particular model and brand of microcontroller. Therefore, I try to present the usage of a microcontroller in a generic way, rather than focusing on the features of a particular part number.

After the different attributes of a microcontroller are discussed, this chapter presents some criteria to assist you in selecting a microcontroller appropriate for your needs.

Comparing a Microcontroller to a Logic Chip

In many ways, a microcontroller is similar to a logic chip. Just like a logic chip, a microcontroller requires power and ground, has input and output pins, and needs a 0.1 µF ceramic bypass/decoupling capacitor near the power pin. The addition of a bulk capacitor (for example, a 10 µF tantalum) is recommended when switching larger currents or operating at faster speeds. These capacitors provide the same benefits as C1 and C2 (recall Figure 11-10) did for the 74AC14 logic chip in Chapter 11.

Unlike an off-the-shelf logic chip, you can program most of the pins on a microcontroller to perform whatever function you desire. In a sense, a microcontroller allows you to create your own custom chip whose diverse or complex functions wouldn't be available in an off-the-shelf standard logic chip.

Choosing a Logic Chip Over a Microcontroller

Because of the wide variety of logic chips and microcontrollers, it's tricky to generalize when comparing them. However, logic chips do have some attributes that are superior to microcontrollers in certain ways:

- Logic chips are inexpensive.

- Logic chips tend to be available in low-density hobbyist-friendly packages, such as 8-pin, 14-pin, and 16-pin DIP and SOIC.

- Logic chips are available in industry-standardized formats with consistent pin definitions.

- Standardized logic chips are readily available from numerous suppliers and manufacturers.

- A specific logic chip design (such as 74xx14) tends to be available for decades. On the other hand, specific microcontroller part numbers have a reputation for going out of production in a matter of years, necessitating that builders stock an adequate personal supply.

- Logic chips tend to be easier for the builder to learn and connect because the pins aren't configurable and the function of the chip is fairly rudimentary.

- Logic chips start up faster on power-up because they don't have to run an internal program to set up pins and variables (and because they don't have to wait for a clock signal to stabilize).

- Logic chips react faster to changes in their inputs because they don't have to run a program to determine how to react.

- Logic chips and interface chips tend to operate under a wider range of acceptable voltages.

- Logic chips use less power, especially when the inputs don't change. A microcontroller needs to constantly run a program even when the inputs are unchanged (there are ways for a microcontroller to enter a sleep or low power state and wait for pin changes).

- Logic chip pins tend to be able to provide more powerful output current.

- Logic chips are self-contained and stand-alone. Some microcontrollers require extra components, such as a low-voltage monitor and clock.

- Because they're less complicated, logic chips tend to have few or no defects or bugs. On the other hand, complex microcontrollers often undergo post-release revisions (mask set changes) by the manufacturer to correct errors.

- Logic chips require no programming or special development tools.

For these reasons, you'll still find logic chips scattered throughout modern designs.

If you have a simple task that's directly suited to the intended use of an existing off-the-shelf logic chip, don't hesitate to employ a logic chip. Logic and interface chips remain excellent choices for functioning immediately from power-up to power-down, for consuming ultralow power from a rarely changing state, for isolating or buffering signals, and/or for driving higher currents.

Choosing a Microcontroller Over a Logic Chip

With all of those advantages, you might think that the popularity of logic chips would remain unchallenged. However, the advantages of microcontrollers are in the categories that usually count the most:

- A single microcontroller can replace the functionality of multiple logic chips. This saves space, power, weight, soldering/manufacturing time, and expense; this also reduces the variety of parts that have to be on hand or stocked.

- You can quickly alter the function of the final product with software, rather than having to resolder wires, replace chips, make a new printed circuit board, drill new holes, and so on.

- Off-the-shelf logic chips simply aren't available to perform more complex functions. Although a variety of logic chips can be interconnected to perform complex functions, the resulting circuit quickly becomes convoluted.

For these reasons, microcontrollers (and programmable logic devices) have supplanted logic chips as the chip of choice in almost all circuits. Microcontrollers have led to the obsolescence of many of less mainstream logic chips over the past 10–15 years.

With the exception of the simpler robots specifically designed for my books, all of my robots include at least one microcontroller. The capabilities and flexibility of a microcontroller really bring a robot to life.

However, the strengths of a microcontroller shouldn't cause you to shy away from including logic chips, interface chips, analog chips, analog circuits, or discrete transistors where appropriate. Just like through-hole and surface-mount package technology, there are advantages to mixing and matching semiconductor technologies.

Programming a Microcontroller

Nearly all factory-fresh microcontrollers arrive without any program in them whatsoever. Wiring a blank microcontroller produces boring results. The configurable pins are usually designed to start as inputs at power-up. Without any output pins, the chip does nothing but listen to the inputs and constantly reset itself as it encounters improper (random garbage) instructions.

It's up to you, the developer, to give each microcontroller its purpose.

Storing Programs

Most modern microcontrollers contain some form of internal nonvolatile memory for storing programs. The program remains inside of the chip even when power is turned off or the chip is removed from the circuit. So, once you've programmed a microcontroller, you can move it from circuit to circuit, power it up, and have the program start running immediately. This really provides the sense of having created a custom chip.

The two most popular reprogrammable nonvolatile memory technologies in use today in microcontrollers are electrically erasable programmable read-only memory (EEPROM) and Flash. These allow the chips to be programmed and reprogrammed over and over again, between ten thousand and a million times or more. The program or other memory contents can be read an infinite number of times and remains intact for decades.

 CAUTION *Some older or cheaper microcontrollers are one-time programmable (OTP). After the part is programmed once, it stays that way forever. Unless your code is perfect the first time you write it, you don't want to purchase an OTP microcontroller. OTP microcontrollers are appropriate for mass-produced items.*

Sizing Up Program Storage

The amount of built-in program storage in a microcontroller tends to be fairly limited. The least expensive microcontrollers may contain only 1 KB (1024 bytes) of program storage. The Motorola KX8 ($5) has 8 KB of program storage. More expensive microcontrollers (greater than $10) can have 60 KB or even 128 KB of program storage.

If greater amounts of program storage are required, high-end microcontrollers provide pins for accessing external memory. Ironically, the high-end microcontrollers can actually have less built-in program storage because they devote more of the semiconductor die to other features. These high-end microcontrollers are expected to be connected to external memory, so the lack of built-in program storage isn't a serious issue.

As little as 1 KB of program storage? For those of you accustomed to computers with 512 MB of RAM and 100 GB hard disks—don't panic!

Microcontroller code tends to be fairly compact. You haven't got images or a hefty operating system clogging it up. Briefly surveying some of my code, I found that none of my robot code exceeded 8 KB (see Table 15-1).

Table 15-1. Size of Programs in Various Robots

Robot Name	Object Code Size
Carefree	419 bytes
Have a Nice Day	1,693 bytes
Hard2C	2,673 bytes
Roundabout	3,774 bytes
Bugdozer	4,388 bytes
Sweet	4,868 bytes
Soup	7,162 bytes

The final three robots listed in Table 15-1 have LCD screens. Much of the program space is consumed by the verbose text that appears on the screens. Personally, I've not yet reached the point with any robot that I had to eliminate code for it to fit within built-in nonvolatile memory. However, microcontrollers from some manufacturers are more restrictive with program space, and it's not uncommon to hear programmers groan as they hit the limit.

Writing Programs

A wide variety of programming languages are available for microcontrollers. Assembly, C, and BASIC are the most common languages. Assembly is the lowest level and arguably the most powerful, but it's also the most complicated and least friendly. BASIC is popular with beginners and for people needing to crank out a straightforward device. C is the most widely selected language by those with software backgrounds. Some of the newer languages (C++, Java) are just entering the microcontroller marketplace, but they struggle somewhat with the limited speed and memory available on microcontrollers.

Complete microcontroller development environments (editors, compilers, debuggers, and software downloads) are available for different operating systems. Microsoft Windows is the most supported, with Apple Mac OS and Linux being somewhat less supported.

You can find appropriate programming software and tools by visiting the Web site of the microcontroller manufacturer. The manufacturers also have programming manuals, technical datasheets, and sample code. Very popular microcontrollers are fortunate enough to have third parties write magazine articles or even entire books about programming them. For less popular microcontrollers, many independent builders post code snippets or even entire programs online.

Working Without a Net

Developing code for a microcontroller is similar to writing a program for a standard personal computer. You've got a text editor in which you type all of your code. You've usually got a project file with settings and links to a bunch of source files. You select Compile from a menu. And when the syntax errors are corrected, you can try running the program, either simulated on the PC or on the microcontroller itself.

The major difference between writing for a PC and writing for a microcontroller is that most (but not all) low-end microcontrollers lack operating systems or even code libraries. You pretty much have to write everything from scratch. No existing math routines, no built-in string routines, no common display routines, nothing!

For many hobbyists, that's the most interesting and challenging part of working with a microcontroller. I really enjoy knowing that every byte of code in that robot is mine (no one else is messing it up). I control every pin, the processor spends time only on the tasks I think are important, and I can tweak and fix anything that's worth my time.

Then again, some hobbyists would prefer to concentrate only on the robot portions of the code. For those individuals, a high-level language with a preloaded microcontroller is more appropriate than a raw, blank microcontroller. For example, the Parallax BASIC Stamp would be a good choice.

Compiling and Downloading the Program

Getting the code from the PC to the microcontroller is fairly easy. Again, you write and compile a program for your microcontroller using a standard personal computer. Then, you attach a programming board (see Figure 15-2), specific to your chosen microcontroller, to the serial port (usually) on the computer. The development environment downloads the compiled program (object code) to the microcontroller sitting in a socket on the board. After that, you can remove the microcontroller and install it in your robot or other electronic project.

For unabashed do-it-yourselfers, many manufacturers publish schematics for making simple programming boards using off-the-shelf components. You can save some money, but it can be frustrating if you encounter any problems getting the code to the microcontroller. You'll constantly be questioning whether your homemade programming board is the source of the problem.

Debugging the Program

Many programming boards include a debugging cable that attaches to the robot (or other electronic project) where the microcontroller would normally be installed. Some programming boards even allow the microcontroller to be programmed and debugged while installed in the robot. Using your personal computer, you can then step through the code and see the values of the pins just as the microcontroller sees them. This is incredibly helpful, especially if your robot doesn't include some sort of display for showing diagnostic messages.

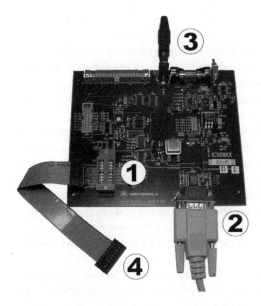

Figure 15-2. A programming and debugging board for the Motorola KX8. It contains a socket to hold the microcontroller being programmed ①, a serial cable to connect to a computer during programming and debugging ②, a power supply ③, and a cable that connects to the robot in place of the microcontroller during debugging ④.

If your microcontroller programming board doesn't provide in-circuit debugging, or if for some reason an issue can't be easily re-created in such an environment, there are a couple of less sophisticated debugging techniques that can be helpful.

Lighting Up an LED

The simplest debugging technique is to attach an LED (with a current-limiting resistor) to one pin on the microcontroller (see Figure 15-3) and then have some piece of code turn on the LED when a certain event occurs.

The code to light up the debug LED would be something like the following:

1. On power up, set pin 2 (or whatever) low (0 V) and make it an output. The LED is off.

2. Anywhere in the code where you want to flag an error or indicate that a piece of code was executed, set pin 2 to high (5 V). The LED turns on.

Now, all you have to do is sit back and watch to see if your LED gets turned on! With multiple LEDs connected to multiple pins, you can flag all sorts of events or stages of successful code completion. "Ah ha! The red LED turned on, so I know the microcontroller got through all of the initialization code, but the green LED didn't turn on, so procedure XYZ isn't getting called."

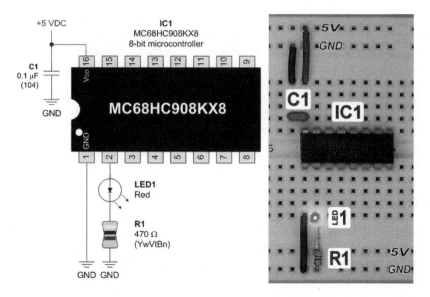

Figure 15-3. A schematic of a microcontroller with an LED attached for debugging (left). The schematic implemented on a solderless breadboard (right). (To simplify the circuit on the solderless breadboard, R1 is soldered to one lead of LED1, just like in Figure 11-7 in Chapter 11.)

 NOTE *As with any chip, be sure to review the microcontroller's datasheet to determine the maximum total current the chip can output from all pins combined. Even if each pin is within current limits, it may be that the total current from all pins is excessive. Normally you won't be driving more than three or four LEDs directly per chip, so this isn't usually an issue.*

This debugging technique is so reassuring that perhaps it should be the first piece of code you try on your new microcontroller. You'll know that you've successfully set up the board and downloaded code if the LED turns on.

Changing a Pin

The LED example seems simple enough, but if you've never worked with a microcontroller before, you may be asking "How exactly do I change a pin to an output?" or "How exactly do I set the output high or low?" Obviously, it depends on the particular microcontroller.

Generally, the manufacturer defines the pins just like global variables (at specific memory addresses) and builds those definitions into the language, header file, or development environment. By putting a 0 or a 1 into the bit of the associated global variable, the pin turns from an input to an output. By putting a 0 or a 1 into a different bit or different global variable, the output turns low (0 V) or high (5 V). Reading that bit from the global variable returns a 0 or a 1 depending on whether whatever is connected to that input pin is low (0 V) or high (5 V).

There's no magic to this. The pins are connected to transistors that are wired to a specific memory address. The manufacturer simply tells you to which memory location the pins are wired.

Higher-level languages, such as BASIC, often provide simplified commands to make it easier for the programmer to write code, rather than having to wrangle bits. But, in the end, the commands are still performing the same task of turning a bit on or off at a predefined memory address, which is attached to some transistors, which are attached to a pin.

Creating a Heartbeat

A slightly more sophisticated LED debugging technique is to include a counter or timer in your code to blink an LED or other indicator in the main loop. This continually demonstrates that the microcontroller is operating properly and isn't hung or stuck in an infinite loop in a subroutine. The following is one way to write the pseudo-code.

SETUP (the beginning of the program):

1. Set pin 2 to low (0 V), and make it an output. The heartbeat LED is off.

2. Create a global variable, HeartBeat, and set it to 0.

3. Continue with the rest of the initialization and setup, if any.

MAIN LOOP (repeats forever):

4. If HeartBeat isn't 0, then decrease HeartBeat by 1 and go to step 8.

5. HeartBeat is 0, so it's time to blink the heartbeat LED. If pin 2 is low (0 V), set it to high (5 V). The heartbeat LED turns on. Go to step 7.

6. Pin 2 must already be high (5 V), so set it to low (0 V). The heartbeat LED turns off.

7. Set HeartBeat to some large value, such as 500, so that the heartbeat LED takes a noticeable amount of time between blinking on and off.

8. Continue with the rest of the main loop, calling subroutines and performing actions for the robot or device.

9. Go to step 4.

This sample code has the disadvantage of blinking based on the number of times the main loop has executed, not based on an accurate timer. Therefore, when subroutines or other robotic duties consume processing time, the interval between blinks increases. Later in this chapter, you'll see how to make the heartbeat more regular by using an interrupt timer.

You can implement an LED heartbeat using little space on the circuit board (see the left side of Figure 15-4). Rather than using an LED for the heartbeat, you could attach a self-oscillating buzzer and turn it off and on like an LED. Or would that be too annoying?

For more sophisticated robots that have LCD displays, you can literally have a heartbeat (see the middle and right sides of Figure 15-4) appear on the display. LCDs have the advantage of consuming much less power. In fact, a 4-character by 20-character LCD display generally consumes the same amount of power as a single LED.

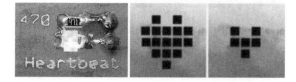

Figure 15-4. A blinking heartbeat LED implemented with surface-mount components takes up very little space. A quick peek at the heartbeat LED immediately reveals whether the microcontroller is receiving power and operating (left). Bugdozer, Soup, and Sweet all display a little heart in the corner of their LCD (middle and right). The heart goes from big to small and small to big once a second. If the microcontroller wasn't operating properly, the heartbeat wouldn't be the correct speed or wouldn't occur at all.

No matter how you choose to implement a heartbeat, it can be a reassuring indicator that the microcontroller is receiving power and that legitimate code is executing.

Driving a Display

The ultimate debugging tool is to actually have the robot output a message to a display. Actually, you can build up from the earlier "multiple LED" example by connecting seven pins from the microcontroller to seven LEDs arranged in the shape of an "8". Ready-made multisegment LEDs are readily available from electronic suppliers (see Figure 15-5).

Figure 15-5. Various seven-segment (or greater) LEDs for alphanumeric displays

Depending on which LED segments are turned on, the microcontroller can indicate various numbers from 0–9 and even some letters (see Figure 15-6). By adding additional multisegment LEDs, you can spell out messages.

Figure 15-6. Seven-segment LEDs displaying numbers and letters. The "8" shape shows all seven LED segments lit at the same time whereas the hyphen (-) has only the middle LED segment lit.

There's a significant downside to using multisegment LEDs: You'll quickly run out of microcontroller pins. Integrated display modules are available that permit the microcontroller to output data over a few pins and have another chip (or microcontroller) display that data as a message. Another option is to use a serial-to-parallel interface chip, such as the 74HC595, to convert a stream of data from the microcontroller into many output pins on the interface chip.

Exploring Common Microcontroller Features

The microcontroller market is a multibillion-dollar business. For that reason, there's a huge variety of microcontrollers, with new models and increasing capabilities adding to the list everyday. It isn't possible to describe all of the features and variations available. However, the following sections provide an overview of the most common microcontroller features.

Microcontroller Packages

Similar to off-the-shelf logic chips, microcontrollers are available in a wide variety of packages and sizes (see Figure 15-7).

In some cases, microcontrollers with identical capabilities are available in a couple of different types of packages (② and ⑤). In some cases, the microcontrollers are nearly identical—except one package includes additional pins (③ and ⑥). In other cases, the microcontrollers may differ considerably with different support modules and amounts of memory (① versus ② versus ③ versus ④). Just like you would for logic chips, consult the manufacturer's datasheets to determine the amount of memory, pinouts, and features of each part number and package.

Figure 15-7. Some example microcontroller packages, all from the same line of Motorola 8-bit microcontrollers. Through-hole packages: 8-pin dual-inline package (DIP) QT2 ①, 16-pin DIP KX8 ②, 40-pin DIP GP32 ③, and 42-pin shrink dual-inline package (SDIP) SR12 ④. Surface-mount packages: 16-pin small outline package (SOIC) KX8 ⑤, 44-pin quad flat pack (QFP) GP32 ⑥, 48-pin low quad flat pack (LQFP) SR12 ⑦.

There are benefits to learning and sticking with the same family of microcontrollers. In many cases, routines written for one chip in the family also work with other chips in the family. Depending upon price and feature set required for a particular project, you can select a different chip from that family without completely rewriting your code.

Microcontroller Pins

The pins on a microcontroller are programmable. The manufacturer's datasheet indicates the different functionality available for each pin. With the exception of a few dedicated pins (power, ground, and so on), most microcontroller pins can be configured at least as either inputs or outputs. Some pins on the microcontroller are also configurable to take advantage of special onboard modules, such as serial ports or analog-to-digital converters (ADCs).

Input Pins

Input pins on a microcontroller are similar to those available on logic chips. The input pins read a voltage near ground (0 V) as low or a 0 bit. The input pins read a voltage near the regulated voltage (usually 5 V) as high or a 1 bit. These are considered digital inputs. Voltages in the middle (such as 2.5 V) are undefined and may read as either low or high.

Analog-to-Digital Input Pins

Analog input pins are also available on some microcontrollers. These analog-to-digital input pins can convert a voltage (say, from 0 V to 5 V) to a numeric range (say, from 0 to 255) instead of just a digital 0- or 1-bit value. In this example, a voltage of 2.5 V applied to an analog-to-digital input pin would be read by the microcontroller as 128.

Although most ADCs produce 8-bit values (2^8 equals 256, which equals 0 to 255), higher-end microcontroller can resolve 10 bits or even 12 bits (2^{12} equals 4,096, which equals 0 to 4,095). That means an 8-bit 5 V ADC reads a voltage in 5 V divided by 256, which equals 0.02 V increments, but a 12-bit 5 V ADC can read a voltage in 5 V divided by 4,096, which equals 0.0012 V increments. A 12-bit ADC is necessary only if, for example, your robot needs to distinguish between 2.5 V and 2.5013 V. However, if distinguishing between 2.5 V and 2.52 V is more than enough for your application, then a standard 8-bit ADC is perfectly adequate.

Robots love analog-to-digital inputs! You'll explore connecting sensors to analog-to-digital input pins in subsequent chapters.

Interrupt Input Pins

Some digital input pins are connected to interrupts. When the voltage on the input changes from low to high or from high to low, the microcontroller interrupts what it was working on, runs a subroutine related to the pin that changed (you provide the subroutine), and then resumes what it was originally working on.

Interrupts can be very useful. Rather than having to check the value of a pin every time through the main loop, the program can ignore the pin until an interrupt occurs. For example, buttons on a robot aren't pressed that often. With interrupt-enabled inputs, the buttons can be ignored until they're actually pressed.

Another benefit of interrupts is that they immediately inform the microcontroller of a change in pin states. If you have a time-critical task, an interrupt-enabled input pin is the way to go.

For example, let's say you're trying to determine the robot's speed by counting the time between marks (an "encoder") on the robot's wheels. The moment a mark appears, a voltage change occurs in the wheel's optical sensor, which connects to an interrupt-enabled input pin on the microcontroller. The voltage change causes the microcontroller to interrupt the current task and launch your subroutine, which stores the exact time that the pin changed. Elsewhere in your program you can subtract the times of the most recent pin changes and multiply that by the diameter of the robot's wheel, and that equals the approximate linear speed.

Most microcontrollers include at least one dedicated interrupt pin. Some microcontrollers also include additional configurable interrupt pins for processing keypad or keyboard events or for stopping a built-in timer (often called *input capture*) the moment a pin changes states.

Reset Pin

Another common input pin found on many microcontrollers is the reset pin. Depending on the microcontroller, bringing this pin high or low (usually through a push button connected to 5 V or ground) causes the microcontroller to immediately start running its program all over again, almost like power had been turned off and on. This is similar to rebooting a computer.

The reset pin is often used by programming boards to stop the microcontroller and to begin downloading new software. The reset pin is a kinder and gentler way to restart the robot's brain, without having to cycle power on other components on that same board.

Reusing the Reset Pin

If you're stuck with a dedicated (nonconfigurable) reset pin, and if you've run out of other pins, you can find ingenious ways of being able to use the reset pin. It's especially beneficial if the microcontroller provides a flag (a bit) to indicate whether the program was restarted because of power cycling (turning power off and on again), toggling the reset pin, or receiving a program error. At the beginning of the program, the robot can check to see if the reset pin had been pressed, and if so, it can take certain actions.

A good example would be a sumo robot. On power-up, if the reset pin hadn't been pressed, the robot enables the sensors and displays the distance to the opponent. This allows the builder to place the robot in the ring and line up the robot for the start of the match. Then, upon pressing the reset button, the start of the robot's program would see that a reset had occurred and would then start the five-second countdown for the start of the match.

Another way to reuse the reset pin (even without the microcontroller providing a flag to indicate reset had been pressed) is to have the robot check the value of certain sensors at start-up. For example, you could configure a line-following robot for dark line following if the sensors were dark upon program start or light line following if the sensors were light upon program start. For robots with distance sensors, you could put your hand at a certain distance and press the reset button for the robot to enter a particular mode.

Configurable Pull-Up and Pull-Down Resistors on Input Pins

Advanced microcontrollers have built-in configurable pull-up or pull-down resistors on their input pins. Recall that CMOS-based inputs require some sort of voltage on their inputs to prevent stray voltages from randomly toggling the input value. With built-in pull-up/pull-down resistors, your software can turn them on at start-up to provide default input values without having to add extra resistors to your circuit board. Not surprisingly, dedicated reset and interrupt pins usually have built-in pull-up or pull-down resistors that are enabled to "not reset" and "not interrupt" by default.

You can disable configurable pull-up and pull-down resistors when you don't want them. You don't want pull-up/pull-down resistors when the microcontroller's pin is going to be configured to be anything other than a *digital* input. For example, you don't want a resistor's default voltage competing with an output, and you don't want it combining with and altering the voltage being read on an analog input.

Another occasion when you want to disable built-in pull-up/pull-down resistors is when another chip is always connected to the microcontroller's input pin. In that case, no default value is necessary, and the extra power consumption of the resistor is undesirable.

However, when there are extra pins on the microcontroller that you aren't going to use, either configure the pin as an input and enable the built-in pull-up/pull-down resistor or configure the pin as an output.

Output Pins

Like input pins, microcontroller output pins are similar to those on logic chips. You can set an output pin to either low (0 V) or high (5 V, or whatever the power pin on the microcontroller is receiving).

Output pins are usually digital—that is, low or high, 0 or 1, or 0 V or 5 V—not values in-between. A few microcontrollers provide analog outputs whose voltage can be varied.

Avoiding Glitches When Configuring an Output Pin

Most microcontrollers power up with all of the configurable pins set to inputs. This prevents the microcontroller from delivering the wrong output values to the rest of the circuit before your program has a chance to fully configure the microcontroller.

For example, imagine if some microcontroller pins were connected to a motor driver. You'd prefer that the microcontroller said nothing (inputs only) to the motor driver rather than outputting an incorrect value that would start the motors moving. You've probably placed some pull-up or pull-down resistors on the motor driver inputs to establish default (no movement) values.

After power-up, but before your program switches a pin from an input to an output, first write the desired output value to the pin. It might seem a little weird to write a value to an (currently) input pin, but most microcontrollers retain this written value to use when the pin changes to an output. Otherwise, how does the microcontroller know whether the output pin should start out low (0 V) or high (5 V) when it's first enabled?

If you fail to write an output value before switching the pin to an output, there may be a brief period in which the output pin changes from some random output value to your desired output value. This may be inconsequential depending on what's connected to that output pin. For example, an LED might blink at start-up—who cares? However, if that output pin is connected to a motor driver, you don't want a glitch.

Higher-Current Output Pins

Because they're designed for low-powered digital signals, many microcontrollers can provide only a few milliamps of output current. This is fine for microcontrollers connected to logic chips, motor drivers, and so on. However, this doesn't provide enough current to brightly light an LED. The most obvious symptom of an overloaded output is when the voltage on the microcontroller's digital output pin isn't "digital"; it's somewhere between 0 V and 5 V.

Many microcontrollers now include pins capable of driving higher currents, up to 25 mA. Some microcontrollers include this feature on only certain pins, so be sure to plan your layout accordingly. If your microcontroller doesn't include any (or enough) high-current output pins, you can always connect the microcontroller's output pin to a transistor or higher-drive logic chip (such as a 74AC14).

Pulse-Width Output

For a robot, one of the most desirable types of output pins on a microcontroller is a pulse-width modulator (PWM). With a PWM, you can configure the output pin to provide an on/off signal at a programmable frequency with a programmable duty cycle (percent of off time versus percent of on time).

For example, a PWM can generate the 38 kHz square wave illustrated in Figure 12-4 in Chapter 12. In fact, a single PWM microcontroller output pin can replace the first four pins on the 74AC14 for the infrared reflector detector circuit. A PWM significantly reduces circuit complexity and cost so that the potentiometer (R6), resistor (R5), and capacitor (C5) from the circuit in Figure 11-10 in Chapter 11 wouldn't be necessary.

The microcontroller's signal doesn't need tuning. Actually, the robot can purposely disable or detune the signal if desired.

Using Only One Infrared Detector by Using Two PWM Output Pins

It's possible to use only one infrared detector and still be able to differentiate between objects on both sides by using two PWM output pins from a microcontroller. The schematic appears in Figure 15-8.

Place one infrared emitter on each side of the single infrared detector (see Figure 15-9). One pin on the microcontroller emits a 38 kHz signal to only one of the infrared emitters and listens to the detector to see if an obstacle is on that side of the robot. Then, the microcontroller emits a 38 kHz signal to the other infrared emitter only and again listens to the detector to see if an obstacle is on that side of the robot.

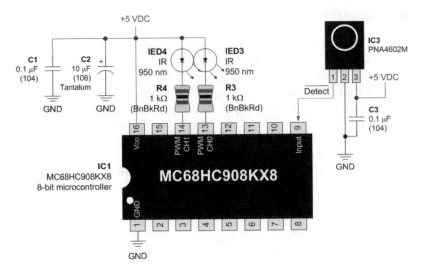

Figure 15-8. Schematic of an example microcontroller, with two emitters connected to PWM outputs but only one detector

Figure 15-9. The pulse emitted from the microcontroller to the left infrared emitter doesn't bounce off of any objects on the left side (left). The PNA4602M detector in middle doesn't detected anything. The pulse emitted from the microcontroller to the right infrared emitter bounces off of an object on the right side and into the PNA4602M detector (right).

The microcontroller can also turn on both PWM signals at the same time so both infrared emitters are active. This produces a wide detection radius that might pick up faint objects that neither emitter alone could illuminate.

In this setup, the cost, space, weight, and power consumption of one detector has been eliminated. It also prevents cross contamination of one side's detector with the other side's emitter. Furthermore, the robot emits the 38 kHz signal only when it wants to read the detector, thus reducing power consumption and making itself less obvious to an opponent (in robot sumo, perhaps).

Using a PWM for Other Purposes

The usefulness of pulse width modulators isn't limited to infrared detectors by any means. You can use PWMs for motor speed control and for creating analog output voltages (in combinations with a resistor and capacitor like in Figures 14-9 and 14-10 in Chapter 14). In fact, you'll use a PWM for making music in a later chapter.

Software-Generated PWMs

If your microcontroller doesn't include built-in PWM output pins, you can still emulate the function in software by toggling the value of the output pin back and forth between high to low as desired. The disadvantage is that your program needs to spend a lot more time toggling the output pins, and the signal can be affected when the microcontroller is interrupted to perform another task.

Combinations of Input and Output Pins: Serial Ports

Some microcontrollers include built-in modules that use a combination of input and output pins. A good example is a serial port. The microcontroller can include hardware that, when enabled, automatically converts an incoming stream of pulses into a byte and automatically converts a byte into an outgoing stream of pulses. Thus, you can achieve serial communication with other chips or with a computer with very little time spent in software.

There are many different types of serial protocols: I^2C, SPI, CAN, LIN, USB, and so on. A few serial protocols use only a single pin, switching it from an input to an output when necessary. Most serial protocols use at least two pins, with one dedicated to input and one dedicated to output. Some serial protocols are very fast (megabits per second) while others have slower bit rates (300, 2400, 9600, and so on).

It's possible to emulate most types of serial communication on a microcontroller using software only (*bit banging*). The downside is that the microcontroller has to be tied up in that subroutine or the subroutine has to use complex timers to interrupt other processes to read the input pins or toggle the output pins. If you plan on using some form of serial communication in your robot, it's best to look for a chip containing a dedicated serial module that matches the parts with which you want to communicate.

Another important point about serial communication on a microcontroller is that the microcontroller usually provides only the logical capabilities, not necessarily the correct voltage ranges or connectors. Therefore, expect to add an interface chip designed to isolate (protect) the microcontroller and to translate the voltages. A good example is the Maxim MAX232 interface chip, which is designed to convert a microcontroller's 0 V and 5 V serial signal into voltages that a computer's RS232 serial ports can understand.

Microcontroller Memory

It's time to transition from the outside of the microcontroller (the package and the pins) to the features within the microcontroller. You'll begin with the memory.

Just like a computer, microcontrollers have two types of memory: nonvolatile and volatile. The contents of nonvolatile memory are retained even without power, such as a hard disk on a computer. Conversely, the contents of volatile memory are lost when the chip is powered down, such as random access memory (RAM) on a computer.

Volatile memory must provide some advantages over nonvolatile memory; otherwise everyone would just use nonvolatile memory. Currently, volatile memory is faster and has no limit to the number of times it can be written to and read from.

The amount of built-in memory available on microcontrollers is increasing, even as microcontroller prices are decreasing. You want to be sure to purchase a microcontroller that has enough memory (both volatile and nonvolatile), but try to avoid wasting money by buying capacity you don't need. One solution is to select a microcontroller family that contains the same part with multiple sizes of memory so you can simply swap in a more expensive part if you find you've run out of room.

There's a limit to the amount of memory a microcontroller can access, depending on the address bus size of the microcontroller. For example, most 8-bit microcontrollers contain a 16-bit address bus. As such, they can only access 2^{16}, which equals 65,536 memory addresses. There are techniques to overcome this limit by swapping memory in and out of address space. But, generally speaking, low-end microcontrollers can't directly access as much memory as high-end microcontrollers can.

Nonvolatile Memory

Built-in nonvolatile microcontroller memory for program storage was discussed earlier in the chapter. In addition to storing programs, nonvolatile memory can also be used for storing tables, text, songs, and other data.

Many microcontrollers can write to their built-in nonvolatile storage. This means you can use the nonvolatile storage for storing changeable settings or for recoding data or logs. For example, a microcontroller could chart temperature or other sensor information during operation and write the data to its nonvolatile memory. Later, you could download that data downloaded to a computer.

Supplementing with External Nonvolatile Memory

External nonvolatile memory (see Figure 15-10) is readily available. However, unless the microcontroller has address and data bus pins (a set of ten or more dedicated pins) for accessing external memory, that external storage isn't directly usable for programs. A workaround is to read in programs from external storage and then run the programs internally. If you think about it, that's just what computers do—the programs are read from hard disks into RAM and then run in RAM. On most microcontrollers, nonbus external memory is usually reserved for settings or other nonprogram data.

Figure 15-10. External nonvolatile memory. A 25C320 32 Kb SPI-serial EEPROM (left). The 24xxx series is available for I²C and 2-wire serial access. The 93xxx series is available for three-wire serial access. A DS1230 256 Kb parallel SRAM with built-in lithium battery backup (right). This has the high-speed and unlimited-write benefits of volatile memory, yet the memory contents are retained for up to ten years without power.

External serial EEPROMs are inexpensive, come in hobbyist-friendly eight-pin DIP or eight-pin SOIC packages, and are commonly available with up to 512 Kb (64 KB) of memory. You can use multiple serial EEPROMs if you require more memory.

TIP *For some reason, external memory chips are normally specified in bits, not bytes. Don't order 32 kilobits (Kb) of memory and expect to receive 32 kilobytes (KB) of memory. In other words, 8 bits equals 1 byte. So, 32 Kb equals only 4 KB.*

External serial-accessible memory is slower to access but requires few microcontroller pins (usually two or three). Parallel-accessible external memory is much, much faster but requires many more (10 to 64) pins and sometimes requires interface chips (latches, buffers). If the microcontroller supports an external bus, programs can be run directly from external parallel-accessible memory.

Volatile Memory

Built-in volatile memory (RAM) is usually at a premium in a microcontroller. The lack of RAM can be a serious problem on low-end microcontrollers because all global variables and the stack (local variables, subroutine return addresses, temporary register storage) are stored in RAM. Therefore, the lack of RAM can limit the functionality of a robot. When using a microcontroller, you'll often find yourself trading algorithm speed for a reduction in RAM usage.

Just like nonvolatile memory, the more expensive microcontrollers tend to have more built-in RAM, and higher-end microcontrollers have bus pins to access external RAM. If you need more than a couple hundred bytes of RAM, you should consider a higher-end microcontroller with external RAM. External serial-accessible RAM isn't generally available; it's almost all parallel-accessible RAM.

Briefly surveying some of my robots, I found that global variable usage varied significantly depending on the robot (see Table 15-2). Note that the stack uses any remaining memory. Unlike nonvolatile storage, I constantly find myself trying to reduce the amount of RAM usage.

Table 15-2. RAM Usage for Global Variables in Various Robots

Robot Name	Total Size of All Global Variables
Carefree	12 bytes
Roundabout	38 bytes
Hard2C	46 bytes
Have a Nice Day	59 bytes
Bugdozer	111 bytes
Soup	155 bytes
Sweet	174 bytes

The Motorola KX8 includes 192 bytes of RAM and meets the requirements of most of the robots listed in Table 15-2. The top-of-the-line microcontroller in that family includes 4,096 bytes of RAM.

Microcontroller Instruction Size

Microcontrollers are usually classified based on the number of bits they can manipulate with a single instruction (command). For example, an 8-bit microcontroller can read, alter, and write 8 bits (1 byte) at a time. Although a few compound instructions may be available, most instructions are limited to handling 2^8 numbers, such as 0 to 255 or -128 to 127. This doesn't mean you can't program the microcontroller to compute larger values; it's just that it takes more than one instruction to do so.

A 16-bit microcontroller can handle 2^{16} numbers, such as 0 to 65,535. A 32-bit microcontroller can handle 2^{32} numbers, such as 0 to 4,294,967,295. Modern personal computers contain 32-bit microprocessors. Microprocessors are similar to microcontrollers except that microprocessors are optimized to be the heart of a much larger system; therefore, most microprocessors don't waste die space with built-in memory and modules. Conversely, microcontrollers contain built-in memory, serial ports, analog-to-digital ports, pull-ups, and other features designed for nearly stand-alone operation.

Hobby robots containing microcontrollers are usually either 8-bit or 16-bit. The advantages of 16-bit microcontrollers are that the commands are more powerful and can handle larger numbers, making code shorter and less complex. The disadvantages of 16-bit microcontrollers are that they're more expensive and less available in hobbyist-friendly packages. Give me a 16-bit (or 32-bit) microcontroller with the same modules, package, and price as a KX8, and I'd buy it. Put another way, robot builders don't choose 8-bit microcontrollers because they want to work in 8-bit chunks; it's the other factors that are the selection points.

Microcontroller Instruction Complexity

If you're going to program your robot using assembly language, be sure to examine the microcontroller's complete instruction list before choosing that microcontroller. For example, some microcontrollers don't include instructions for multiplication and division (there are ways to perform those math operations through bit-shifting, addition, and subtraction). On the other hand, if you plan on using a higher-level language, such as BASIC or C, then multiplication and division algorithms are usually included, regardless of the microcontroller's instruction set.

Microcontroller Speed

Although a modern personal computer runs at several gigahertz, a modern microcontroller runs only in the low megahertz range. Microcontrollers commonly run at between 1 MHz and 16 MHz, with some topping out at about 40 MHz. The Motorola KX8 can operate at up to 8 MHz.

To understand this gap, you need to consider where microcontrollers are most often installed. Microcontrollers are commonly used in battery-powered devices where long battery life (low power consumption) is important. Microcontrollers are also contained in a variety of products (automobiles, alarm systems, washing machines, refrigerators, toys) where generated electrical noise could interfere with other products and where electrical noise reduction techniques (metal shielding, capacitors, chokes) would prohibitively increase costs in a competitive consumer product. The slower pace (low megahertz range) of most microcontrollers results in lower power usage and lower electromagnetic emissions. Speed is generally a secondary concern in such products.

All of this is fortunate for us robot builders because peculiar effects occur at higher frequencies. Believe me, you don't want to try to design and etch a gigahertz-capable circuit board in your basement.

Comparing Clock Speed

As you're probably aware, a computer's total speed can't be determined by simply looking at megahertz or gigahertz. This frequency rating, expressed in hertz (cycles per second), tells you only how often the system clock (or "drumbeat") occurs.

 NOTE *The term clock can be confusing. Don't think of it in common human terms as something for telling the time of the day. Although you can purchase an external chip to provide your robot with the current date and time, a microcontroller clock is more like the second hand (or nanosecond hand) that ticks away, providing a master signal to synchronize all of the internal modules within the microcontroller.*

Depending upon the chip, the number of data bits per instruction, and the support hardware, one computer may be able to get more work done in a single cycle than another computer. This is also true for microcontrollers. An 8 MHz 8-bit microcontroller can be slower than a 4 MHz 16-bit microcontroller with built-in support modules.

Microcontroller designers have applied some tricks to increase total speed without increasing the clock frequency. For example, it used to be that a single instruction would often take multiple instruction cycles to complete. Newer microcontroller use fancy techniques so that most, if not all, instructions take only a single instruction cycle. That means a newer 8-bit microcontroller might easily be faster than a slightly older 8-bit microcontroller, even with the same software, the same support modules, and the same megahertz clock rate.

Again, this is good for robot builders because we get "faster" chips without an increase in external frequencies. Keep this in mind when selecting a microcontroller—you can't simply compare megahertz ratings to determine the fastest chip.

Generating a Clock Signal

The clock signal, or "drumbeat," for a microcontroller is usually generated externally by a crystal or canned oscillator (see Figure 15-11). By changing the crystal or oscillator, you can control the speed of the microcontroller. The slower the microcontroller runs, the lower the power usage and the lower the electrical emissions. Therefore, on a low-power solar robot, you might choose to run a microcontroller at only 1 MHz, for example, even if it was rated to run at up to 8 MHz.

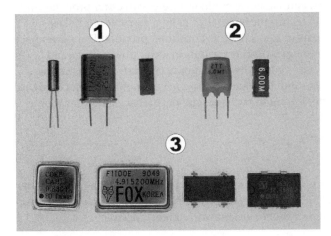

Figure 15-11. Microcontroller clock options. Crystals ① are inexpensive (about $1 to $1.50) and accurate, but they require resistors, capacitors, and microcontrollers with driving gates to create a clock signal (top row). Ceramic resonators ② are less expensive (about $0.50 to $0.75) although less accurate (about 0.5 percent). Canned oscillators ③ combine accurate crystals with an integrated circuit to create strong clock signals in a stand-alone package (no additional components required) (bottom row). Canned oscillators are more expensive (about $2.50 to $3.50).

There are usually dedicated pin(s) on a microcontroller for receiving the clock signal. Referring to Figure 15-1, where is the input pin for the clock signal on the KX8? Well, it actually has a couple of configurable pins that could receive a clock signal if desired. But, even better, the KX8 has an internal clock generator that can create its own clock signal!

An internally generated clock signal has many benefits. No crystal or canned oscillator means the following:

- Lower cost, more board space, less soldering, less complex board design, less to debug, and lighter weight

- Less electrical noise because the clock signal is generated and used entirely within the microcontroller

- You can choose a clock rate programmatically that might not be available in a standard crystal or canned oscillator

- More microcontroller pins are available

Some microcontrollers, such as the KX8, even allow the internally generated clock speed to be altered on the fly. That is, the microcontroller can be running at a sluggish pace in the kilohertz range while idle. Then, the microcontroller can slam into high gear and run at full speed during periods of heightened activity.

The major downside to an internally generated clock is that it isn't terribly accurate. It may vary slightly from beat to beat, and the long-term rate may be off by as much as ±25 percent on the KX8. With tuning, the KX8 can be within about 5 percent of the expected rate. That's fine for most purposes. However, if you need a more accurate clock, use an external crystal or oscillator instead.

Using the Clock As a Timer

The clock signal is required by the microcontroller to synchronize all of the internal circuits and operations. The clock signal has a side benefit in that it can be used as a timer.

Most microcontrollers include a timer (based on the clock signal) that can be configured to interrupt the program and call one of your subroutines at regular intervals. For example, a timer could be set to trigger 1,000 times a second (1,000 Hz, or 1 kHz). From there, the interrupt subroutine would decrease several counters until they reach zero. Elsewhere in the program, different procedures in the robot would examine their counters and take action when they reach zero. The procedures then reload their counter with a new value and wait for it to reach zero again.

Recall the heartbeat example earlier in the chapter. The following is a more accurate heartbeat that uses an interrupt timer:

SETUP (the beginning of the program):

1. Set pin 2 to low (0 V), and make it an output. The heartbeat LED is off. (Notice that you set the pin value before making it an output to prevent an output glitch.)

2. Create a global variable, HeartBeat, and set it to 0.

3. Set the microcontroller's interrupt timer to call MY_TIMER_ROUTINE 1,000 times a second.

4. Continue with the rest of the initialization and setup, if any. Go to step 8 (the main loop).

MY_TIMER_ROUTINE (automatically called 1,000 times a second):

5. If HeartBeat isn't 0, then decrease HeartBeat by 1.

6. Check and decrease any other counters here. Try not to perform too much work during an interrupt because, after all, you did rudely interrupt some other process.

7. Return to the original task that was going on before the interrupt. You don't have to keep track of which task was interrupted—returning to the original task is a built-in instruction in the microcontroller.

MAIN LOOP (repeats forever):

8. If HeartBeat isn't 0, then go to step 12.

9. HeartBeat is 0, so it's time to blink the heartbeat LED. If pin 2 is low (0 V), set it to high (5 V). The heartbeat LED turns on. Go to step 11.

10. Pin 2 must already be high (5 V), so set it to low (0 V). The heartbeat LED turns off.

11. Set HeartBeat to 500, so the heartbeat LED switches states every 500 divided by 1,000 Hz, which equals a half second. This results in one complete blink (a half second on and a half second off) every second.

12. Continue with the rest of the main loop, calling subroutines and performing actions for the robot or device.

13. Go to step 8.

You could further increase the accuracy of the blink timing by actually blinking in the interrupt routine, rather than waiting an unknown amount of time to hit the main loop. However, this would cause the heartbeat to keep blinking even if the robot's program got stuck in a subroutine because the interrupt routine would continue to get called 1,000 times a second. You want this heartbeat to represent a properly functioning program that's regularly executing the main loop.

There are other reasons not to perform too much actual work in the interrupt routine. First, the regularly executing program might have been halfway done with switching some pins around (motor driver controls for example) when the interrupt occurs. You want the interrupt to perform the minimum amount of work so that the interruption is short.

Second, if you're like me, I like to have code for each part of my robot in its own file. I don't want my interrupt routine to contain little pieces of code related to all of the sections of the robot. It's much cleaner for the interrupt timer simply to decrease a bunch of counters and allow each subroutine to deal with the meaning of the counters on their own time.

Special Watchdogs

Some microcontrollers contain an optional ("watchdog") timer that resets (restarts) the microcontroller if the timer hasn't been read by the main loop after a certain length of time. Thus, if the microcontroller's program gets stuck in an infinite loop in a subroutine, it will have failed to read the watchdog timer, and the program will get restarted.

The watchdog timer is a nice feature for rescuing a stranded robot. It's especially nice if the microcontroller sets a flag so the start of the program can determine why it was reset. For example, a sumo robot could immediately start fighting if it was reset because of an infinite loop. Instead of a "hung" robot being a stationary target for an opponent, it would resume fighting after a brief pause.

If your microcontroller doesn't include a watchdog timer, you can create one using the standard interrupt timer. Simply decrement a counter in the interrupt routine but constantly store a large value in that counter in the main loop. If, for whatever reason, the main loop fails to execute, eventually the interrupt routine will have decreased the counter to zero. In that event, simply have the interrupt routine call the first line of code in the robot's program (usually setup), and the robot's program will start over.

Low-Voltage Watchdog

Another type of watchdog module built into many microcontrollers is a low-voltage detector. Unrelated to timers, this built-in module constantly monitors the microcontroller's power supply pin and halts the microcontroller if the voltage drops below the minimum operating specification.

By halting the microcontroller, the low-voltage watchdog prevents the microcontroller from executing improperly, perhaps setting pins to undesired states or overwriting the program in nonvolatile memory. The low-voltage module regularly kicks in during power-up and power-down, thus making the circuit safe for robot builders who like using huge values for bulk capacitors.

Choosing a Microcontroller

If you don't already have a favorite microcontroller, I suggest you consider the following selection criteria:

Can you get the part? Does your favorite retailer/electronics supplier stock the microcontroller? It's one thing to browse the selection listed at a manufacturer's Web site. However, it's totally another thing to actually find the part for sale.

Can you get the accessories? Does anyone stock a programming board and program language for the microcontroller? Because a programming board is a one-time purchase, it isn't as important if you have to purchase it from someone other than your favorite supplier.

Can you get help? Does the manufacturer provide complete, well-written documentation and technical notes? Does a friend, colleague, or local club member use that microcontroller? Is there a decent support group available online?

Does the part fit? Is the microcontroller available in a package that you can use (through-hole or surface-mount with relatively large pins)? Does it operate in the voltage range available on your robot and appropriate for your sensors (usually 5 V)?

If you answer "no" to any of the previous questions, you'll probably want to keep looking for a different microcontroller.

Is this a popular microcontroller and popular manufacturer? The purchase volume of a hobbyist is unlikely to influence a manufacturer or keep them afloat. Learning all about your microcontroller is going to take a large investment of your brainpower and time. Therefore, you want to back a winner that's going to stick around, maintain the existing line, and produce upgraded models.

From that point on, choosing between the remaining candidate microcontrollers becomes a question of cost and capabilities.

Running Out Of...

Things you'll wish your microcontroller had more of (in descending order of what I always run out of) include the following:

- Pins

- RAM

- PWMs

- High-current pins

- ADCs

- Speed

- Nonvolatile memory (toward the top on some people's wish lists)

- Independent timers

- Serial ports

- Pins (it's worth mentioning again)

Other thoughts include the following:

- I wouldn't be interested in a microcontroller that didn't have some ADCs.

- I wouldn't be interested in a microcontroller that didn't have at least one timer. With at least one timer, you can create additional subtimers using counters.

- Built-in pull-up or pull-down resistors are really nice, but external resistors are acceptable.

- For most uses, speed is less important than you might think. Because they're fairly cheap, multiple microcontrollers can be used to distribute workload if necessary.

- PWM and serial communication can be emulated in software, if absolutely necessary. But they sure are nice to have built into the microcontroller.

- A built-in clock generator is a nice feature. That's one less component to add to the board.

Recommending Motorola Microcontrollers

If I had to start over, I would still choose the Motorola 68HC908 family of microcontrollers. They're inexpensive, reliable, and generally available. They have excellent documentation, contain a rich feature set, are fast, and are part of a continually upgraded product line.

NOTE *I work for Motorola, but not in a semiconductor-related part of the business. Additionally, Motorola is spinning off their semiconductor division. I did take a harder look at Motorola's microcontrollers because I'm an employee, but my recommendation is based on the aforementioned characteristics. As an added bonus, I grew up programming Apple II and Commodore 64 computers using the 6502 and 6510 assembly languages, which closely match the 68xx microcontroller line.*

Because Motorola 8-bit microcontrollers are the most popular choices of appliance manufacturers and the automobile industry, the microcontrollers are going to continue to be supported and will continue to be on the cutting edge of technology for a long time to come.

As a hobbyist, however, I have run into some obstacles common to dealing with a product made by a large corporation:

- The programming boards aren't readily available through retail channels. They can be difficult to obtain if you miss purchasing one of the boards shortly after product introduction. Motorola is overcoming this by introducing a generic programmer for all 8-bit microcontrollers in its new HCS line.

- The price of a programming board for each model of chip is about $350. This may not be a big deal if your company is buying the board, but it hurts if the money is coming from your personal pocketbook. Again, Motorola is overcoming this obstacle by introducing one generic programming board for the entire HCS line.

- The price of the full best-in-class-C development environment is several thousand dollars (disgusting!). On the other hand, the full assembler and 4 KB C compiler are free.

- The microcontrollers are moving away from hobbyist-friendly configurations (DIP and SOIC at 5 V) to commercial and industrial configurations (tiny surface-mount packages at 3.3 V or less). Then again, this is how the whole industry is headed. Also, with due respect, Motorola continues to maintain a selection of microcontrollers in through-hole packages.

- Lastly, many of the pins on the HC series are reused during programming and debugging, making it difficult to design a circuit that can be debugged on the robot. Motorola is again overcoming this obstacle by using a single dedicated programming/debugging pin on their new HCS line.

Recommending the Parallax BASIC Stamp

From far away, the Parallax BASIC Stamp II (BS2) appears to be a 24-pin DIP microcontroller. Upon closer inspection (see Figure 15-12), the BASIC Stamp is revealed to be a complete circuit board containing a microcontroller, a power supply, a nonvolatile program storage, and a serial port interface.

Figure 15-12. The Parallax BASIC Stamp II consists of a microcontroller ①, 20 MHz microcontroller clock (ceramic resonator) ②, low-dropout low-quiescent 5 V voltage regulator ③, 15 µF 16 WV bulk capacitor ④, detector to halt the microcontroller if voltage drops below 4 V ⑤, transistors ⑥ ⑧ for converting computer serial port signals, 4.7 kΩ pull-up resistors to provide default input values ⑦, and a 2 KB serial EEPROM for user program storage ⑨.

This ingenious design combines the simplicity of a single-part through-hole DIP with the density of surface-mount components to provide a nearly complete robot brain. With the addition of a couple of buttons, sensors, motor drivers, battery connector, and bulk capacitor, you've got a complete robot circuit.

Parallax BASIC Stamps are extremely popular with the hobbyist community. Accessories, source code, documentation, and support are readily available. The quality and continued growth by Parallax is unrivaled. The setup, programming, and debugging couldn't be simpler.

The cost of a stand-alone programming board is reasonable, from $65 to $89. Parallax has many kits, including starter kits and robots, that incorporate a programming board in the kit. The full programming language and debugging environment is free, and updates are available online.

There are some downsides to using BASIC Stamps:

- The cost per microcontroller is quite high, about $34 to $99. So, most hobbyists reuse the same microcontroller from robot to robot or from project to project.

- The BASIC Stamp is relatively slow. Newer varieties are faster, but a standard microcontroller can outpace a BASIC Stamp. You need to ask yourself whether you really need that much speed. Surprisingly, most hobbyist robots don't require much speed.

- The BASIC Stamp tends to be single-task orientated. This is one of those classic trade-offs between ease of use and complete control. Still, in the hands of an expert, the BASIC stamp can be made to perform multitasking.

- There isn't much room per program (nonvolatile memory). A BASIC Stamp program currently can't exceed 2 KB.

- There isn't much room for variables (RAM or volatile memory). BASIC Stamp variables are limited to 26, plus up to 128 bytes of scratchpad on the newer chips.

The last two bullet points are common laments for all microcontrollers. That being said, the BASIC Stamp tends to be slightly constrictive.

All in all, I heartily recommend a BASIC Stamp as a pleasant and powerful "microcontroller." They're probably the fastest way to prototype and create a simple to moderately complex robot.

Asking Around

As stated earlier, it's really important that you select a microcontroller you'll be able to use. I've concentrated on the Motorola and Parallax microcontrollers because they're the ones with which I'm most familiar. The other two most popular robot brains are the Microchip PICmicro microcontroller and the LEGO MINDSTORMS RCX. But there are many others available, including the OOPic, Atmel AVR, BasicX24, Athena, AMR Gadgets, Basic Atom-28, MVS Mega, and so on (see the advertisements in *Nuts & Volts*).

Some people avoid the limitations of a microcontroller by supplementing with the more powerful processing and memory capacities of a handheld computer (Palm, Windows Pocket PC), laptop, or even a portable game machine (Nintendo Game Boy).

For additional recommendations, just ask around. Talk to members of your local robot club or post a message on a robot mailing list.

Graduating Your Robot

At this point, I hope you're convinced of the splendid usefulness of a microcontroller and have a basic understanding of a microcontroller's major features and functions. In the next chapter, you'll apply a microcontroller to Roundabout to demonstrate the ease in which a microcontroller can expand a robot's repertoire.

CHAPTER 16

Building Roundabout's Daughterboard

Covers Connecting Two Parallel Circuit Boards, Using Boardmount Sockets, Selecting Screws, Reheating Solder Joints, Intercepting Inputs to Reroute Control, Software Debouncing, Using DIP Switches, and Implementing the Expansion Connector

THE MAIN CIRCUIT BOARD of an electronic device is usually called the *motherboard*. As you saw in Chapters 13 and 14, Roundabout's motherboard contains many effective subcircuits: a voltage regulator, two motor drivers, and a pair of infrared reflector detectors. However, Roundabout's brain is the weak point. With such simple logic, the 74AC14 can get the robot stuck during exploration.

You can't modify the "programming" of the 74AC14 logic chip. Therefore, what you'd like to do is to replace the brain but leave the other subcircuits intact. Unfortunately, there isn't any room remaining on the motherboard to add a microcontroller.

There's a creative option for upgrading Roundabout without discarding the existing motherboard. It turns out that all of the control signals and wires arrive at the 74AC14's socket. So, why not remove the 74AC14 and, in its place, snap in a connection to another board with a better brain? The second board is called the *daughterboard*.

This chapter describes Roundabout's daughterboard, pictured in Figure 16-1. The daughterboard includes a microcontroller ①, push button ②, settings DIP switch ③, expansion connector (for connecting floor sensors or other circuits) ④, audio amplifier ⑤ (for making music), volume control ⑥, speaker connector ⑦, and a 5.6 V zener diode ⑧ to protect against overvoltage.

Moving the 74AC14 chip ⑨ from the motherboard to the daughterboard salvages it. The 74AC14 chip no longer makes decisions, but it does continue to generate the 38 kHz signal and to drive the infrared emitters and bicolor LEDs.

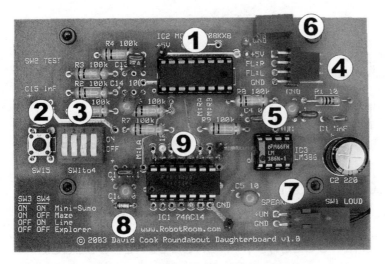

Figure 16-1. An overview of Roundabout's daughterboard

With the addition of the daughterboard, the overall transformation of Roundabout is remarkable. The robot is much more sophisticated and versatile.

Converting to a Two-Story Configuration

The most important feature of the daughterboard is a microcontroller that replaces the brain functions of the 74AC14. In this case, I selected a Motorola MC68HC908KX8 (KX8) microcontroller. However, a Parallax BASIC Stamp or a Microchip PICmicro would work just as well.

The daughterboard design could have stopped there. With the inclusion of a microcontroller, you can overcome Roundabout's stalling, and the robot would be a capable explorer. But why punch out only a dormer when you can build an entire second story (see Figure 16-2)?

Replacing the DIP Socket

The 74AC14 14-pin DIP socket on the motherboard is designed to hold the thin pins of a chip. A ribbon cable with a 14-pin DIP connector (similar to the cable ④ pictured in Figure 15-2 in Chapter 15 coming off of the microcontroller programming board) would be an adequate choice to bring the lines from the motherboard's 74AC14 DIP socket to the daughterboard. But because this robot rambles around, I was concerned that the DIP connector on the ribbon cable might wiggle loose from the DIP socket. Therefore, I chose to replace the DIP socket entirely with something deeper and more substantial (see Figure 16-3).

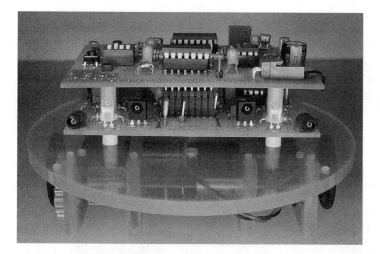

Figure 16-2. Roundabout's daughterboard (top) snaps in place where the 74AC14 logic chip sat on the motherboard (bottom). Notice that the PNA4602M infrared detectors are short and flush on the motherboard—not as tall as they were on the previous version of Roundabout. This was necessary for a compact design but has the added benefit of reducing electrical noise and false detections that can occur with long leads.

Figure 16-3. Boardmount socket (left) compatible with 0.1 inch (2.54 mm) spaced, 0.025 inch square-pin male headers (shown being inserted at right).

Using Boardmount Sockets

Boardmount sockets (also called *female headers*) with holes spaced every 0.1 inches are compatible with the male headers described in Chapter 14. Boardmount sockets are available in different lengths and heights, as a single row or double row, and with either tin or gold plating. I usually purchase a single row of 36 tin-plated boardmount sockets ($1.87 to $1.98; #929974-01-36 at Digi-Key and #517-974-01-36 at Mouser). Avoid "screw-machined" sockets because they have round holes that don't accept the square pins of most male headers.

Dividing Boardmount Sockets

Like male headers, boardmount sockets can be purchased in longer lengths and cut down as desired. Usually one socket is wasted in the process because it's difficult to cleanly separate adjoining sockets. Therefore, it's easier to simply cut down the center of one socket (see Figure 16-4) and sand or file the edges so that the sockets on either side are complete and undamaged.

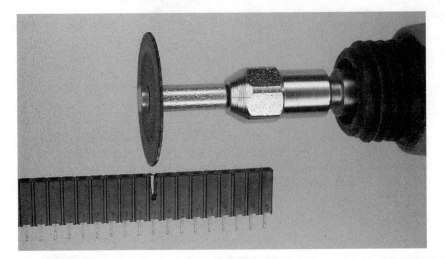

Figure 16-4. Cutting apart a strip of boardmount sockets using a Dremel. One socket is sacrificed in the process. During cutting, the strip should be held in a vise (omitted in this figure for clarity).

Depending upon the type of plastic housing, it may be easier to cut sockets apart using a Dremel with a cutoff disc, rather than a wire cutter or nippy cutter. Scoring the groove between sockets with a razor blade and then snapping them apart can also work, but it's more time-consuming.

Connecting with Boardmount Sockets

Many builders use the combination of male headers and boardmount sockets to create inexpensive connectors on their robots. Simply solder wires onto a strip of male headers and perhaps cover the solder joints with heat-shrink tubing (see Figure 16-5).

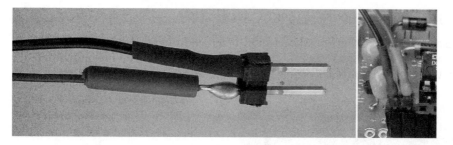

Figure 16-5. Male header with wires soldered on and covered with heat-shrink tubing; one tube hasn't been shrunk yet and is pulled off to show the solder joint (left). Male header with wires, partially inserted into boardmount socket (right).

Removable Installation of Components in Boardmount Sockets

Another application of boardmount sockets is in holding discrete components. Lightspeed, a solar roller robot, has sockets for inserting and removing components related to the power charging circuit (see Figure 16-6). You can easily modify this "solar engine" to store different amounts of energy (by adding or removing capacitors) or to trip at different voltage levels (by swapping out voltage detector ICs) to optimize performance for track conditions on race day.

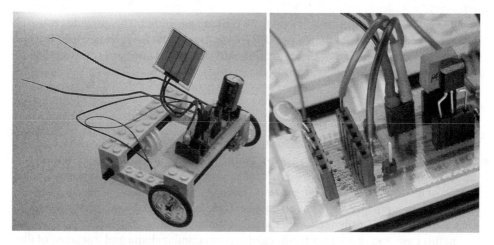

Figure 16-6. Lightspeed, a solar-powered robot (left), has components inserted in female header sockets spaced 0.1 inch apart (right). You can add or remove capacitors to alter charge and discharge time.

Making the Motherboard Signals Accessible

After desoldering and removing the 14-pin DIP socket from Roundabout's motherboard, a 16-pin boardmount socket is installed (see Figure 16-7) on the motherboard. This new socket consists of two single rows of eight sockets each.

Figure 16-7. A 16-pin male-header-compatible boardmount socket replaces the 14-pin DIP socket that originally held the 74AC14 logic chip.

By using two eight-pin sockets, up to 16 pins are permitted. This provides two more connections than did the 14-pin DIP socket. One of the new connections is wired to unregulated voltage so that the daughterboard can access raw battery power. The other spare socket hole ended up unused.

Restoring the 74AC14, If Desired

Unfortunately, the 74AC14 chip sits loosely in the motherboard's new boardmount socket because the pins on a chip are too skinny for the square holes on the board-mount sockets. Because the chip doesn't make proper contact, the motherboard-only version of the robot would no longer work. However, you can use a 14-pin (illustrated) or 16-pin wire-wrap DIP socket as an adapter (see Figure 16-8) if you want to test or use the motherboard-only version of the robot for any reason.

In this case, you're taking advantage of the rectangular shape and thickness of the wire-wrap pins to fit in the boardmount sockets. In standard usage, a wire-wrap socket is inserted through a circuit board, and the long pin lengths permit multiple wires to be wrapped around the pins for prototyping purposes. Rectangular header-compatible 14-pin wire-wrap sockets are available at several electronic suppliers ($0.90 to $3.02; #WWICS-14 at All Electronics, #C8114 at Digi-Key, and #19ICW14 at Electronix Express).

Figure 16-8. The square pins of a wire-wrap DIP socket fit snuggly in the 16-pin header-compatible boardmount socket to permit the 74AC14 to be restored to the motherboard. Be careful not to insert the 14-pin wire-wrap socket into the wrong holes because one of the far-right "spare" holes connects to unregulated power, which would damage the chip.

A disadvantage of the long pins of a wire-wrap socket (when installed on Roundabout) is that the chip ends up raised above the motherboard more than necessary. From a clearance and electrical noise perspective, it'd be more desirable for the socket to sit flush. On the other hand, the vertical space provides plentiful access to all of the pins, making it easy to connect them to the probes of a multimeter or an oscilloscope.

Connecting the Boards

At this point, Roundabout's motherboard contains a 16-pin boardmount socket that can connect to a 74AC14 with wire-wrap adapter (thus restoring the original Roundabout circuit) or can connect to male headers on the daughterboard (thus providing power, signals, and control lines to and from a new brain). Because of the height of the components and motor/battery connectors on the motherboard, extra-tall male header pins are required to provide a large enough gap (18 mm or more) between the motherboard and daughterboard when snapped together.

Aligning and Connecting the Boards with Dual-Stop Male Headers

I ran across some 15-mm tall male headers that include two pairs of plastic stops (see Figure 16-9). When inserted into 8-mm tall female sockets, the total height from the bottom of the socket to the top of the second plastic stop is just taller than 17.1 mm. That's barely close enough to the desired 18-mm gap to permit the boards to fit together without squishing or bending components.

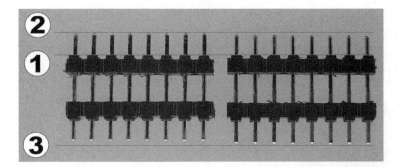

Figure 16-9. Extra-tall (15 mm) 8-pin male headers with dual plastic stops. In this figure, the left and right headers don't line up nicely with each other because the header on the right is "upside down." Just make sure to properly orient the headers before soldering them onto a board.

Unlike most male headers, the ones in Figure 16-9 include two plastic stops. This is a nice feature for keeping the motherboard and daughterboard level and parallel to each other.

Obtaining or Making Dual-Stop Male Headers

I've been unable to locate a retail supplier of these exact dual-stop male headers. Part #SHS-12 from All Electronics is almost perfect but is 2 mm too short. Unless you have 11-mm tall boardmount sockets, there won't be a large enough gap to bring the motherboard and daughterboard together without squishing the components on the motherboard.

Extra-tall single-stop male headers, such as #S1042-36 from Digi-Key, are satisfactory. Using a pair of pliers, you can remove all of the pins from the plastic stop of one row of headers and push that plastic stop onto another row of headers to make your own dual-stop male headers. Make sure to align the plastic stops equidistant from the ends of the pins or else the resulting connection may be tilted.

Orientating a Pair of Headers Before Soldering

At first glance, the top and bottom plastic stops on factory-made dual-stop male headers may appear to be located the same distance from the ends of the pins. However, look carefully to determine if the headers actually have a "top" and "bottom."

For example, back in Figure 16-9, notice how nicely the plastic stops have been aligned ① between the pair of headers. Yet, the top pins ② don't line up, and the bottom pins ③ don't line up between the pair of headers. In this case, the right header is simply upside down with respect to the left header. The ends of the pins and the plastic stops actually lined up nicely after they were arranged in the same orientation. If your headers still don't line up with each other, use pliers to move the plastic stops as needed.

Use a pen to mark the top plastic stop on each header (see Figure 16-10) to avoid soldering a header in an upside-down orientation with respect to the other header.

Even with an upside-down header, both headers may still be able to sit flush and level, depending on the depth of the boardmount socket. But why take the chance of ending up with a tilted board or partially inserted header?

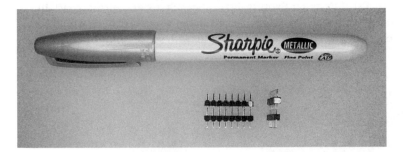

Figure 16-10. Mark the top of each dual-stop header so that the ends of the pins and the locations of the plastic stops match each other after being soldered onto the daughterboard. Marks from a black permanent marker won't be visible on black plastic. Fortunately, Sharpie has introduced a metallic-colored permanent marker that provides excellent contrast on dark surfaces. Light-colored paint pens also work well.

Securing the Daughterboard to the Motherboard

Before soldering the male headers onto the daughterboard, test the fit of the daughterboard to the motherboard. Although the headers and sockets provide a firm enough fit for prototyping, the boards should be physically held together using bolts (see Figure 16-11) when the robot is actually running. In other words, the headers and sockets should be relied upon only to make an electrical connection between the boards, not a physical connection.

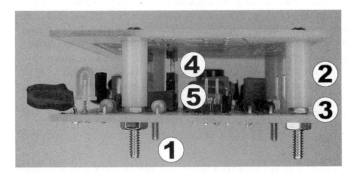

Figure 16-11. Motherboard (bottom) and daughterboard (top), held together by four bolts ①. Round plastic spacers ② keep the boards parallel and prevent the bolts from clamping the boards together too closely. Washers or extra nuts ③ may be necessary to make the gap the correct height so that the daughterboard headers ④ fit snuggly into the motherboard sockets ⑤.

Experimenting with Anodized Aluminum Socket Head Cap Screws

Usually, I use ordinary-looking #4-40 stainless-steel machine screws on my robots. However, I recently ran across some very attractive #4-40 anodized-aluminum cap screws (see Figure 16-12) at Fastener Express (`http://www.fastener-express.com/`). In addition to the usual silver, these screws are also available in red and blue, which can add a nice touch to any robot. The screws are available with socket, button, washer, or flat heads.

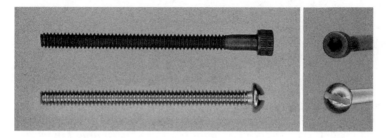

Figure 16-12. Red aluminum anodized cap screw with socket head (top). Stainless steel machine screw with slotted head (below)

The red anodized aluminum socket head screws look gorgeous on Roundabout with a red fluorescent acrylic body. Although the motherboard and daughterboard are bolted together during soldering, they'll eventually be screwed together onto Roundabout's center platform.

NOTE *The difference between a bolt and a screw is that a bolt uses a nut to clamp the workpieces together whereas a screw interlocks threads with the workpiece. In Chapter 5, Figure 5-20 shows a screw. If the workpieces don't have threads tapped in them, and a nut had been used to clamp the two pieces together, then that same fastener in Figure 5-20 would have been called a bolt. So, some threaded fasteners can be either a bolt or a screw depending on how they're used. If your friend asks you if it's a bolt or a screw, reply, "I won't know until I use it." Of course, some threaded fasteners are clearly designed to be used as screws (such as wood screws that dig into the workpiece) or bolts (such as heavy-duty construction bolts where threads in the workpiece wouldn't provide enough gripping force such that a nut and washer are required).*

Table 16-1 compares the attributes of different screw materials. Although anodized aluminum cap screws are attractive and lightweight, the table shows that they're unfortunately more expensive and less durable when compared with more common screw materials.

Table 16-1. Screw Materials (As Compared to Steel)

Material	Density	Durability	Price	Corrosion	Magnetic	Conductive
Steel	1X, Moderate	Moderate	1X, Inexpensive	Corrodes	Magnetic	Conductive
Stainless steel	1X, Moderate	Toughest	2X, Moderate	Resistant	Usually nonmagnetic	Conductive
Brass	1.1X, Heavier	Less moderate	3X to 5X, More expensive	Resistant	Nonmagnetic	Conductive
Anodized aluminum	0.35X, Light	Wears down	5X to 10X, Most expensive	Resistant	Nonmagnetic	Nonconductive
Nylon	0.15X, Lightest	Weakest	3.5X, More expensive	Resistant	Nonmagnetic	Nonconductive

Carbon, alloy, plated, and stainless steel screws are readily available in the widest variety of styles and lengths. Unless you're mass-producing cost-sensitive equipment, choose stainless steel screws over other types of steel for the benefits of increased durability and corrosion resistance.

Nylon doesn't conduct electricity (it's an electrical insulator) and therefore may be useful in isolating circuits. Note that anodized aluminum screws aren't electrically conductive because of their relatively thick oxide layer. However, the aluminum underneath is electrically conductive and can be exposed when scratched.

Nylon and aluminum screws are the lightest weight, and their weaker durability isn't usually a factor in lunch-box-sized robots. However, avoid using long nylon screws because the heads tend to torque off. Also, avoid using aluminum for screws that have to be removed and inserted multiple times because the threads tend to wear down quickly.

Soldering the Male Headers

Recall that the 74AC14 has been removed from the motherboard to provide the 74AC14's power, signals, and other connections to the daughterboard. Even though you don't want the 74AC14 logic chip to control the robot anymore, it did provide the valuable services of generating a 38 kHz signal for the infrared emitters and driving the bicolor LEDs. You'd like to install the 74AC14 on the daughterboard to continue to provide those functions.

To conserve space, I arranged for the ends of the male headers to come up beneath a 14-pin DIP socket on the daughterboard, which will then hold the 74AC14. This makes sense because the motherboard's male headers provide all of the connections that the 74AC14 needs, thus the circuit traces between the daughterboard's DIP socket and the motherboard's male headers are direct and short. Although successful in saving board space, it's a little awkward to solder male headers on one side of the daughterboard and a DIP socket on the other side.

Soldering While Bolted

To ensure that the male headers are soldered perpendicular to the board, solder them when the two boards are secured with bolts in place (see Figure 16-13).

Figure 16-13. Notice the bolts are installed during soldering to hold the daughter-board headers at the correct (perpendicular) angle for a perfect fit with the already-soldered boardmount sockets on the motherboard.

Trimming the Solder Joints

After soldering, trim the soldered ends of the headers flush with the daughterboard (see Figure 16-14). This permits a DIP socket to fit over that location, conserving board space.

Figure 16-14. Trimming solder joints flush with nippy cutters

Reheating the Solder Joints

Trimmed solder joints can be somewhat jagged (see the top of Figure 16-15). Smooth the solder joints by reheating each one with a soldering iron (see the bottom of Figure 16-15). Don't add more solder. Just touch the tip of the soldering iron to each solder joint until the solder melts and forms a silky surface. This relieves any stress or cracks that may have formed because of trimming.

Figure 16-15. Solder joints before reheating (top). Those same solder joints after reheating (bottom).

TIP *After soldering and trimming a circuit board, I always reheat each solder joint (trimmed or not) to ensure that each connection is solid. It can be frustrating and time-consuming to track down an intermittent or complete failure attributable to a weak solder joint. Save yourself trouble by making a reheating pass part of your assembly process.*

Soldering the New DIP Socket

If you choose to solder a DIP socket (or any other component) over the same board location where the headers come through, then plan each step carefully before soldering. The first time I tried this, I began by soldering both headers in place, but then I had a really difficult time fitting the soldering iron between the header rows to reach the places that each DIP socket pin came through. It would have been better to have soldered a single header, then both sides of the DIP socket, and finally the other header.

Figure 16-16 shows how the pins of the new DIP socket are immediately beside the male header rows. This makes it really simple to directly connect the new DIP socket to the desired pins on the header (and thus to the original locations on the motherboard). In other words, the 74AC14 hasn't been removed from the circuitry; it has just been moved straight up to the second floor.

Figure 16-16. A new DIP socket for the 74AC14 is located on top of the daughter-board. The male headers on the underside of the daughterboard are directly beside the DIP socket pins, with short traces on the circuit board connecting each pin where the original functions of the 74AC14 are to be retained.

Difficulty Accessing the Motherboard

Placing the daughterboard on top of the motherboard has the downside of making it difficult to access components of the motherboard. For example, you must remove the daughterboard to be able to adjust the frequency or brightness potentiometers for the reflector detector circuit. Fortunately, you can restore the 74AC14 to the motherboard if you need to tune the reflector detector circuit.

Relocating the Power Switch

Flipping the power switch is awkward with the daughterboard stacked on top of it (see Figure 16-17). So, desolder the switch from the motherboard and install a connector in its place. Epoxy a small piece of plastic with two screw holes onto the power switch and install it toward the rear of the robot. Wire the power switch to the power-switch connector on the motherboard.

Figure 16-17. The power switch on the motherboard is no longer finger-friendly with the daughterboard stacked above it (left). The power switch moved to the rear of the robot, with wires connected to the original location on the motherboard (right)

Perilously Stacking Sockets

In early testing of the daughterboard, one of the motors activated intermittently when it should have been idle. The voltage values on the daughterboard indicated that the microcontroller was indeed properly commanding the motor drivers to be in brake mode. Therefore, I needed to read the voltages on the motherboard to determine if the correct command signals were actually reaching the motor drivers.

Unfortunately, there isn't enough space between the motherboard and daughterboard for a multimeter test probe to reach the interior chips. Because the motherboard uses through-hole components, it's possible to remove both the motherboard and daughterboard from the robot to test the traces underneath the motherboard. But I really don't want to disassemble the robot every time I need to check a voltage on the motherboard.

An acceptable solution is to insert a bunch of boardmount sockets between the motherboard and daughterboard (see Figure 16-18). Admittedly this isn't the most physically stable arrangement, but it works well enough for testing.

Shading the Infrared Reflector Detectors

An advantage of having the daughterboard over the motherboard is that the daughterboard partially blocks overhead ambient light from reaching the infrared reflector detectors. In Chapter 14, one of the problems discovered with Roundabout was that fluorescent lighting interfered with the proper operation of the PNA4602M infrared detectors.

Figure 16-18. "Carmen Miranda" configuration. Multiple boardmount sockets temporarily stacked on top of each other raises up the daughterboard to provide access to components on the motherboard.

To further improve in shielding the sensors, the underside of the daughterboard includes a wide trace toward the front (see Figure 16-19). This trace is connected to ground, thus establishing a fixed voltage (0 V) at that point, rather than permitting a random fluctuation because of electrical noise and leakage.

Figure 16-19. A wide copper trace on the front underside of the daughterboard helps screen out light and electrical interference from reaching the infrared detectors.

Because the board is slightly translucent wherever there aren't copper traces, the underside of the board can be painted flat black (see Figure 16-20) to reduce the amount of light seeping through. Give the paint plenty of time to dry before applying power to the board.

One problem with painting a circuit board is that it will be difficult to unsolder any painted joints. So, be sure that your board is functioning properly before committing to a paint job. On the other hand, perhaps the paint job is overkill.

Figure 16-20. The front underside of the daughterboard painted black to provide additional reduction in sensor interference because of ambient overhead lighting

Intercepting Signals: Meeting the New Boss

For the moment, ignore the rest of the daughterboard and concentrate on the 74AC14 and the microcontroller. The primary reason for the daughterboard is to hand over control of the robot to a microcontroller. You can accomplish this by judiciously disconnecting certain wires before they reach the 74AC14 and providing those connections to the microcontroller instead.

Retaining Valuable Functions

Most of the pins on the header continue to be connected directly to the 74AC14. In fact, the 74AC14 retains all of its connections except for four inputs (pins 5, 9, 11, and 13). See Figure 16-21.

This arrangement permits the 74AC14 to continue to provide many valuable functions. The 74AC14 continues to generate the 38 kHz signal (pins 1 to 4) for the infrared emitters. The 74AC14 also continues to drive the motors and bicolor LEDs (pins 6, 8, 10, and 12), which is important because the microcontroller can't provide the same high current output that the 74AC14 can.

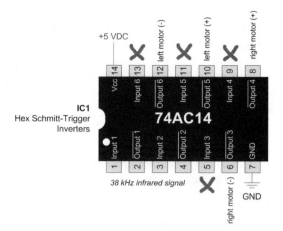

Figure 16-21. Almost all of the 74AC14 pins are unchanged from when the chip was originally installed on the motherboard. Only four inputs have been disconnected from their original sources.

Rerouting the Infrared Detection Signals

The left and right detection signals from the PNA4602M infrared detectors are no longer connected to pins 9 and 13 of the 74AC14. Instead, those traces come from the header and are delivered to the microcontroller. Only the microcontroller knows what the infrared detectors sees now and can choose to respond to, filter, or ignore that information according to a program. Output pins on the microcontroller are connected to pins 9 and 13 of the 74AC14, so the microcontroller can still pass along the detect signals if desired.

Catching and Disrupting the Stalled State

By intercepting the detection signals, the microcontroller now has the ability to recognize a 50 percent partial detection condition (which would stall the motors) and provide a different signal to the 74AC14 (thus continuing to drive the motors).

During normal conditions, the microcontroller passes the detection signals to the 74AC14 most of the time. In this case, the robot would behave as it had with just the motherboard.

To recognize a 50 percent partial detection condition, the microcontroller counts the amount of time that the detect signals are high and low over a period of time (say $\frac{1}{10}$ of a second). If the detect signals change multiple times and are evenly high and low (between 40 percent and 60 percent) on both detectors, the microcontroller recognizes that this is the state that causes both motors to stop and the robot to stall.

In a stalled state, the microcontroller feeds a false signal to the 74AC14 to keep the motors moving. The microcontroller continues to feed a false signal to the 74AC14 until such time as at least one of the detectors provides a solid high or low signal. At that point, the robot resumes normal operation.

This simple counting algorithm prevents the robot from stalling, without reducing the original room-exploring capabilities.

Rerouting the Motor and Bipolar Controls

Recall that an inverter chip, such as the 74AC14, simply takes an input voltage and provides the opposite voltage (high or low) on the associated output pin. The 74AC14 is still connected to the motor drivers and the bicolor LEDs. However, the associated input pins (5, 9, 11, and 13) to the motor drivers are now connected to output pins on the microcontroller. This means the microcontroller can provide any output pattern it wants, and the 74AC14 will flip the voltage and pass it along to the motor drivers and bicolor LEDs.

Although it'd be nicer if the 74AC14 didn't flip the voltage, it doesn't make that much of a difference. The real value is that the 74AC14 provides higher current to drive the bipolar LEDs, relieving the microcontroller of that load.

Producing (Almost) Complete Control

When installed on the motherboard, the 74AC14 logic chip brain generated nothing more than a chain reaction. The PNA4602M signal came in, was flipped and sent to one motor wire, and then was flipped again and sent to the other motor wire. The motors wires were linked to each other and to the PNA4602M.

But now the PNA4602M signal and each motor wire are no longer linked to one another. The microcontroller controls each motor wire independently. That means the microcontroller can set the motor wires high/low (clockwise) and low/high (counterclockwise) like before or set the motor wires high/high or low/low to brake. The directional LEDs work just as before, green with "forward" motor rotation and red with "backward" motor rotation, but they turn off when the motor is in high or low brake mode.

Roundabout isn't stuck with just forward and reverse anymore! In fact, Roundabout isn't stuck being a room-exploring robot because the microcontroller can command the motors however it pleases.

Expanding Functionality

As discussed earlier in the chapter, Roundabout's daughterboard contains additional features beyond a 74AC14 and a microcontroller. The board includes some switches, an audio amplifier, and an expansion connector.

Examining the Microcontroller Pins

The Motorola KX8 microcontroller is a 16-pin chip. I chose to wire the microcontroller as shown in Figure 16-22.

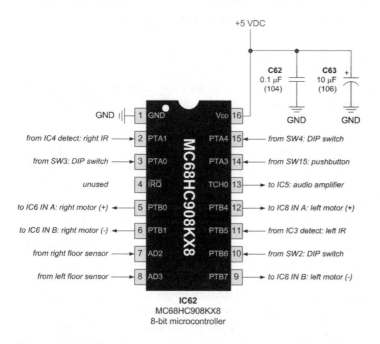

Figure 16-22. The pins as configured on the microcontroller (IC62) for Roundabout. (The motor control signals actually route through the 74AC14 rather than going directly to the motor driver chips.)

Powering the Microcontroller

Two nonconfigurable pins are used for power (pin 16) and ground (pin 1). A 0.1 µF decoupling/bypass capacitor (C62) is included as per normal practice. An optional 10 µF bulk capacitor (C63) is also included, even though the 74AC14 actually performs the higher current switching on behalf of the microcontroller.

Leaving the Interrupt Pin Unused

The microcontroller's interrupt pin is unused by this robot. A good choice would have been to connect the interrupt pin to the daughterboard's push button, but I held off thinking I was going to find something more useful. I didn't. Oh, well.

You can't configure the interrupt pin as an output or a standard input. So, there it sits, lonely and dejected.

Detecting Walls and Obstacles

The detect output from the left PNA4602M infrared detector (IC3) on the motherboard feeds into input pin 11 on the microcontroller. The right infrared detector (IC4) feeds into input pin 2. There wasn't any significant reason for these pin assignments other than the circuit board traces routed easily to those locations.

Controlling the Motors and Bipolar LEDs

You can control each wire of each motor independently to produce clockwise, counter-clockwise, and brake. Coast isn't available because of limitations of the motor driver chips on the motherboard.

Microcontroller output pins 9 and 12 control the left motor. Microcontroller output pins 5 and 6 control the right motor. These pins were selected so that all four motor pins appear in the same byte in memory (which happens to be labeled "PTB") on this microcontroller. Therefore, all four motor pins can be modified with a single command to write a byte to that location.

If multiple commands had been required because of motor wires being at multiple memory locations, the robot might sometimes briefly move in an undesired manner during the time it takes to change each pin individually. Each single instruction on this microcontroller takes only 125 ns, so any transitional indiscretions would have been unnoticeable to the human eye, unless an interrupt had occurred in the middle of the commands. Of course, you can temporarily disable interrupts to avoid such situations.

All in all, it's simpler and faster to have all motor pins appear at the same memory address. Setting a single byte (actually, only four particular bits) commands both motors at the same time.

Controlling the Bipolar LEDs

The motor controlling output pins on the microcontroller are connected to input pins on the 74AC14. The 74AC14 has output pins connected to the motor driver chips and to the bipolar LEDs. Therefore, the same microcontroller pins that control the motors also control the bipolar LEDs.

Some minor rearrangements of the pins on the motherboard's connector can permit the microcontroller to have somewhat independent control of the motors and the bipolar LEDs. However, generally speaking, the motors and bipolar LEDs are inexorably partnered in this design.

Reading the Push Button

Input pin 14 reads the push button on the daughterboard. When the push button is pressed, it connects input pin 14 to ground, causing the microcontroller to read a zero value. When the push button is released, a 100 kΩ pull-up resistor defaults the value to 5 V, causing the microcontroller to read a one value.

You can use the push button for any purpose relevant to the particular program running in the microcontroller. Mostly I program the push button to tell Roundabout to begin its task. This way, unlike the motherboard-only version of Roundabout, the robot doesn't immediately start moving when the power switch is turned on. At power-up, the program in the microcontroller patiently waits until input pin 14 reads zero.

Actually, the program only "arms" the start routine when the button is pressed (zero) but waits until the button is released (one) to actually trigger the start of action. There are two reasons for waiting for the button release. First, it's a little disconcerting for the robot to start moving while your finger is still in contact with the button. Second, during robot sumo contests, many contestants are unsure if they fully pressed the start button to begin the mandatory five-second countdown. However, if you first press the button to arm the robot, you can be completely confident in your ability to release the button.

Debouncing an Input

Recall Figure 6-12 from Chapter 6. A push button or switch can generate a fairly noisy signal when pressed or released. If the microcontroller is doing nothing more than waiting for the first zero value, then the noise that follows the zero value is irrelevant and can be ignored. However, if the quantity of push button presses are going to be counted, or if the push button is going to be used to step through a series of stages, then the noisy signal may fool the microcontroller into thinking the button has been pressed multiple times.

There are a couple of ways to debounce a switch. Figures 6-6 and 6-7 in Chapter 6 presented a hardware solution that involved the relatively slow charging and discharging of a capacitor to absorb spikes or rapid transitions.

For its push button, Roundabout includes an almost identical hardware debouncing circuit (see Figure 16-23). However, to save board space, Roundabout's circuit omits the LED. Additionally, the resistor value (R65) has been increased and the capacitor value (C65) has been decreased from the earlier circuit, so the resistor and capacitor match component values found elsewhere on Roundabout. Reusing the same component values saves money because you can purchase them in larger quantities, and it avoids component installation mix-ups because there are fewer different values lying around.

This debouncing circuit is reusable in other robots and electronic projects. Pull-up resistor R65 provides a default high-value voltage. When SW65 is pressed, the microcontroller's pin is connected to ground, providing a low voltage. When SW65 is released, the voltage rises relatively slowly as C65 charges up. You might think that R65 would immediately provide a 5 V signal, but the large 100 kΩ resistance means that almost all of the current from R65 is consumed by C65 as it charges.

Any spikes and rapid unintentional switch bounces simply increase or decrease the voltage on C65 by a small amount. Eventually, C65 reaches a voltage high enough for a microcontroller or logic chip to read the value as 1. Thus, increasing the transition time and averaging out the voltages from the spikes and dips eliminates most false switching signals.

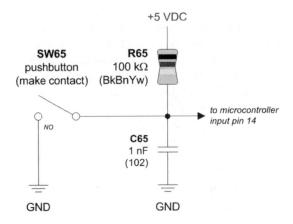

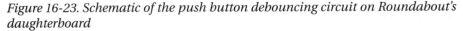

Figure 16-23. Schematic of the push button debouncing circuit on Roundabout's daughterboard

Adding the Push Button to the Daughterboard

There are a lot of tiny push buttons available on the market. Depending on the size and function, they may be called *momentary tactile switches* or *keyswitches*. The left side of Figure 16-24 is a push button from Mouser ($0.22, #653-B3F-1020). You can obtain similar-sized push buttons from other suppliers ($0.25 to $0.30; #FSM-4 or #MPB-129 at All Electronics, #EG1828 at Digi-Key, #N17DTS63K at Electronix Express, and #SWT5 at Solarbotics). Feel free to be creative in selecting a push button; there are all sorts of sizes, colors, and styles.

For this circuit, the push button should be *normally open* (NO, or *make* contact). This means that the button makes an electrical connection only when the button is pressed. The other type of push button is called *normally closed* (NC, or *break* contact). Obviously that type of push button makes a connection when idle and disconnects when pressed.

Most momentary tactile push buttons have four leads for physical stability on the board. The leads are usually connected in pairs, so only two leads (one lead on each side) need to be wired to the circuit. Use a multimeter to determine which two leads are connected and disconnected when the button (or "actuator") is pressed (see the right side of Figure 16-24).

Providing Options with a DIP Switch

A DIP switch is nothing more than a bunch of tiny switches in a dual-inline package. Similar to push buttons, DIP switches are available in many sizes and styles. Roundabout uses a plain four single-pole single-throw (SPST) DIP switch ($0.50 to $0.92; #DWS-4 at All Electronics, #GH1104 at Digi-Key, and #N17DIP4SS at Electronix Express). See the left side of Figure 16-25.

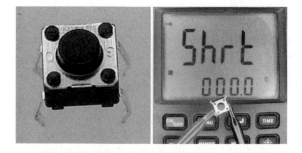

Figure 16-24. A tiny push button (left). A push button being tested with a multimeter (right). Connect one probe to a lead on one side of the push button and the other probe to a lead on the other side, then press and release the push button to see the resistance change. If the resistance doesn't change, try each combination of leads until you find the correct pair. This test works best on a multimeter with a continuity mode that beeps when the resistance drops to near 0 Ω.

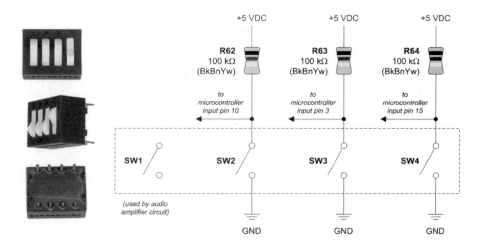

Figure 16-25. Three views of a DIP switch containing four independent switches (left). Schematic showing the three rightmost switches in the DIP being pulled up with 100 kΩ resistors when they aren't switched to ground (right).

A DIP switch can be read by the microcontroller in the same way it reads any other switch or push button. In this case, independent pull-up resistors (R62, R63, and R64) provide high values to input pins 3, 10, and 15 of the microcontroller. When the user toggles a particular switch, it connects the associated microcontroller input pin to ground. The microcontroller's program simply reads each of the input pins, seeing either 0 or 1, to determine which DIP switches are set on or off.

A capacitor or other form of hardware debouncing isn't required here because, unlike a push button, the number of times the DIP switch changes states isn't important. It might be important for a robot to know how many times a button was pushed, but the robot cares only about the final, settled state of the DIP switches. In other words, momentary fluctuations or extra "bounces" don't matter.

Debouncing Through Software

For really noisy switches, especially push buttons, hardware debouncing can be highly beneficial. Another approach, software debouncing, can be used with or without hardware debouncing to ignore false signals. An advantage of software debouncing is that there's no hardware cost (if you don't include the cost of the microcontroller's memory/program space and some processor time).

Generally, you accomplish software debouncing by doing multiple reads of an input pin over some period of time and then accepting the input value only when it hasn't changed during all of those reads. In other words, the input value is relied upon only when it's consistent—which occurs after the bouncing has stopped.

Roundabout sets a timer whenever a button or switch input value changes. If the input value changes again before the timer has expired, the timer gets reset to its full value again. The timer expires only when the pin hasn't changed states at all during that time, so the voltage at that input pin must have finally settled down, and the value can then be relied upon.

Another software debouncing method is to read an input pin ten times (or whatever) and add one to a variable every time the pin is high. At the end of all of the reads, if the variable is greater than five (or whatever), then the average value of the input pin must have been high. You could add software hysteresis that would accept only a count of three or less for low when the prior accepted input state was high and would only accept a count of seven or more for high when the prior accepted input state was low.

Almost all methods of hardware and software debouncing involve some element of time. The longer the time period (or number of reads), the less likely that false switch values will be accepted. Unfortunately, the longer the time period, the less immediately responsive the circuit will be to a button press and the less likely it is to accept true multiple push button presses when the user is pressing rapidly.

It might seem like software debouncing can be a pain. But you can write a generic subroutine that reads the input pins and regularly updates the debounced results to a global variable. The remainder of the robot code reads the debounced global, not the pins directly, thus simplifying the majority of the code.

Avoiding Intermittent Switch Changes

Roundabout uses a combination of three DIP switches to set the robot's behavior or primary task. With one set of DIP switch values, the robot is a room explorer while with another set of values, the robot is a sumo warrior. Other settings direct the robot to access programs that cause it to follow lines or solve mazes. Using a DIP switch allows the same robot to execute a wide variety of behaviors.

However, if any one of the DIP switches exhibits any sort of reliability problems, the robot could briefly switch modes during operation. For example, if the DIP switch setting "off on on" represents robot sumo and "off off on" represents line following, then a loose switch could briefly change a sumo robot into a line-following robot in the middle of a battle.

Therefore, it's a good idea to apply software debouncing even for switches that aren't expected to change often or that otherwise are acceptable to bounce for a short

while after being toggled by a user. The software debouncing routine ignores temporary or intermittent glitches in an otherwise clean signal.

In the last example, a random brief misfire from a loose DIP switch would automatically be stripped by a software debouncing algorithm so that the mode portion of
the robot would never see the intermittent fluctuation and wouldn't change modes in
the middle of a battle. Of course, an even safer approach is for the robot not to read the
DIP switches after the push button has been pressed to start a battle. The robot would
require power to be cycled (turned off and on again) to reread the mode setting from
the DIP switch.

Making Music

Pin 13 on the KX8 microcontroller includes a built-in PWM (pulse-width modulator).
Hardware-based PWMs can generate tones with negligible processor effort. Therefore,
the audio amplifier chip on the daughterboard is connected to pin 13. Chapter 18
covers music generation in more detail.

Remaining Pins Available for Expansion

Besides the unused interrupt pin, two pins remain available on the microcontroller.
You can configure pins 7 and 8 as digital inputs (high or low), as digital outputs (high
or low), or as 8-bit analog inputs (0 V to 5 V converted into values from 0 to 255).

The versatility of these pins made them prime candidates to bring out to an
expansion connector on the daughterboard. The connector itself is a four-pin Molex at
a right angle (see Figure 16-26) to keep down the robot's profile and prevent wires from
sticking out of the top. The first pin on the connector is tied to 5 V, and the last pin on
the connector is tied to ground so that the expansion circuit can receive power.

*Figure 16-26. Right-angle four-pin Molex connector leads to a floor-sensor expan-
sion module. Pins top to bottom: +5V regulated power, floor right (FL:R) connects to
pin 7 of the microcontroller, floor left (FL:L) connects to pin 8 of the microcontroller,
and GND (0 V).*

The middle two connector pins are connected to pins 7 and 8 on the microcontroller. In the next chapter, a floor sensor circuit uses pins 7 and 8 as analog inputs to
read the left and right brightness.

Upgrading a Robot

It's amazing to see how easy it is to dramatically enhance the potential of a robot after you've built the basic features (voltage regulator, motor drivers, and primary sensors). This is one of the reasons that many robot builders choose to use ready-made modules for the base functions, so they can concentrate their efforts on custom building the more specific modules for their particular robot.

In this chapter, a prime location (the 74AC14 DIP socket) on the motherboard was tapped for its centralized collection of signals, controls, and power lines. Installing a boardmount socket permits the daughterboard to be stacked on top of the motherboard.

From that point, the 74AC14 was reused for many of its features, such as frequency generation and LED current driving, but not for its brainpower. The IR detector inputs were redirected to a modifiable chip, the KX8 microcontroller.

The microcontroller improves motor control by adding brake mode, as well as eliminating motor stalling by decoupling the direct cascade from the IR detectors. By applying simple filtering algorithms, not only can you clean up the IR detection signals, but you can also eliminate the noisy inputs from push buttons and DIP switches.

In the next chapter, you'll put the DIP switches to good use to exhibit the versatility of the robot's hardware under programmable microcontroller control. The addition of floor sensors will improve the robot's understanding of the world, whereas the playing of music may improve the world's (or at least the builder's) understanding of the robot.

Adding the Floor Sensor Module

Includes Photoresistors, Voltage Dividers, Light Meter, TAOS TSL257 Light-to-Voltage Amplified Photodiode IC, Semicircular Breadboard, Baffles, Line-Following Algorithm, and Robot Sumo Suggestions

IN THE PREVIOUS CHAPTER, Roundabout gained a daughterboard containing a microcontroller. With the microcontroller, Roundabout uses the same motors, motor drivers, voltage regulator, and sensors to explore rooms without stalling.

By adding a few more parts, Roundabout can receive enough input to perform other tasks, such as following a line or participating in a robot sumo contest. This chapter presents a simple floor reflectivity sensor circuit that connects to the expansion connector on Roundabout's daughterboard.

The front underside of Roundabout is prime real estate—open territory yearning to be filled with circuitry. Installation of the "brightness" detection circuit at that location provides Roundabout with the ability to sense the reflectivity of the floor on the left and right sides of the robot.

Unlike the digital (0 and 1) values read from the infrared reflector detectors, the floor reflectivity circuit produces a range of values from 0 to 255 when read through a microcontroller's 8-bit analog-to-digital converter (ADC) input pins. The floor reflectivity circuit needs only to deliver a voltage anywhere from 0 V to 5 V, which varies with the lightness/darkness of the floor.

Like the voltage regulator, motor driver, and infrared detection circuits, the floor sensor circuit is an independent robotic module. Its usefulness isn't limited to Roundabout because you can easily connect the floor sensor circuit to other microcontrollers or robots.

Sensing Brightness with Photoresistors

Photoresistors (also called *photocells, photoconductors,* or *light-dependent resistors*) are very popular electronic components for sensing brightness. In particular, cadmium-sulfide or cadmium-sulfoselenide (CdS) photoresistors (see Figure 17-1) appear in most inexpensive light-triggered consumer electronic devices, such as automatic nightlights.

Figure 17-1. Different sizes of cadmium-sulfide photoresistors, from 4 mm to 25 mm. The most popular size (the fourth photoresistor from the left) is about 7 mm.

Photoresistors are nonpolarized. That is, you can connect either lead to either higher or lower voltage potential. Photoresistors function with either AC or DC voltage.

The face of a photoresistor contains a photoconductive gap (the wavy line) separating the two metallic electrodes (see Figure 17-2). Interdigitating (wavy halves fitting into the other) increases the total photoconductive perimeter between the two sides, which lowers the overall resistance. Conversely, a straighter gap has a lower perimeter, which results in a higher overall resistance.

Figure 17-2. Different gap or grid patterns. Given the same photoconductive base material, the leftmost pattern (narrow and wavy) provides a lower resistance but lower permitted voltage. The rightmost pattern (wide and straight) provides a higher permitted voltage but also a higher resistance.

Another factor is the width of the gap. An increase in gap width corresponds to an increase in resistance, but it also permits a greater maximum allowable voltage to be applied. The manufacturer can tailor the attributes of the photoresistor by varying the waviness, gap width, and chemical composition of the photoconductive material.

It isn't possible to determine the exact attributes of a photoresistor just from its appearance, mainly because you can't tell the chemical composition of the photoconductive material. Instead, refer to the manufacturer's datasheet and then perform test measurements yourself.

Converting Varying Resistance into Varying Voltage Through a Voltage Divider

Although technically semiconductors, treat cadmium-sulfide photoresistors like variable resistors (such as potentiometers) in a circuit. Place the photoresistor in series with a fixed resistor, apply a voltage to one end, apply ground to the other end, and measure the voltage at the midpoint between the resistors (see Figure 17-3).

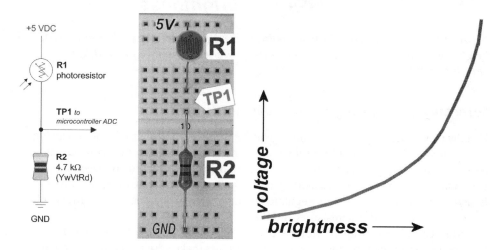

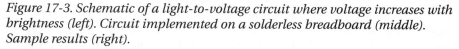

Figure 17-3. Schematic of a light-to-voltage circuit where voltage increases with brightness (left). Circuit implemented on a solderless breadboard (middle). Sample results (right).

This is called a *voltage divider circuit*. The applied voltage divides up between the two resistors (one fixed, one changing with light). A cadmium-sulfide photoresistor decreases in resistance as more light strikes its surface and increases resistance with less light. Therefore, the photoresistor receives a lesser share of the voltage than the fixed resistor in lighter conditions and a greater share of the voltage than the fixed resistor in darker conditions.

If the photoresistor connects to the top of the voltage divider (as in Figure 17-3), the voltage at the midpoint increases with an increase in light. If the photoresistor connects to the bottom of the voltage divider (as in Figure 17-4), the voltage at the midpoint decreases with an increase in light. Select either circuit based on your personal preference or particular application.

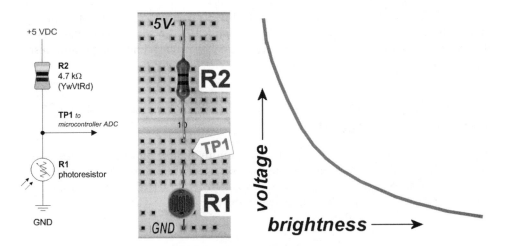

Figure 17-4. Schematic of a light-to-voltage circuit where voltage decreases with brightness (left). Circuit implemented on a solderless breadboard (middle). Graph of results (right)

Selecting a Voltage for the Voltage Divider

Usually you'll want to apply a regulated voltage (such as +5 VDC) to the light-sensing voltage divider so that the midpoint voltage varies only with light, not with declining battery voltage. However, you can get away with using unregulated voltage as long as the voltage reference for the measuring chip (such as a microcontroller or comparator) is also connected to the same unregulated voltage. That way, a decline in battery voltage evenly affects both the resistors and the measurement scale.

Most cadmium-sulfide photoresistors can handle 50 V, so that's not going to be a limiting factor for most battery-powered robots. Just make sure the voltage applied doesn't cause the voltage at the midpoint of the voltage divider to exceed the maximum input voltage of the measuring chip. Usually it's best just to apply the same regulated low voltage (5 V, 3.3 V, or whatever) to the voltage divider that the microcontroller or other voltage-measuring chip is receiving.

Selecting a Resistor for the Voltage Divider

For a photocell voltage divider, 4.7 kΩ is a decent fixed-resistor value for most circuits. It reduces the current flowing through the light-sensing circuit yet allows enough current to flow into the input pin so that most ADCs can read the voltage.

If the datasheet of your ADC specifies that it requires a lower impedance (such as 1 kΩ), feel free to substitute that resistor value. Of course, power consumption will increase. Older, faster, or higher-resolution (more bits) ADCs tend to require lower impedances.

Experiment with different fixed resistors to complement your photoresistor under expected lighting conditions. Perhaps the best fixed-resistor value is one that both meets the needs of the ADC and matches the resistance of the photoresistor when the amount of light it's receiving is in the middle of the desired range. When the photoresistor and fixed resistor have the same resistance, then the voltage at the midpoint is exactly half the total applied voltage. For example, if a photoresistor reads 2.2 kΩ under moderate light, then partnering it with a 2.2 kΩ fixed resistor results in a 2.5 V reading from a 5 V applied voltage under moderate light.

Staying Below the Maximum Power Dissipation Rating of the Photoresistor

The photoresistor manufacturer usually provides a maximum power dissipation rating in milliwatts (mW). To determine if your circuit complies with that rating, perform the following worst-case calculation:

```
maximum photoresistor power dissipation in mW =
    ((½ voltage in volts × ½ voltage in volts) ÷ fixed resistor in ohms)
    × 1000
```
Example circuit for 5 V:
```
maximum power dissipation in mW = ((2.5 V × 2.5 V) ÷ 4700 Ω) × 1000
maximum power dissipation in mW = 1.33 mW
```
Example circuit with 1 kΩ resistor for more sensitive ADC:
```
power dissipation in mW = ((2.5 V × 2.5 V) ÷ 1000 Ω) × 1000
power dissipation in mW = 6.25 mW
```

The worst-case power dissipation across the photoresistor, described by that formula, occurs when the photoresistor matches the resistance of the fixed resistor. The photoresistor dissipates less power when the photoresistor's resistance is less than (brighter conditions) the fixed resistor because less voltage (and thus less power) drops across the photoresistor. The photoresistor also dissipates less power when the photoresistor's resistance is greater than (darker conditions) the fixed resistor because less current (and thus less power) flows in total.

Most cadmium-sulfide photoresistors have a continuous power dissipation rating between 10 mW and 250 mW in free air at room temperature (25° C). All things being equal, physically larger photoresistors have higher power ratings than smaller photoresistors. But as you can tell from the example calculations, continuously exceeding maximum power dissipation isn't a likely problem for 5 V circuits.

Photoresistor Response Is Nonlinear

Lux is a unit that describes the amount of human-perceived light falling on a location regardless of where the light is coming from and regardless of how many light sources are contributing. This is otherwise known as *illuminance*. You can measure lux using a light meter (see Figure 17-5), available at photography stores or electronics suppliers ($65.95; #01LX101 at Electronix Express).

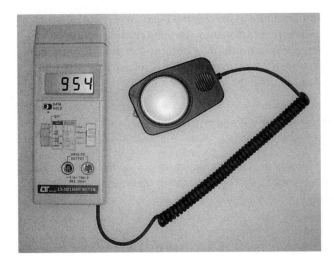

Figure 17-5. Digital light meter

Interestingly, photoresistors don't change resistance in a linear manner with respect to a change in light. For example, going from 500 lux down to 400 lux, a sample photoresistor may increase in resistance by 10 percent. But going from 200 lux down to 100 lux, that same photoresistor may increase in resistance by 50 percent.

The left side of Figure 17-6 shows a graph of a sample resistance change with respect to a change in light. It's that same familiar curve from Figure 17-3 and Figure 17-4.

The right side of Figure 17-6 shows a graph of results from the same photoresistor, but this time plotting the base 10 logarithms of the resistance and light. This results in a generally linear representation of the photoresistor's behavior.

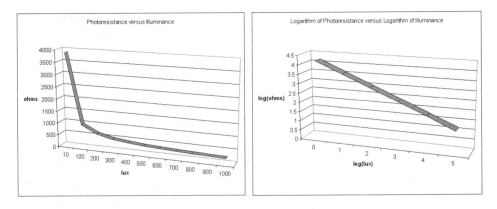

Figure 17-6. A graph of photoresistance versus illuminance for a sample photoresistor (left). The shape is nonlinear (it curves). A graph of the logarithm of the photoresistance versus the logarithm of illuminance for that same sample photoresistor (right). The shape is near-linear. (Note that the scale of the graph on the right is much larger than the graph on the left.)

If you carefully examine the gridlines on photoresistor datasheets, you'll find the "graph paper" or grid lines are expressed in logs. For those people who look only at the line on the graph and not the axis labels, this can cause confusion in thinking that the photoresistor's response is linear.

Graphing the Response of a Specific Photoresistor

You can create a reasonably accurate graph of a particular photoresistor's response based on two measurements of resistance and light, usually at 10 lux and 100 lux. You can call these sample measurements *light10/resistance10* and *light100/resistance100*, respectively. During illuminance and resistance measurements, your setup must be opaquely covered to prevent ambient (room) lighting from altering the measurements.

Using a light meter, first measure the light arriving at a location from a single controllable light source, such as a white LED. Use a potentiometer as the current-limiting resistor to the white LED to adjust the light level.

After reaching a target level (say, 10 lux), place the sample photoresistor in the exact location where the light meter was. If placed closer, the photoresistor would receive more light (greater lux). If placed farther away, the photoresistor would receive less light (lesser lux). Use a multimeter in ohm mode to measure the resistance of the sample photoresistor (no voltage divider circuit is necessary) being illuminated by the white LED.

Calculating Sensitivity

With the two measured data points (resistance at 10 lux and resistance at 100 lux), you can calculate the sensitivity of the photoresistor. This value is called the gamma, or γ.

```
sensitivity =
    absolute value ((log(resistance100 in ohms) - log(resistance10 in ohms))
    ÷ (log(light100 in lux) - log(light10 in lux)))
```

The larger the sensitivity, the more the resistance of the photoresistor changes with respect to light. For example, a 0.8 γ photoresistor changes resistance at a steeper rate than a 0.6 γ photoresistor.

Whether greater sensitivity is desirable depends on your particular circuit. Would you prefer a range of 5 kΩ to 50 kΩ for particular lighting or a more sensitive 1 kΩ to 100 kΩ for that same lighting?

This isn't a cop-out. It really does depend. There are times when a sensitive photoresistor can be considered "overly sensitive" for a particular application. For example, if the sensitive photoresistor changed from 120,000 kΩ to 18 Ω over a fairly narrow range of lighting, then a 4.7 kΩ fixed-resistor 5 V voltage divider circuit would rapidly sweep from 5 V to 0 V. An 8-bit ADC can't tell the difference between 4.981 V and 4.99 V. So any change in lighting beyond those points would be unperceivable to the robot.

Calculating Any Resistance for a Given Illuminance

After measuring a couple of data points and computing the photoresistor's sensitivity, you can calculate the approximate resistance for any illuminance. Pick any light value desired, and plug it into this formula to calculate the resulting resistance:

```
resistance in ohms at desired light level =
    10^(log(desired light level in lux) - ((log(resistance100 in ohms)
    - log(light100 in lux))×sensitivity))
```

I've found predicted values to be fairly close to measured values. Keep in mind that as the predicted values extend further away from any actual measured values, the less accurate the predicted values will be.

Recognizing Inconsistency Between Photoresistors

Resistance varies significantly from photoresistor to photoresistor, even if they're all the same model from the same manufacturer. It isn't uncommon for a manufacturer to quote resistances that vary ±50 percent between 10 lux and 100 lux. For example, if that model of photoresistor was quoted at 10 kΩ at 100 lux, any of the photoresistors of that model could actually be between 5 kΩ and 15 kΩ at 100 lux! Variance increases with less light.

Furthermore, the sensitivity of the photoresistors differs (called the *tolerance of the gamma*) within the same model. Thus, two photoresistors that measure the same resistance at 10 lux can have a noticeable difference in resistance at 100 lux.

Lastly, photoresistor quality control can be poor. I find about 10 percent of production-quality photoresistors are outside the variances and tolerances specified. In fact, they're usually so bad that they just aren't usable and should be discarded.

Testing Variance

I ordered 36 photoresistors with the same part number from the same manufacturer at the same time. Four (11 percent) of the photoresisters were so far out of range or had such little change in resistance with change in light (sensitivity) that they were discarded as defective. Of the 32 that remained, I measured (not calculated) each photoresistor's resistance at five light levels between 100 lux and 1,000 lux from a calibrated white light source on the same day at room temperature. At the end of all of the tests, I retested a few of the first photoresistors to verify that any unintended changes in test equipment (circuit heating up, LED fading) hadn't significantly affected the test results (they hadn't).

The distribution of results was generally as expected (see Figure 17-7). There are fewer photoresistors with greater variation and more that are clumped together in the middle. Although not discernable in this reduced view, many of the lines cross over each other from one end of the graph to the other. This is caused by variations in sensitivity (gamma).

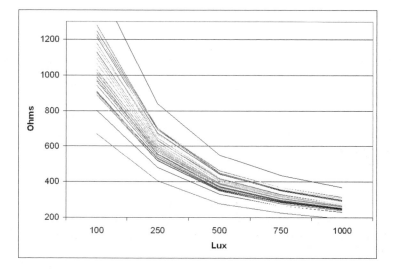

Figure 17-7. A graph of the responses of 32 production-quality photoresistors of the same model from the same manufacturer ordered at the same time

The graph should serve as a reminder to treat each photoresistor as unique and to carefully test a photoresistor before selecting it for use in a robot. Furthermore, you should consider testing a batch of photoresistors to select matching pairs or sets.

Rising and Falling Resistance Speeds

Probably the most often cited disadvantage of photoresistors is their relatively slow reaction time in response to changes in light. The sluggishness becomes more pronounced under darker conditions.

Although it varies based on the photoresistor's chemistry and manufacturer, a photoresistor's resistance fall time tends to be specified between 20 ms and 40 ms at 10 lux. The resistance rise time tends to be specified between 50 ms and 100 ms at 10 lux. Photoresistors react faster to an increase in brightness (decreasing resistance) than to a decrease in brightness (increasing resistance). Put another way, the resistance falls about two to three times faster than it rises.

For example, in Figure 17-8, an LED provides 100 lux of illumination on a sample photoresistor. The LED is turned on and off about six times a second (6 Hz). The photoresistor is connected to a 4.7 kΩ voltage divider (recall Figure 17-3) so that the voltage reading increases when the LED turns on. The oscilloscope shows that the resistance falls (voltage rises) to about 10 percent peak in about 30 ms. Also, the oscilloscope shows that the resistance rises (voltage falls) to about 90 percent peak in about 80 ms.

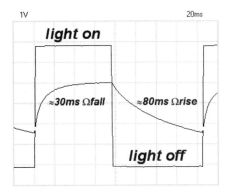

Figure 17-8. An oscilloscope trace demonstrating that a photoresistor takes a fairly long time to react to a change in brightness. If the photoresistor reacted more quickly, the curved, sloping lines would be much more square in relation to the light turning on and off.

This means that photoresistors aren't a good choice for high-speed circuits; they react too slowly. Photoresistors are perfectly acceptable for many robotic applications and beginner circuits. However, consider other light-sensing technologies for more sophisticated robot designs.

Reusing the Balanced Brightness-Sensing Circuit

Sandwich, from *Robot Building for Beginners* (Apress, 2002), uses a photoresistor circuit for following lines. The circuit at the end of Chapter 14 of that book would work acceptably for Roundabout, as long as the circuit is run from regulated 5 V rather than 9 V. TP1 would connect to pin 7 on Roundabout's microcontroller, and TP2 would connect to pin 8.

Because that circuit has already been presented in my previous book, and because I've just spent the last few pages deriding photoresistors, I'll present something more advanced for this book.

Sensing Brightness with a Photodiode IC

Photodiodes react up to 1,000 times faster than photoresistors. A photodiode is usually connected to some sort of an amplifier (a transistor or an op amp) and conversion circuit to increase the signal gain and convert the current to a voltage.

TAOS (http://www.taosinc.com/) produces a light-to-voltage photodiode-based sensor in a neat, complete package (see Figure 17-9). Connect one pin to ground, and connect one pin to power; the third pin outputs a voltage related to the amount of light sensed. What could be easier?

The TAOS TSL257 (Future/Active $1.43) photosensor responds to a wide range of wavelengths, from visible to infrared. The same package is available with color filters for sensing red (TSLR257), green (TSLG257), and blue (TSLB257).

Figure 17-9. Pinout of the TAOS TSLx257 series light-to-voltage converter

Presenting the Floor Reflectivity Circuit

Figure 17-10 shows the schematic for the floor reflectivity circuit. A white LED on each side reflects light off of the floor and into each TSL257 sensor. Current-limiting resistors (R85, R88) prevent the brightness adjusting potentiometers (R86, R87) from being dialed to the point that either white LED could become damaged. Decoupling/bypass capacitors (C86, C87) are included on the TSL257 power supply lines, per standard practice.

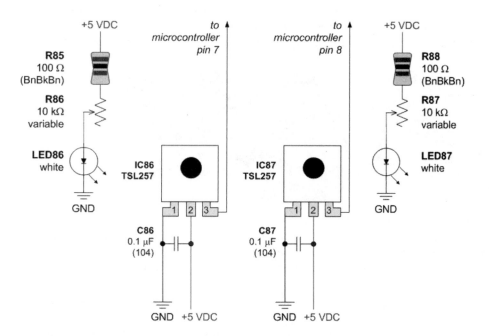

Figure 17-10. Schematic of the floor reflectivity circuit that uses two brightness-adjustable white LEDs to reflect light off of the floor and into TSL257 light-to-voltage converters

There are two sensors and two adjustable white LEDs so that the left side and right side of the floor can be detected independently. This provides the robot with the ability to follow a line or to pick an optimal (less bright) direction to turn away from the border of a sumo ring.

TIP *The resistance values for R86 and R87 may seem really large, but it turns out the TSL257 photosensors are extremely sensitive to light. Therefore, it doesn't take much current to provide enough light from the white LEDs to illuminate the floor at the proper level for the sensors to see.*

White LEDs have come down in price considerably. They now cost between $1 and $2. Although you could use colored LEDs or even infrared LEDs in this circuit, they won't produce a broad enough spectrum for the robot to see what you see. For example, low-mask blue tape may look dark to a robot when illuminated with red LEDs because the blue tape likely reflects only the blue portion of the visible light spectrum.

Implementing the Floor Reflectivity Circuit

The floor reflectivity circuit easily fits in the space available at the underside of the front of Roundabout (see Figure 17-11). You could position the TSL257 sensors farther away from each other—more toward the sides. But too large of a gap between the sensors would cause the robot to oscillate (steer back and forth) during line following.

Figure 17-11. The floor reflectivity circuit installed underneath Roundabout. A right-angle Molex connector ① connects the circuit to the expansion connector on Roundabout's daughterboard. (Alternatively, because the daughterboard already has a connector, you could solder the wires directly to this floor-sensor board.)

Cutting Out a Semicircular Breadboard

The space underneath the front of the robot provides enough room to fit a rectangular circuit board within the borders of the circular central platform. However, if the corners of the circuit board stick out, they'd partially defeat the purpose of having a circular robot because the circuit board corners would lodge against obstacles and prevent the robot from being able to rotate in place.

Instead of using a rectangular circuit board, you can cut a semicircular circuit board from a standard blank perfboard (see Figure 17-12).

Figure 17-12. A semicircular circuit board (bottom) cut out from a standard 0.1 inch rectangular perfboard.

Follow these steps:

1. Place the blank rectangular perfboard underneath the front of your robot. Mark the desired shape of the board with a pencil, using the edge of the robot's platform as a guide.

2. Move the marked perfboard to your workbench. Always put on a dust mask before cutting or drilling circuit board material because breathing the dust from the laminate isn't healthy for you.

3. Use a coping saw, jigsaw, router, or high-speed rotary tool (Dremel) to roughly cut out the semicircle.

4. With a file or sandpaper, smooth the board edges as desired.

Baffling the Board

To accurately judge the lightness/darkness of the floor, the TSL257 sensors should be permitted to see only white LED light reflecting off of the floor. Light coming directly from the LEDs or reflected light originating from the room can easily saturate the sensors so that they constantly provide a 5 V reading regardless of the lightness/darkness of the floor itself.

The solution is to put protective baffles or enclosures around the sensors and around the entire floor reflectivity circuit to block uncontrolled light (see Figure 17-13).

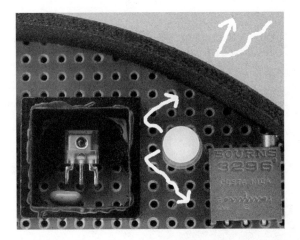

Figure 17-13. External light is blocked by an opaque barrier glued to the outer edge of the circuit board. Direct light from the white LED is blocked by a small opaque plastic baffle. Therefore, the only significant light sensed by the TSL257 will be reflected off of the floor from the output-adjusted white LED.

Putting on a Black Skirt

An external barrier or skirt should surround the outer edge (see Figure 17-14) of the floor reflectivity circuit board and prevent ambient lighting from reflecting off of the floor directly beneath the sensors. Also, a barrier sheet should cover the top of the board; otherwise light can accidentally seep in through the circuit board's component holes (see Figure 17-15). You can make the barriers from any nonelectrically conductive flexible opaque material. Foam sheet, felt, fabric, construction paper, or thin plastic may all be suitable materials if they're opaque enough.

You can find a flexible, black, 2-mm thick, foam sheet at most local craft stores. Flexi-Foam #15200-55 from Fibre-Craft (http://www.fibrecraft.com/) costs about $0.59. After cutting out a strip of the foam sheet and mocking it up on the board to check the length, glue the foam sheet to the underside or outside edge of the circuit board using a thin layer of gel-type cyanoacrylate-based glue (superglue).

Much to my surprise, cyanoacrylate glue really holds foam and circuit board material together well. In fact, you should first finish soldering and testing your circuit before fully gluing the foam sheet to the sensor board. Perhaps tack the foam sheet in a few spots for temporary testing.

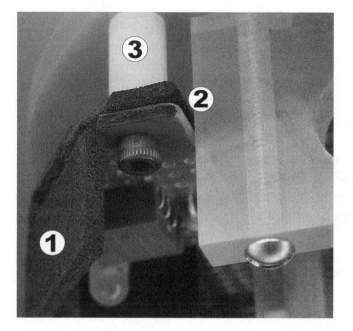

Figure 17-14. Black foam sheet glued underneath the edge of the board ① and covering the top of the board ② prevents ambient light from affecting the sensors. (Note the white plastic spacer ③ between the floor reflectivity circuit board and the robot's center platform. By varying the length of the spacer, you can control the board's distance from the floor. You want to ensure enough distance to allow light to reflect from the white LED and back into the TSL257 sensor.)

Figure 17-15. Two views of Roundabout with the floor reflectivity circuit installed

Gutting a LEGO Brick

For the sensor baffle, a fairly small, opaque, rectangular piece is needed that will be rigid enough not to curl or get bent over the TSL257 sensor when the robot eventually runs over an obstacle. The baffle needs to be able to be glued and should be reasonably lightweight.

A 2 by 2 LU (LEGO unit) black LEGO brick is perfect! The conversion process is fairly simply (see Figure 17-16).

Figure 17-16. Drilling, filling, and/or milling a standard black LEGO brick into a sensor baffle. What I like most about this picture is that the LEGO brick looks like a shocked face at the end of the process. "Ah! What have you done to me?"

Follow these steps:

1. Begin by milling/drilling out the underside circular post of the LEGO brick.

2. Flip the brick over and sand, file, or mill off the top posts so that the block sits flush. This saves vertical space and makes it easier to glue.

3. Drill, file, or mill out a hole in the bottom of the brick to permit the sensor leads to reach the breadboard.

A neat trick when machining a LEGO brick is to use other LEGO bricks to help secure and keep the machined brick level (see Figure 17-17). Just be sure to tighten the vise enough to compress the sides of the top brick to prevent it from slipping out.

Tuning and Testing the Floor Reflectivity Circuit

After soldering, baffling, and installing the floor reflectivity circuit, you must adjust each white LED's potentiometer to provide the correct amount of light. At first, this might seem like a difficult task because the robot doesn't have an LCD or multisegment LED to provide feedback as to the values it's reading. But there's an easy way to display the values.

Simply connect multimeter test probes to the ground pin and either the left or right floor sensor pin (see Figure 17-18) on the daughterboard's expansion connector. Set the multimeter to voltage measuring mode.

Figure 17-17. Milling off the top posts of a LEGO brick. Place additional LEGO bricks underneath in the vise to secure, level, and raise the top brick to the proper height.

Figure 17-18. Connecting multimeter test probes to the expansion connector on the daughterboard. The multimeter displays the floor sensor's output voltage.

Tuning Just Below 5 V on a Maximally Reflective Surface

Place the robot on several sheets of white paper or a white diffusely reflective surface. Check the voltage reading on the meter. Odds are that the value will be pinned near 5 V. If your meter reads "4.94 V" or something close, that's still probably the maximum voltage output of the TSL257.

Turn down the brightness of the associated white LED (the left side if you're testing the left sensor output) by adjusting the associated potentiometer. Because of the black skirt and location of the sensor board, this was too awkward for me to do while the robot was in position. I simply picked up the robot, made a couple of turns on the multiturn potentiometer, and placed the robot back onto the white paper. However, you may want to cut or drill little holes in the skirt to be able to adjust the potentiometers with a tiny screwdriver while the robot is in position.

Keep adjusting the associated white LED until the voltage reading drops below 4.5 V. At this point you know the sensor isn't saturated. Now you can just slightly increase the brightness of the LED to bring the sensor closer to 5 V if you want.

Repeat this process until both the left and right floor sensors are fine-tuned to just barely provide their peak reading on a bright surface.

Testing on a Minimally Reflective Surface

Place the robot on a dark, dull surface and measure the voltage of both floor sensors. Preferably both sensors read less than 0.5 V.

If the sensor voltages seem too high (more than 1 V), try covering the robot with an opaque covering. If the voltage drops noticeably while the robot is covered, then ambient lighting reaching the floor sensors is raising the floor sensor readings. Some increase, such as a couple of tenths of a volt, is tolerable.

If the floor sensors are being significantly affected by ambient lighting, but you think that the floor reflectivity circuit board appears to be adequately covered, remember that the TSL257 is sensitive to infrared as well as visible light. It may be that the material you've chosen for the skirt and baffle doesn't block infrared.

On the other hand, if the voltage doesn't drop when the robot is seriously shrouded (say, by a metal box), then check the circuit wiring and possibly reduce the brightness of the white LEDs. Also, make sure the dark test surface is fairly dull. A shiny or mirrored surfaced can reflect a lot more light than you know.

Following a Line

Now that Roundabout has a floor sensor, the robot can follow a line on the floor. A rudimentary algorithm is as follows:

1. Read the DIP switches.

2. If the first DIP switch is set to on, then the robot is configured to autodetect the line/floor brightness. Go to step 5.

    If the program reaches this point, the DIP switches aren't configured for autodetection. In competitions, it's probably safer to use DIP switches to specify whether the line is light or dark because the autodetect algorithm may not work in untested conditions.

3. If the second DIP switch is set to on, then the robot is configured to follow a light line. Set the global variable, gDarkLine = FALSE. Go to step 10.

4. If the program reaches here, the second DIP switch must have been set to off, so the robot is configured to follow a dark line. Set gDarkLine = TRUE. Go to step 10.

Autodetection of Line Brightness

A really fancy autodetect algorithm might have the robot spin in a complete circle to detect the minimum, maximum, and average floor reflectivity readings. If the average reading is closer to the minimum value, the floor is dark and the line is light. If the average reading is closer to the maximum value, the floor is light and the line is dark.

A simpler approach is to assume that the human operator has placed the robot so that the line is centered between the floor sensors at the start. The sensors see the lightness/darkness of the floor to the left and the right of the line. If the floor reflectivity is below 50 percent of the maximum ADC value, the floor is assumed to be dark and the line is assumed to be light.

5. Read the left floor sensor (0 V to 5 V equals 0 to 255 on an 8-bit ADC in this example) into the global variable gLeftFloorSensor.

6. Read the right floor sensor into the global variable gRightFloorSensor.

7. Add gLeftFloorSensor and gRightFloorSensor together. The resulting number is between 0 and 510.

8. If the sum of both sensors is less than 50 percent reflectivity (2.5 V equals 127.5; two sensors with 127.5 added together are going to equal 255 or more), then the floor is dark, so the line must be light. Set gDarkLine = FALSE. Go to step 10.

9. For the program to get here, the total must have been equal to or more than 50 percent reflectivity, so the floor must be light and the line must be dark. Set gDarkLine = TRUE.

Reading Floor Sensor Values

Converting analog values to digital (0 to 255) takes more time than simply reading a digital input (0/1). Therefore, it's faster to regularly read the floor sensor values into global variables and have the rest of the algorithm read those global variables. Think of it as taking a snapshot of the floor sensors at a particular moment and referring to that snapshot when making steering decisions.

10. Read the left floor sensor into the global variable gLeftFloorSensor and the right floor sensor into the global variable gRightFloorSensor.

Inverting Sensor Values

Here comes a really cool trick. It'd be a pain to constantly check whether the robot should be following a light line or dark line throughout the entire line-following algorithm. Because the floor sensor values are read into global variables, and because the line-following algorithm reads those variables instead of the floor sensor pins directly, you can alter the global variables so that you can simplify the line-following algorithm:

11. If gDarkLine = TRUE, go to step 14.

12. gLeftFloorSensor = 255 - gLeftFloorSensor.

13. gRightFloorSensor = 255 - gRightFloorSensor.

 TIP *Depending on your choice of microcontroller and programming language, an exclusive-or (also called EOR or XOR) instruction may be faster than subtracting the sensor values from 255. It achieves the same mathematical result.*

If not already set for a dark line (in which case the program would have gone to step 14 after carrying out step 11), steps 12 and 13 invert the sensor global variables to cause all dark inputs to appear to be light, and all light inputs to appear to be dark. The "snapshot" has been flipped from a light line on a dark background to a dark line on a light background.

For example, if gLeftFloorSensor was 255, it's now 0 (255 minus 255 equals 0). If gLeftFloorSensor was 0, it's now 255 (255 minus 0 equals 255). If gLeftFloorSensor was 10, it's now 245 (255 minus 10 equals 245).

From this point on, the robot can always execute a dark line–following algorithm because all light lines seen by the sensor will now appear to be dark lines. If this makes your head spin, try thinking about it this way: The robot's job is to follow a dark line. If the line was dark to begin with, great! If the line was light to begin with, it's converted to a dark internally. In either case, the line now appears dark to the robot and thus can be followed using a single dark line–following algorithm.

Following the Dark Line

Now the robot needs to determine if the sensor values are close enough to be considered equal, which suggests that the line is currently centered between the sensors:

14. Subtract gLeftFloorSensor from gRightFloorSensor. If less than zero, subtract gRightFloorSensor from gLeftFloorSensor instead. The resulting number indicates how near the sensor values are to each other.

15. If the sensor values are within 30 (or whatever) of each other, then they pretty much see the same brightness. Unless the robot has driven off into la-la land, the line is probably centered between the sensors. Set both motors to forward to drive straight ahead. Go to step 10.

Centering Over the Dark Line

At this point the sensor values aren't close to each other (otherwise step 15 would have executed). This means that the line, or at least part of the line, is underneath one of the sensors and the robot needs to make a course correction to recenter over the line:

16. If gLeftFloorSensor is less than gRightFloorSensor, then some or all of the dark line is under the left sensor. Set the left motor to reverse and the right motor to forward to rotate the robot to the left. Go to step 10.

17. If step 16 didn't execute, then the only remaining possibility is that some or all of the dark line is under the right sensor. Set the left motor to forward and the right motor to reverse to rotate the robot to the right. Go to step 10.

Steps 16 and 17 aren't time dependent. The robot repeats steps 10 through 16 (or 17) to continue to rotate either left or right until the sensor values are near each other again, which kicks in step 15 to move forward.

If you find that the robot stays in one place alternately between rotating left and rotating right, then you need to increase the nearness value (30 in step 15) until the robot spends at least some of the time moving forward.

Improving the Line-Following Algorithm

The rudimentary line-following algorithm works acceptably for most courses. The algorithm isn't particular smooth or efficient and isn't designed to handle broken lines or to hunt for the line if the robot has accidentally wandered off of the course.

A robot with a microcontroller has the advantage of being able to contain more sophisticated and successful algorithms. This feature is completely independent from the existing circuits and hardware.

Given the detailed brightness information coming in from the left and right sensors, the motors could be powered more gradually, rather than full forward and full reverse, depending on the ratio of the sensors to each other. The resulting movements would be more graceful. Without all the exaggerated back and forth rotations, the robot would spend more time going forward, thus increasing overall speed.

Competing in Robot Sumo

Robot sumo is a nonviolent pushing contest where two robots try to push each other out of a ring. More details about robot sumo appear in an illustrated guide on my Web site (http://www.robotroom.com/SumoRules.html).

The first characteristic of a successful sumo robot is to ensure that the robot won't mistakenly drive out of the ring on its own. The ring is made from a dark material with a light border. The floor reflectivity sensors make detection of the ring border easy. The robot need only back up or turn around when the floor sensor voltage rises higher than 50 percent.

The second characteristic of a successful sumo robot is to push the opponent. Of course, it helps a lot if the sumo robot can find the opponent in the first place! The infrared reflector detector sensors are excellent for locating walls, obstacles, or, in this case, opponent robots. With an otherwise bare sumo ring, the robot merely drives around (or spins in place) until the infrared detectors trip and then drives forward to push.

Entering Roundabout in Robot Sumo

As built, Roundabout doesn't have the proper physical body for robot sumo. Roundabout's body is too large to qualify for mini-sumo dimensions and too small to be competitive against standard-sized sumo opponents. Furthermore, Roundabout's round shape is designed to slide off of obstacles, not to square them up for pushing.

However, the size and functions of Roundabout's *circuitry* are excellent fits for robot sumo. Placing the circuit boards atop a smaller body with an opponent-toppling scoop easily creates a competitive mini-sumo robot (see Figure 17-19).

Figure 17-19. Roundabout's stock circuitry installed on a mini-sumo body

To improve targeting, a small black baffle ① optically separates the left and right infrared detectors. The difference in the view of the detectors has a more pronounced influence on navigation than the narrowness of the beam from the emitters.

Underneath the front scoop, the floor reflectivity circuit ② can detect the white edge of the sumo ring. Be sure to place the floor sensor circuit as close to the front of the scoop as possible so the robot will stop before the tip of the scoop passes over the lip of the sumo ring edge.

Roundabout Sumo has its motors built into the wheels (see Chapter 5) for a compact solution with a low center of gravity. I selected Copal 50:1 gearmotors ($26.99 from RobotMarketPlace.com) because they met the necessary dimensions and speeds. Insert the ends of the motors into a plastic block ③ with a large hole (the same diameter as the motors) drilled through it. A pair of setscrews on the back and the front of the block secure the motors in place.

The complete, functioning robot weighs only 350 grams. However, it's to your advantage to maximize the robot's mass to make it more difficult for a competitor to push. A brass block ④ has been attached beneath the motors to bring the robot up to the 500-gram mini-sumo maximum limit. This location provides the robot with a low center of gravity (more difficult to tip over) and an increase in traction (because the mass pulls down on the wheels, not the front scoop).

The power switch resides in the difficult-to-reach location ⑤ on the motherboard. This decreases the likelihood of an opponent's appendage accidentally powering off Roundabout. In that same vein, you could improve this body by adding a rigid covering over the exposed wires and circuit board.

Strategizing with DIP Switch Settings

Robot sumo is divided into two major categories, autonomous and remote controlled. Remote-controlled sumo robots are similar to remote-control cars, where the human guides the robot to the opponent. Opponent sensors and ring border sensors aren't necessary on such robots. (However, the judicious inclusion of some autonomous functions, which operate much faster than any human operator could hope to match, can provide a competitive advantage.)

Conversely, the autonomous robots are self-controlled, usually with a microcontroller, just like Roundabout. Most winning robots contain a variety of onboard sensors, such as the infrared reflector detector and floor reflectivity circuit. All external guidance during the round is forbidden.

However, that doesn't mean an autonomous sumo robot need be completely devoid of human-perceived information. You can use DIP switches to select the best algorithm available from those that have been programmed into an autonomous robot in advance. Depending on the opponent, the human operator simply sets the DIP switches before the start of the round or match.

Some contests permit the operator to continue to press buttons or alter settings up until the moment the start button is pressed. In that case, DIP switches could be set with the robot in place in the sumo ring to suggest whether the opponent was straight ahead, to the right, or to the left. Check with the event organizers to determine if this is considered fair.

Expanding Possibilities

This chapter described an add-on floor-sensing module that expands Roundabout's capabilities. Whether you use discrete components such as cadmium-sulfide photoresistors in voltage dividers or amplified photodiodes in integrated packages, the ability for the robot to sense brightness is one of the most fundamentally useful types of functions.

The expansion connector on Roundabout's daughterboard and brightness sensors aren't limited to sensing reflectivity off of the floor. That same technology can detect a stripe, or multiple stripes, on each wheel and by counting can determine the speed or number of rotations of each wheel. Or, you can install brightness detectors on the sides of the robot to aid navigation through shadow detection.

CHAPTER 18

Cooking Up Some Robot Stew

Covers LM386 Audio Amplifier, Music Through PWM, Roundabout Pro, Angle Stock Motor Mounts and More, Smooth Wheels, Spring Tubing Whiskers, Lever Switches, and Wireless Video

AS I APPROACH THE END of writing a book, I find I have accumulated a pile of parts or ideas that never ended up getting squeezed into a prior chapter. The concepts are often not meaty enough to fill an entire chapter, but they're still worth mentioning. I can either throw away the leftovers or serve them up as a single meal. Guess what I decided to do? Make robot stew!

Your feast begins with an appetizer—an audio circuit for playing tones or tunes. Roundabout includes this circuit on its daughterboard.

You'll then be served side dishes of family-size Roundabout Pro along with tasty motor mounts that illustrate several ways to hold a motor to the body of a robot. Mounting motors was the hardest task for me when I was first starting out, but it turns out there's a great way (angle stock) to precisely attach motors with little machining.

The main course is a big helping of Carefree, a solar robot. Actually, the emphasis is on Carefree's sensors, more than anything else.

For dessert, I hope you'll imbibe in some wireless video. There's a relatively low-cost and electrically painless way to add a video camera to any lunch-box-sized or larger robot.

Making Music

Roundabout has the ability to play tones or music as it drives around. Although the sounds are primarily designed to increase the robot's entertainment factor, it can be a unique debugging tool as well. Unlike an LED display, which blurs on a fast-moving robot, playing different sounds for different events can effectively communicate the robot's thought process, even when you can't observe the robot directly.

Presenting the Audio Circuit

The audio circuit consists of a single output pin from the microcontroller, connected to an audio amplifier chip, which connects to a speaker. The circuit (see Figure 18-1) is based on a 250 mW LM386-1 audio-amplifier chip in an eight-pin DIP ($0.39 to $0.61; #LM386N-1 at All Electronics, #LM386N-1 at Digi-Key, #N10386N-1 at Electronix Express, and #LM386N-1 at Jameco). Higher-wattage chips, the LM386N-3 (500 mW) and LM386N-4 (750 mW), are drop-in compatible if you want louder audio volume.

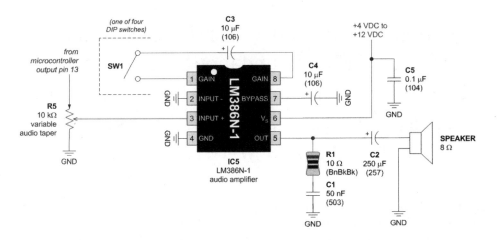

Figure 18-1. The schematic for Roundabout's audio circuit

Implementing the Audio Circuit

The components in this audio circuit match those recommended in the manufacturer's datasheet. A 0.1 µF ceramic decoupling/bypass capacitor (C5) has been added per standard practice.

Turning the Volume

The volume control potentiometer (R5) really ought to be an "audio" (nonlinear taper) potentiometer rather than the standard linear-taper potentiometer (such as the trim-pots used throughout this book). Audio potentiometers change resistance logarithmically to match the way our ears perceive differences in volume.

A standard linear-taper potentiometer works tolerably in this circuit. Dial adjustments made toward one extreme of a linear range don't result in any apparent volume difference, but that same amount of dial adjustment made on the other end of the linear range results in huge differences of apparent volume. The only reason I chose to use a linear taper in this circuit is that I wanted to conserve space, yet I couldn't find a nonlinear trimpot.

Listening to Binary

The third pin of the volume-control potentiometer (R5) should connect to ground, as shown in Figure 18-1. The volume control acts as a voltage divider, causing the voltage of the output of the microcontroller to be reduced before reaching the audio amplifier.

An interesting effect occurs if you eliminate the volume-control trimpot (connecting the microcontroller's output pin directly into the audio input) or if you fail to connect the third pin of the trimpot to ground. As the microcontroller is powering up, or when the microcontroller is being programmed or debugged by the programming board, the microcontroller's pin is in an "input" (or hi-z) state, not an output. As such, the audio input pin is temporarily not connected to an output, resulting in a floating state. So, the audio amplifier chip amplifies the electrical noise of the microcontroller or the programming board's connecting cable. You end up hearing tones, not unlike a dial-up modem, of the circuitry in action.

When the third pin of the volume-control potentiometer is connected to ground, the input of the audio amplifier input is connected to ground when the microcontroller's pin isn't in an output state. There's some resistance between the audio amplifier input and ground, but that simply acts as a pull-down resistor.

Boosting Loudness

In most circuits, an audio amplifier input connects to a weak signal, such as a radio demodulator or a microphone. To deal with extreme cases, the LM386 chip features a 200-gain mode instead of the default 20-gain mode. For example, the higher gain mode is useful when the audio amplifier input is connected to a microphone listening for a far-away smoke-detector alarm on a fire-fighting robot circuit such as in Figure 8-6 in Chapter 8. The extra gain is unnecessary for Roundabout because even the wimpy 8 mA CMOS output pin on a microcontroller is more than enough of a signal to produce a strong, clean sound.

That being said, Roundabout still permits the 200-gain feature to be enabled through SW1 of the DIP switch on Roundabout. Recall that DIP switches are just tiny switches combined in a single package. Rather than using all of the switches for configuration settings, one switch connects/disconnects pin 1 of the LM386 to a 10 μF capacitor to pin 8 of the LM386, thus enabling/disabling the 200-gain feature.

Normally, I'll have the volume control on the robot dialed low enough to not bother other people in my house when I'm experimenting. But when someone is foolish enough to walk into my "laboratory," I flip SW1 to instantly enable Roundabout's screech at its full glory. Then, when the visitor thinks it's no longer impolite to flee, I flip off SW1 to restore standard gain (standard volume), without ever altering the carefully adjusted dial setting on the volume-control trimpot.

Driving a Speaker

In many ways, an audio amplifier performs the same function as a motor driver does: It takes a relatively weak signal from the microcontroller and boosts it to the level required by the destination device, whether that's a speaker or a motor. In fact, notice in Figure 18-1 that the audio amplifier chip receives unregulated power to supply to the speaker, just like a motor driver chip receives unregulated power to supply to the motors.

Selecting a Speaker

A commonly specified characteristic of a speaker is its impedance (resistance). The LM386 should be connected to an 8 Ω speaker. You can salvage appropriately small 8 Ω speakers from old PCs or consumer electronic devices (see left side of Figure 18-2). Check the back of the speaker to see if it's labeled "8 Ω."

Roundabout uses a compact, encased speaker ($1.25; #SK-94 at All Electronics). Most miniature speakers are vulnerable to physical damage on an open-frame robot. However, this particular speaker features an attractive protective cover (see the right side of Figure 18-2). To prevent the robot from being too tall and to avoid taking up too much room on the daughterboard, the speaker has been epoxied to a piece of plastic and screwed in from below at the rear of the robot.

Figure 18-2. An ordinary 8 Ω speaker removed from a discarded personal computer (left). A compact speaker with protective cover that's glued to a piece of plastic and screwed in from underneath (right). Note the square trimpot (R5) at the top right of the picture, which adjusts the volume.

Choosing an Audio Amplifier Chip Instead of a Simple Transistor

Unlike ordinary transistors or op amps, an audio amplifier chip is designed to distort the original signal as little as possible during amplification. Additionally, an audio amplifier provides the same level of gain across most audible frequencies. In doing so, one note (middle C, for example) is played at the same volume level as another note (such as F, up about an octave and a half). Lastly, an audio amplifier filters (rejects) as much of the power supply electrical noise as possible, rather than amplifying it. By doing so, electrical noises aren't magnified along with the intended sound, which would otherwise result in hiss.

Instead of using an audio amplifier chip, you could use a transistor or even a motor driver chip (I suppose) to drive the speaker. In fact, Figure 9-6 from Chapter 9 works acceptably with a speaker instead of a motor for M1. You're trading simplicity and low cost for sound quality. The distortions aren't noticeable for robot beeps, but they might be noticeable on digitized sounds or prerecorded voices.

Seeing Sound

The square wave generated by the microcontroller to make sound isn't complex (see Figure 18-3). You'll notice this looks very much the same as the 38 kHz square wave generated by the 74AC14 chip (Chapters 11 and 12) to be delivered to infrared emitters for the infrared reflector detector circuit. However, in this case, the square wave is at a much lower frequency, about 261 Hz, which can be heard by human beings. In all other respects, the signals are identical.

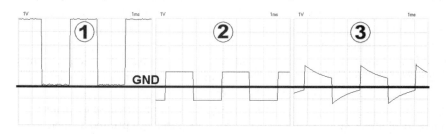

Figure 18-3. A simple square wave ① in the audio range (middle C) generated by the microcontroller and fed into the audio amplifier's input (left). The LM386's output pin drives capacitor C2 to convert the signal into digital AC ② (middle). The reduction in peak-to-peak voltage is because of the volume control. The inductive and electromagnetic attributes of the speaker affect the output to alter the final waveform ③ (right).

Sounds made by instruments (including the human voice) have very complex waveforms that include varying attack, sustain, and decay portions, as well as multiple frequencies. But Roundabout's microcontroller's tones are pure digital: suddenly on and suddenly off. As such, the microcontroller's music sounds tinny, like a cell phone ring or a musical birthday card.

Still, Roundabout's sounds are more than enough to be useful for debugging. Furthermore, the robot's music is mildly entertaining, even after the tenth time listening to it. If desired, you could dedicate more processor power and memory to create more complex sounds.

Playing a Note

You can find a list of frequencies for musical notes on the Internet. I copied the American Standard Pitch frequencies into a spreadsheet (available at http://www .robotroom.com/IRBGoodies.html#FREQ), applied a formula to calculate the correct numerical values based on the clock frequency of the KX8 microcontroller, and pasted the resulting table into the robot's source code. When a robot wants to play a note, it looks in the table to determine the frequency in a numeric format.

Playing a Tune

Despite some piano lessons as a child, I began this book with no musical expertise whatsoever. I fumbled my way through converting some simple songs from music sheets into the robot.

To play a single note, the robot needs to know only the frequency to play (the pitch and octave) and the amount of time to play it (duration). To create a song, you simply string note information together, with quiet pauses (rests) at certain points in the music. When the robot is done playing the first note for the listed duration, it goes to the next, and so on.

Often, a program specifies a song as a simple text string, such as "4AQ 4GQ 4FQ 4GQ 4AQ 4AQ 4AH 4GQ 4GQ 4GH 4AQ 5CQ 5CH" for "Mary Had a Little Lamb." In this example, the first number in each sequence is the octave (1 to 8), the letter is the pitch (A to F), and the last letter is the duration (whole, half, quarter, and so on). The program looks up the table row for the octave and the table column for the pitch, and thus it determines the frequency. The duration letter translates into some hard-coded length of time, such as one second for a whole note.

You can download beginner's sheet music from the Web or purchase a learner's guide from a local music store. Using an overhead transparency, I printed a cheat sheet to slide along the printed music to quickly indicate the pitch and octave (see Figure 18-4). After writing down the number of the octave and the letter of the pitch of each note, I typed the song into a string in the source code. When the robot wants to play a song, it simply passes that string into the song-playing routine, which then passes a few characters at a time into the note-playing routine.

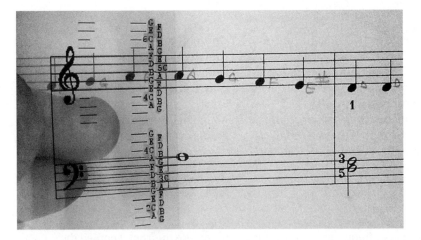

Figure 18-4. Transparency cheat sheet to quickly transcribe notes on a music sheet. There's no reason you couldn't print the cheat sheet on plain paper, except with a transparency you can see the sharps and flats on the left side of the music sheet.

I initially encountered a small problem with the song-playing algorithm: It immediately started the next note after the current note's duration had completed. As such, each note ran immediately into the next (legato), which made it sound a little like drunken jazz (no offense intended to drunken jazz players). This problem was easily corrected by having the song-playing routine insert a brief amount of quiet (output pin set to ground) between notes.

Playing Tunes Simultaneous to Robot Action

Roundabout has a very cool feature regarding the way it plays sounds. Roundabout can drive around performing its usual duties while simultaneously playing a tune. Some robots must stop what they're doing, play the song or tone, and then continue driving. Roundabout's ability to multitask is largely accomplished by using built-in microcontroller hardware for generating each note.

The Motorola KX8 chip has a hardware-based pulse-width modulator (PWM). The PWM is provided with a single number that sets the frequency, and the PWM will continue to wiggle the output pin high and low at that rate until told to stop. As such, the robot's program need only stuff the proper number for the frequency of the note into the PWM, set a timer for the duration of the note, and then continue with the rest of the program. When the timer goes off, an interrupt subroutine gets called that plugs in the next note, and so on, until the string containing the song has been exhausted.

It's possible to play a tune while performing other tasks without a hardware-based PWM. However, it would require a much shorter timer that would interrupt the microcontroller's regularly scheduled operations every time it needed to flip the output pin high or low to generate the proper frequency. The robot's overall processing speed would be somewhat reduced by the work required.

All in all, I'm very happy with the way the music module turned out. I recommend it for any robot.

Scaling Up

Roundabout's daughterboard significantly added to the robot's abilities. Eventually, however, a 7-cm radius body limits the amount of additional features and circuits you can tack onto it. So, I decided to start making a larger version, Roundabout Pro, with a 10-cm radius body. Your math teacher would be proud of you for calculating that the robot's platform area will actually double going from 7 cm to 10 cm.

All of the circuits described earlier in this book work equally well on Roundabout Pro. So, you may choose to build this larger body instead of the smaller body described in Chapter 13.

Creating a Double Platform

By stacking two sheets of plastic together during machining and drilling, I created two identical Roundabout Pro platforms at the same time. But, instead of making two robots, the total circuit board and robot accessory area doubled again by placing one platform on top of the other (see Figure 18-5).

Figure 18-5. Roundabout Pro's body features a lot of space for robot parts by connecting two platforms together. You can mount battery packs, circuit boards, and sensors above and below each platform.

To keep the robot lightweight, the platforms are made from ³⁄₁₆-inch thick acrylonitrile-butadiene-styrene (ABS) thermoplastic. ABS is moderately priced, easy to machine, much less brittle than acrylic, and retains tapped threads unlike expanded PVC (Sintra).

A 12-inch wide, 24-inch long, ¼-inch thick sheet of black ABS from McMaster-Carr (#8586K372) is $19.32. However, you might want to first visit the online auctions of Machinist Materials to see if some surplus sheets are available for cheaper.

Sliding Around

Instead of sliding around on screw heads like Roundabout, Roundabout Pro has four free-turning wheels. Two of the wheels are in the front and two of the wheels are in the back to balance the motorized LEGO wheels in the center. The sliding wheels are made of Teflon rods (see the bottom of Figure 18-5 and Figure 18-6) with holes drilled in the middle for a screw axle. When the robot turns in a direction that the rod isn't able to roll, the Teflon simply slides.

Figure 18-6. Side view of Roundabout Pro with sliding wheels in the front and back for balance

Providing Greater Headroom with Homemade Spacers

To increase the amount of vertical space between the platforms, one usually inserts off-the-shelf spacers. Unfortunately, even the longest #4 screw spacers didn't provide enough of a gap to be useful. I briefly considered mini M&M's candy tubes like on Sandwich, but the availability of extra-long #4-40 screws was still a limiting factor. Instead of sticking with a #4-40 screw, you could install a larger-diameter screw (such as ¼ inch) because larger-diameter screws are commonly available in longer lengths.

There's an alternative. If you're comfortable with the process of making homemade motor couplers out of aluminum or plastic rods, as shown in the first chapters of this book, then you possess the skill set to drill relatively shallow holes in both ends of a rod and thread the holes to accept screws. In doing so, you can create very long spacers in a variety of colors and styles, with reasonably short-length (½ inch or shorter) screws (see Figure 18-7).

Figure 18-7. The end of a rod being milled flat while being held in a V-block clamp (left). The finished rod with holes drilled and tapped at the top and bottom (right)

To create extra-long spacers, a hacksaw or cutoff wheel first cuts a rod into multiple equal-length pieces. That process usually leaves the ends of the rods in rough shape, which isn't conducive to the parallel alignment of the platforms. So, use a mill or a file to smooth and flatten the ends of the rods.

To center a rod for drilling, you can create a fixture as described in Chapter 3. You needn't be overly concerned with centering these holes since the rods aren't going to be attached to a spinning motor. But if the holes are seriously off-center, the spacers will be tilted or won't screw in all the way.

Wheel Slots

Thinking back on Roundabout, recall that its wheels are exposed on the sides. In the course of exploration, the wheels and gears occasionally snag on an obstacle. To reduce this problem, Roundabout Pro's wheels are contained within the perimeter of the platforms through slots (see Figure 18-8).

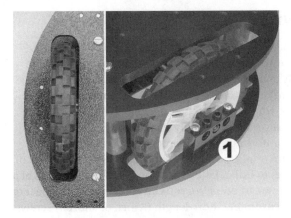

Figure 18-8. Roundabout Pro features wheels that make contact with the ground through slots in the platforms. LEGO bricks ① support the outer end of the wheel axle. Two screws hold the bricks in place.

Slotted wheels have several advantages. First, this design permits one platform to be located beneath the motors and couplers. That leaves very little uncovered on the underside of the robot, reducing the risk of obstacle damage to the motors, wires, batteries, and so on. Second, the edges of the platform are more likely to slide against an obstacle or wall, instead of the face of the wheel doing so.

Supporting Both Ends of the Axle

On Roundabout Pro, a load-bearing structure supports the outside end of the wheel axle (see ① in Figure 18-8). On larger robots, axle support protects the delicate gearbox against stress and prevents the axle from bowing or breaking. Smaller and lighter robots, such as the standard model of Roundabout, can get away with unsupported axles.

Figure 18-9 shows Roundabout Pro's drive train with the top platform removed. This provides an excellent view of the motor, motor mount, LEGO coupler (from Chapters 2 through 4), LEGO wheel, and LEGO brick support.

Figure 18-9. Three views of Roundabout Pro's motor, motor mount, coupler, wheel, and LEGO-brick bearing block

Although the drive train looks precise in Figure 18-9, small errors in alignment necessitate a slight loosening of the screws that hold the LEGO-brick bearing blocks. By not imposing a clamping force, the block can shimmy during the robot's movement to reduce friction and wear.

One downside to wheel slots is that the wheel can't be simply pulled off for maintenance because the sides of the slots prevent removal. Looking at Figure 18-9, consider that a fairly long axle runs from the coupler to the bearing block, and think of how you might remove the wheel. Because the motors are end to end, the only suitable way to remove the wheel is to unscrew both the motor mount and the bearing block and lift the entire motor drive assembly up and out of the slot.

Mounting Motors

Over the years, I've experimented with and seen a wide variety of ways to secure a motor to a robot's body. Sandwich has perhaps the easiest motor mounts—simply drill holes in the sides of a box-shaped body. Roundabout uses a moderately difficult method although the results are technically attractive and fairly accurate.

In the next sections, you'll explore three other ways to mount a motor. Additionally, I'll describe an alternate LEGO coupler for motors with small-diameter shafts.

Mounting with Angle Stock

Roundabout Pro features my favorite way to mount a motor: using ready-made angle stock (see Figure 18-10). A few cuts with a hacksaw and a few holes with a drill are all it takes to create a precise and strong motor mount.

Figure 18-10. A motor screwed onto aluminum angle stock, ready to be attached perfectly parallel to the robot's platform

Purchasing Aluminum Angle Stock

Angle stock looks like the letter *L* (see Figure 18-11). It's available in aluminum, brass, steel, and even some plastics. Aluminum is probably the best choice of materials because it's lightweight, inexpensive, easy to machine, and wicks away motor heat.

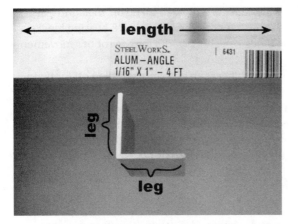

Figure 18-11. Aluminum angle stock. Depending on the seller, the sides may be referred to as legs or as height and depth or height and width.

Some robot builders try to bend a flat sheet of aluminum to make their own angle stock, but it rarely turns out at a crisp right (90-degree) angle and the material tends to be stressed. Because the quality of these motor mounts depends on the quality of the angle stock, it's preferable to buy the correct stock material rather than try to bend your own.

Aluminum angle is available at local hardware stores, which is where I purchased mine. Or, 8 feet of 1-inch leg, ¹⁄₁₆-inch thick aluminum angle is $9.40 from McMaster-Carr (#88805K47). Or, 4 feet of 1-inch leg, ⅛-inch thick (twice as thick) aluminum angle is $9.42 from MSC Industrial Supply. You can even get ¼-inch thick angle with up to 4-inch legs.

If you plan on tapping threads in the screw holes on your motor mounts, then select thicker angle stock, such as ¼ inch. If you plan on having the screws thread into the robot's platform or if you're going to be using bolts and nuts, then perhaps select a thinner angle stock that's easier to machine and weighs less.

Preparing the Proper Lengths

With a hacksaw and a vise, simply cut the angle stock to the length desired for each motor. Look back at the left side of Figure 18-9 to see that extra length on both sides of the motor diameter must be included to accommodate the platform screws.

After cutting down the material, the lengths of each motor mount may be slightly different, and the ends may be tilted and ragged (see Figure 18-12). Fortunately, neither the length nor the tilt has any effect on the resulting precision of the motor mount. However, you don't want to cut your hand (or wires) on the sharp edges, so use a mill, file, or sandpaper to smooth the sides.

Figure 18-12. The edges may be ragged (left) after cutting. Although not necessary for motor performance, you can square the sharp edges of the angle stock with a milling machine (middle) or smooth them with either sandpaper or a file (right).

Drilling Holes with a Template

As with platforms and other robot body parts, a computer-generated template (see Figure 18-13) can assist you in drilling holes accurately for the motor mounts. Try to obtain the manufacturer's datasheet for your robot's motors to learn the exact placement of mounting holes. Drill these holes in one leg of the angle stock to permit the motor to be attached with screws.

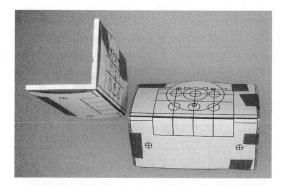

Figure 18-13. Taping paper templates onto cut-angle stock to aim the drill. (Whoops! Neither tape job is holding the template flat and tight to the material surface. I'd better redo that in order to drill accurate holes.)

The underside of the motor mount should contain two or more holes for attaching the motor mount to the robot's platform or body. Four holes may be appropriate for more powerful motors. In any case, don't forget to drill a center hole for the motor shaft.

Purposely Incorporating Wiggle Room by Drilling Unthreaded Oversized Holes

It's inevitable that some minor errors are going to creep into the drive train because of drilling errors and part tolerances. Although the manufactured angle stock already avoids some errors, there can still be problems with the motor being the wrong distance from the wheel or gear, not facing parallel, or the center of the motor shaft being at the wrong height compared to the center of the wheel or gear. Therefore, it's wise to make motor mounts that are designed to be adjustable to make corrections.

All of the motor mount's screw holes should be unthreaded and drilled slightly oversize. The motor screws and body screws should pass through the motor mount and thread into the motor and robot platform respectively, with pan-head screws providing a clamping force, as illustrated in Figure 5-20 in Chapter 5. This arrangement permits the motor and motor mount to be wiggled into alignment to compensate for errors and then to have the screws tightened to hold the motor and mount in that position.

Lastly, these types of mounts permit washers or rubber liners to be easily inserted between the motor and the mount and between the robot platform and the mount. Not only is this useful to adjust height or distance, but also the inserted material can absorb vibrations and shocks. You can take this example to the extreme by inserting springs between the robot's body and the motor mount.

Saving Space with Right Angle Gearing

I think angle stock is probably the best way to build motor mounts. But perhaps there are arrangements where a different kind of motor mount would come in handy.

Hard2C, a mini-sumo robot, has a slightly unusual motor mount. This motor mount is designed to conserve width in the robot, which is important, because the dimensions of sumo robots are restricted.

Notching and Grooving

A single piece of aluminum sheet has holes drilled in it for both motors and their securing screws. Using a single solid flat piece guarantees that the motors are parallel to each other.

Make a notch in the middle of the aluminum piece (see Figure 18-14). The width of the notch matches the width of a rectangular block. A groove is made in the rectangular block, and the pieces mate together. In some ways, this is reminiscent of a balsa glider airplane kit.

Figure 18-14. A single piece of aluminum with both motors secured (and then gears attached) has a notch that fits into a groove in a rectangular block.

Inserting Wheel Axles

With the aluminum piece fully inserted in the rectangular block, axles with wheels and gears are inserted into holes in the rectangular block (see Figure 18-15). Assuming a reasonably precise groove and axle hole, the gears should mesh well. Because the wheels and gears are press fit on the LEGO axles, they can be nudged to tighten or loosen the meshing.

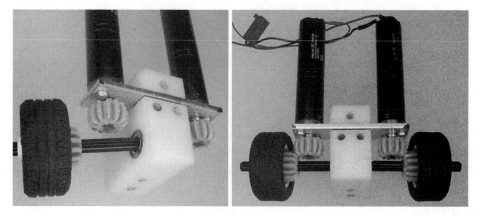

Figure 18-15. Inserting axles into the rectangular block so that the LEGO bevel gears mesh

Reducing Friction

In an attempt to reduce friction losses, Hard2C includes miniature ball bearings on both ends of each axle. This ended up being a waste. There just isn't enough force on the axle to cause the bearings to turn.

The rectangular center block is made from nylon and the LEGO axle is made of polypropylene, both of which are really slippery materials. The axle would probably slip better in the unadorned block than with the stainless steel bearings.

Placing the Drive Train into the Robot's Body

This motor mount ① and overall drive train arrangement works very well in a constrained sumo robot body (see Figure 18-16). There's room on both sides for 9 V batteries ② and a voltage regulator power supply in the middle ③.

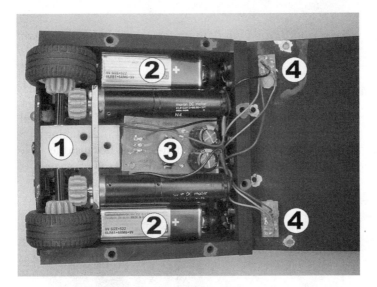

Figure 18-16. Drive train installed in Hard2C

Figure 18-16 is actually a photograph from underneath the robot. You can see the reflective floor sensors ④ for detecting the edge of the sumo ring attached to the bottom lid of the robot.

Adapting a Small-Diameter Motor Shaft and Integrated Mount for LEGO Compatibility

For the final motor mount, this one takes advantage of the specific features on a salvaged gearmotor made by Nihon Mini-Motor Company. These popular gearmotors appear from time to time at B.G. Micro (http://www.bgmicro.com/) as part of a lens assembly. When obtained in that manner, the motor usually comes with numerous external gears and plates (see left side of Figure 18-17) that are easily removed (pull off the gears and unscrew the plates) until only the distinct gearmotor remains.

Figure 18-17. Nihon gearmotor with external gears, slip clutch, and miscellaneous attachments (left). Stand-alone gearmotor after removal of external items (right).

Altering the Gearmotor Shaft

Now place a LEGO combination cross axle/connector peg over the gearmotor shaft (peek ahead at Figure 18-20). However, depending on the version of the salvaged Nihon gearmotor you obtain, the gearmotor shaft will likely need some slight alterations to result in a snug fit.

Using a Dremel with a cutoff disc, trim the narrow-diameter motor shaft to no more than 6.75 mm in length, as illustrated in Figure 18-18. You can test the fit by sliding the shaft into the cross axle peg. Make sure the narrow-diameter portion of the shaft goes in all the way.

Figure 18-18. Specifications for the Nihon gearmotor shaft after being altered to reduce the shaft length and diameter

Grinding the Shaft

After shortening the narrow-diameter portion of the shaft, grind down the wider-diameter portion of the shaft until its diameter is about 4.8 mm (refer to Figure 18-18). Test the fit by sliding a 7/32-inch diameter telescoping (0.014-inch thick walls) brass tube over the shaft. The first wide-diameter section of the shaft should fit within the brass tube. This brass tubing is the same kind used to make telescoping-tube couplers, as described in Chapter 2, with complete instructions in *Robot Building for Beginners* (Apress, 2002).

To perform the motor shaft grinding, I used a Dremel #8215 aluminum-oxide grinding stone while holding the motor with a vise (see Figure 18-19). To reduce the shaft diameter evenly all the way around, power the gearmotor with a battery during grinding.

Figure 18-19. Grinding down the wide portion of the shaft with a Dremel grinding stone accessory. The gearmotor is powered by a rechargeable 9 V battery (about 7.2 V) to rotate the motor shaft during grinding to ensure the reduction is even all of the way around. The grinding process produces spectacular sparks.

Adding Tubing

The motor shaft and half of the LEGO cross-axle peg are surrounded by 7/32-inch diameter hollow brass tubing (see Figure 18-20) to provide coupler strength, to hold the pieces parallel, and to contain the epoxy during gluing. Cut a piece of tubing to about 9 mm in length using a cutoff disc. If you prefer to use a hacksaw or other bladed device, insert a wooden rod inside of the tubing during cutting to prevent the tube walls from bending or collapsing.

After cutting the tube to the proper length, file or sand the edges smooth. Then, test the fit of the pieces together before filling the inside with epoxy. You might want to make a Teflon gluing fixture, as described at the end of Chapter 5, to ensure that the parts are as straight as possible. Because the cross-axle peg is loose on the motor shaft before gluing, it could become affixed at an angle, resulting in angular offset at the attached wheel or gear.

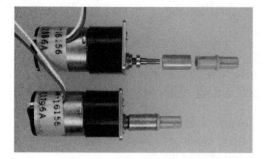

Figure 18-20. Adapting the Nihon motor shaft for LEGO compatibility by placing a cut length of brass tube and a LEGO cross-axle peg over the existing motor shaft. They're retained in place by filling the inside with epoxy.

Unlike other couplers in this book, this coupler doesn't use a setscrew. So, you can't remove this coupler from the motor shaft after gluing, except by destructive means.

Attaching the Motor with a Peg-Based Mount

A 5-mm to 6-mm thick piece of material provides just about the correct amount of thickness for a LEGO friction-lock connector peg to securely pop out one side (see Figure 18-21). A thinner piece would probably work just fine, as long as the holes are drilled so that the connector pegs are tight; otherwise the attached motor will slide and wiggle during operation.

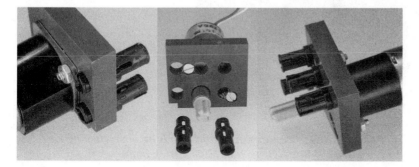

Figure 18-21. Holes drilled in a piece of PVC plastic accept LEGO friction-lock connector pegs. The plastic piece is screwed to the integrated mounting plate on the Nihon motor. The LEGO pegs are arranged to snap the whole assembly onto a Technic LEGO brick.

Drill some ¾₆-inch holes (you can use a #12 drill if you find the holes too tight to fit the pegs) all the way through the mounting piece, spacing the holes like a LEGO Technic brick. Although I drilled five holes surrounding the motor shaft/brass coupler hole, you may choose any arrangement or location depending on how and where you want the motor to connect to a LEGO brick.

You'll also need to drill some holes for the tiny screws that clamp the integrated Nihon motor mount to the thicker mounting piece. I initially wanted to tap the thicker mounting piece and insert the screws from the motor's side. But, because of all of the holes and their proximity to each other, a bolt and nut clamping arrangement seemed more secure.

Not surprisingly, these motor mounts are intended for attaching a motor to a LEGO-based body. Specifically, these motor mounts and motors are installed on Carefree, the robot described in the next section of this chapter.

Roaming the Solar Terrain

Carefree (see Figure 18-22) is an experiment in combining a microcontroller with an unregulated low-power source, such as a solar panel. The robot roams around brightly lit rooms or outdoors on flat surfaces, such as a patio or a driveway. The robot detects walls and obstacles with physical contact sensors (whiskers and touch switches) because infrared emitters aren't bright enough for their reflections to be detected in sunlight. Using a pair of cadmium-sulfide photoresistors to seek light for its solar panel, this robot can wander around while *usually* avoiding getting trapped.

Figure 18-22. Carefree features two solar panels and two long obstacle whiskers. The motherboard is screwed onto a lightweight LEGO brick body.

Selecting Wheels for a Smooth Ride

Carefree has four LEGO wheels: two "30.4 by 14," hollow, smooth, plastic front wheels and two "30.4 by 14 VR" rubber rear wheels (see Figure 18-23). These small-diameter wheels provide the robot with a low, slow, higher-torque ride, appropriate for this robot's solar questing.

Figure 18-23. Slippery LEGO front wheel (left) and grippy LEGO rear wheel (right)

The unpowered, smooth, slippery front wheels perform particularly well. Most robots have a flat piece of plastic or complex omnidirectional balls on which to slide. These wheels are thin and hollow and thus extremely light in weight. They roll when moving forward and slide when turning. I highly recommend giving them a try on one of your smaller robots.

Unlike the front wheels, the rear wheels have rubber tires that grip well. Because the robot's motors drive the rear wheels, it's important that those wheels have good traction.

Detecting Obstacles

Carefree has six obstacle sensors: front and floor detection lever switches, two spring whiskers, and two cadmium-sulfide photoresistors (see Figure 18-24). Can you guess which are the most effective in detecting obstacles? It's surprising. Read on!

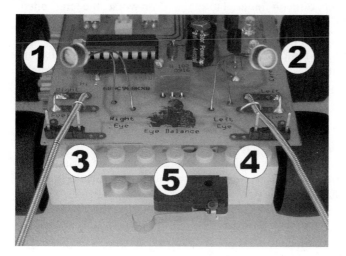

Figure 18-24. Cadmium-sulfide photoresistors (① and ②), whisker sensors (③ and ④), front lever switch (⑤), and floor lever switch (underneath, not pictured)

Looking for Light and Sensing Shadows

Carefree's cadmium-sulfide photoresistors are wired into voltage dividers (as discussed in Chapter 17) and connected to the microcontroller's ADC inputs. The photoresistors are primarily designed to guide the robot to light sources for fueling the solar panels. Oddly enough, *the photoresistors are somewhat effective at helping the robot avoid obstacles by detecting shadows.*

Feeling Around with Whisker Sensors

The whisker sensors are made from stainless-steel spring tubing purchased from Solarbotics, #TACT1, which costs $0.50 for 10 inches.

The spring tubing barely droops under its own weight. It remains virtually straight over a distance of 6 cm. Yet the springiness is such that it easily twists and flexes under stress and immediately bounces back into shape when the force is removed.

If the spring tubing is bent far enough and with enough force, it can be permanently bent into a position. Although permanent bends are easily performed by hand or with a tool, the robot possesses a fraction of the strength necessary to cause unwanted permanent bends.

Using Spring Tubing

The following are a couple of tips on using spring tubing to make whisker sensors:

1. Don't cut the spring tubing with standard wire cutters because the jaws of the cutter will be damaged. With the tubing held in vise, use tin snips or metal sheers. Frankly, bolt cutters wouldn't be out of the question.

2. Stainless steel is a very difficult material to solder. Even worse, the long coiled shape of the spring tubing conducts away heat. That makes the whiskers really, really difficult to solder! The Solarbotics Web site suggests using silver-alloy solder with a high-temperature soldering iron. You might try scuffing up the metal somewhat with sandpaper or a file. After multiple failed attempts, I resorted to crimping the whiskers to the board by soldering a loop of noninsulated solid wire across the whiskers (see Figure 18-25).

Carefree's whiskers rest on the plastic insulating portion of a four-pin, 0.1 inch spaced, male header with the middle two pins removed (clearly too wide). It looks a little like a goal post. The idea is that when something pushes against the spring tubing, the spring tubing presses against the metal pins of the header, forming an electrical path just like a switch.

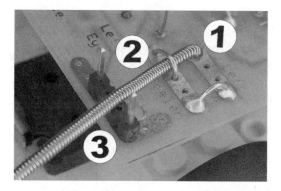

Figure 18-25. Each whisker is made from stainless-steel spring tubing stuck into a hole in the circuit board ①, crimped in place with a wire loop ②, and then passed through the center of a four-pin header with the center two pins removed ③.

Unfortunately, the spring tubing tends to flex and twist so easily that the robot really has to be pressed up against something in order for the spring tubing to make contact. In fact, sometimes a whisker will get flexed outward against an obstacle just as Carefree was turning away. Upon moving forward, the whisker can get bent backward enough to then register a contact (see Figure 18-26) even though the robot actually had a clear path.

Figure 18-26. Carefree's left whisker bent back by on obstacle on the left side. The robot actually has a clear path ahead, but the whisker registers a false contact as Carefree tries to move forward.

Instead of using Carefree's whisker and four-pin header configuration, try passing the stainless-steel spring tubing through the center of a metal tube (like those used for telescoping motor couplers) or a narrow loop of wire. Although I was very impressed with the spring tubing itself, my implementation of whiskers left a lot to be desired. As such, *Carefree almost never successfully detects obstacles with its whiskers.*

There's still value in the whiskers—not for obstacle detection but for obstacle avoidance. The whiskers tend to gently nudge and push the robot away from obstacles and walls. It's almost like a person in a boat using an oar to shove away from shore.

Lever Switches

Carefree contains two lever (snap action) switches attached to the main body for obstacle detection. One switch is in the front, and one switch is underneath.

Mounting the Lever Switch Sensors

The switches are glued to LEGO bricks (see Figure 18-27) with cyanoacrylate-based glue (superglue). This type of adhesive works well on most LEGO parts.

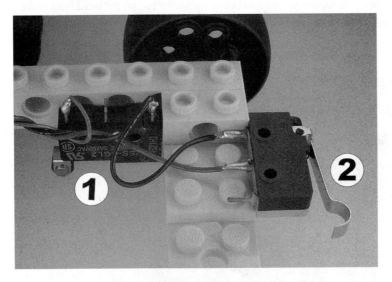

Figure 18-27. Two lever switches glued to the LEGO body. One switch is mounted facing down ① to detect contact with the floor. The other switch is mounted facing forward ② to detect frontal collisions.

I usually avoid permanently gluing anything to a robot's body. However, it seemed a bit odd to screw the switches onto LEGO bricks, whose very purpose is to be easily attached or detached. Because LEGO bricks are widely available, they can be inexpensively replaced along with the switches if necessary.

The front switch, which is normally not pressed (normally open), detects collisions with objects that press against it. Unfortunately, a thin pole, such as a chair or desk leg, can pass undetected between the switch and a front wheel. Attaching a Popsicle stick or other flat bar to the front switch would allow a greater area of detection. However, I've seen more than one front bumper get torn off of other robots because the bumper catches on the edge of something as the robot backs up or turns away.

All in all, the unadorned front bumper switch on Carefree is fairly ineffective.

Detecting Lift Off

The second lever switch, facing down, is normally pressed in by the weight of the robot against the floor. This switch has a small roller manufactured on it, which reduces friction and wear on the lever arm as the robot drives around.

Because this is a solar robot without an off switch, the floor-detecting switch was originally intended to allow the robot to automatically turn itself off when picked up. Alas, during test runs, the robot regularly turned itself off when it ran into an object that caused the front end to lift off the ground.

However, the lack-of-floor detection capability soon turned out to be the most beneficial obstacle avoidance feature. By reprogramming the microcontroller software, the robot was made to back up and turn away whenever the floor-detection switch detected the robot lifting up. *The floor-detection lever switch turns out to be a much more effective obstacle detector than any of the other sensors.* See Figure 18-28.

Figure 18-28. Carefree is initially unable to detect the monster's leg located between the front bumper switch and the wheel. The whiskers were also useless in this example. Fortunately, the lever switch underneath the robot detects the robot's front end sliding up the monster's leg and off of the ground. This enables the robot to back up until the front end again contacts the ground and then to turn away. Good thing Carefree has rear-wheel drive!

Standing in a Robot's Shoes for a While

I have always wanted to mount a video or digital camera onto a robot to provide the robot with vision. Unfortunately, the processing horsepower required is way beyond most microcontrollers. However, there's an off-the-shelf way to see from the robot's point of view, even if just for fun and debugging rather than real robotic vision.

Adding a Wireless Video Camera to Any Existing Robot

A complete wireless video camera system is available for $99 from Circuit Specialists (http://www.circuitspecialists.com/), #GFP-2400. The receiver has standard RCA jacks for connecting to a VCR or television. The transmitter and antenna (see Figure 18-29) are built into the camera itself, making for a compact solution.

Figure 18-29. Roundabout equipped with a CCTV-2400TRX/C161 color video camera with microphone and integrated 2.4 GHz wireless transmitter

The robot merely has to supply a secure location for mounting the camera and enough power (270 mA at 9 V). A 9 V battery (not shared to power the robot) is adequate for short-term use, but a six-pack of AA cells or two fully charged lithium-polymer cells in series (8.4 V) is preferable.

Exploring with Wireless Video

It's a lot of fun to see what the robot sees. Robot sumo is a blast!

On the more practical side, some of the robot's decisions no longer seem so quirky when viewed at the robot's level. Floor vents, baseboards, and furniture overhangs never entered my mind before. Don't underestimate the effects of bumpy terrain on sensors until you've experienced the tilting and jarring first hand.

You could place some small color LEDs at the bottom of the video camera's view to provide debugging information on the television screen as the robot drives around. This is easier to do if you design the robot with a location for the video camera in mind from the very beginning.

My video camera happens to have a built-in microphone, which really enhances telepresence. You can hear the motors whirring and the sounds of the robot smacking into things. The music and tones from the robot don't fade with the robot's distance from the television because the camera's microphone is near the robot's speaker the whole time.

Exploring Yourself with Wireless Video

One final thought on using wireless video: The next time you're pondering your robot, it may be pondering you! See Figure 18-30.

Figure 18-30. Author adjusting a robot equipped with a video camera

Thank You

Thank you, dear reader, for spending a few afternoons in my home laboratory. I hope this book has sparked some exciting ideas or suggested some useful new techniques and parts. One of the nicest things about building robots for a hobby is getting to share scientific experiences with fellow builders.

Internet References

THIS APPENDIX CONTAINS LINKS to Web sites where you can find more information about robot building. Some Web site links are case-sensitive. Be sure to type the Web address exactly as it appears in this appendix.

Table A-1 provides links to my Web site, Table A-2 provides links to retail robots and parts, Table A-3 provides links to the LEGO site, Table A-4 provides links to tools and materials, Table A-5 provides links to retail electronic parts, and Table A-6 provides links to manufacturers, and Table A-7 provides miscellaneous links.

Table A-1. Author

Robot Room	http://www.robotroom.com/
Errata, updates, resources for this book	http://www.robotroom.com/IRBGoodies.html
Musical notes spreadsheet	http://www.robotroom.com/IRBGoodies.html#FREQ
Printed circuit boards	http://www.robotroom.com/PCB.html
Robot sumo rules and guide	http://www.robotroom.com/SumoRules.html
Roundabout KX8 source code	http://www.robotroom.com/IRBGoodies.html#SOURCE
Roundabout printed circuit boards	http://www.robotroom.com/IRBGoodies.html#PCBs
Sandwich, the line-following robot	http://www.robotroom.com/Sandwich.html

Table A-2. Retail Robots and Robot Parts

Acroname	http://www.acroname.com/
Mark III	http://www.junun.org/MarkIII/Store.jsp
Parallax	http://www.parallax.com/
Solarbotics	http://www.solarbotics.com/

Table A-3. LEGO Links

Bricklink	http://www.bricklink.com/
LEGO MINDSTORMS	http://mindstorms.lego.com/
Steve Hassenplug	http://www.geocities.com/stevehassenplug/

Table A-4. Tools and Materials

Fastener Express	http://www.fastener-express.com/
Machinist Materials	http://www.machinistmaterials.com/
McMaster-Carr	http://www.mcmaster.com/
Micro-Mark	http://www.micromark.com/
MSC Industrial Supply	http://www.mscdirect.com/
Online Metals	http://www.onlinemetals.com/
U.S. Plastic Corp.	http://www.usplastic.com/

Table A-5. Retail Electronic Parts

All Electronics	http://www.allelectronics.com/
B.G. Micro	http://www.bgmicro.com/
Circuit Specialists	http://www.circuitspecialists.com/
Digi-Key	http://www.digikey.com/
Electronix Express	http://www.elexp.com/
Jameco	http://www.jameco.com/
Mouser	http://www.mouser.com/
RadioShack	http://www.radioshack.com/

Table A-6. Manufacturers

Bourns	http://www.bourns.com/
Dremel	http://www.dremel.com/
Fibre-Craft	http://www.fibrecraft.com/
International Rectifier	http://www.irf.com/
IXYS	http://www.ixys.com/
Maxim	http://www.maxim-ic.com/
Microchip	http://www.microchip.com/
Motorola	http://e-www.motorola.com/
National Semiconductor	http://www.national.com/
Texas Advanced Optoelectronic Solutions	http://www.taosinc.com/
Texas Instruments	http://www.ti.com/
Tyco/Raychem	http://www.circuitprotection.com/

Table A-7. Other

BEAM robots	http://www.solarbotics.net/
ChiBots	http://www.chibots.org/

Index

Numbers

7805 linear voltage regulator, 96–102

   assisting batteries and voltage regulator, 98–99

   building 7805-based power supply, 100–102

   protecting against reverse flows, 99–100

   substituting LM2940 or LP2954 for, 102–3

A

ABS (acrylonitrile-butadiene-styrene), 24, 57, 400

acetal (Delrin), 24, 57, 280

AC power adapters, 86–87

Acroname, 421

acrylic (Plexiglas), 14, 24, 57, 279

acrylonitrile-butadiene-styrene (ABS), 24, 57, 400

active reflective sensor system, 222

ADCs (analog-to-digital converters), 321, 322

adhesive, 55

alkaline batteries, 117

All Electronics, 422

alloy screws, 48, 352

aluminum, 33, 57, 58, 244

aluminum angle stock, 403–4

aluminum anodized cap screw, 350

aluminum electrolytic capacitors, 101, 123, 126, 128, 229

aluminum screws, 352

American Standard Pitch frequencies, 397

ammeters, 290

analog-to-digital converters (ADCs), 321, 322

analog-to-digital input pins, 322

angle stock, mounting motors with, 403–6

   drilling holes with template, 405

   preparing proper lengths, 404–5

   purchasing aluminum angle stock, 403–4

   purposely incorporating wiggle room, 406

angular offset, 18–20

anodes, 81–82

anodized aluminum socket head cap screws, 350–52

antistatic foam, 246

Apple Mac OS, 314

assembling modular robots. *See* modular robots, assembling

assembly programming language, 314

audio. *See* music

audio amplifier, 396, 397

audio amplifier chips, 396–97

autonomous robots, 391

avalanche point, 137

B

baffles, 292, 381–84

ball-end mill, 65

ball-grid arrays (BGAs), 93

BASIC programming language, 314, 318, 331

batteries, 85–86

    12 V batteries, 117

    9 V batteries, 116–17

    alkaline batteries, 117

    checking voltage and polarity, 289

    increasing lifetime of, 123

    letter designation for, 75

    voltage regulators, 95–96

BEAM robots, 422

bearings, 52–53

belts on pulleys, 270

BGAs (ball-grid arrays), 93

B.G. Micro, 409, 422

BiCMOS (bipolar combined with MOSFET technology) logic chips, 144–45

bipolar LEDs, 362

bit banging, 327

black paint, 242

blind holes, 46

blink timing, 334

blocks, placing robot on, 289

boardmount sockets, 343–45

    connecting with, 344

    dividing, 344

    removable installation of components in, 344

body diodes, 185

bolts, 350

bottom-style taps, 45, 46

Bourns, Inc., 422

Bourns 3296W series multiturn potentiometer, 226

Bourns 3386W series single-turn trimming potentiometer, 226

Bourns MultiFuse resettable overcurrent protectors, 136

breadboards. *See* solderless breadboards

breakaway headers, 307

break-beam sensors, 243

breakdown voltage, 137

Bricklink, 421

bright-finish drills, 33

brightness, sensing

    with photodiode IC, 378–86. *See also* floor reflectivity circuit

    with photoresistors, 370–78

        converting varying resistance into varying voltage, 371–73

        nonlinear photoresistor response, 373–76

        recognizing inconsistency between photoresistors, 375–77

        reusing balanced brightness-sensing circuit, 378

bulk capacitors, 122

bypass capacitors, 129–30

C

C++ programming language, 314

cadmium-sulfide photoresistors, 412, 413, 414

cadmium-sulfoselenide (CdS) photoresistors, 373

cameras, 418–19

canned oscillators, 75, 332, 333

capacitors, 98

  for 7805-based power supply, 101

  common capacitor multipliers, 80

  input/output

    delayed power-off, 123–25

    implementing higher margins of safety for tantalum capacitors, 127

    increasing battery lifetime, 123

    reducing turn-off time, 125–26

    selecting bulk capacitors, 126

  letter designation for, 75

  selecting construction, 80

  selecting working voltage and temperature, 80

cap screws, 350, 350–52

carbon-film resistors, 78

carbon screws, 352

Carefree robot, 412–14

"Carmen Miranda" configuration, 357

cathodes, 81–82

CdS (cadmium-sulfoselenide) photoresistors, 373

center platforms, 263–64

center punch, 261–62

ceramic resonators, 332

chamfered threads, 45

Chicago Area Robotics Club (ChiBots), 3, 422

circuit boards, 7

circuit breakers, 75

circuitry of Roundabout robot, 250–54

  controlling direction with simple logic, 251–54

  supplying power, 250–51

Circuit Specialists, 418, 422

clamps, 138

CMOS (HC) chips, 164

cobalt drills, 33

colored lens, 88

compiling programs, 315

conventional milling, 62

countersinking, 66

couplers, 11–20. *See also* hub-adapter couplers

  adding Lego axle, 48–50

  comparing homemade coupler technologies, 12–14

  defined, 11

  drill holes, 14–20

    aligning hole angles and hole centers, 15–20

    connecting setscrew hole to motor shaft hole, 15

  drilling solid rods for

    gathering tools and parts, 21–22

    preparing lengths of solid rods, 22–27

  installing setscrew, 43–48

    determining location for setscrew, 43–44

    drilling setscrew hole, 44–45

    selecting setscrew, 47–48

    tapping setscrew hole, 45–46

  making coupler fixtures, 27–36

    adding setscrew to, 38

    cutting block, 29–30

    drilling coupler rod hole, 32–36

    drilling motor-shaft and LEGO axle coupler holes, 38–41

    drilling setscrew hole, 30–31

(continued)

couplers *(continued)*

    enlarging tight fits, 37

    repositioning fixture, 38

    tapping setscrew hole, 31–32

  overview, 11–12

  solid-rod couplers, 13–14, 20

  telescoping-tube couplers, 12–13, 20

C programming language, 314, 331

crankshaft, 32

cross talk, 227

crystal, 332, 333

current

  limiting, 152, 379

  supplying more to motors, 144–45

  watching during power-up, 290–91

cutoff disc machine, 4

cutting oil, 46

cyanoacrylate-based glue (superglue), 70, 382, 416

D

daughterboard, Roundabout's, 341–68

  connecting boards, 347–55

    with dual-stop male headers, 347–49

    securing daughterboard to motherboard, 349–52

    soldering male headers, 352–54

    soldering new DIP socket, 354–55

  expanding functionality, 360–67

    controlling bipolar LEDs, 362

    controlling motors, 362

    detecting walls and obstacles, 362

    examining microcontroller pins, 361

    leaving interrupt pin unused, 361

    making music, 367

    powering microcontroller, 361

    providing options with DIP switch, 364–67

    reading push button, 362–64

    remaining pins available for expansion, 367

  intercepting signals, 358–60

    catching and disrupting stalled state, 359–60

    producing (almost) complete control, 360

    rerouting infrared detection signals, 359

    rerouting motor and bipolar controls, 360

    retaining valuable functions, 358–59

  overview, 341–42

  replacing DIP socket, 342–47

    making motherboard signals accessible, 346–47

    using boardmount sockets, 343–45

  shading infrared reflector detectors, 356–58

  upgrading robots, 368

debouncing circuit, 363

debugging programs, 315–20

  changing pins, 317–18

  creating heartbeats, 318–19

  driving a display, 319–20

  LED use, 316–17

decoupling/bypass capacitors, 379

Delrin (acetal), 24, 57, 280

detecting obstacles. *See* obstacle detection

detection ambiguity, reducing, 302–8

detectors. *See* sensors

Devcon epoxy, 49

Digi-Key Corporation, 81, 422

Digital light meter, 374

diodes, 75, 81–82

DIP sockets

    replacing, 342–47

        making motherboard signals
           accessible, 346–47

        using boardmount sockets, 343–45

    soldering, 354–55

DIP switch

    providing options with, 364–67

    strategizing with settings
        (in robot sumo), 391

discrete bipolar H-bridge, 207

dividing boardmount sockets, 344

double-pole double-throw (DPDT)
    switch, 125–26

downloading programs, 315

DPDT (double-pole double-throw)
    switch, 125–26

drawing program, 259

Dremel, 344, 422

Dremel grinding stone, 410

drill bits, 13

drill machine, 13

drill press, 13

drills, 13

drill sizes, 30

drive train, 408

driving motors. *See* motor drivers

driving speakers, 395–97

drunkard's walk, 300–301

dual-stop male headers, 347–49

E

eBay, 256

EEPROM (electrically erasable
    programmable read-only memory),
    313, 329

effective series resistance (ESR), 228

EG1903 slide switch, 102

electrically erasable programmable read-
    only memory (EEPROM), 313, 329

electronics, 89–93. *See also* schematics

    avoiding obsolete technology, 90

    learning curve issues, 89

    using surface-mount components,
        90–93

Electronix Express, 422

emitters. *See* sensors

EOR (exclusive-or) instruction, 388

epoxy, 49–50, 70

equivalent series resistance (ESR), 122

ESR (effective series resistance), 228

ESR (equivalent series resistance), 122

exclusive-or (EOR or XOR) instruction,
    388

external serial-accessible memory, 329

F

Fastener Express, 350, 422

female headers. *See* boardmount sockets

Fibre-Craft, 382, 422

filing, 26, 27

fixtures, 27, 28

Flash, 313

Flexi-Foam, 382

floor reflectivity circuit, 380–86, 391

    cutting out semicircular breadboard, 380–81

    overview, 379–80

    protective baffles, 381–84

    tuning and testing, 384–86

floor sensor circuit, 391

floor sensor module, 369–92.
    See also floor reflectivity circuit

    competing in robot sumo, 389–91

        entering Roundabout, 390–91

        strategizing with DIP switch settings, 391

    expanding possibilities, 392

    following lines, 386–89

        autodetection of line brightness, 387

        centering over dark line, 389

        following dark line, 388–89

        improving line-following algorithm, 389

        inverting sensor values, 388

        reading floor sensor values, 387

    overview, 369

    sensing brightness with photodiode IC, 378–86

    sensing brightness with photoresistors, 370–78

        converting varying resistance into varying voltage, 371–73

        nonlinear photoresistor response, 373–76

        recognizing inconsistency between photoresistors, 376–77

        reusing balanced brightness-sensing circuit, 378

fluorescent acrylic, 13

flyback diodes, 153, 185

four-pin Molex connector, 367

frequencies for musical notes, 397–98

friction, reducing, 408

FU5505 MOSFET, 106–7, 116

Full House, 300–301

functionality of Roundabout robot, expanding, 360–67

    controlling bipolar LEDs, 362

    controlling motors, 362

    detecting walls and obstacles, 362

    examining microcontroller pins, 361

    leaving interrupt pin unused, 361

    making music, 367

    powering microcontroller, 361

    providing options with DIP switch, 364–67

    reading push button, 362–64

    remaining pins available for expansion, 367

fuses, 132

G

gamma, 375

gearhead motors, 146

gearmotors, 408–9

gearmotors, availability of, 255–57

gears, and parallel offset, 18

gluing, 55, 70–72

Gould, Stephen Jay, 300–301

grinding stone, 70, 410

H

hacksaws, 25, 42

half bridge, 156–57

Hard2C robot, 243, 406

Hassenplug, Steve, 421

H-bridge chips, 77

H-bridge motor drivers, 158–63

   coasting with, 161–62

   combinations of, 162

   enumerating other H-bridge combinations, 162–63

   implementing, 163

   slowing down with electronic brake, 160–61

   spinning clockwise with, 158–59

   spinning counterclockwise with, 159

HC (high-speed CMOS chips), 139

heartbeats, 318–19

heat sinks, 113

higher-current output pins, 325

high-speed CMOS chips (HC), 139

HSS drills, 33

hub-adapter couplers, 54–72

   adapting motor shaft's outer diameter to wheel's inner diameter, 54–55

   coring Lego hubs, 67–70

      drilling out center of hub, 69

      sanding away remains of hub center, 70

      securing hub during machining, 68

      selecting Silver & Deming drill, 68–69

   coupler rod, 55–56

   fitting and gluing parts together, 70–72

   hub-adapter discs, 56–67

      choosing raw material, 57–58

      choosing shape, 56–57

      cutting raw sheet to size, 58

      determining size, 57

      drilling center hole, 59

      drilling screw holes, 63–65

      finishing, 65–67

      measuring oversize, 59–60

      milling circles with rotary table, 60–63

hysteresis, 239

I

IC4 and IC3 detectors, 251

IED3 emitter, 304

IED4 emitter, 304, 305

IEDs, 82

illuminance, 373, 374

impedance (resistance), 396

inductors, letter designation for, 75

infrared detection signals, rerouting, 359

infrared-emitting diodes, letter designation for, 75

infrared light, 242–43, 296

infrared modulated obstacles, opponent, and wall detector, 213–32

   completing reflector detector circuit, 222–30

      implementing 38 kHz reflector detector on solderless breadboard, 224–30

      reflector detector schematic, 222–24

   detecting modulated infrared with popular module, 214–17

   expanding detection circuit to include LED indicator, 218–21

      adding a 74AC14 inverter chip to drive LED, 218

      examining indicator circuit, 218–21

   overview, 213–14

infrared reflector detector, fine-tuning, 291

initial wattage, 287

input capture, 322

input/output capacitors, 122–27

    delayed power-off, 123–25

    implementing higher margins of safety for tantalum capacitors, 127

    increasing battery lifetime, 123

    reducing turn-off time, 125–26

    selecting bulk capacitors, 126

input pins, 321–24

integrated circuits, letter designation for, 75

intercepting signals, 358–60

    catching and disrupting stalled state, 359–60

    producing (almost) complete control, 360

    rerouting infrared detection signals, 359

    rerouting motor and bipolar controls, 360

    retaining valuable functions, 358–59

interface, 163

International Rectifier, 170, 422

interrupter, 243

interrupt pins, 322, 361

IRFU5505 MOSFET, 183, 185, 186

IRLU024N MOSFET, 174, 176, 185, 186

iron, 24

IXDF404PI chip, 187

IXDN404PI chip, 170, 171, 196–97

IXYS Corporation, 422

J

Jameco 106526 infrared LED, 244

Jameco Electronics, 256, 422

jam nuts, 62, 63

Java programming language, 314

jigs, 28

jobber-length drills, 32–33

jog in crossing wires, 74–75

K

kerosene, 32

keyswitches, 364

kilohm resistances, 77

KX8 microcontroller, 330, 342, 361, 367, 398

L

lack-of-floor detection capability, 417

lathes, 60

LDO (low dropout) regulators, 102, 103

LEDs

    bicolor, flipping, 291

    infrared, purchasing, 225–26

    schematic symbol and label for, 82

    use in debugging programs, 316–17

left-hand rotation drills, 32

LEGO bricks, 52, 53. *See also* floor sensor module

LEGO cross axles, 12

LEGO gears, 267–70

LEGO MINDSTORMS, 339, 421

LEGO moving parts, limits of, 270–71

LEGO Technic pin friction connector, 40

LEGO unit (LU), 267

LEGO wheels, 54

level shifter, 163

lever switches, 416–17

lever switch sensors, mounting, 416–17

LEXAN (polycarbonate), 14, 24, 230

light-dependent resistors. *See* photoresistors

light-emitting diodes, letter designation for, 75

Lightspeed robot, 345

light-to-voltage circuit, 372

linear-taper potentiometer, 394

linear voltage-regulated power supplies, 112–17

  5 V linear regulator selection, 118

  7805 linear voltage regulator, 96–102

    assisting batteries and voltage regulator, 98–99

    building 7805-based power supply, 100–102

    protecting against reverse flows, 99–100

    substituting LM2940 or LP2954 for, 102–3

  consuming quiescent current, 113–14

  isolating power and noise, 114–16

  protecting against reverse batteries, 112

  protecting against short circuits, 112

  protecting against thermal overload, 112–13

  reducing minimum required unregulated voltage, 102–12

    analyzing minimum input voltage, 107–10

    increasing resistance at lower voltages, 105

    input/output voltage results, 110–12

    selecting low-resistance P-channel power MOSFET, 106–7

    substituting LM2940 or LP2954 for 7805, 102–3

    substituting power MOSFET for 1N5817, 103–5

  selecting, 116–17

  simplicity/low cost of complete circuit, 113

lines, following, 386–89

  autodetection of line brightness, 387

  centering over dark line, 389

  following dark line, 388–89

  improving line-following algorithm, 389

  inverting sensor values, 388

  reading floor sensor values, 387

Linux operating system, 314

LM1117 voltage regulator, 118

LM2940 voltage regulator, 112, 113, 114, 117

LM386 chip, 395

LM386N-3 chip, 394

LM386N-4 chip, 394

LNA2903L infrared LED, 226

logic chips, 143, 144

logic errors, causing with motor noise, 145

low dropout (LDO) regulators, 102, 103

LP2954 voltage regulator, 112, 114, 117

lubrication, 46

lux, 373, 375

Lynxmotion, 256

M

Machine-screw length drill, 33

machining, 3–8

  miniature milling machines, 5–8

  stocking machine shop, 3–4

Machinist Materials, 28, 71, 422

Mac OS, 314

male headers

    dual-stop, 347–49

    soldering, 352–54

Mark III Robot Store, 421

MAX232 chip, 327

MAX4427 chip, 170

MAX603 voltage regulator, 122

MAX8881EUT50 voltage regulator, 118

Maxim Integrated Products, 422

MC33887 MOSFET H-bridge motor
    driver, 199–206, 210

    implementing, 202–3

    pins, 201–2

    sensing motor current, 204–6

McMaster-Carr Machinist Materials, 400,
    404, 422

megohm resistances, 77

memory of microcontrollers, 313–14,
    327–30

    nonvolatile memory, 328–29

    volatile memory, 329–30

metallized polyester, 128, 230

metal oxide semiconductor field effect
    transistor. *See* MOSFETs

Microchip PICmicro microcontroller,
    339, 342

Microchip Technology, 170, 422

microcontrollers, 143, 144, 309–40

    choosing, 335–40

        advice from others, 339–40

        important features, 336–37

        Motorola microcontrollers, 337–38

        Parallax BASIC Stamp, 338–39

    comparing to logic chip, 310–12

        choosing logic chip over
            microcontroller, 311–12

        choosing microcontroller over logic
            chip, 312

    instruction complexity, 331

    instruction size, 330–31

    memory, 327–30

        nonvolatile memory, 328–29

        volatile memory, 329–30

    overview, 309

    packages, 320–21

    pins, 321–27

        input pins, 321–24

        output pins, 324–27

    powering, 361

    programming, 313–20. *See also*
        debugging programs

        compiling and downloading
            program, 315

        difference from writing for PC, 315

        sizing up program storage, 313–14

        storing programs, 313

        writing programs, 314

    speed, 331–35

        comparing clock speed, 331–32

        generating clock signal, 332–33

        using clock as timer, 333–35

    watchdogs timers, 335

MicroLux milling/drilling machine, 5, 6,
    60

Micro-Mark, 5, 422

micromultipliers, 80

microphones, 419

Microsoft Visio application, 258

Microsoft Windows operating system, 314

miniature milling machines, 5–8

misaligned shaft and axle holes, 17

modular robots, assembling, 1–10

applying parts and techniques to other robots, 9–10

building modules, 1–3

grouping machining parts, 8

grouping stand-alone electronic modules, 8–9

machining, 3–8

miniature milling machines, 5–8

stocking machine shop, 3–4

overview, 1

process of, 9

testing robots, 9

Molex connector, 367, 380

momentary tactile switches, 364

MOSFETs, 77, 173–93

MOSFET H-bridge, 184–89

adding Schottky diodes, 185–86

interfacing to, 186–89

N-channel power MOSFET, 174–77

connecting gate, 175–77

controlling transistor switch with voltage, 174

revising to include a pull-down resistor, 181–82

P-channel power MOSFET, 103–5, 182, 183

for powering full circuits, 104

providing default input value with resistor, 177–81

choosing between no resistor, pull-up resistor, pull-down resistor, 180–81

choosing value for pull-up/pull-down resistor, 179–80

setting input high by default with pull-up resistor, 177–78

setting input low by default with pull-down resistor, 178–79

selecting power MOSFETs, 189–93

parallel MOSFET transistors vs. parallel bipolar transistors, 193

resistance of MOSFET, 190–93

motherboards, 341. *See also* daughterboard, Roundabout's

motor bracket, 44

motor drivers, 143–72, 173–212. *See also* MOSFETs

driving motors with chips, 194–206. *See also* MC33887 MOSFET H-bridge motor driver

4427-family as stand-alone motor driver, 195–97

getting bipolar H-bridge on chip, 197–99

ideal setup, 194–95

driving with single transistor, 149–56

NPN bipolar single-transistor motor-driver circuit, 150–54

PNP bipolar single-transistor motor-driver circuit, 154–56

evaluating, 206–11

four modes of, 146–49

H-bridge motor driver, 158–63

coasting with, 161–62

enumerating other H-bridge combinations, 162–63

implementing, 163

slowing down with electronic brake, 160–61

spinning clockwise with, 158–59

spinning counterclockwise with, 159

(continued)

motor drivers *(continued)*

    interfacing with high side, 163–71

        avoiding interface by not regulating logic chips, 164

        avoiding interface by regulating H-bridge, 164

        interfacing PNP via NPN, 164–68

        using interface chip, 168–71

    mastering motor control, 171–72

    overview, 143, 173

    putting NPN and PNP motor drivers together, 156–58

        avoiding short circuit, 157–58

        implementation, 156–57

    reasons for using, 143–46

        causing logic errors with motor noise, 145

        running motors at higher voltages, 144

        supplying more current to motors, 144–45

        supplying motor power from unregulated vs. regulated power, 145–46

motor mounts, 271–82, 406. *See also* motors, mounting

    defining motor-mount dimensions, 271–72

    drilling all of motor mounts at same time, 273–77

    making holes to secure motor mounts to center platform, 278–82

    preparing raw material, 272

    revealing finished motor mounts, 282

    selecting ready-made material instead of milling, 273

Motorola Corporation, 422

Motorola KX8 microcontroller, 330, 342, 361, 367, 399

Motorola microcontrollers, 337–38

motors. *See also* wheels, building motors inside of

    building mechanism, 264–67

    causing logic errors with noise from, 145

    connections, mixing up, 292–93

    controlling, 362

    letter designation for, 75

    rerouting controls, 360

    vibrating, 16

motors, mounting, 403–12

    with angle stock, 403–6

        drilling holes with template, 405

        preparing proper lengths, 404–5

        purchasing aluminum angle stock, 403–4

        purposely incorporating wiggle room, 406

    lever switch sensors, 416–17

    making LEGO-compatible, 408–12

        adding tubing, 410–11

        altering gearmotor shaft, 409

        attaching motor with peg-based mount, 411–12

        grinding shaft, 410

    saving space with right angle gearing, 406–8

        inserting wheel axles, 407

        notching and grooving, 406–7

        placing drive train into robot's body, 408

        reducing friction, 408

mounting. *See also* motors, mounting

Mouser Electronics, 422

MSC Industrial Supply, 404, 422

multimeters, 375

multisegment LEDs, 319–20

music, 367, 393–99

    driving speakers, 395–97

    implementing audio circuit, 394

    playing notes, 397–98

    playing tunes, 398–99

    presenting audio circuit, 394

    seeing sound, 397

    turning volume, 394–95

        boosting loudness, 395

        listening to binary, 395

Musical notes spreadsheet, 421

N

N08L5013IRAB infrared LED, 226

N17SLDH251 power switch, 102

Nano capacitances, 80

National Semiconductor, 422

natural polycarbonate, 14

N-channel power MOSFET, 174–77

    connecting gate, 175–77

    controlling transistor switch with voltage, 174

    with pull-down resistor, 182

Nickel-metal hydride (NiMH) rechargeable batteries, 117

Nihon gearmotor, 409

Nihon Mini-Motor Company, 408

Nihon motor mount, 412

noisy signal, 363

nonlinear photoresistor response, 373–76

nonpolarized capacitors, 79

nonvolatile memory, 328–29

notes, playing, 397–98

NPN motor drivers

    overview, 150–54

    working with PNP motor driver, 156–58

        avoiding short circuit, 157–58

        implementation, 156–57

nuts, 350

nylon, 24, 57

nylon screws, 352

O

obstacle detection, 413–17

    lever switches, 416–17

    looking for light/sensing shadows, 414

    using spring tubing, 414–16

    whisker sensors, 414

ohmmeters, 286, 288

oil, cutting, 46

one-time programmable (OTP), 313

Online Metals, 28, 58, 422

operating systems, 314

oscilloscopes, 89, 124, 238, 377–78

OTP (one-time programmable), 313

output pins, 324–27

overcurrent protection, 131, 133–36

P

Panasonic PNA4602M Photo IC, 214–17

parabolic drills, 33

Parallax, Inc., 421

Parallax BASIC Stamp microcontroller, 338–39, 342

parallel, 27

parallel-accessible external memory, 329

parallel offset, 17

    between holes and coupler body, 16–17

    between holes of couplers, 17–18

PCBs (printed circuit boards), 90, 92, 93, 421

P-channel power MOSFET, 102, 183–84

photocells. *See* photoresistors

photoconductors. *See* photoresistors

photodiode IC, sensing brightness with. *See* floor reflectivity circuit

photodiodes, 242

photoresistors

   letter designation for, 75

   sensing brightness with, 370–78

      converting varying resistance into varying voltage, 371–73

      nonlinear photoresistor response, 373–76

      recognizing inconsistency between photoresistors, 375–77

      reusing balanced brightness-sensing circuit, 378

Pico capacitances, 80

pins, 321–27

   examining, 361

   input pins, 321–24

   output pins, 324–27

plastics, 14, 24, 57, 279

plated screws, 352

Plexiglas (acrylic), 14, 24, 57, 279

plug-style taps, 45, 46

PNP motor drivers

   overview, 154–56

   working with NPN motor driver, 156–58

      avoiding short circuit, 157–58

      implementation, 156–57

polarized capacitors, 79

polycarbonate (LEXAN), 14, 24, 230

polyethylene, 24, 57

polymeric positive temperature coefficient overcurrent-protection devices. *See* PPTC overcurrent-protection devices

polypropylene, 24, 57, 230, 280

potentiometers, 75, 226–27, 233, 375

power, unregulated vs. regulated, 145–46

power distribution buses, 85–86

power supply, 121–42. *See also* linear voltage-regulated power supplies

   adding voodoo capacitors, 127–28

   bulking up input/output capacitors, 122–27

      delayed power-off, 123–25

      higher safety margins for tantalum capacitors, 127

      increasing battery lifetime, 123

      reducing turn-off time, 125–26

      selecting bulk capacitors, 126

   bypass/decoupling capacitors, 128–31

      bypassing long path to power supply, 129–30

      decoupling noise at each source, 130

      selecting, 130–31

   overview, 121

   preventing damage from overvoltage in regulated circuit, 136–40

      choosing appropriate breakdown voltage, 139

      zener diodes, 136–40

   preventing damage from short circuits or overcurrent, 131–36

      with auto-resetting PPTC device, 132–36

      deciding if overcurrent protection is required, 131

with fuse, 132

with manually reset circuit breaker, 132

power-up, watching current usage during, 290–91

PPTC overcurrent-protection devices, 132

installing, 133–34

selecting, 134–36

precession, 19

printed circuit boards (PCBs), 90, 92, 93, 421

protective baffles, 381–84

PTFE (Teflon), 24, 57, 71, 280

pull-down resistors

choosing between no resistor and, 180–81

choosing value for, 179–80

on input pins, 323–24

pull-up resistors, 178–79

choosing between no resistor and, 180–81

choosing value for, 179–80

on input pins, 323–24

setting input high by default with, 177–78

pulse-width modulator (PWM), 325, 367, 399

push button, 362–64

PVC, 24, 57

PWM (pulse-width modulator), 325, 367

Q

quick-setting epoxy, 49

quiescent current, 113

R

RadioShack, 86, 422

RAM (random access memory), 328, 329

Rayovac rechargeable nickel-metal hydride (NiMH) 9 V battery, 86

RC (resistor-capacitor) time formula, 126

red LEDs, 91

reflector detector, 233–46

limitations of, 242–45

failing provide range value, 246

failing to detect certain kinds of objects, 242–43

failing to detect objects far away/very close, 243–46

failing to work outdoors or under bright lights, 242

overview, 233

preparing for practical robot application, 246

tuning in 38 kHz, 233–41

diagnosing problems encountered in circuit tuning, 239–41

revealing the purpose of a Schmitt-trigger inverter, 238–39

selecting halfway between start/end of detection, 234–37

using multimeter with frequency detection, 237–38

using oscilloscope, 238

regulated power supply, 96

reheating solder joints, 360

Remote-controlled sumo robots, 391

rerouting

infrared detection signals, 359

motor and bipolar controls, 360

reset pins, 323

resistance, 396

resistor-capacitor (RC) time formula, 126

resistor multipliers, 77

resistors

    coloring, 77–78

    color value bands, 78

    letter designation for, 75

    selecting construction, tolerance, wattage, 77–78

    substituting lower-wattage resistors, 77–78

resources for this book, 421

reversing robot, 293

right angle gearing, 406–8

    inserting wheel axles, 407

    notching and grooving, 406–7

    placing drive train into robot's body, 408

    reducing friction, 408

right-hand rotation drills, 32

Robot Room Web site, 421

robot sumo, 389–91

    entering Roundabout in robot sumo, 390–91

    rules and guide, 421

    strategizing with DIP switch settings, 391

rods. *See* solid rods

rotary tables

    adapting for small pieces, 60

    milling circles with, 60–63

rotating robot, 295

rotational error (runout), 37, 40

rotation drills, 32

Roundabout Pro robot, 399–403

    creating double platform, 399–400

    providing greater headroom with homemade spacers, 401

sliding around, 400

supporting both ends of axle, 402–3

wheel slots, 401–2

Roundabout robot, 2, 247–84. *See also* daughterboard, Roundabout's; floor sensor module; Roundabout Pro robot; test driving Roundabout

    building body, 254–82

        characteristics of body, 257–58

        constructing center platform, 263–64

        gearmotor availability, 255–57

        limits of LEGO moving parts, 270–71

        motor mechanism, 264–67

        selecting LEGO gears, 267–70

    circuitry, 250–54

        controlling direction with simple logic, 251–54

        supplying power, 250–51

    designing body, 258–63

        attaching template, 260

        creating template, 258–59

        printing template, 260

        punching holes for better centering, 261–62

        removing tape before machining sides, 262–63

        squaring template with workpiece, 260–61

    KX8 source code, 421

    making motor mounts, 271–82

        defining motor-mount dimensions, 271–72

        drilling all of motor mounts at same time, 273–77

making holes to secure motor mounts to center platform, 278–82

preparing raw material, 272

revealing finished motor mounts, 282

selecting ready-made material instead of milling, 273

overview, 247–48

printed circuit boards, 421

summarizing, 282–84

viewing from above and beneath, 249

viewing from side, 248–49

rubber-grip material, 27

runout (rotational error), 37, 40

S

sag, 122

Sandwich robot, 248, 378, 421

schematics, 73–84

connecting wires, 74–75

designating parts, 75–76

labeling parts, 76–82

labeling capacitors, 79–81

labeling LEDs and IEDs, 81–82

labeling resistors, 76–79

specifying power supply, 82–84

Schmitt-trigger inputs, 239, 302–3

Schmitt-trigger inverter, 238–39

Schottky diodes, 153, 185, 185–86

"screw-machined" sockets, 343

screw-machine length, 32

screws, difference from bolts, 350

semicircular breadboards, 380–81

semicircular circuit board, 381

sensors, testing, 292

Sequoia Group, 256

serial ports, 321

serial protocols, 327

setscrews, 28. *See also* couplers

sheet music, 398

Sherline rotary table, 60

short circuits, 132–36

short length, 32–33

shunts, 306

signals, intercepting

catching and disrupting stalled state, 359–60

producing (almost) complete control, 360

rerouting infrared detection signals, 359

rerouting motor and bipolar controls, 360

retaining valuable functions, 358–59

Silver & Deming drill, 68, 69

silver mica, 230

single-pole single-throw (SPST) DIP switch, 364

single transistors, driving motors with, 149–56

NPN bipolar single-transistor motor-driver circuit, 150–54

PNP bipolar single-transistor motor-driver circuit, 154–56

slotted heads, 47

slotted wheels, 401–3

slow-motion robot, 294

SN754410 chip, 198–99, 207–8, 210

snappable headers, 307

socket head cap screws, 350–52

soft tires, 19

Solarbotics Ltd., 256, 414, 421

solar panel implementation, 412–17

    detecting obstacles, 413–17

        lever switches, 416–17

        looking for light/sensing shadows, 414

        using spring tubing, 414–16

        whisker sensors, 414

    selecting wheels, 412–13

solar panels, 412, 414

soldering

    DIP sockets, 354–55

    male headers, 352–54

solder joints, 360

solderless breadboards, 84–88

    adding amenities, 88

    powering, 86–87

    selecting, 84

    setting up to match photographs, 85–88

solid-rod couplers, 13–14, 20, 55, 56

solid rods for couplers, drilling

    gathering tools and parts, 21–22

    preparing lengths of solid rods, 22–27

sound. *See* music

Soup robot

    comparison to Roundabout, 10

    gliding on screw heads, 280

    limits of LEGO moving parts, 270–71

    mounting motors with screws, 266

    overview of parts, 10

    parallel offset motors of, 265

speakers, driving, 395–97

speed of microcontrollers, 331–35

    comparing clock speed, 331–32

    generating clock signal, 332–33

    using clock as a timer, 333–35

split-point, 32

split-point drill, 34

spotting drill, 35, 39

spring tubing, 414–16

SPST (single-pole single-throw) DIP switch, 364

stainless steel screws, 48, 352

stalled state, 359–60

stalling robot, 294

stand-alone electronic modules, grouping, 8–9

standard-length (jobber-length) drills, 33

standard taps, 45

starter taps, 45

steel, 24

stubby length, 32–33

sumo. *See* robot sumo

superglue (cyanoacrylate-based glue), 70, 382, 416

surface-mount components, 90–93

Surma, Terry, 32

switches, 363

    letter designation for, 75

    lever switches, 416–17

switching regulators, 118

T

tantalum capacitor, 128

tantalum-dipped capacitors, 101

TAOS (Texas Advanced Optoelectronic Solutions), 378, 422

TAOS TSL257 photosensor, 378

taper-style taps, 45, 46

tapping fluid, 31, 32, 46

tap wrench, 31

TC4427 chip, 170

Teflon (PTFE), 24, 57, 71, 280

telescoping-tube couplers, 12–13, 20

templates

    attaching, 260

    creating, 258–59

    drilling holes with, 405

    printing, 260

    squaring with workpiece, 260–61

test driving Roundabout, 285–308

    evaluating performance, 293–300

        challenging Roundabout, 297–300

        encountering problems, 293–96

        exercising all of robot's maneuvers, 296–97

    getting stuck, 300–308

        evaluating drunkard's walk, 300–301

        evaluating Roundabout's walk, 301–2

        reducing detection ambiguity, 302–8

    overview, 285

    preparing for, 285–91

        checking battery voltage and polarity, 289

        measuring resistance of complete circuit, 286–89

        placing robot on blocks, 289

        setting all controls to safe or moderate positions, 285–86

        testing one module at time, 286

        watching current usage during power-up, 290–91

    preparing robot and correcting minor glitches, 291–93

        fine-tuning infrared reflector detector, 291

        flipping bicolor LEDs, 291

        mixing up motor connections, 292–93

        testing sensors, 292

testing

    floor reflectivity circuit, 384–86

    robots, 9

test points, letter designation for, 75

Texas Advanced Optoelectronic Solutions (TAOS), 378, 422

Texas Instruments, 422

thermal overload, 112

thermal runaway, 193

threaded fasteners, 350

three-fluted taps, 46

tires, soft, 19. *See also* wheels

titanium aluminum nitride (TiAlN) coatings, 33

titanium carbonitride(TiCN), 33

titanium nitride (TiN), 33

totem pole, 156–57

TPS2812P chip, 170

transistors, letter designation for, 75. *See also* single transistors

transparencies, 260

transparent material, 244

trimming solder joints, 353

TSL257 sensor, 380, 384

T-slots, 60

Tyco/Raychem Electronics, 422

Tyco/Raychem PolySwitch resettable devices, 136

U

UHMW polyethylene nylon, 280

UHMW polyethylene strips, 273

United States Plastic Corporation, 71

unregulated power supply, 95, 145–46

updates for this book, 421

upgrading robots, 368

U.S. Plastic Corp, 422

V

V-block, 24, 68

VCO (voltage-controlled oscillator), 222, 240

vertical milling machine, 26

V-grooved vise, 24, 25

vibrating motors, 16

video cameras, 418–19

Visio application, 258

volatile memory, 328, 329–30

voltage-controlled oscillator (VCO), 222, 240

voltage divider circuit, 371

voltage regulators. *See also* linear voltage-regulated power supplies

    letter designation for, 75

    overview, 95–96

voltages, running motors at higher, 144

volume, 394–95

    boosting loudness, 395

    listening to binary, 395

W

watchdogs timers, 335

water-clear lens, 88

wheels

    axle holes too small/large, 296

    building motors inside of, 51–72. *See also* hub-adapter couplers

        bent shafts, 52–53

        overview, 51–52

    problems with rotation, 297

    selecting (for use with solar power), 412–13

    slots for (Roundabout Pro robot), 401–2

whisker sensors, 413, 414–16

Windows operating system, 314

wireless video cameras, 418–19

wiring diagrams. *See* schematics

X

XOR (exclusive-or) instruction, 388

Z

zener diodes, 75, 136–40, 288

zinc-plated steel screws, 48